Ungrounded Empires

The Cultural Politics of
Modern Chinese Transnationalism

Aihwa Ong and Donald M. Nonini, editors

ROUTLEDGE
NEW YORK   LONDON

Published in 1997 by
Routledge
29 West 35th Street
New York, NY 10001

Published in Great Britain by
Routledge
11 New Fetter Lane
London EC4P 4EE

Library of Congress Cataloging-in-Publication Data

Ong, Aihwa.
    Ungrounded Empires: The cultural politics of modern Chinese
transnationalism / Aihwa Ong and Donald M. Nonini, editors.
        p.   cm.
    Includes bibliographical references and index.
    ISBN (invalid) 0–415–91542–2 (hardcover). — ISBN (invalid)
0–415–91543–0 (pbk.)
    1. Chinese—Foreign countries—Ethnic identity.   2. China—
Civilization.   3. Nationalism—China.   4. Chinese—Foreign
countries—Economic conditions.   I. Nonini, Donald Macon.
II. Title
DS732.055   1996
909′.04951082—dc20
                                                           96–30223
                                                           CIP

Acknowledgements

This book grew out of a conference on overseas Chinese capitalism held in August 1994 in Singapore, hosted by the National University of Singapore (NUS). The symposium was jointly convened by Aihwa Ong, who invited participants from North America and Asia, and Tong Chee Kiong, who invited participants from Singapore and oversaw administrative and logistical support for the meeting. We thank the Pacific Rim Research Program of the University of California at Berkeley, and the Department of Sociology of the National University of Singapore for financial support for the conference.

The formal acknowledgements above hardly state fully our sense of appreciation to certain persons who made the meeting possible. Above all, special thanks go to Dr. Tong Chee Kiong, deputy head of the Department of Sociology, National University of Singapore, and to Dr. Ong Jin Hui, professor and head of the Department of Sociology at NUS. Tong Chee Kiong and other faculty of the National University of Singapore were the most gracious hosts that participants could ask for, as well as contributors to the intellectual productivity of the conference.

Lisa Hoffman, a graduate student in the Department of Anthropology at the University of California at Berkeley, served as rapporteur for the conference, and we thank her for her skillful work. In a crucial phase of preparing the manuscript, we benefited from the invaluable contribution of Kathleen Erwin's fine and skilled work on our page proofs. We also thank Suzanne Calpestri for suggesting the title *Ungrounded Empires*.

Acknowledgments

Part of the costs of publication have been borne by the University Research Council, University of North Carolina at Chapel Hill, and we are grateful for the publication subvention grant the council provided.

We would like to thank the participants in the conference, not all of whom could be represented in this volume, for five days of intensive discussion. Although the participants come from different fields, the center of gravity is in cultural anthropology. Fruitful dialogues with cultural studies, history, sociology, and development studies are reflected in this volume, especially with the inclusion of chapters by two historians, Prasenjit Duara and Carl Trocki, who were not among the conference participants. The authors in the current volume share an interdisciplinary approach and a belief in innovative methodology for the study of the Chinese diaspora, capitalism, and cultural diversity in the late twentieth century.

Finally, we thank Robert R. Ng for making the maps for our book, and we thank Sandy Smith-Nonini. We are grateful to both of them and to our kids, Pamela Hui-hui, Ben Jiaming, and Roque Antonio, for supporting us with their time and love, while making things difficult enough to help us maintain a sense of humor and some perspective on our work throughout.

A. O. and D. N.

Table of Contents

Ungrounded Empires

Introduction

Chinese Transnationalism as
an Alternative Modernity

Chinese Transnationalism as an Alternative Modernity

Donald M. Nonini and Aihwa Ong

When, in the summer of 1993, Chinese people from the ill-fated freighter *Golden Venture* were washed ashore on a New York beach, Americans learned about a far-flung Chinese network that smuggled human cargo. Most of the boat people were from Fujian province in southern China, and their smugglers were Taiwanese from across the Straits. Market reforms in coastal China have, ironically, fueled a "get-rich" fever, making Fujianese eager to resume their distinctive, centuries-old tradition of going overseas to make a fortune. Many turn to smuggling syndicates, which have connections in Taiwan, Hong Kong, Southeast Asia, and Central and South America, to slip them into the United States. After the U.S. immigration service cracked down on the freighters, smugglers instead sent their clients, armed with false documents made in Hong Kong or São Paulo, through American airports.

While most Chinese businesses are above board, the interceptions of Fujianese boat people provide a glimpse of the global scope of many Chinese businesses, their historical roots in diaspora, their operational flexibility and spatial mobility, and their capacities to circumvent disciplining by nation-states. Boat people, whether from Fujian or from Vietnam, represent a tiny drop in the latest wave of Chinese emigration throughout the world, prompted by the changing world economy. This particular conjunction of events, whereby Chinese from China and elsewhere in Asia are caught up in the migrations, dislocations, and cultural upheavals associated with the "hypermodernity" of late capitalism (Pred and Watts 1993), challenges conventional, long-standing ideas about Chinese culture and identity. These events demonstrate that "Chinese-

3

ness" is no longer, if it ever was, a property or essence of a person calculated by that person's having more or fewer "Chinese" values or
norms, but instead can be understood only in terms of the multiplicity of
ways in which "being Chinese" is an inscribed relation of persons and
groups to forces and processes associated with global capitalism and its
modernities.

Another example of the new Chinese transnationalism is the staging
of meetings exclusively confined to ethnic Chinese entrepreneurs from
all over the world. First hosted in 1991 by the Singapore Chinese Chamber of Commerce, the World Chinese Entrepreneurs Convention attracted some eight hundred delegates from seventy-five cities in thirty
countries—from China to California, Guam to Greece, Malaysia to
Mauritius. Subsequent meetings, held every two years, took place in
Hong Kong and Bangkok. At the first gathering, the chairman welcomed
delegates by saying:

> Today, there are some twenty-five million ethnic Chinese outside of China,
> the bulk of whom are concentrated around the fast-growing Pacific Rim. In-
> dividually and collectively, they are well-placed to play a key role in realizing
> the potential and promise of globalization, particularly in making the Pacific
> Century come true. (SCCCI 1991, 7)

These are instances of the global reorientation of Chinese that we seek to
examine, even as we also aspire to decode various representations (such
as this one) that cast the new transnationalism in a range of prideful, celebratory, or triumphal terms. The chairman's words about placement,
"the Pacific Rim," globalization, and "the Pacific Century" are tropes
that instruct us to view new ways of being Chinese as inseparable from
far-flung capitalist processes.

We ground our study of Chinese transnationalism as a culturally distinctive domain within the strategies of accumulation of the new capitalism—both Chinese and non-Chinese—emerging over the last two
decades in the Asia-Pacific region (hereafter, "Asia Pacific"). Over the
same period, transnational phenomena among Chinese—called diasporas, transnational publics, global and regional imaginaries, dispersed
gender and family structures, and, above all else, new Chinese subjectivities found in the global arena—have excited both popular interest and
scholarly attention and controversy. In this book we hold that it is impossible to understand such transnational phenomena unless strategies of
accumulation by Chinese under capitalism are examined, for such strategies penetrate these phenomena and are in turn affected by them. In this
way, the essays of this book contextualize the study of the modern Chi-

nese diaspora of the last two centuries and the subsequent changes in Chinese political and economic activities, and in cultural identities, within specific historical and regional settings. But taken collectively, these essays accomplish even more: they point to the necessity of reconceptualizing the relationship between the study of Chinese identities and the place-bound theorizations of a preglobal social science, implied in such terms as *territory, region, nationality,* and *ethnicity.* These essays invoke the imperative of finding a new theoretical discourse for comprehending not only Chinese transnationalism but other transnationalisms as well, suggest new concepts for this project, and sketch out new lines of inquiry.

Drawing on ethnographic research in Asia Pacific sites, the essays in this book illuminate, for various sites and from varying perspectives, transformations in relations among Chinese communities and organizations, the nation-states of the Asia Pacific, and capitalist activity, and describe the new cultural identities these transformations have called into existence. The contributors to this book fruitfully combine in various registers anthropological and cultural-studies approaches with an interpretive political economy. In so doing, they point to the need for a new theoretical language in order to adequately confront the deterritorialized relations constituting Chinese transnationalism while grounding them in specific times and spaces. In this book we move with the Chinese diaspora from China's heartland, through south China, across the waters to Southeast Asia, and northwest across the Pacific to North America (see figure 1). By studying the connections of diverse cultural representations—connoted by restlessness, mobility, and novelty—to the political economy of Chinese transnationalism, our essays also convey forcefully the dimensions of human agency, cultural politics, and indeed pathos present within what has conventionally been seen as the "natural" and unhuman operation of global market forces and profits.

Diaspora Chinese Studies: From Trading Minorities to "Residual Chinese" to Triumphal Moderns

There are alternative perspectives to ours on diaspora Chinese, their emigration, their status as minorities within nation-states, and their economic organization at both the family and regional levels. To a large extent, these approaches are inflections of Euro-American visions of Asian emigration and of "Chinese culture" in Asia. There are at least three approaches in the social science literature. First, there were early

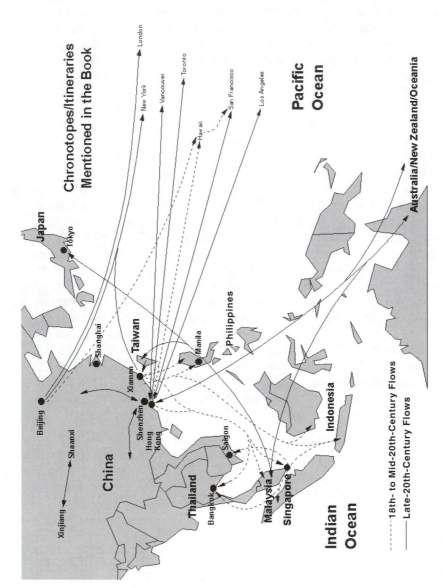

Figure 1.

(1950–1960s) anthropological and sociological studies that focused on enduring Chinese cultural values and organization in the midst of geographic, social, and economic change in the colonial world (Newell 1962; Dewey 1962; Freedman 1957, 1979a; Skinner 1957, 1958; Crissman 1967; Purcell 1960, 1965; T'ien 1953; W. Willmott 1967; D. Willmott 1960). These overlapped with a second focus on Chinese as urban trading minorities and on their ethnic statuses within the late colonial and newly independent nation-states of Southeast Asia (Dewey 1962; Crissman 1967; Skinner 1968; Wickberg 1965; Amyot 1973). Scholars from both approaches were concerned and at times obsessed with two recurring issues: How were the loyalties to Euro-American economic and political hegemony on the part of cosmopolitan and highly urbanized Chinese to be vouchsafed, given the "subversive" menace posed by Chinese Communism (and Mao's millions on the march) to the political stability of the decolonizing and ex-colonial state regimes of Southeast Asia? And how were culturally and racially distinct Chinese trading minorities to be "integrated" into the capitalist modernization projects of these regimes, given the latter's indigenous majorities?

These obsessions of a cold war–era evolutionist Parsonian social science, elaborated within the burgeoning fields of East Asian and Southeast Asian area studies during the period of American world hegemony, explain the major theoretical emphasis on the "norms" and "values" of "Chinese culture" (Farquhar and Hevia 1993). The norms and values were those of commercialism (Freedman 1979b [1959]; Skinner 1957; Olsen 1972); of familism (Amyot 1973), and of loyalty to native place in China (Skinner 1957; Crissman 1967). And it was out of such obsessions that the field of "overseas Chinese" studies was born: Chinese not residing in China—but in Hong Kong, Taiwan, and Southeast Asia—constituted, in the words of the eminent sinological anthropologist Maurice Freedman (1979c, 414, 416), a "residual China"—an imperfect replication of the template or real "Chinese culture" in China, which was temporarily not accessible to inquiring social scientists because of the closing of the Bamboo Curtain. Overseas Chinese studies was thus adopted as the semilegitimate stepchild of a sinological anthropology, that was by then flourishing.

Subsequently a third scholarly approach to diaspora Chinese studies has arisen. By the late 1970s and early 1980s, it was evident that—with the exception of the tragic massacre of thousands of Chinese (and all of the organized Left) in Indonesia in 1965–1966, and irrespective of the outcomes of a so-called "integrative revolution" (Geertz 1973) and "modernization"—overseas Chinese were in Southeast Asian nation-states to stay for some time, and, on the whole, were doing quite well for themselves economically. Studies of overseas Chinese conducted between the 1950s and the 1970s were therefore succeeded by a body of social science and policy-oriented studies that sought to explain the economic success of overseas Chinese, who began to be seen less as "overseas" as such, and more as Southeast Asian, Malaysian, Philippine, Canadian, and so on. Following the adaptationist and rationalist paradigms then current, these sought to explain such success primarily in terms of cultural strategies, focusing on family firm behavior, *xinyong* ("creditworthiness"), and *guanxi* (particularist relations) (Tong 1991; Lim and Gosling 1983; Wong 1988; Cushman and Wang 1988; Hamilton 1991; Mackie 1993; McVey 1993). During this period, it was considered almost heresy to propose what much evidence pointed to—that there were large numbers of overseas Chinese who were lower-class, had prospered little despite capitalist growth in colonial and postcolonial Southeast Asia, and often held critical views about it (Simoniya 1961; Nonini 1988, 1993b).

Over the last decade, as East Asian and ASEAN[1] capitalist economies have flourished, with Chinese entrepreneurs playing pivotal roles within them, these social scientific studies have been followed by a business-school crowd eager to provide a cultural explanation and justification for East Asian development (Goldberg 1985; Berger and Hsiao 1988; Yoshihara 1988; Tai 1989; Redding 1990; Kotkin 1992; Kao 1993) as well as, in some instances, to sound dire warnings of the decline of the West (Fallows 1994). In this literature, much has been made of the supposed Confucian contribution to East Asian economic success (Berger and Hsiao 1988; Tai 1989; Redding 1990); some have even gone so far as to link an East Asian "Confucian culture area" and "chopstick culture" to capitalist prosperity in the region (Nakajima 1994).

A recent perspective is represented by journalistic and popular texts that tend toward exegesis of the Chinese diaspora and economic success (Pan 1994; Chan and Chiang 1994), and by equally self-important tracts on the Chinese cultural periphery as a revolutionary force in Asian modernity (L.-c. Wang 1991; G. Wang 1991a; Tu 1991). Although inflected by Euro-American assumptions about modernism, such writings veer uneasily between cultural chauvinism and Enlightenment ideals, and they reveal the lack of a critical distance that one might hope for among disapora Chinese intellectuals (but see Ang 1993). These works presuppose by their ritual invocation of and obsessive return to family values, *guanxi* particularism, and communal humanism, that there are intrinsic and timeless features of Chinese culture, which persist even in the midst of non-Chinese society (G. Wang 1991b). Even when cross-cultural borrowings and exchanges are acknowledged, the essentializing

Orientalist binary opposition of East versus West is restored in such neo-Confucian triumphalist visions. And with the opening of south China to capitalist penetration (see Ong 1993 and the essays by Lee and Hsing in this volume) and the commercial and touristic excitement generated by it, those who were previously referred to as Southeast Asian, Malaysian, or Indonesian Chinese, or in another setting as Taiwanese, are newly positioned as "Chinese not resident in China." This renaming is not a matter of popular self-referencing so much as the reworking of an elite rhetoric of representation, and theoretically it is a regressive move come full circle: from "overseas Chinese" (*huaqiao* in Mandarin)[2] back to "Chinese living overseas" (*haiwai huaren*).[3] Again, China is reinstalled as primal source and center, the Middle Kingdom, *fons et origo* of "Chinese culture."

In contrast, in this book we fruitfully view "Chinese culture," Chinese family values, *guanxi,* "Confucian capitalism," and so on as discursive tropes, each with a genealogy, each having been constantly cast and recast in cultural terms both by Chinese and by Westerners, including academics. For instance, the forms or practices of family values and *guanxi* networks become inseparable from the multiple cultural constructions of them (Yang 1994), and these enter into struggles over representation played out in various cultural fields, including those of academic life (Bourdieu 1991). Therefore, their study invariably involves a reflexive aspect. In the essays in this book, the authors argue that these tropes and the discourses underlying them do not merely explain Chinese identity, networks, and economic activity; rather, such discourses and their connections to power in large part *constitute* Chinese identities and transnational practices, and are therefore in need of deconstruction and study. This is the project we seek to initiate.

Transnationalism, Ethnography, Alternative Modernities

Flexible Accumulation, Third Cultures, Deterritorialized Ethnographies

A constellation of technical, financial, and institutional innovations that have occurred since the early 1970s has led to a shift in late capitalism from mass industrial production to globalized regimes of flexible accumulation (Harvey 1989; Lipietz 1986). Flexible accumulation, according to David Harvey (1989, 147), "rests on flexibility with respect to labor processes, labor markets, products, and patterns of consumption. It is characterized by the emergence of entirely new sectors of production, new ways of providing financial services, new markets, and, above all, greatly intensified rates of commercial, technological, and organizational innovation." Fundamentally, these changes are associated with the enhanced and increased mobility of people, commodities, ideas, and capital on a global scale: Late capitalism shows new capacities to annihilate space in configuring industrial production, distributing goods and services, and creating new markets (and new classes of commodities, such as "experience"), and to speed the velocity of turnover in the production, consumption, and distribution of commodities. We can thus speak of the simultaneous implosion of space and the speedup of all aspects of economic (and hence cultural) life, in this latest episode of what Harvey (1989) refers to as "time-space compression."

For our purposes, these developments have two important implications. First, they have called forth new kinds of social organization that require intercultural communication and are deterritorialized, flexible, and highly mobile. Labor markets have been reorganized by new forms of labor regulation—subcontracting (at times, to more than one level), outsourcing, employment of large numbers of temporary, part-time, and seasonal workers, and putting-out and "home work" arrangements. As a result of the implosion of space that characterizes flexibility, production processes have been increasingly segmented, deskilled, and globalized into a new international division of labor increasingly independent of specific places and their populations across the world. At the same time, a proliferation and segmentation of new commodity markets, of global scope, have promoted and in turn been fed by new lifestyle consumer constituencies.

But, as Doreen Massey (1993) has recently observed, time-space compression has its own "power-geometry." Speedups, accelerated turnover times, and increased mobility do not affect all persons and groups equally. Older asymmetrical power relations are reinforced, while new ones have emerged. Women, particularly young women, have become the largest section of local populations to be drafted as temporary, contingent, and part-time laborers for industrial subcontractors and other firms using the forms of labor regulation characterizing flexible accumulation (Ong 1991). In addition, various sorts of semi-unfree laborers—children, convicts, undocumented transnational labor migrants, and others—have come to be employed in large numbers. For women and semi-unfree laborers, modes of labor regulation extend beyond the capitalist workplace per se to domestic units and to capitalist nation-states—the latter engaging in forms of discursive inscription and control (Ong 1990, 1991).

Juxtaposed—in time, but not in space—to the rise of these unskilled and semiskilled laborers are the new transnational functionaries associated with the globalization of capitalist production, distribution, marketing, finance, and consumption. With globalization there has been the appearance of new managerial, financial, legal, technical, and commercial service professionals, and of design professionals in architecture and advertising. These transnational professionals and technocrats provide the managerial and other integrative competencies called forth by the organizational and technical innovations of flexibility (Featherstone 1990, 7–8). They have evolved new, distinctive lifestyles grounded in high mobility (both spatial and in terms of careers), new patterns of urban residence, and new kinds of social interaction defined by a consumerist ethic. These professionals have come to form what Weber (1978) called "status groups," yet ones sharing common class privileges as members of a globalized capitalist managerial elite.

Whether as members of the contingent workforces of subcontractors or as technocratic elites, diaspora Chinese have found themselves in novel social arrangements. The newness of these arrangements has largely gone unnoticed, for their distinctive strategies of accumulation are obscured because they take the guise of "traditional" patterns of family and of networking based on *guanxi* particularism (see below).

A second implication of these changes is that "third cultures" have emerged out of the social arrangements associated with flexibility. Writing of global cultural flows that are relatively independent of the controls of nation-states, Mike Featherstone coins the term "third culture" (1990). Third cultures are the products of the globalization associated with late capitalism, and they arise out of the new transnational economic processes that transcend the porous political boundaries of nation-states even as they now penetrate them. According to Featherstone, third cultures arise when groups face problems of intercultural communication at first hand and confront the necessity of continually moving to and fro between different cultures, each to some extent spatially defined. Modern Chinese transnationalism can be considered one such third culture, an emergent global form that moreover provides alternative visions in late capitalism to Western modernity and generates new and distinctive social arrangements, cultural discourses, practices, and subjectivities. Perhaps most crucial, new identities are thereby constituted—"new types of flexible personal controls, dispositions and means of orientation, in effect a new kind of habitus" (Featherstone 1990, 8). As we argue later, these transformations have been mapped onto preexisting patterns of dispersion, mobility, and displacement among diaspora Chinese, who since the 1970s have come to play nodal and pivotal roles in the emergence of the new flexible capitalism of the Asia Pacific.

In this book, our ethnographic and historical reflections about and contextualizations of Chinese transnationalism as a third culture have two related objectives. On one hand, by grounding our study of diaspora Chinese in the historical conditions of colonialism, postcolonialism, and late capitalism, we break with the Orientalist approach that depends on a timeless, irreducible East-West divide in culture and consciousness. On the other, we also intervene in debates on flexible accumulation, its concomitant displacements, flexibilities, habitus, and postmodern cultural forms, which have up to now been limited to Western societies (Jameson 1991; Harvey 1989; Gilroy 1991, 1993; Pred and Watts 1993). Such studies as they now stand are at implicit risk of taking as universal the culturally distinct experiences of America and Europe as they have made a transition from Fordism to flexible accumulation or from modernity to postmodernity. In contrast, drawing on rich ethnographic and historical research on persons moving across (as much as dwelling in) the Asia Pacific, our book introduces the multifaceted and shifting experiences of diaspora Chinese living under, yet reworking, the conditions of flexibility—prototypical moderns possessing more than a "double consciousness" (Gilroy 1993). They face many directions at once—toward China, other Asian countries, and the West—with multiple perspectives on modernities, perspectives often gained at great cost through their passage via itineraries marked by sojourning, absence, nostalgia, and at times exile and loss.

We thus take modern Chinese transnationalism to be a recent global phenomenon with historical roots in premodern trade systems, European colonialism, and more recent American geopolitical domination of the Pacific. In this regard, unlike previous approaches, we decenter the Middle Kingdom as the ultimate analytical reference for an understanding of diaspora Chinese (Chow 1993). The reader will notice that this volume contains several essays from studies based in China (by Liu, Lee, Yang, and Hsing) as seen *within* the Chinese diaspora, but we do not thereby accord China a privileged ontological or epistemological position; it is one among many sites within and across which Chinese transnational practices are played out. Instead, by providing a systematic view of modernities in the Asia Pacific—modernities constituted out of the multiple conflicts, exploitations, and embraces between and among Asians, Europeans, and North Americans over the past century—we ground Chinese transnationalism in the geopolitical context of late-twentieth-century Asian modernity. Arif Dirlik (1993) has argued that the idea of the Pacific Rim must be deconstructed as a figure of American hegemony, and a post-Orientalist approach must attend to its reconstruction as an Asian cultural space of capitalism. We agree with Dirlik's position and seek in our essays to go beyond the analyses of written texts in his two edited volumes (Dirlik 1993, Wilson and Dirlik 1994) by providing ethnographic detail about the necessary social and cultural contexts for particular Chinese transnational practices across this transformed space. We, with Wilson and Dirlik (1994), call for the humanization—and transformation—of the so-called global system of late capitalism, in Asia and elsewhere. Our essays seek to do this through their rich ethnographic treatment of Chinese transnationalism, which conveys the particular impasses, contradictions, and pathos of Chinese who are living and thinking transnationally. The essays thereby challenge reigning scholarly and popular fetishizations of a market system that is seen as natural and, if not yet universal, inevitable.

On the other hand, the essays in this book by and large also depart from a recent dominant theoretical trend within anthropology. In that discipline, calls for greater attempts to engage in ethnographic research within a global political economy framework (Wolf 1983; Marcus and Fischer 1986) have not been borne out. The earlier promise of ethnographies' investigating the cultural and social effects of transnational industries in third world societies (Fernandez-Kelly 1983; Scott 1985; but see Ong 1987; Wolf 1992; and Freeman forthcoming) has lately been diluted by an American cultural studies approach that treats transnationalism as a set of abstracted, dematerialized cultural flows, giving scant attention either to the concrete, everyday changes in peoples' lives or to the structural reconfigurations that accompany global capitalism. The new journal *Public Culture* has fostered interesting and important work on transnational mass media, publics, and cultural politics (e.g., Appadurai 1993; Abu-Lughod 1993; Rouse 1995), thus carving out a new area for anthropological investigation. But what has often dropped out of this approach is an interest in describing the ways in which people's everyday lives are transformed by the effects of global capitalism, how their own agencies are implicated in the making of these effects, and the social relationships in which these agencies are embedded. While we have learned much from and value the focus on social imaginaries, new globalized literary and aesthetic genres, and abstracted culture flows, we are apprehensive about the limitations of what might be called lite anthropology, and we seek in this book an engagement with what Clifford Geertz (1973), perhaps mindful of missed opportunities, calls "the hard surfaces of daily life" that can impart a concrete yet open-ended sense of the predicaments, struggles, and human dilemmas of late-twentieth-century societies. At the same time, we attempt to carry this through without reducing ethnography to the study of a spatially delimited, fixed, and local "Other" set outside of our own time

(Fabian 1983). Here we take seriously James Clifford's recent (1992) injunction to consider "travel" as an important alternative locus to "the village" for contemporary ethnography. In example after example, our essays explore these relations—studied in the form of the movements of Taiwanese entrepreneurs into and out of south China, the sojourns of Malaysian Chinese migrant laborers in Japanese urban space, the "bosses" commuting between Hong Kong and the Pacific coast of the United States, and so on.

Furthermore, Chinese transnationalist discourses and practices are grounded in intertwined political, economic, and cultural processes that are reworking every aspect of life in a world no longer clearly divided into a Western core and global peripheries elsewhere. Thus the transformations of the last two decades associated with flexible accumulation have led to the emergence of a polycentric global capitalism with multiple nodes of geopolitical and economic power (Ong 1993), with new "global cities" such as New York and Tokyo (Sassen 1991), new urban centers for export-oriented industrialization and trade such as Hong Kong, São Paulo, and Singapore, and the newly defined regions on which these centers draw. Complementary to this has been the formation of strong modern states in East Asia (Korea, Taiwan) and the ASEAN region, with forceful policies aimed at regulating national cultural life. These economic and political reconfigurings have called forth (though not determined) new, condensed cultural formations across the Asia Pacific: new centers of intellectual and cultural as well as economic innovation, new publics and public spheres, new cultural commodities, and new forms of cultural production in literature, journalism, and the electronic media. We might cite as examples in the realm of academia the recent (1993) establishment of the journal *positions* or the *Trajectories* conference in cultural studies held in Taipei in the summer of 1995; they mark the increased salience of these new, alternative positions for cultural geopolitics and theorization. And in the realm of business-speak, this is what talk about "the Pacific Century" reflects—a total transformation in the world balance of forces in all dimensions of cultural life, not just in economics and politics.

In this book we address Chinese transnationalism as an outcome of these transformations, as a phenomenon of late modernity. We contend that, in fact, many modernities constitute the distinctive formation of Chinese transnationalism, in the particular human experiences of change, the elite narrations that define what is modern in Asia, and the workings of late capitalism that form the context and cause of such cultural ferment and struggles at individual, national, regional, and international levels.

One modernity, many modernities?

Marshall Berman (1982) calls modernity the body of experience whereby women and men find themselves to be subjects in and objects of a world in flux, where "all that is solid melts into air." Speaking from a Euro-American viewpoint, Berman maintains that modern life is suffused with the fleeting and the fragmentary, that renewal and disintegration are universal, that all peoples are united by "a unity of disunity."

We see the experiences of fragmentation, flux, and the contingent among diaspora Chinese as being grounded in the institutional changes associated with late capitalism (Harvey 1989) and the repositioning of powers within and between nation-states. Scholars have paid increasing attention to the modernities that are produced out of the articulations, productions, and struggles between capitalist forces and local communities in different parts of the the world (Ong 1987, 1991, 1993; Nonini 1993a; Ong and Peletz 1995; Gilroy 1991, 1993). Allan Pred and Michael Watts (1993) refer to the confrontations between local cultural forms and the global forces associated with capitalism as the reworking of "multiple modernities." But where their approach seems to suggest that modernities in non-Western countries are only reactive formations or resistances to Euro-American capitalism, we see these instead as cultural forms that are organically produced in relation to other regional forces in the polycentric world of late capitalism; forces with new cultural ecumenes independent of older centers of power have arisen.

This points to why the essays of this book go beyond Berman's focus on the experiential condition of modernity to consider metanarratives of modernity in Asia, discourses that play a reflexive role in the experience of a modernity that is distinct from that of the West, though historically connected to it. Narratives of difference intervene in the modern experience of unsettling transitoriness, playing a key role in providing a sense of larger purpose, identity, and historical continuity—that is, ideological framing (Bhaba 1990). Elite production of what constitutes progress, the future, and the nation freely detaches, deploys, reinvents, and legitimizes selected cultural fragments as the composite, essential, and primordial "tradition" and "culture" of a people (Hobsbawm and Ranger 1983; Clifford 1988; Anderson 1991). Such production of narratives is tied to the formation and elaboration of the disciplinary powers of modernity. For instance, Thai elite appropriations of the (originally Euro-American) modern disciplines of mapping, cadastral surveying, and geography have constructed the "geobody" of Thailand as a nation, and thereby the history of the geobody; Thai traditions, customs, populations, and essences, like boundaries, were being constituted even as Siam was mapped into Thailand (Thongchai 1994). Yet, for Thailand, there have been other less nationalist or less elite narratives of modernity that have contested the one that has become hegemonic.

In a similar way, the discourse of "Chinese culture" provides the raw materials for the making of different narrations of modernity. In the case of both Thailand and overseas Chinese, imaginings of what is modern are what Michel Foucault (1978, 1980, 1991) calls "regimes of truth" that seek to objectify, discriminate, and normalize power relations. Such knowledge-power systems are engaged in the work of constructing "imagined communities"—not only ones framed by visions of national territories and borders (Anderson 1991), but also other collectivities—for instance, those created by travel and trade, and those mobilized in dispersion. Overseas Chinese have played an affirmative role in the making of such discourses of modernity, being positioned centrally in their regimes of truth as "modern Asians," "successful entrepreneurs," or "Confucian capitalists." However, contrasting antagonistic narratives of modernity—those of non-Chinese indigenist rhetorics—have also stationed transnational Chinese on the margins of the community and inscribed them as stigmatized, undesirable, or disloyal Others.

The making of these alternative modernities cannot be understood independent of the cultural reworkings brought on by capitalism's own dynamic and by the tensions between this dynamic and nation-state projects of control and regulation. Chinese transnationalism is thus an interplay between strategies of accumulation and the experiences of dislocation, discussed earlier, and the different constructions of modernity by capitalist interests and by nation-states. There are also oppositional narratives of modernity expressed by subalterns divided along class, ethnic, and gender lines, who are marginalized or even suppressed and elided by the dominant constructions of modernity (see Scott 1985; Ong 1987; Nonini 1993a, 1993b). Discourses of modernity in the Asia Pacific are produced in different sites of power, and they refer to each other as much as to the West. The essays in this book deal with modern Chinese transnationalism at the levels of human agency, subject-making, the modern projects of nation-states, and the modernist imaginings of mobile, border-crossing capitalism. We maintain that capitalism in the Asia Pacific and its accompanying institutions and practices—flexibility, travel, consumption, multiculturalism, and mass media—are reworking Chinese identities and subjectivities.

Themes

The essays in this book seek to identify for a range of sites the precursors and contemporary forms of a distinctively modern Chinese transnationalism, and the instrumentalities and identifications that constitute it. While the authors take different approaches, we share a fruitful mix of ethnographic theory, political economy, Foucauldian analytics, and cultural studies. Ultimately, in looking at Chinese transnationalism, we are concerned with specific processes by which diaspora Chinese are subjectified: the dimensions of self-making, and of being made for persons who are subjects within the multiple and mobile domains of late capitalism.

The chronotopes of modern Chinese transnationalism

We find it useful in considering the variety of diaspora Chinese mobility and experience recounted in this book to deploy Bakhtin's notion of the chronotope—a configuration of spatial and temporal indicators for a setting in which, and about which, certain activities take place and certain stories are told. While the authors ground their observations in diverse historical, colonial, and postcolonial contexts, our chronotopes are not, however, locales or sites, but rather time-bound, irreversible paths or itineraries of connection between places that are spanned by imagined and remembered narratives of Chinese transnational practices and discourses. In this sense, Chinese transnational chronotopes are defined by the ways in which different kinds of Chinese crisscross the globe. They have been merchants plying trade in the nineteenth century and tax farmers in European colonies (as in the essay by Trocki) and nationalists from early modern China visiting Southeast Asia, Hawaii, and San Francisco (as in the essay by Duara). As well, they traverse and pass in and out of contemporary China—as migrant female workers from the "north" coming into Shenzhen (studied by Lee), as Beijing scholars sojourning in London, and as Shaanxi villagers in Xinjiang (see the essay by Liu). They travel over vast spaces as overseas bosses from Taiwan based in south China (described by Hsing), as labor migrants to Japan (see Nonini's essay), as thoroughly modern Asians based in Manila and Bangkok (see the essay by Blanc), and as Hong Kong businesspeople and professionals settling in Vancouver (see Mitchell's essay). And they pass over paths of imagination and desire from China to Hong Kong, Taiwan, and New York, as media-captivated cosmopolitans in Shanghai (see Yang's essay) and as national political and economic elites fashioning alternative discourses of modernity (see the essay by Ong).

In thinking about the chronotopes of modern Chinese transnationalism, we begin by positing a *transition between premodernity and moder-*

nity in what has come to be known as the Asia Pacific. Chinese involvement in trade, commerce, and military expeditions (for example, that of the eunuch admiral Zhenghe), encounters with European and American colonial powers, and experiences of travel, study, trade, and sojourn within imperial China all clearly predated *modern* Chinese transnationalism. We resist calling these practices premodern transnationalism since that would presuppose the existence of something like modern nation-states, and yet the formation of nation-states whose administrative powers are linked to industrialism and urbanism (Giddens 1985, 172–97) as well as the emergence of nationalism have both been central to the making of modernity. We therefore conceive of these practices as precursors to modern Chinese transnationalism, out of which the latter arose. Thus the early trade across boundaries of colonial empires by Chinese merchants organized in *kongsis* (see Trocki's essay) is an example of these processes, as is the emergence of contending modern nationalisms in China vis-à-vis earlier forms and their dissemination throughout the diaspora (see Duara's essay). These are discussed in the essays in part 1 of the book.

Diasporas and the diacritics of difference
Joining a recent theoretical project (Clifford 1995; van der Veer 1995; Tölölyan 1991; Safran 1991; Rouse 1991), we seek to resurrect to theoretical respectability the theme of diaspora. If one adhered to the earlier paradigm of overseas Chinese studies in which to be Chinese "overseas" was to be part of an imperfect residual China, diaspora might be seen as a negatively defined and inferior phenomenon. But central to this book is an affirmative view of diaspora as a pattern that marks a common condition of communities, persons, and groups separated by space, an arrangement, moreover, that these persons see themselves as sharing ("we Chinese . . ."). This pattern is continually reconstituted by the literal travel of Chinese persons across and throughout the regions of dispersion, and it is characterized by multiplex and varied connections of family ties, kinship, commerce, sentiments and values about native place in China, shared memberships in transnational organizations, and so on.

Moreover, the very deterritorialized (but not dematerialized) social instititions of the Chinese diaspora in the Asia Pacific set off Chinese from non-Chinese in two related ways and provide constraints on the strategies of accumulation by Chinese (see Clifford 1995, 307). First, there have been various indigenist ideological discourses that have centered legitimate identities for non-Chinese on being "native," *bumiputra* ("princes of the soil" in Malay), or, as in the case of the western United

States in the late nineteenth century, not Oriental and not alien. These discourses have emerged vis-à-vis the perceived dangers of Chinese mobility, and their articulation has been related to episodic economic and political crises of modern capitalisms and nationalisms throughout the Asia Pacific. These discourses have frequently crystallized around racist tropes of threat, disorder, and destruction (such as those of the Yellow Peril, of "Oriental hordes," of being "swamped" by Chinese, and others) that belie fearful visions of hidden yet somehow massed Chinese powers coordinated across the diaspora. Second, there have been the nation-states of the Asia Pacific whose regimes of discipline for "citizens" and "subjects" have been threatened by the mobile cosmopolitanism of diaspora Chinese. Governing power in some of these nation-states has at times been directly captured by the advocates of indigenist ideologies, as in the case of Malaysia (studied by Nonini in this volume); at other times, leaders of these nation-states have had to accommodate to them; at yet others, leaders among diaspora Chinese, in what is apparently a long-standing strategy (Skinner 1968), have colluded with sympathetic non-Chinese to discipline other Chinese in the direction of non-Chinese prejudices (as in the instance studied by Mitchell in this book).

Mobility, modernity, power:
The wildness of Chinese transnationalism

A principal theme that unifies the essays of this book is the mobility of diaspora Chinese, which manifests a wildness, danger, and unpredictability that challenges and undermines modern imperial regimes of truth and power. The essays in this book demonstrate that by means of strategies of transnational mobility, Chinese have eluded, taken tactical advantage of, temporized before, redefined, and overcome the disciplinings of modern regimes of colonial empires, postcolonial nation-states, and international capitalism. These mobile practices have intersected with the impositions of modern regimes of truth and knowledge to take the form of a guerrilla transnationalism.

Chinese transnationalism has an unpredictable wildness and danger to it in that diaspora Chinese have reworked the definitions of them imposed by these regimes as "local" and locatable. As the essays by both Duara and Trocki suggest, until the 1970s, European, American, and Japanese empires could seek only to partially domesticate and harness Chinese transnational strategies of mobility, never completely dominate them. Since the 1970s, with the emergence of regimes of flexible accumulation, the distinctive transnational strategies of diaspora Chinese have converged even more closely with the circuits of accumulation within flexible capitalism across the Asia Pacific. The last three decades have witnessed both the rise of Japanese transnational corporations to regional economic dominance and the emergence of strong modern states in the ASEAN countries, China, Taiwan, and South Korea. Both processes have brought on the installation of widely ranging nation-state regimes that mobilize the biopower and labor power of populations, constitute nationalities and citizenships, regulate genders and ethnicities, and organize space through bureaucratic technologies of inscription and control. At the same time, however, the trends toward capitalist globalization, its institutional flexibilities such as subcontracting, the opening of new commodity markets, instantaneous fax communication, the demand for migrant labor, and rapid air travel have acted as foils to these new nation-state technologies of regulation—and Chinese transnationalists have taken ample advantage of them. Although constrained by nation-state regimes to operate obliquely rather than confront them head on, diaspora Chinese have nonetheless acted effectively to enact their own strategies of accumulation.

The potential of wild and dangerously innovative powers associated with Chinese diasporic mobility has now therefore been incorporated into the open-ended logics of flexible capitalism itself. Thus, for instance, the commercial and real-estate holdings of Liem Sioe Leong conform to, yet transcend, the postcolonial orderings of the Indonesian state and of ASEAN; Taiwanese investors in Guangdong form new links with local officials that explicitly repudiate the older cold war divisions between the Peoples Republic of China and Taiwan, which even the gerontocrats of both now concede are obsolete (see Hsing's essay); new syntheses in consumption patterns among Chinese trendsetters in Thailand set off a thoroughly contemporary Asian modernity that is emulated elsewhere in the region, even as such syntheses threaten to displace indigenist identifications (see Blanc's essay). In these and a multitude of other examples, Chinese transnational practices represent forms of power that collude with the contemporary regimes of truth and power organizing the new flexible capitalisms and modern nation-states, but also act obliquely to them, and systematically set out to transgress the shifting boundaries set by both. It is precisely for this reason that we have entitled this book *Ungrounded Empires,* to refer to the new deterritorialized and protean structures of domination that span the Asia Pacific and within which diaspora Chinese act—empires that constantly change shape, being constituted by Chinese transnational practices in the ether of airspaces, international time-zones, migrant labor contracts, mass media images, virtual companies, and electronic transactions, and operating across all recognized borderlines.

The uses of "family" and guanxi: *Flexibility and violence*

Yet another theme of this book is the ways in which the contemporary regime of flexible accumulation has called forth new deployments of "family" and of *guanxi* particularist relations from within the accumulation strategies of transnational Chinese. In this regard, we need to move beyond the economism of Harvey's (1989) analysis. Family and *guanxi* relations among diaspora Chinese represent a long-standing habitus whose very flexibilities have now been placed in the service of accumulation strategies under the novel conditions of late capitalism, and in the process are thereby being reworked themselves. Thus, as noted earlier, diaspora Chinese have taken advantage of these conditions to move their children into the ranks of the global professional elites (see the essays by Nonini and Mitchell). Even more important are the ways in which their transnational practices centered on family and *guanxi* relations have thoroughly intermeshed with the tendency toward subcontracting and, in fact, have underwritten it—whether they are subcontractors as such, the laborers employed by them, the human cargo they smuggle, or so on.

Taken as authentic features of an essential "Chinese culture," both the Chinese family and *guanxi* particularism have been thoroughly fetishized as objects of cultural analysis by scholars studying overseas Chinese. In particular, familism, *guanxi*, *ganqing* ("sentiment"), and *xinyong* ("trust" or "credit") had been emphasized by an earlier generation of functionalist scholars as crucial to Chinese business operation (De Glopper 1972; Silin 1972; Amyot 1973; Young 1974). Later scholars have thoroughly integrated these traits as explanatory elements within the postwar celebratory narratives of Chinese business success associated with the economic rise of the Asia Pacific (Berger and Hsiao 1988; Tai 1989; Hamilton 1991). The needs of the Chinese family are seen as focal to the hard work and business acumen to which overseas Chinese everywhere are prone; *guanxi* particularist relations between businessmen are viewed as positive attributes crucial to the trust and credit that make the Chinese commercial world go round, provide them with access to inside information and commercial contacts, and so on.

But these scholars have thus failed to acknowledge two phenomena— the ways in which both Chinese "family" and *guanxi* are central discursive constructs within the newly self-confident regional imaginary of a "Greater China" and "the glow of Chinese fraternity" (see Ong's essay in this volume), and the ways in which flexible accumulation and its transnational imperatives have recast the structure and meaning of both. In their idealizations of family, *guanxi*, fraternity, and so on, these scholars have colluded with political and economic elites in promoting the first, while completely missing the second. The essays in part 2 of this book challenge such fetishizations by situating the forms of Chinese families and of *guanxi* practices implicated in transnational ventures within the new constraints of flexible capitalism, and by pointing to the "symbolic violence" (Bourdieu 1991)[4] centrally implicated in the workings of both.

The tactical practices of family and *guanxi* euphemized in discourse (Yang 1994) show amoral tactics of domination, violence, exploitation, and duplicity, both outside this discourse and within it. Outside it: *guanxi* discourse demarcates various relationships of comity and privilege with specific kinds of people ("brothers," classmates, people with the same China native place). But this by implication excludes numerous others with whom one has no acknowledged relationship—such as a female clerical employee, a non-Chinese manual laborer, or a poorer customer to whom one sells adulterated goods. These people can be legitimately taken advantage of, exploited, disciplined, abused, or cheated. Within it: Most *guanxi* relationships are articulated between putative status equals (classmates, workmates, people with the same surname) or between persons with a distinct but supposedly benevolent difference in status: teacher and student, for instance. Yet the supposed equality or benign status difference euphemizes relations of domination where de facto differences in power and capital are misrecognized or not acknowledged in public by both sides. Take the relationship built on having the same native place, *tongxiang guanxi*: We read of such domination within the *kongsi* described by Trocki, the Shenzhen factory studied by Lee, and among the Hong Kong immigrants to Vancouver discussed by Mitchell.

The flexible tactics of accumulation among Chinese transnationalists are evident in the uses to which Chinese put their family and *guanxi* networks in subcontracting throughout the Asia Pacific and beyond.[5] These uses of networks interest us precisely because of their informality and their related capacity to span space and to connect individuals and groups who occupy different positions in national spaces. Examples of these tactics and their applications to subcontracting are discussed in the preface and essays of part 2.

A question we have so far finessed is, In Chinese accumulation strategies, what is being accumulated? Succinctly stated the answer is, capital. But here we imply not Marx's idea that capital has a single form—material wealth—but rather the idea from Bourdieu (1986) that there is a variety of capitals—economic, cultural, symbolic, educational, social, and linguistic. For Bourdieu, such capitals are different, mutually convertible kinds of culturally defined resources that can be converted into personal power, thereby supporting one's life chances or social trajectory (Postone, LiPuma, and Calhoun 1993, 4–5). Thus, for example, the educational capital of a university degree can be converted, under specific conditions, into economic capital (wealth), social capital (prestige), and eligibility for legal citizenship (see Ong 1992 and Nonini's essay in this volume).

Localizations, identities, and
effects of regimes of truth and power

How can the complex tactical practices of Chinese transnationalism best be theoretically conceptualized? Returning to our earlier discussion of diaspora Chinese mobility, and taking up concepts broached in Nonini's essay in this volume, we propose that there are several contemporary regimes of truth and power to which diaspora Chinese are subject and whose effects constrain their strategies and hence tactics of accumulation. We identify three such regimes: the regime of the Chinese family, the regime of the capitalist workplace, and the regime of the nation-state. Each regime disciplines persons under its control in different ways to form acceptable and normal subjectivities as, for example, industrious workers or conscientious managers, dutiful daughters or providing fathers, and loyal citizens or economically desirable immigrants. For its effects, each kind of regime requires *the localization of disciplinable subjects*—that persons be locatable and confinable, if not actually confined, to specific spaces defined functionally by these regimes: the home, the factory, the nation.

For example, modern nation-state regimes promulgate and inscribe normalizing discourses of the citizen and the nation on the bodies and subjectivities of person-subjects through various disciplining practices as diverse as saluting a flag, marching in an army parade, being entered as an item in a government dossier, dancing in a national folkloric festival, or learning to speak a national language. These practices require for their effects that subjects be defined probabilistically—for example, as citizen or alien, immigrant or indigene—in ways with knowable spatial referents. For instance, citizens go to police stations and voting registrars while undocumented workers do not; indigenes enter government schools not open to most students of immigrant descent. In short, the modern nation-state regime requires for its effects that the subjects its discourses and disciplines construct be generally localizable.

Under these conditions, Chinese transnationalists seek to elude the localizations imposed on them by nation-state regimes by, above all, moving between national spaces, playing off one nation-state regime against another, seeking tactical advantage—knowing that it is easier to become a citizen here than there, that there are more legal and political rights in country X than in country Y, and so on (Ong 1993). Some, such as illegal migrants, also may seek to hide their civil status. Yet, obviously, not all Chinese transnationalists are alike. Each is systematically advantaged or disadvantaged by his or her positions within not only nation-states but also the capitalist workplace and the family. Like nation-state regimes, workplace and familistic regimes each serve up relative agents and those relatively acted on, relative victimizers and relative victims—managers and day laborers, older married men and younger unmarried women, for example. The effects of workplace and familistic regimes are also probabilistic and operate through localization—regulating subjectivities and bodies by allotting them to specific proper spaces and putting them "in their place."

Whereas for persons who are not mobile, these three regimes operate in tandem, for persons engaged in transnational moves, it is possible to take advantage of the disjunctures in space, and therefore in power, between them. Nonini writes in his essay in this volume that Chinese transnationalists engage in strategies of capital accumulation "that seek to resist the localizations these overlapping regimes require of them as disciplinable subjects, while appropriating for their own uses the effects of the localizations these regimes have upon other disciplinable subjects." Therefore, if our conceptualization of the tactics centered on localization is valid, there is no *general* description possible of how transitional practices work for all transnational Chinese, for this depends on how persons defined by specific categories (gender, class, nationality, age, among others), and thus unequal in their capacity to avoid localization while taking advantage of *others* being localized, strategize to avail themselves of family and *guanxi* network resources to accumulate various kinds of capital. In part 3, the preface and essays by Nonini and Mitchell focus in different ways on nation-state regimes, their localizations, and Chinese tactics for dealing with them, and provide other examples illustrating the theoretical perspective developed here.

Imaginaries, subject-making, and identifications
What are the implications of such transnational tactics for modern Chinese identities and subjectivities? In recasting the analysis of identities and subjectivities, we reject the conventional assumption that a person simply "has" or "possesses" an identity. Roger Rouse (1995) notes the presumption of liberal discourse that identity "is something that unproblematically connects individuals to society," with individuals who share some common trait thereby having an "identity" as members of a particular group in society. In contrast, critical anthropology, feminism, and cultural studies have come to view identities and bodies, though variously marked, possessed, and experienced, as unstable formations constituted within webs of power relations (Ong 1987; Laclau and Mouffe 1985; De Lauretis 1986; Williams 1989; Moore 1994; Ong and Peletz 1995). Different identities—gender, race, nationality, subculture, domi-

nant culture—intersect in and constitute an individual. A person is therefore a site of differences; someone can be simultaneously Indonesian, Chinese, working-class, and a mother, as well as all of these together. What is invoked, or when, depends on particular circumstances and the configuration of social relations that constitute our everyday world.

The essays in part 4 push further the theme of multiplicity and instability in identities by examining how they are shaped by the intersections between localizing regimes of truth, on the one hand, and the articulations, practices, and deterritorialized imaginaries of subjects who operate in reference to a transnational world, on the other. The different subject-positions of diaspora Chinese, formed by their allegiances to various places as well as by a propensity to sojourning as a way of life, engender contradictory subjectivities that are at once fluid, fragmentary, but also enabling of an agency to circumvent certain modalities of control while taking advantage of others. We must therefore attend to the various governmentalities whereby they undergo subjectification, or the processes of the subject's being made and self-made (Foucault 1991). These dialectical processes of disciplining and self-identification are produced at the intersections of regulation by nation-states and individuals' attempts to circumvent or redirect control as well as to (re)imagine their lives in different visions of modernity.

As part of projects of state formation (Corrigan and Sayer 1985), from the mid-1970s onward new Asian nation-state regimes have sought to discipline and instill in citizen-subjects a sense of guided cultural orientation and affluence within limits (Chun 1994; Chua 1991; Wee 1993; Tremewan 1994). Over the same period, however, the sense of ethnicity and nationality as something tied to a particular history and place has begun to be undermined by booming commodity markets, American mass culture, and increased travel overseas. Modern communications, mass media, global mass culture, and flexible capitalism—the constituent elements that go to make up globalization (Hall 1991, 22–23)—have intruded into the body politic of the nation-state to create transnational publics. An intersection and mixing of different flows of information, images, ideas, and peoples, transnational publics provide alternatives to state ideologies for remaking identity, thus eroding not only the nation-state but also "the national identities which are associated with it" (Hall 1991, 25). The different publics engendered by modern air travel, satellite communications, and flexible capitalism enable capitalist systems to exploit different forms of labor, and to mix and transfer them across geopolitical spaces. Such flexible strategies inculcate new positions and subjectivities—Chinese as workers or employers moving in and out of old locales (for example, Malaysian Chinese in Japan or New Zealand, as described in Nonini's essay) and as consumers (such as mainland Chinese fantasizing through karaoke or television about overseas Chinese modernity, as discussed in Yang's essay). Transnational publics are forming new Chinese subjectivities that are increasingly independent of place, self-consciously postmodern, and subversive of national regimes of truth.

Imaginaries inspired by mass comsumption, pastiche culture, fantasies of other places, and unruly desires can be disciplined either to support hegemonic views of regimes of truth (as in the Michael Fay affair in Singapore) or to undermine them (see Ong's essay). Whether nurtured by nostalgia for vanishing cultures, fired by consumer restlessness, or impelled by spiritual homelessness, such alternative imaginaries can cast identities beyond the inscriptions and identifications made by states. The concept of imaginaries therefore conveys the agency of diaspora subjects, who, while being made by state and capitalist regimes of truth, can play with different cultural fragments in a way that allows them to segue from one discourse to another, experiment with alternative forms of identification, shrug in and out of identities, or evade imposed forms of identifications.

The proliferation of different ways of being Chinese—through accumulation strategies, mobility, and modern mass media—has engendered complex, shifting, and fragmented subjectivities that are at once specific yet global. In the realm of imagination, mainland Chinese dream about futures that can be captured through gaining a "PR" (permanent residence) in the United States (see Liu's essay), while a Sino-Thai executive working the China-Thailand import-export markets can play simultaneously at being Chinese, Teochew, modern Asian, and loyal Thai (see Blanc's essay). Thus there are multiple subjective senses of Chineseness that appear to be based not on the possession of some reified Chinese culture but on a propensity to seek opportunities elsewhere, a spatial projection of economic and social desires across geopolitical divides, and a bricolage with different modes of political inclusion and exclusion.

Chinese in their transnational practice thereby draw on their participation in the proliferation of difference in the global economy. Their sense of fragmentation and even displacement comes out of an ever-increasing sense of being alternatively embedded in and disembedded from various social relationships (Giddens 1991) and the inescapable tension between identification with specific places (or families) and the postmodern flux of many places and many identifications. In this, the subjectivities of modern Chinese transnationalists are not all that different from those of many in the West, and in some ways diaspora Chinese are even more ultra-modern in their global maneuvers (Ong 1993). What is distinctive is the particular history of the Chinese diaspora, the specific roles of Chinese in the flexible capitalism of the Asia Pacific, and the ways Chinese have themselves come to experience and interpret it. Yet these all testify to the generically modern condition that transnational Chinese share with many other peoples: always already being "out of place."

Notes

[1] ASEAN, the Association of Southeast Asian Nations, consists of Singapore, Malaysia, Philippines, Indonesia, and Thailand. As of this writing, Vietnam has just joined ASEAN.

[2] In this book we provide transcriptions of Chinese terms for English readers in Mandarin pinyin, rather than for some so-called "dialect" such as Cantonese or Hokkien, except in a few cases where proper names and certain terms (e.g., *kongsi*) have well-known alternative transcriptions, or where contributors have, due to concerns about representation, insisted on "dialect"-based transcriptions. Thus in using pinyin transcriptions because they are widely understood, we do not privilege Mandarin as a mode of representation over other equally legitimate languages spoken by diasporic Chinese (on Taiwan see Murray and Hong 1994, 9–15).

[3] "Don't call us 'overseas Chinese' because the term carries a historical baggage, referring to *huaqiao*, or sojourners who harbour deep desires for China. Call us 'Chinese overseas' instead as that is more factual, and simply means we are *haiwai hauren*, or Chinese living overseas" (Lee 1994).

[4] Bourdieu (1991, 51) writes that "*intimidation*, a symbolic violence which is not aware of what it is (to the extent that it implies no *act of intimidation*), can only be exerted on a person predisposed (in his habitus) to feel it, whereas others will ignore it." Intimidation operates within a broader process of stigmatizing and marginalizing the category of persons intimidated, depriving them of access to resources available to others.

[5] Within anthropology and sociology, a network is defined as a set of persons, each connected to every other either directly or through one or more nodal individuals, who are the "anchors" of the network. Networks are therefore ego-centered (Whitten and Wolfe 1973; Mitchell 1974; Mayer 1966; Cook and Whitmeyer 1992).

References

Abu-Lughod, Lila. 1993. "Writing Against Culture." In R. Fox, ed., *Recapturing Anthropology: Working in the Present*, pp. 137–62. Santa Fe, NM: School of American Research.

Amyot, Jacques. 1973. *The Manila Chinese: Familism in the Philippine Environment.* Quezon City: Ateneo de Manila.

Anderson, 1991. *Imagined Communities: Reflections on the Origin and Spread of Nationalism.* Rev. ed. London: Verso.

Ang, Ien. 1993. "To Be or Not to Be Chinese: Diaspora, Culture, and Postmodern Ethnicity." *Southeast Asian Journal of Social Science* 21, no. 1: 1–17.

Appadurai, Arjun. 1993. "Global Ethnoscapes: Notes and Queries for a Transnational Anthropology." In R. Fox, ed., *Recapturing Anthropology: Working in the Present*, pp. 191–210. Santa Fe, NM: School of American Research.

Berger, Peter L., and Hsin-Huang Michael Hsiao, eds. 1988. *In Search of an East Asian Development Model*. New Brunswick, NJ: Transcation.

Berman, Marshall. 1982. *All That Is Solid Melts into Air: The Experience of Modernity*. New York: Penguin.

Bhabha, Homi K. 1990. "DissemiNation: Time, Narrative, and the Margins of the Modern Nation." In H. K. Bhabha, ed., *Nation and Narration*, pp. 291–322. London: Routledge.

Bourdieu, Pierre. 1986. "The Forms of Capital." In J. G. Richardson, ed., *Handbook of Theory and Research for the Sociology of Education*, pp. 241–58. New York: Greenwood.

———. 1991. *Language and Symbolic Power*. Edited by J. B. Thompson, Cambridge, MA: Harvard University Press.

Chan, Kwok Bun, and Claire S. N. Chiang. 1994. *Stepping Out: The Making of Chinese Entrepreneurs*. Singapore: Simon and Schuster.

Chow, Rey. 1993. *Writing Diaspora: Tactics of Intervention in Contemporary Cultural Studies*. Bloomington: Indiana University Press.

Chua Beng-Huat. 1991. "Depoliticized but Ideologically Successful: The Public Housing Programme in Singapore." *International Journal of Urban and Regional Research* 15, no. 1: 24–41.

Chun, Allen. 1994. "From Nationalism to Nationalizing: Cultural Imagination and State Formation in Postwar Taiwan." *Australian Journal of Chinese Affairs* 31: 49–72.

Clifford, James. 1988. *The Predicament of Culture: Twentieth-Century Ethnography, Literature, and Art*. Cambridge, MA: Harvard University Press.

———. 1992. "Traveling Cultures." In L. Grossberg, C. Nelson, and P. Treichler, eds., *Cultural Studies*, pp. 96–116. New York: Routledge.

———. 1995. "Diasporas." *Cultural Anthropology* 9, no. 3: 302–38.

Cook, K. S., and J. M. Whitmeyer. 1992. "Two Approaches to Social Structure: Exchange Theory and Network Analysis." *Annual Review of Sociology* 18: 109–27.

Corrigan, Philip, and Derek Sayer. 1985. *The Great Arch: English State Formation as Cultural Revolution*. Oxford: Basil Blackwell.

Crissman, Lawrence. 1967. "The Segmentary Structure of Urban Overseas Chinese Communities." *Man* (n.s.) 2, no. 2: 185–204.

Cushman, Jennifer, and Wang Gungwu. 1988. *Changing Identities of the Southeast Asian Chinese Since World War II*. Hong Kong: Hong Kong University Press.

De Glopper, Donald. 1972. "Doing Business in Lukang." In W. E. Willmott, ed., *Economic Organization in Chinese Society*, pp. 297–326. Stanford: Stanford University Press.

De Lauretis, Teresa, ed. 1986. *Feminist Studies/Cultural Studies*. London: Macmillan.

Dewey, Alice. 1962. "Trade and Social Control in Java." *Journal of the Royal Anthropological Institute* 92, no. 2: 177–90.

Dirlik, Arif. 1993. "Introducing the Pacific." In Arif Dirlik, ed., *What Is in a Rim? Critical Perspectives on the Pacific Region Idea*, pp. 3–12. Boulder, CO: Westview.

Fabian, Johannes. 1983. *Time and the Other: How Anthrology Makes Its Object*. New York: Columbia University Press.

Fallows, James. 1994. *Looking at the Sun: The Rise of the New East Asian Economic and Political System*. New York: Pantheon.

Farquhar, Judith B., and James L. Hevia. 1993. "Culture and Postwar American Historiography of China." *positions* 1, No. 2: 486–525.

Featherstone, Mike. 1990. "Global Culture: An Introduction." *Theory, Culture, and Society* 7: 1–14.

Fernandez-Kelly, Maria Patricia. 1983. *For We Are Sold, I and My People: Women and Industry in Mexico's Frontier*. Albany: State University of New York Press.

Foucault, Michel. 1978. *History of Sexuality, Vol. 1*. Translated by Michael Hurley. New York: Pantheon.

———. 1980. *Knowledge/Power: Selected Interviews and Other Writings, 1972–1977*. Edited and translated by Colin Gordin. New York: Pantheon.

———. 1991. "Governmentality." In G. Burchell, C. Gordon, and P. Miller, eds. *The Foucault Effect: Studies in Governmentality*, pp. 87–104. Chicago: University of Chicago Press.

Freedman, Maurice. 1957. *Chinese Family and Marriage in Singapore*. Colonial Research Studies no. 20. London: Colonial Office.

———. 1979a. *The Study of Chinese Society: Essays by Maurice Freedman*. Edited by G. William Skinner. Stanford: Stanford University Press.

———. 1979b. [1959]: "The Handling of Money: A Note on the Background to the Economic Sophistication of Overseas Chinese." In *The Study of Chinese Society: Essays by Maurice Freedman*, pp. 22–26. Edited by G. William Skinner. Stanford: Stanford University Press.

———. 1979c [1970]. "Why China?" In *The Study of Chinese Society: Essays by Maurice Freedman*, pp. 407–422. Edited by G. William Skinner. Stanford: Stanford University Press.

Freeman, Carla S. Forthcoming. *High Tech and High Heels in the Global Economy: Women, Work, and Off-shore Informatics in Barbados*. Durham, NC: Duke University Press.

Geertz, Clifford. 1973. *The Interpretation of Cultures: Selected Essays*. New York: Basic Books.

Giddens, Anthony. 1985. *The Nation-State and Violence: Volume II of a Contemporary Critique of Historical Materialism*. Berkeley: University of California Press.

———. 1991. *Modernity and Identity*. Stanford: Stanford University Press.

Gilroy, Paul. 1991. *"There Ain't No Black in the Union Jack": The Cultural Politics of Race and Nation*. Chicago: University of Chicago Press.

———. 1993. *The Black Atlantic: Modernity and Double Consciousness*. Cambridge, MA: Harvard University Press.

Goldberg, Michael A. 1985. *The Chinese Connection: Getting Plugged In to Pacific Rim Real Estate, Trade, and Capital Markets*. Vancouver: University of British Columbia Press.

Hall, Stuart. 1991. "The Local and the Global: Globalization and Ethnicity." In A. D. King, ed., *Culture, Globalization, and the World System: Contemporary Conditions for the Representation of Identity*, pp. 19–39. London: Macmillan.

Hamilton, Gary, ed. 1991. *Business Networks and Economic Development in East and Southeast Asia*. Hongkong: Centre of Asian Studies, University of Hong Kong.

Harvey, David. 1989. *The Condition of Postmodernity*. Oxford: Basil Blackwell.

Hobsbawm, Eric, and Terence Ranger. 1983. *The Invention of Tradition*. Cambridge: Cambridge University Press.

Jameson, Fredric. 1991. "The Cultural Logic of Late Capitalism." In *Postmodernism, Or the Cultural Logic of Late Capitalism*, pp. 1–54. Durham, NC: Duke University Press.

Kao, John. 1993. "The Worldwide Web of Chinese Business." *Harvard Business Review* (March–April): 24–37.

Kotkin, Joel. 1992. *Tribes: How Race, Religion, and Identity Determine Success in the New Global Economy*. New York: Random House.

Laclau, Ernesto, and Chantal Mouffe. 1985. *Hegemony and Socialist Strategy: Towards a Radical Democratic Politics*. London: Verso.

Lee, Michelle. 1994. "Name Change." *Singapore Sunday Straits Times*, August 8.

Lim, Linda Y. C., and L. A. Peter Gosling, eds. 1983. *The Chinese in Southeast Asia*. 2 vols. Singapore: Maruzen Asia.

Lipietz, Alain. 1986. "New Tendencies in the International Division of Labor: Regimes of Accumulation and Modes of Regulation." In A. Scott and M. Storper, eds., *Production, Work, Territory: The Geographical Anatomy of Capitalism*, pp. 16–40. Boston: Allen and Unwin.

Mackie, Jamie. 1993. "Changing Patterns of Chinese Big Business in Southeast Asia." In R. McVey, ed., *Southeast Asian Capitalists*, pp. 161–90. Ithaca, NY: Southeast Asia Program, Cornell University.

Marcus, George, and Michael Fischer. 1986. *Anthropology as Cultural Critique: An Experimental Moment in the Human Sciences*. Chicago: University of Chicago Press.

Massey, Doreen. 1993. "Power-Geometry and Progressive Sense of Place." In J. Bird et al., eds., *Mapping the Futures: Local Cultures, Global Change*, pp. 59–69. New York: Routledge.

Mayer, Adrian C. 1966. "The Significance of Quasi-groups in the Study of Complex Societies." In M. Banton, ed., *The Social Anthropology of Complex Societies*, pp. 97–122. London: Tavistock Publications.

McVey, Ruth. 1993. "The Materialization of the Southeast Asian Entrepreneur." In R. McVey, ed., *Southeast Asian Capitalists*, pp. 7–33. Ithaca, NY: Southeast Asia Program, Cornell University.

Mitchell, J. Clyde. 1974. "Social Networks." *Annual Review of Anthropology* 3: 279–99.

Moore, Henrietta L. 1994. *A Passion for Difference*. Bloomington: Indiana University Press.

Murray, Stephen O., and Keelung Hong. 1994. *Taiwanese Culture, Taiwanese Society: A Critical Review of Social Science Research Done on Taiwan*. Lanham, MD: University Press of America.

Nakajima, Mineo. 1994. "Economic Development in East Asia and Confucian Ethics." *Social Compass* 41, no. 1: 113–19.

Newell, William H. 1962. *Treacherous River: A Study of Rural Chinese in North Malaya*. Kuala Lumpur: University of Malaya Press.

Nonini, Donald M. 1988. "Class Consciousness, Ethnicity, and Class Differences Among Malaysian Chinese in the Post-War Period." In J. Cushman and G. Wang, eds., *Changing Identities of the Southeast Asian Chinese Since World War II*, p. 299. Hong Kong: Hong Kong University Press.

———. 1993a. "On the Outs on the Rim: An Ethnographic Grounding of the 'Asia Pacific' Imaginary." In Arif Dirlik, ed., *What Is in a Rim? Critical Perspectives on the Pacific Region Idea*, pp. 29–50. Boulder, CO: Westview.

———. 1993b. "Popular Sources of Chinese Labor Militancy in Colonial Malaya." In C. Guerin-Gonzales and C. Strikwerda, eds., *The Politics of Immigrant Workers: Labor Activism and Migration in the World Economy Since 1830*, pp. 215–44. New York: Holmes and Meier.

Olsen, Stephen M. 1972. "The Inculcation of Economic Values in Taipei Business Families." In W. E. Willmott, ed., *Economic Organization in Chinese Society*, pp. 261–96. Stanford: Stanford University Press.

Ong, Aihwa. 1987. *Spirits of Resistance and Capitalist Discipline: Factory Women in Malaysia*. Albany: State University of New York Press.

———. 1990. "State vs. Islam: Malay Families, Women's Bodies and the Body Politic in Malaysia." *American Ethnologist* 17, no. 2: 258–76.

———. 1991. "The Gender and Labor Politics of Postmodernity." *Annual Review of Anthropology* 20: 279–309.

———. 1992. "Limits to Cultural Accumulation: Chinese Capitalists on the American Pacific Rim." *Annals of the New York Academy of Sciences* 645: 125–145.

———. 1993. "On the Edge of Empires: Flexible Citizenship Among Chinese in Diaspora." *Positions* 1, no. 3: 745–78.

Ong, Aihwa, and Michael G. Peletz, eds. 1995. *Bewitching Women, Pious Men: Gender and Body Politics in Southeast Asia*. Berkeley: University of California Press.

Pan, Lynn. 1994. *Sons of the Yellow Emperor: A History of the Chinese Diaspora*. New York: Kodansha International.

Postone, Moishe, Edward LiPuma, and Craig Calhoun. 1993. "Introduction: Bourdieu and Social Theory." In C. Calhoun, E. LiPuma, and M. Postone, eds., *Bourdieu: Critical Perspectives*, pp. 1–13. Chicago: University of Chicago Press.

Pred, Allan, and Michael John Watts. 1993. *Reworking Modernity: Capitalisms and Symbolic Discontent*. New Brunswick: Rutgers University Press.

Purcell, Victor. 1960. *The Chinese in Modern Malaya*. Singapore: Oxford University Press.

———. 1965. *The Chinese in Southeast Asia*. 2nd ed. Kuala Lumpur: Oxford University Press.

Redding, S. Gordon. 1990. *The Spirit of Chinese Capitalism*. Berlin: Walter de Gruyter.

Rouse, Roger. 1991. "Mexican Migration and the Social Space of Postmodernism." *Diaspora* 1, no. 1: 8–23.

———. 1995. "Questions of Identity: Personhood and Collectivity in Transnational Migration to the United States." *Critique of Anthropology* 15, no. 1: 351–80.

Safran, William. 1991. "Diasporas in Modern Societies: Myths of Homeland and Return." *Diaspora* 1, no. 1: 93–99.

31

Sassen, Saskia. 1991. *The Global City: New York, London, Tokyo.* Princeton: Princeton University Press.

SCCCI (Singapore Chinese Chamber of Commerce and Industry). 1991. *First World Chinese Entrepreneurs Convention: A Global Network.* Edited by F. Hu, Singapore: Kim Hup Lee.

Scott, James C. 1985. *Weapons of the Weak: Everyday Forms of Peasant Resistance.* New Haven: Yale University Press.

Silin, Robert. 1972. "Marketing and Credit in a Hong Kong Wholesale Market." In W. E. Willmott, ed., *Economic Organization in Chinese Society*, pp. 327–52. Stanford: Stanford University Press.

Simoniya, N. A. 1961. *Overseas Chinese in Southeast Asia—A Russian Study.* Data Papers no. 45. Ithaca, NY: Southeast Asia Program, Deptartment of Far Eastern Studies, Cornell University.

Skinner, G. William. 1957. *Chinese Society in Thailand.* Ithaca, NY: Cornell University Press.

———. 1958. *Leadership and Power in the Chinese Community in Thailand.* Ithaca, NY: Cornell University Press.

———. 1968. "Overseas Chinese Leadership: Paradigm for A Paradox." In G. Wijeyewardene, ed., *Leadership and Authority*, pp. 191–207. Singapore: University of Malaya Press.

Tai, Hung-chao, ed. 1989. *Confucianism and Economic Development: An Oriental Alternative?* Washington, DC: Washington Institute for Values in Public Policy.

Thongchai Winichakul, 1994. *Siam Mapped: A History of the Geo-Body of a Nation.* Honolulu: University of Hawaii Press.

T'ien, Ju-k'ang. 1953. *The Chinese of Sarawak.* London: London School of Economics and Political Science.

Tölölian, Khachig. 1991. "The Nation State and Its Others: In Lieu of a Preface." *Diaspora* 1, no. 1: 3–7.

Tong, Chee-kiong. 1991. "Centripetal Authority, Differentiated Networks: The Social Organization of Chinese Firms in Singapore." In G. Hamilton, ed., *Business Networks and Economic Development in East and Southeast Asia*, pp. 176–200. Hong Kong: Centre of Asian Studies, University of Hong Kong.

Tremewan, Chris. 1994. *The Political Economy of Social Control in Singapore.* New York: St. Martin's.

Tu, Wei-ming. 1991. "Cultural China: The Periphery as the Center." *Daedalus* 120, no. 2: 1–32.

van der Veer, Peter. 1995. *Nation and Migration: The Politics of Space in the South Asian Diaspora.* Philadelphia: University of Pennsylvania Press.

Wang, Gungwu. 1991a. "Little Dragons on the Confucian Periphery." In G. Wang, ed., *China and the Overseas Chinese.* Singapore: Times Academic Press.

———. 1991b. "Among Non-Chinese." *Daedalus* 120, no. 2: 135–58.

Wang, Ling-chi. 1991. "Roots and Changing Identity of the Chinese in the United States." *Daedalus* 120, no. 2: 181–206.

Weber, Max. 1978. *Economy and Society: An Outline of Interpretive Sociology.* Edited by G. Roth and C. Wittich. Berkeley: University of California Press.

Wee, C.-J. W.-L. 1993. "Contending with Primordialism: The 'Modern' Construction of Postcolonial Singapore." *positions* 1, no. 3: 715–44.

Whitten, Norman E., and A. W. Wolfe. 1973. "Network Analysis." In John J. Honigman, ed., *Handbook of Cultural and Social Anthropology*, pp. 717–46. Chicago: Rand-McNally.

Wickberg, Edgar. 1965. *The Chinese in Philippine Life, 1850–1898*. New Haven: Yale University Press.

Williams, Brackette. 1989. "A Class Act: Anthropology and the Race to Nation Across Ethnic Terrain." *Annual Review of Anthropology* 18: 401–44.

Willmott, Donald E. 1960. *The Chinese of Semarang*. Ithaca, NY: Cornell University Press.

Willmott, William E. 1967. *The Chinese in Cambodia*. Vancouver: University of British Columbia Publications Centre.

Wilson, Rob, and Arif Dirlik, eds. 1994. *Asia/Pacific as Space of Cultural Production*. Special issue of *Boundary 2* 21, no. 1.

Wolf, Diane. 1992. *Factory Daughters: Gender, Household Dynamics, and Rural Industrialization in Java*. Berkeley: University of California Press.

Wolf, Eric. 1983. *Europe and the People Without History*. Berkeley: University of California Press.

Wong, Siu-lun. 1988. "The Applicability of Asian Family Values to Other Sociocultural Settings." In P. L. Berger and H.-H. M. Hsiao, eds., *In Search of an East Asian Development Model*, pp. 134–154. New Brunswick, NJ: Transaction Books.

Yang, Mayfair Mei-hui. 1994. *Gifts, Favors, and Banquets: The Art of Social Relationships in China*. Ithaca, NY: Cornell University Press.

Yoshihara, Kunio. 1988. *The Rise of Ersatz Capitalism in South-East Asia*. Singapore: Oxford.

Young, John A. 1974. *Business and Sentiment in a Chinese Market Town*. (Asian Folklore and Social Life Monographs, 60.) Taipei: The Orient Cultural Service.

Part 1

Transiting to Modernity:
The Wildness and Power of
Early Chinese Transnationalism

Preface

By the modern colonial period, Chinese outside of China, like other Asian peoples, resisted the localizations imposed on them by Euro-American and Japanese colonial empires in Asia by employing their border-crossing practices to undermine laterally the association between authoritative mobility and imperial power.

Both essays in Part 1 substantiate this, though in different ways. The essay by Duara points to the late nineteenth and early twentieth centuries as a period when new, alternative political logics and rhetorics from China itself confronted Euro-American colonial empires in the Asia Pacific during a time prior to their own consolidation. The representatives of three factions of modern nationalists from China moved across permeable colonial boundaries and spaces to engage in an extraterritorial rivalry with one another for the loyalties of diasporic Chinese positioned in these spaces: the emissaries of the Chinese emperor, nationalist reformers such as Liang Qichao and Kang Youwei, and revolutionary nationalists such as Hu Hanmin and Sun Yat-sen. These three factions made conflicting rhetorical claims vis-à-vis one another on diasporic Chinese as *huaqiao*, citizens of a larger modern Chinese nation, but in so doing were all subversive in challenging Euro-American colonial sovereignty by calling for the movement of diasporic Chinese bodies and economic capital out of the Euro-American colonies through campaigns of patriotic return, investment, and so on.

The merchants discussed by Trocki in his essay were organized into *kongsis* or "companies," and plied their trade in men (indentured laborers) between China and Southeast Asia and in commodities (gambier and pepper; later, rubber; and throughout, opium) across the boundaries of British, Dutch, and French empires in Southeast Asia. Chinese merchants, called *taukehs* in Hokkien, sought to take advantage of two problems of European rule—the need to recruit "Oriental" labor to open up colonial frontiers for European profit-taking, and the need to raise revenues in Asia rather than the metropole to subsidize the colonial administration. The latter problem was solved by letting out "opium farms"—an early modern form of subcontracting dealing in opium for addicted laborers—to Chinese merchants. However, by the early years of the twentieth century, Chinese flows in men, opium, and capital came to be seen as unauthorized movements across and beyond administered colonial spaces, posing a danger to colonial order and to the burgeoning racial "color line" that by then had come to buttress it, and the colonial authorities took steps to curb their border-crossing activities. Nonetheless, similar transgressions by Chinese have continued under the conditions of middle and late modernity.

As discussed in the introduction, we contend that the wildness and unpredictability of Chinese transnationalism has since the mid-1970s been harnessed and put to use by the forces of global capitalism and late modernity. The social, cultural, and spatial features of contemporary Chinese transnationalism, its connections to nation-state regimes of truth and power, and the implications of its workings for the (self-) making of new Chinese subjects are the topics investigated in the essays in parts 2, 3, and 4.

Chapter One

Nationalists Among Transnationals: Overseas Chinese and the Idea of China, 1900–1911[1]

Prasenjit Duara

The problem with modern *territorial* nationalism is that while it is the only acceptable form of sovereignty in the modern world, it is an inadequate basis of affective identification within the nation-state. Thus, the modern nation-state seeks to deploy the frequently older, extraterritorial narratives of racial and cultural community to serve its own needs. This essay will explore how, and with what difficulties, a territorially limited sovereignty, the early twentieth-century Chinese nation, sought to turn the energies and loyalties of deracinated transnational communities, the overseas Chinese, toward its interests. I will consider the efforts of three nationalist groups between 1900 and 1911: the late Qing imperial state, the constitutional monarchists and reformers led by Kang Youwei, and the republican revolutionaries led by Sun Yat-sen and others. Given that there are several important works on the history of Chinese nationalism among the overseas Chinese themselves, especially as it developed in Singapore, Malaya, and the United States (including Hawaii) (see especially Ma 1990; Yen 1976; and Huang 1993), I will not dwell on that topic. My goal is to probe the discursive and cultural means that the mainland nationalist groups utilized to mobilize the emigrants to the national cause.

All three mainland groups appealed to the overseas Chinese principally for financial contributions for their projects and investments in China and elsewhere, which they believed would strengthen the Chinese nation. I am concerned with the different political and rhetorical mechanisms whereby the nationalist groups exchanged symbolic values in order to secure material support from the overseas Chinese. All three groups sought to create a strong nation-state in China, and the overseas Chinese were expected to contribute to this project because they were Chinese. Yet the meaning of Chineseness itself was by no means clear, not only because emigrants themselves had multiple and ambiguous identities but especially because it was a time when such meaning was itself changing rapidly in China. The task of each of the three nationalist groups was to secure and fix a sense of Chineseness, but each had to fix this identity in the face of a preexisting multiplicity and ambiguity of identities as well as in relation to conflicting interpretations of Chineseness espoused by the others.

The Nationalist Cultural Project

In a recent work on nationalism (Duara 1995, 65–69), I have discussed the problem of how small activist groups seek to transform the identities of communities by changing the perception of social boundaries of this community from being soft to hard. A survey of the Chinese diaspora in Southeast Asia and the United States in the period under review suggests that the model of soft and hard boundaries is particularly useful in understanding the relationships between the nationalist groups mentioned above and these communities. The various cultural practices of a community—such as language, eating habits, and marriage taboos— also constitute the boundaries that mark that community.

From a historical perspective, these boundaries are never fixed but are mobile, in the sense both that their valence changes over time and that at any given point in time they signify a variable degree of openness to different Others. Thus these boundaries may be perceived as permeable or soft in certain respects and rigid with respect to other people and times. Activist groups with a totalizing vision of community seek to eliminate these permeable boundaries or transform them into the hardened boundaries of a closed community. They do so in accordance with a narrative that privileges one organizing institution or practice—such as race or fictive kinship—over all others.

Diasporic Chinese often organized themselves as several simultaneously different communities: as linguistic groups, such as Cantonese *bendi*, Hakka, Chaozhou, and Hokkien, with dialects and languages that were mostly mutually incomprehensible; as surname groups; as territorial or native-place communities; as secretive versus public sodalities; and as class-differentiated groups, among others (Ma 1990, 7–29; Yen 1976, 4–15, 286–89; Freedman 1979). An individual might have belonged to several of these communities, thus crossing some permeable boundaries while encountering other, harder boundaries. At the same time, diasporic communities were also differentiated by how they perceived their boundaries with the surrounding communities and cultures—depending often on the nature of the indigenous or colonial polity and racial division of labor (see Alatas 1977, 75–76, 85–89). Thus Chinese in Thailand tended to assimilate with local Thais (or exhibit biculturalism), Peranakans in Indonesia to remain aloof from the local culture, and Chinese in the Philippines to emerge as a *mestizo* group halfway between the above two (Purcell 1965, 30–36; Lee 1978, 4–5). Chinese Christians in North America (Ma 1990, 21–22, 36) or Malaccan Babas and other Straits-born Chinese who intermarried with local Malays and later became anglicized had different and changing attitudes from those more recently arrived (*xinke*) from China (Freeman 1979, 63–64). If we imagine a baseline scenario of the diaspora before the arrival of mainland nationalist forces, it would be this image of multi-strandedness and shifting boundaries. The activists sought to transform these multiple, mobile identifications into a Chineseness that eliminated or reduced internal boundaries, on the one hand, and hardened the boundaries between Chinese and non-Chinese, on the other.

Wang Gungwu (1991a) has characterized the dominant pattern of Chinese immigration to Southeast Asia from at least the nineteenth century (though he finds it to be much older) as the *huashang*, or Chinese trader, mode. There is also the *huagong* or Chinese labor, mode, which emerged between the 1850s and the 1920s, but the *huashang* mode is more basic and continues to this day. It is one in which kinsmen of successful traders follow the pioneers or are brought in to establish or extend business networks. There is a sense in which this group remains Chinese because of the functional significance of family and native-place ties; at the same time, they demonstrate a certain flexibility, especially toward the political authorities of the host countries, whether colonial or indigenous. Wang's strong emphasis on the *huashang* mode as the dominant mode or even model of Chinese society overseas reinforces my basic point that the sense of Chineseness with which the majority of Chinese abroad lived was one with relatively open boundaries. In this context, Freedman's revelation that the culturally adaptive Baba Chinese were also highly influential among the later immigrants and absorbed the more successful among them as Baba because they were wealthy, influential, and had marriageable daughters underscores the correlation between adaptability and success (Freedman 1979, 63–64).

Wang contrasts the *huashang* mode with what he defines as the *huaqiao* pattern, which became most visible between 1900 and the 1950s but which has had rather less staying power than the *huashang* mode (Wang 1991a, 6–8). Clarifying his very specific terminological choice of *huaqiao* for this phenomenon rather than its more common usage as a general term for the diaspora as a whole, Wang traces its origins to the influx of nationalist activists and ideology at the end of the nineteenth century. *Huaqiao*, which may be literally rendered as "Chinese sojourner," was introduced to unify the various terms that the diaspora used to refer to themselves, such as Min Guangren, Min Yueren, and Tangren—ways of identifying the people of Guangdong and Fujian. The new national signifier, *huaqiao*, implied first that the *hauqiao* owed their allegiance to China and the Qing state (and after 1911, to the Republic) and entailed certain legal rights and responsibilities toward the Chinese state. More important than the legal dimension was the political and ideological one, whereby the primary loyalty of all Chinese was owed to China. *Huaqiao* were mobilized, especially through education campaigns—often directed against local authorities opposed to education in Chinese—to instill this sense of loyalty and re-sinicize those who had been acculturated to local or Western ways (Wang 1991a, 8–9). It is precisely this process of fixing the meaning and hardening the boundaries of Chineseness that I shall explore in this essay.

Imperial Nationalism: Mobilizing Culture

Consider the Qing state (1644–1911) first. Although republican historiography—which has dominated much professional historiography in China and elsewhere—has tended to demonize the Qing as a foreign (Manchu), barbarian power that sold out the nation to Western imperialist powers, it is also clear that in its last decade the Qing state launched a program of strengthening the nation-state vis-à-vis the imperialist powers. It did so by trying to maximize and define its territorial boundaries, by strengthening national defenses, and by undertaking a comprehensive reform program in education, commerce, law, and local self-government (Pomeranz 1993; Duara 1988). For these purposes, it needed to expand its revenue base, especially since much of its existing revenue was pledged to servicing the foreign debt incurred through military defeats. It was in this context of national and state strengthening that it turned to the overseas Chinese (among other sources) for revenue.

Until the mid-nineteenth century, the Qing state banned emigration and regarded emigrants as pariahs and pirates. It often executed repatriated emigrants in order to deter potential travelers from leaving the empire. In the early period of Qing rule, overseas Chinese were associated with Ming loyalists and with secret-society efforts to overthrow the Qing.

After it succeeded in quelling the opposition to its rule in Taiwan led by Koxinga (Zheng Chenggong) in 1683, that source of the policy against emigrants evaporated, but the ban continued to be strict (Zhuang 1989, 101–4). Overseas Chinese were regarded as people who had moved out of the ambit of civilization and, indeed, had betrayed this civilization. When complaints about the Dutch massacre of Chinese in Batavia in 1740 reached the Qing court, the Qianlong emperor displayed a lack of interest, saying that "they had deserted their ancestors' graves to seek profits abroad" (quoted in Tsai 1979, 499). The conversion of overseas Chinese to foreign religions such as Christianity and Islam, their association with "barbarians" such as the Dutch, and their participation in rebellions on the Burmese and Vietnamese borders earned them the opprobrium of *hanjian*, or traitor to the Han (Zhuang 1989, 102–4).

With growing awareness of the world system of modern nation-states and the discursive seachange accompanying it, the imperial state reversed its policy toward emigrants by the 1880s. Not only did it remove the ban on emigration and seek to oversee the coolie trade (Tsai 1979, 502) but also, following the nation-state model, beginning in 1878 it established consulates in Southeast Asia and America to address the needs of its "nationals" abroad. The concern behind the imperial state's setting up consulates was as much the need to care for its overseas nationals as it was to benefit from their presence and wealth. The writings of imperial officials—in particular, provincial governors and governor-generals—through the 1880s (Zhuang 1989, 140–41) and later were dominated by the interest in *huaqiao* as contributing to national strength. They sought both financial support for state-dominated ventures and technical skills in shipbuilding and armament production from the *huaqiao* (Zhuang 1989, 139–41). Their ideas were dominated by the "self-strengthening" school, which sought to build up the military strength of the imperial state while preserving essential Confucian values. The practical manifestation of this ideal was the establishment of enterprises run by merchants but supervised by officials (*guandu shangban*). Self-strengthening officials such as Li Hongzhang sought to enlist *huaqiao* help for the China Maritime Stem Navigation Company to compete with Western shipping interests and support the company's overseas expansion (Yen 1982a, 217–18). *Huaqiao* were also expected to serve as spies. Wu Zengying wrote:

Nanyang is surrounded by islands on the east and the west, exactly like a Great Wall of the sea (*haishang changcheng*). . . . We should send delegates to these places to sign treaties that would forbid mistreatment of our merchants. We should also grant the outstanding ones among them the consul's posts and have them investigate the physical features of their host country, its population distribution and the depths of its waterways. In addition, they can keep an eye on the Westerners and inform us of any suspicious move. (Quoted in Zhuang 1989, 141)

With the New Policy reforms in 1902, Qing policies toward *huaqiao* began to focus increasingly on soliciting commercial involvement within China. Special opportunities to invest in mining and railroads were granted in order to prevent foreigners from monopolizing these areas. In 1903 Zhang Bishi, a scholar-official well-connected to overseas merchants, was appointed as imperial commissioner to inspect overseas commercial affairs. Six special missions of imperial envoys and many smaller delegations to drum up investment were organized in Southeast Asia, and millions of dollars were actually raised through these means (Yen 1982a, 224–28). The missions to solicit investments were conducted in conjunction with the other measure to raise money: the sale of brevet ranks and titles. Although this policy predated the investment missions, the campaign to solicit investments in the 1900s was often directly coordinated with the offer of honors and titles. During the last decade of the Qing state, the sale of titles grew rapidly, as did the value and rank of the honors. After 1907, those who invested over two thousand yuan in a modern enterprise in China received the first rank (Zhuang 1989, 257). Titles were also purchased for three generations of ancestors, and ranked *huaqiao* could don "dynastic costumes" when receiving Qing delegates and celebrating imperial holidays (Zhuang 1989, 255–57).

In Singapore and Malaya, ranks and titles were purchased not only by rich merchants but also by ordinary ones. Only 17 percent of the purchasers were wealthy merchants, who paid over a thousand taels for each title. The remaining 83 percent were ordinary traders, who paid under 680 Mexican dollars (each dollar was worth slightly under one tael) and could afford only one title or rank (Yen 1970, 25–26). The popularity of purchased ranks and titles among all classes reveals the enormous prestige of the imperial and Confucian model of Chineseness that prevailed among the Chinese communities in Southeast Asia. It was a model that appealed to the upwardly and rapidly mobile, self-made men who could distinguish themselves with the symbols—the caps and gowns—of the elite from the old country. Moreover, as Yen Ching-hwang has argued, these titles—which were repeatedly cited for ranking purposes by the local *huaqiao* newspapers—also certified local leadership in the community (Yen 1970, 27–32; see also Huang 1993, 303–23).

The popularity of these imperial symbols must be understood in the context of a larger effort (indeed, a campaign) by the imperial Confucian establishment to instill Confucian virtues among the Nanyang overseas Chinese population in the late nineteenth century. While the early stages of this movement were designed to wean overseas Chinese away from both Malayization and Westernization (or Islam and Christianity) by introducing an upper-class or gentry model of Chineseness, by the late 1900s this model was in effective competition with the narratives of both the reformers and the revolutionaries (Huang 1993, 273–81). At around the same time that the imperial consul was established in Singapore in the late 1880s, a Confucian revival movement emerged in Singapore and Malaya, led by gentry-style societies such as the Laoshanshe and charitable societies such as Tongshanshe. This movement, which was strongly backed by the Singapore consul, was devoted to the building of Confucian temples, the creation of literary societies, and the teaching of the sixteen maxims of the Kangxi emperor in community centers (implying rejection of Christianity and Islam). Merchants financed the effort, while visiting scholar-officials and imported Confucian teachers furnished the doctrinal leadership. At the same time, the Qing consuls in Singapore and Malaya also played a big role in organizing celebrations for imperial birthdays, Confucian ceremonies, literary contests, and, of course, the sale of titles and honors (Yen 1982b, 401–15).

I argue here that the Qing effort to install a gentry model of Chinese community amounted to an effort to construct a Confucian nationalism. Through these efforts, not only could the Qing state garner funds to strengthen the emerging nation-state, but it constructed a Chinese identity that sharply differentiated *huaqiao* from European and local cultures and from revolutionary narratives of Chineseness. The idea of a Confucian nationalism may sound somewhat oxymoronic because we are used to thinking of Confucianism as a universalist and culturalist philosophy of civilization that embraces all who live by its morals, learning, and rituals. Yet while Confucianism may contain within it the ability to accept and transform barbarians, nonetheless it also contained within it the potential to harden the boundaries of a community when an alien culture refused to accept Confucian values on the Chinese community's terms. This was the case with the opposition to the Mongols as well as during the early opposition to the Manchus and to the European powers in the nineteenth century. In these times, the Confucian universe (*tianxia*) itself became a closed political community competing as one among others in a wider universe with other politicized communities (Duara 1995, 56–60).

The imperial state's effort to create a nationalist community amenable to its worldview did not require the construction and mobilization of a *new* narrative, which other activitists required. The ceremonies, temple-building, literary contests, and public lectures activated a latent narrative of civilization associated with the gentry and the imperial establishment with which upwardly mobile traders were already familiar. As we have seen, the Southeast Asian diaspora was composed predominantly of merchants or would-be merchants in the *huashang* mode. In late imperial China, merchants had emerged as among the most persistent emulators and patrons of literati culture and ritual, especially in peripheral regions such as Yunnan and Guangxi (Naquin and Rawski 1987). As Han merchants moved into these peripheries, their often hostile encounters with "barbarian" communities caused them to identify with a model of Chinese civilization based on high gentry culture, which they were able to develop precisely because they operated in a space relatively free from gentry and imperial control. Undoubtedly, the social and political environment of the Chinese diaspora in Southeast Asia was different from the peripheries of the empire. Nonetheless, the cultural pattern established by the emigrating or sojourning merchant continued to have some force in Southeast Asia. While the political power of colonial regimes and the social ties with the local communities did exercise a pull on these merchants, the blockages or limits—in particular, the racial boundaries laid down by colonial ideology (see Alatas 1977)—these same pull factors, the continuing links with Chinese communities and families, and, from the late nineteenth century on, the unexpected attention from the imperial establishment in China made this civilizational model of Chineseness very attractive to the merchant community in this last decade of the Qing.

Reform Nationalists:
Synthesizing Capitalism and Confucianism

The Qing state sought to create a nation by grafting modern institutions onto an older discourse of civilization that would allow the imperial system to retain power. This was not the strategy of the reformers and revolutionaries who sought to found state power and modern society on a radically different discourse: the narrative of linear, progressive history in the Enlightenment mode. This narrative in the late nineteenth and early twentieth centuries was underpinned by the global discourse of social Darwinism, in which nation-states were engaged in a competitive struggle for survival and a nation that was not predatory or imperialistic would be destroyed or colonized by ones that were (Duara 1995, 20–23). For success in this struggle, the revolutionaries, and to a lesser extent the reformers, believed in the need to mold the nation into a homogeneous, cohesive, monoracial body politic, a belief again reinforced by social

Darwinist notions of racial purity and superiority. Revolutionaries such as Wang Jingwei and Zou Rong translated these ideas, derived from Western and Japanese imperialism, into a virulent Han racism that was most proximately anti-Manchu but embedded within the idea of a global hierarchy of races in which the white and yellow races were superior.

The reformer Liang Qichao first created the history of China within the framework of a linear, progressive history affiliated with the history of "civilized" nations of the West (Duara 1995, 33). However, Liang was often torn between whether the Chinese were to be depicted as already civilized, once civilized, or in need of civilizing—a classic nationalist predicament. During the first decade of the twentieth century, when Liang traveled abroad, his writings showed a preoccupation with the struggle between races, and in his overview of the *huaqiao* in San Francisco, he was overwhelmed by what he considered the inferior qualities of the Chinese who lacked the attributes of modern citizens (*shimin*) and were parochial, submissive, and clannish (*zumin*) (Liang 1981, 144–51). At the same time, in his biographies of eight great Chinese colonists, written in 1906, Liang reminds his readers that *huaqiao* did in fact have a glorious history of colonial expansion in Nanyang; he culled these people's lives in order to foster a spirit of heroism among Chinese. The individuals he cited were heroes who ruled as kings of places such as Srivijaya, subdued local "barbarians," and established Chinese colonies (Liang 1906, 81–88; see also Sourcebook, doc. 4.1).

But the distinction between reformers and revolutionaries—which gave the reformers a distinct edge over the revolutionaries with the *huaqiao*—did not arise over their basic discursive affiliation with the new history. It arose over the the fault line within this discourse: the split between the nation as the continuing essence of the past and the nation as revolutionary and modern. The contest between the two positions was about the way in which the nation would be linked to modernity. As we shall see, notions of revolution—the modern as revolutionary—necessarily encounter difficulty in securing the very concept of the nation without some notion of the abiding essence of the national past; paradoxically, this is an essence they are committed to destroying.

The hybrid philosophy of the reformer Kang Youwei deftly straddled this fault line. Most readers are familiar with his narrative of history, which introduced the linear progressivism of Enlightenment history but was periodized in Chinese categories and culminated in the Confucian telos of Datong, or the Great Unity—a utopian world without barriers (K'ang 1958). Specifically, Kang was able to formulate a vision and program of modernity within the framework of Confucian civilization and constitutional monarchy (*xujun gonghe*). During his years of exile from

China in the early 1900s after the failure of the 1898 reforms, this vision was embodied in the Baohuanghui (Society to Protect the Emperor), which had many chapters all over Nanyang and America. The focus on the emperor—especially a constitutional emperor—as symbolic of Chinese civilization did much to address the discursive problem that the revolutionaries would fight so hard to overcome. As a monarch who stood for change, the Guangxu emperor symbolically secured the historical nation at the very heart of progressive change.

This particular resolution of the discursive problem gave Kang the political advantage among *huaqiao*. He could appeal to the monarchism or prestige of the imperial state and the symbols of that ideology in a way that was not available to the revolutionaries, and yet promote reform. On the other hand, the reformers were not constrained in the way that the imperial state, which sought to graft modern institutions on an older discourse of civilization, was constrained in terms of how far it could reform itself without losing power. In their synthesis of the old and the new, the reformers could attract those merchants, would-be merchants, and even secret-society members drawn to the imperial Confucian model while at the same time appealing to the changing consciousness of the people who were, despite or perhaps because of Chinese nationalist education, becoming more aware of the necessity of change. By sharing in imperial prestige but not being held accountable for the actions and policies of the imperial state, the reformers could absorb those increasingly disaffected by national defeats and humiliations for which the Qing court became the lightning rod.

Huang Jianchun suggests that the popularity of Kang among *huaqiao* in Malaya and Singapore derived from his status as the "emperor's mentor" (Huang 1993; 240). Ma (1990) underscores the same point regarding both Kang and Liang in explaining the success of the Baohuanghui among merchants in America, where the Confucian model of civilization continued to be dominant among the elite during the early part of the century. These elites even imported scholarly notables from China to serve as presidents of the native-place associations (*huiguan*) and established gentry-style academies (*shuyuan*) (Ma 1990, 18). Even many members of the secret society, the Zhigongtang, supported the Baohuanghui, distinguishing themselves from the anti-Qing rhetoric of those whom they regarded as their less enlightened brethren in China (Ma 1990; 72–73). While revolutionaries swore the Peach Garden Oath of loyalty to overthrow the Manchu emperor, a group of *huaqiao* in Canada took the oath with Liang Qitian to *restore* the emperor (Ma 1990, 79). Supporters of the Baohuanghui in Nanyang—over thirty thousand from Thailand alone in the 1900—sent floods of letters and cables urging the imperial court to restore power to the Guangxu emperor (Yen 1976, 155, 178). On the day of mourning for his death in 1908, the reformists succeeded in keeping most shops in major Malayan cities and Singapore closed despite the vigorous efforts of revolutionaries to keep them open (Yen 1976, 167–68).

The reformers' synthetic vision of a modern society also targeted professionals—educators, doctors, bureaucrats, and journalists—among the *huaqiao*. They communicated their vision of Chinese modernity by dominating the modern media (newspapers, magazines, and pamphlets) and establishing modern reform societies. In Singapore and Malaya, three of the five newspapers reflected their views (Yen 1976, 52; Huang 1993, 242). As for education, Kang was perhaps responsible for establishing many if not most of the modern Chinese schools in Nanyang and also a normal school in Penang to train teachers for these schools. The reformers controlled the managing boards and the teachers in the majority of these schools (as they did in Canada, Japan, and America also; see Ma 1990, 152) and influenced their curriculum, fostering both Confucian values and modern, scientific education (Yen 1976, 156–57). Through control of the media and education, the reformers sought to install their representation of a Chinese citizen who was to be distinguished not only from the Malay, Thai, European, or American national, but also from the representation of Chineseness cultivated by revolutionaries and the imperial state.

The reformers also tried to mobilize support for their political agenda. In 1908 the Baohuanghui led a boycott of Japanese goods, which drew the support of many *huaqiao* and mobilized them to press the Qing court, through petitions and cables, to convene a national parliament. They persuaded many chambers of commerce in the Straits colonies to join in the twelve-point petition to the Qing government, which included a call to convene a parliament in China (Yen 1976, 160–61; Ma 1990, 127). Over two hundred chapters of the Baohuanghui from five continents endorsed it (Lo 1967, 212). It should be noted that the reformers also addressed the local problems of *huaqiao*. Kang and Liang supported attempts by Chinese in America to change the Chinese Exclusion Act and were generally sensitive to mistreatment of *huaqiao* (Ma 1990, 98–99).

The reformists, especially the Baohuanghui in America, incorporated an economic vision of the Chinese people that responded to the interests of the *huaqiao*. The economic wing of the Baohuanghui, the Commercial Corporation, sponsored investment ventures in China, the United States, Canada, and Mexico as well as in Southeast Asia. The corporation was designed to make the Baohuanghui financially independent by the sale of its shares and to defray the expenses of its cultural arsenal, including the various bookstores, newspapers, and schools. It developed interests or floated companies in banking, mining, real estate, news media, rice brokerage, hotels, restaurants, and other enterprises in which many ordinary *huaqiao* were shareholders (Lo 1967, 195). In the United States for instance, the strongest supporters of the corporation were in places such as Montana, Washington, and Oregon (Lo 1967, 200).

The reformers presented the *huaqiao* with a vision of an expanding economy in China and the opportunities that it provided for them. The Baohuanghui appealed to the Chinese authorities to create chambers of commerce and promote a climate for business ventures (Ma 1990, 76–77). A study of a group of wealthy merchants supporting the reformists (in contrast to those supporting the revolutionaries) in Singapore and Malaya shows that the merchants supporting the reformers not only often held Qing titles or ranks but also had investments and other business interests in China (Yen 1976, 267–76; Huang 1993; 260–75). The Commercial Corporation also undertook business ventures with official liaisons in China—*guandu shangban* types—some of which, however, suffered from scandals and official opposition (Ma 1990 128–29). These various enterprises were extremely successful until about 1908, when a combination of bad economic conditions, overextension, quarrels, and misappropriation on the part of some managers (as well as the appropriation of Mexican properties after the Mexican revolution in 1910) plunged it and the Baohuanghui into a crisis from which it did not recover (Lo 1967, 215).

Thus at least until the end of the decade, the reformers offered a vision of gradualist modernity in which Chinese moral and cultural values were commensurate with a representative, if elitist, polity and expanding capitalism. Speaking crudely, one might say that this vision of modernity could be associated with the gentry-merchant elites in China who were the force behind the movement for provincial consitutional assemblies in the 1900s and who supported the proliferation of modern philanthropic and "redemptive" societies in republican China (see Duara 1996). While in China during the first half of the twentieth century this vision of modernity was frustrated by warfare and obscured by revolutionary narratives of modernity—first of the republicans and then of the May fourth movement—in some ways the vision or model, if not the activists themselves, had greater staying power among the *huaqiao*, where merchants and would-be gentry-merchant elites were more influential in the communities. Indeed, this vision may be the most proximate ancestor of the phenomenon called "Confucian capitalism" in the Pacific Rim today.

Revolutionary Nationalism: Forging a New Narrative

There is a tendency in some of the scholarship to stress the different class bases of the constituencies for the revolutionaries as opposed to the reformers (and of course the supporters of the Qing). The revolutionaries allegedly found their most enthusiastic supporters among the working classes and the petty bourgeoisie, whereas the reformers were supported by the rich merchants. This kind of analysis was perhaps first presented by the revolutionaries themselves—see, for instance, Hu Hanmin's 1936 (Hu 1964) speech in Singapore—who were not disinclined to present themselves as the champions of the poor. It has been taken up in modified form by several academic analysts, especially those sympathetic to the republican or Kuomintang (KMT) view, such as Yen Chinghwang (1976) and Chen Yu-ching (1981).

Although there is some truth in the assertion that most merchants supported either the Qing or the reformers (Huang 1993, 260–71), differentiating the constituencies for the revolutionaries from that of the reformers on a strictly class-based analysis cannot hold up for long. In the first place, the revolutionaries also made appeals to rich merchants, because their needs were principally financial. The founders of the Tongmenghui were well-to-do merchants (Yen 1976, 93) as were the founders of its predecessors, the Xinzhonghui in America (Ma 1990, 61–63), and when the revolutionaries did gain financial contributions in the last year or so before the revolution of 1911, their supporters were often rich merchants—though ones without strong China business interests (Yen 1976, 267–76; Huang 1993, 260–70). More significant, the lower-class constituency was not quite as natural an ally for the revolutionaries as their narrative alleged. As we have seen, ordinary *huaqiao* were greatly attracted to the reformist and even to the Confucian/imperial style.

Revolutionary leader Hu Hanmin, who was sent to organize *huaqiao* for the revolutionary cause in 1908 (Sourcebook, doc. 4.3, 6), was struck by two phenomena: the extent to which many overseas Chinese had lost their Chinese identity, and the extent to which those who remained Chinese were drawn to, or were under the spell of, imperial Confucian culture. The amazement or grief about the loss of Chineseness among overseas Chinese was a recurrent theme among revolutionaries and indexes the rapidity with which the idea of national loyalty had become naturalized or dehistoricized among them. Hu reported that many overseas Chinese from Fujian would find it strange if he asked them their Chinese names (Hu 1964, 476). Another revolutionary, Lu Hun, complained that when asked, those Chinese residing in Java would reply that they were Javanese; those in Singapore, Singaporean; those in Sumatra,

Sumatran (Lu 1910, 3981). Moreover, Hu found them to be superstitious and greedy for the honors and titles of the imperial state. He explained the relative success of the Baohuanghui among the overseas Chinese as a result of their imperial Confucian orientation. Indeed, Hu reported that the only way to identify them as Chinese was by the queue that they sported—a sign, in fact, of submission to the Manchus in China! While Hu decried their lack of a modern republican sensibility, he was thankful that the queue at least continued to identify them as Chinese. Note the circularity of nationalist logic in his subsequent comment that he would have them cut off their queues after they had been made sufficiently Chinese (*zhongguohuale*) (Hu 1964, 476–77).

While some revolutionaries were finding that they had no constituency among *huaqiao*, others began to romanticize the secret societies as their natural allies. The argument that is made most strongly for why the lower classes gave their support to the revolutionaries rests upon the alleged ideological intimacy between the republican revolutionaries and the secret societies—in particular the Hongmen or Tiandihui, which was the most important organization among plantation, mine, or railroad workers in Southeast Asia, the mainland United States, and Hawaii (where it was called the Zhigongtang) (Yen 1976, 14–18, 287–89; Chen Y.-C. 1981, 414–18; Chen C. 1964, 485–87). Chen Chunsheng believed that *huaqiao* were descendants of generations of secret-society revolutionaries devoted to overthrowing the Manchus (Chen C. 1964, 486–7).[2] Yen Ching-hwang notes that the triads had certain affinities with the revolutionaries, such as the notion of egalitarianism and brotherhood as well as their anti-Qing tradition, and reports that the revolutionary organization, the Tongmenghui, was modeled on the secret societies (Yen 1976, 15–18).

The rhetoric of the revolutionaries depicted the secret societies and their emigrant descendants as the source of China's salvation from the Manchus as well as the source of a modernity that Confucianism and the literati were too compromised to bring about. Xihuang Zhengyin's (1910) history of the overseas Chinese in Nanyang traced their origins since the Han dynasty. The author and Lu Hun, who wrote a preface framing the text tightly within the following narrative, lamented the loss of Chinese identity among the overseas Chinese and sought the origins and history of overseas Chinese settlement in order to rally Chinese people both within and outside China to resist the Manchus. Xihuang developed two braided narratives, which addressed two dimensions of a social Darwinian nationalism. The first was the narrative of the *huaqiao* as the last loyalists of the Han race, resisting the two principal barbarian invaders, the Mongols and the Manchus. References abounded to keywords from secret-society ideology, such as *zhong* and *yi* (see Xihuang 1910, 3119) and to Koxinga and Ming Taizu, heros of the societies. The text dwelled at length on the resistance to the Mongols by the southerners who had fled to Southeast Asia, particularly the unsuccessful resistance of Chen Yizhong, who sought to build a military alliance against the Mongols in Java (Xihuang 1910, 3992–3), and that of Koxinga, who led a group of southerners against the Manchus. These Ming loyalists finally fled to Southeast Asia, where they were persecuted by the Dutch colonialists in active collusion with the Manchus (Xihuang 1910, 4002–10).

If the first narrative deplored the victimization of loyalist heroes by foreigners, both barbarian conquerors of China and Western colonialists, the second narrative sought to remind *huaqiao* of their glorious role as pioneering colonizers. Xihuang wrote that geographically, Nanyang had been China's southern screen of defense; historically, it had been China's territory (*lingtu*) for thousands of years. Xihuang also suggested that it had been a place of colonial settlement for no less than seven million (*sic*) Han people. But despite their great numbers, he said, the *huaqiao* succumbed to the tyranny of a small number of Europeans and Americans (Xihuang 1910, 3986–7). Central to this narrative were the reigns of the first two Ming emperors, who conducted the great maritime expeditions across the Indian Ocean, revived Han power in Southeast Asia, and reestablished colonial settlements there. The Ming represented the culmination of an early and interrupted history of Chinese colonization of Nanyang; it was a time when settlers in Nanyang, after ninety years of Mongol rule, were once again able to see the light of day (Xihuang 1910, 3994–6). By their great enterprise of colonizing distant lands (*yuanlüe*), these two emperors were "the great men of national imperialism in world history," comparable not only to the founders of the Han and Tang dynasties but also to Columbus, Magellan, and others (Xihuang 1910, 4110). Indeed, according to Lu Hun, for centuries Nanyang had been China's new "America" (Lu 1910, 3981). As for the settlers, Xihuang recounted the stories of the great pioneers (several of which was culled from Liang Qichao's account, discussed earlier) who ruled Southeast Asian states, and he concluded that despite all odds, these settlers continued the legacy of the Ming. They conquered the savages, reclaimed land, and dominated commerce; the greatness of their civilizing purpose—evidenced by their support for education—was unmatched. In conclusion, he quoted Theodore Roosevelt to the effect that the Chinese, with their adventurous and enterprising character, were most capable of civilizing the barbarians (*kaipi caolai zhi renmin*) (Xihuang 1910, 4112).

The two narratives were joined together causally: The reason that *huaqiao* were not able to defend these southern lands from the Western colonizers was not because they were deficient in any way, but rather because they were denied any support or encouragement from the Qing government; worse, they were been vilified, sabotaged, and persecuted by it. Colonial expansion by the Western powers was made possible only by the support of each of their states, and the condition of the *huaqiao* was the consequence of despotic rule by an alien race (Xihuang 1910, 4111). Thus to restore the Han to their pristine greatness in the progress of world history toward which the *huaqiao* had made such great contributions, it was incumbent upon all Chinese to overthrow the Manchus. The image of Chineseness that the revolutionaries offered the *huaqiao* was one associated not with high cultural traditions but with newly discovered Enlightenment values of adventurousness, enterprise, expansionism. Yet the price of breaking with the gentry culturalist model was to accentuate the racist element: the element of Han greatness versus all primitive peoples.

For all of their discursive ingenuity, the revolutionaries were unable to generate support from more than a very small segment of the populace until 1911. One of the more sympathetic accounts of the republican efforts indicated that even at the time of the 1911 revolution, no more than 0.3 to 0.5 percent of the *huaqiao* population in Singapore and Malaya supported the revolutionary parties (Yen 1976, 263). The establishment of a republican administration in China after 1911 and especially after 1927 deepened support for republicanism, particularly as a result of the proliferation of (Mandarin) Chinese schools across Southeast Asia.

Locality and Transnationalism

Embedded in the efforts of each of the nationalist groups was the appeal to the particular regional loyalty of the *huaqiao*—whether in the Americas or in Nanyang. One reason why Kang and Liang did so much better than Sun Yat-sen in America before 1911, according to Ma (1990), was that both the reformers came from the same native places in Guangdong from which the greatest number of emigrants came, the *sanyi* and *siyi* counties, whereas Sun was from the economically and numerically much weaker Hakka community. The Qing officials most successful in soliciting investment were ones from Fujian and Guangdong; indeed, it was hard to draw *huaqiao* investment to projects that did not involve their home provinces or countries (Yen 1982a, 220–22; Zhuang 1989, 138–39). The divisions among the revolutionaries in Nanyang often broke along native-place lines. Tao Chengzhang rested his case on a progressive southern nationalism that was opposed to the backwardness of the northerners. Even revolutionaries such as Xihuang and Wang Jingwei celebrated the heroism of the southerners who fought the Mongols and Manchus. Here I want to explore a text by the reformer Ou Qujia, who sought to reconcile this localism with nationalism.

Ou was a Cantonese follower of Kang Youwei who was also involved in the Hunan reforms with Liang Qichao in 1897. He became increasingly revolutionary during his post-1898 exile in Japan and the United States but ultimately returned to the reformist view by the time he moved to Southeast Asia in 1907 (Ou 1971, 1). His text, "New Guangdong," first published in the San Francisco *Datong Daily* in 1902, during an alliance between the revolutionaries and reformers, prefigured many of the revolutionary themes regarding secret societies and became a revolutionary classic despite the author's ambivalence about revolution. The piece is more significant, however, because it advocated the independence of provinces and regions in China, to the horror of committed nationalists among both revolutionaries and reformists. More clearly than any other, the text demonstrates the importance of the local origins of the *huaqiao* in shaping the vision of revolution on the mainland.

Ou called for the independence of Guangdong in a rousing rhetoric that celebrated the great wealth, physical resources, talents, and cosmopolitanism of the people of Guangdong, which he saw as the doorway of China to the world. This kind of independence for the provinces and regions of China would enable each "nation" to compete with neighboring ones, absorb the weak, and emerge as equals with the powerful nation-states in the world. This ingenious social Darwinian argument held that China's weakness derived not only from the restraints imposed by the racially alien Manchus but also from the enormous size of the empire, which could not produce the intimacy and feelings for one's own people that the province and region could produce (Ou 1971, 1–8). But while the objective measures for Cantonese independence, or *zili*, were strong, the subjective dispositions of the people had worked against independence and self-reliance. Ou used *zili* creatively to forge a link between political or national independence and the character or spirit of self-reliance—the necessary condition for survival of a species (Ou 1971, 15). He was particularly bitter about the lack of *zili* sentiments among Cantonese merchants at home and abroad who curried favors with Western colonialists, cozied up to government officials, and established intimate familial ties with other races, such as Thais and Vietnamese (Ou 1971, 18).

Ou believed that the best and perhaps only chance to build an independent Guangdong would come from the secret societies, which carried on the heritage of racialist nationalism against the Manchus long after the Confucian literati had been co-opted by the imperial state. Ou suggested that the societies not only were nationalist but also represented the sprouts of a modern polity composed of public associations such as parliaments and political parties. It was only the despotic and alien Qing that forced secrecy upon them; in this light, they should be compared with the Japanese *ronin* or with popular secret societies during the French revolution (Ou 1971, 24–37). Ou confronted the degeneration and divisiveness among the secret societies (even among Cantonese) both at home and abroad—between Hakka, Chaozhou, and *bendi*. Yet he believed that as long as one confined one's sights to the province, the activists could work with the secret societies, remind them of their glorious revolutionary heritage, and unify them as Cantonese sons of the Yellow Emperor (Ou 1971, 39–46). Such was the nature of political loyalties in China that it would be impossible at that point to aim at unification beyond the province and region.

I believe the significance of this text emerges from its tacit acknowledgment of the indeterminacy of political loyalty. Ou was not overly anxious about the chances of eventual unity. To critics who pointed out that his plan would do the work for the imperialists by getting the Chinese to "slice the Chinese melon themselves," he responded that when a people voluntarily secede, it is easier for them to reestablish a federated unity on the model of a German federation and better protect the great unity (*dayitong*) (Ou 1971, 46–48). The issue of Chinese national unity provided a kind of ultimate framework, a distant, deferred horizon—a deferral with which many *huaqiao* presumably did not feel much discomfort. The advocacy of provincial and regional independence, modeled on the language of national independence, doubtless appealed to the sentiments of overseas Chinese, especially secret-society members who were from the region. And yet we cannot say that Ou was appealing to some fundamental or primordial provincialism among the *huaqiao*, although he might have believed that himself. After all, a good part of the text was hortatory: Like nationalist texts, it appealed to the Cantonese to overcome the divisions within themselves. In such ways, the text revealed the insufficiency of the nationalist model for communities of transnationals with multiple identities pulled by global forces as much as by their need for a sense of home that was itself quite elastic.

Conclusion

Nationalism involves fixing fluid identities, refashioning their representations, and rigidifying the perception of boundaries between the self and Other. All three nationalist groups were engaged in this project, but we may wonder about the extent to which they could succeed in fully mobilizing the identities of transnational communities pulled in multiple directions by foreign political authorities, dispersed economic networks, and English-language-based career possibilities for their children. Certainly the broad currents of nationalism in the Chinese diaspora at that time appear to have been quite nonsynchronous with the trajectory of nationalism on the Chinese mainland. Whereas the imperial state was collapsing within China, the imperial narrative of the court and Kang's advocacy of the symbolism of a modern emperor were gaining ground among the *huaqiao*. Although the idea of a republic had captured the imagination of key, if miniscule, segments of the Chinese populace, support for the revolutionaries among *huaqiao* remained largely ineffective until 1911. This nonsynchronicity reflects not some kind of lag among *huaqiao* but rather the different conjuncture of global and domestic forces operating in China as opposed to that among the Chinese overseas.

At the same time, the limited success of some nationalists does indicate the meaningfulness of some of the narratives and representations. Particularly intriguing here is the relative effectiveness of the reformers and constitutional monarchists, in part because theirs is something of a buried history obscured by the later triumph of republican historiography. I have suggested that their fashioning of a vision of modernity— this early synthesis of Confucian capitalism—was particularly suited to the mercantile elites and leaders of these communities. With an eye on contemporary developments, we may ask a last question about this vision: To what extent did the Confucian element in this nationalism, with its supposedly universal yearnings, temper the exclusivism of social Darwinist nationalism, as, for instance, anti-imperialism did for a period? I do not believe that Confucianism, or any other tradition, has an abiding essence, and so its reformulation in the early twentieth century allowed it to coexist with a social Darwinian nationalism. At the same time, it did possess a utopian universalism, particularly in the formulations of Kang Youwei, which made this coexistence extremely uneasy and capable of generating doubts and new openings. We may wonder whether this utopian urge exists any longer in the current reformulation of Confucianism.

And what about the revolutionary republicans? Should we discount their colorful narratives as meaningless gesticulations in the air? Hardly, because as Wang Gungwu has pointed out (Wang 1991b, 28–30), these narratives found their way into Southeast Asian Chinese school textbooks during the republican period at a time when republican leaders such as Sun Yat-sen were becoming greatly popular among the *huaqiao*. Themes that had linked the core images of the secret societies and *huaqiao* to the republican revolution, such as the racial family, fraternity, and colonial mastery, were now instilled in schoolchildren. This point suggests a larger one about the circulation of historical representations of *huaqiao* in later narratives. The first decade of the twentieth century was the era in which the various representations and narratives of the revolutionaries and reformers we have examined were first produced through the media, associations, and schools. Their interiorization as representations of a Chinese national self through formal institutions of modern knowledge production—such as school systems and universities—in later decades possibly deepened the affective power of these images. Even when the narratives that first gave meaning to these images, such as social Darwinism, withered away, these representations continued to serve new functions in the new narratives of transnational capitalism.

Notes

[1] I would like to thank Philip A. Kuhn for his helpful comments on the first draft and for supplying me with many of the sources for this paper, including the materials from the sourcebook he has put together. Apart from furnishing me with the big picture in which I have tried to embed this essay, Donald Nonini and Aihwa Ong also gave me invaluable comments on the first draft. I am also extremely grateful to Li Haiyan for her meticulous and intelligent research assistance.

[2] A recent work by Dian Murray in collaboration with Qin Baoqi suggests that there is little in the historical archive to actually link the secret society, the Tiandihui, with Koxinga and other Ming loyalists. The association appears to be based on the creation myth of the secret society itself and became widely believed in the twentieth century (Murray 1994, 3; see also Duara 1995, ch. 4).

References

Alatas, Syed Hussein. 1977. *The Myth of the Lazy Native*. London: Frank Cass.

Chen, Chunsheng. 1964. "Nanyang huaqiao yu geming" (The Nanyang *huaqiao* and revolution), in Zhonghua Minguo Kaiguo Wushinian Wenxian Bianzhuan Weiyuanhui. Comp. *Zhonghua minguo kaiguo wushinian wenxian.* vol. 1.11 *Gemingzhi changdao yu fazhan* (The propagation and development of the revolution), pp. 484–97. Taipei: Zhengzhong Shuju.

Chen, Yu-ching. 1981. "The Overseas Chinese in the United States and National Revolution, 1894–1912." In *Symposium on the History of the Republic of China*, vol. 1, pp. 406–26. Taipei: Conference on the History of the Republic of China.

Duara, Prasenjit. 1988. *Culture, Power, and the State: Rural North China, 1900–1942*. Stanford: Stanford University Press.

———. 1995. *Rescuing History from the Nation: Questioning Narratives of Modern China*. Chicago: University of Chicago Press.

———. 1996. "Of Authenticity and Woman: Personal Narratives of Middle-Class Women in China." Unpublished manuscript.

Freedman, Maurice. 1979. "Immigrants and Associations: Chinese in Nineteenth-Century Singapore." In *The Study of Chinese Society*, pp. 61–83. Edited by G. William Skinner. Stanford: Stanford University Press.

Hu, Hanmin. 1964. "Nanyang yu zhongguo geming" (Nanyang and the Chinese revolution). In *Zhonghua minguo kaiguo wushinian wenxian*. 1.11 *Gemingzhi changdao yu fazhan*, pp. 457–84.

Huang, Jianchun. 1993. *Wanqing Xinma huaqiao dui guojia rentongzhi yanjiu* (Studies of overseas Chinese attitudes in Singapore and Malaya toward national identity in the late Qing). Taipei: Zhonghua Minguo Haiwai Huaren Yanjiu Xuehui.

K'ang Yu-wei. 1958. *Ta T'ung Shu: The One-World Philosophy of Kang Yu-wei*. Translated by Laurence G. Thompson. London: Allen and Unwin.

Lee, Poh-ping. 1978. *Chinese Society in Nineteenth-Century Singapore*. Kuala Lumpur: Oxford University Press.

Liang Qichao. 1906. "Zhongguo zhimin ba da weiren zhuan" (Eight great Chinese colonists). *Xinmin Congbao* 15: 81–88.

———. 1981. *Xin dalu youji* (Travels in the New World). Changsha: Hunan Renmin Chubanshe.

Lo, Jung-pang, ed. 1967. *K'ang Yu-wei: A Biography and a Symposium*. Tucson: University of Arizona Press.

Lu Hun. 1910. "Xu." *Minbao* 25: 3977–82.

Ma, L. Eve Armentrout. 1990. *Revolutionaries, Monarchists, and Chinatowns: Chinese Politics in the Americas and the 1911 Revolution*. Honolulu: University of Hawaii Press.

Murray, Dian H., in collaboration with Qin Baoqi. 1994. *The Origins of the Tiandihui: The Chinese Triads in Legend and History*. Stanford: Stanford University Press.

Naquin, Susan, and Evelyn S. Rawski, 1987. *Chinese Society in the Eighteenth Century*. New Haven: Yale University Press.

Ou, Qujia. 1971 [1902]. "Xin Guangdong" (New Guangdong). In Zhang Yufa, ed., *Wan qing geming wenxue*, pp. 1–49. Taipei: Xinzhi Zazhishe.

Pomeranz, Kenneth. 1993. *The Making of a Hinterland: State, Society, and Economy in Inland North China, 1853–1937*. Berkeley: University of California Press.

Purcell, Victor. 1965. *The Chinese in Southeast Asia*. Kuala Lumpur: Oxford University Press.

Sourcebook. 1995. History 1834, "Chinese Emigration in Modern Times" Copyright 1994. President and Fellows of Harvard College.

Tsai, Shih-shan H. 1979. "Preserving the Dragon Seeds: The Evolution of Ch'ing Emigration Policy." *Asian Profile* vol. 7 no. 6: 497–506.

Wang, Gungwu. 1991a. "Patterns of Chinese Migration in Historical Perspective." In *China and the Overseas Chinese*, pp. 3–21. Singapore: Times Academic Press.

———. 1991b. "Southeast Asian Huaqiao in Chinese History-Writing." In *China and the Overseas Chinese*, pp. 22–40. Singapore: Times Academic Press.

Xihuang Zhengyin. 1910. "Nanyang huaqiao shilue" (A brief history of overseas Chinese in Southeast Asia). *Minbao* 25: 3983–4011, 26: 4087–126.

Yen Ching-hwang. 1970. "Ch'ing Sale of Honors and the Chinese Leadership in Singapore and Malaya (1877–1912)." *Journal of Southeast Asian Studies* 1, no. 2: 20–32.

———. 1976. *The Overseas Chinese and the 1911 Revolution, with Special Reference to Singapore and Malaya*. Kuala Lumpur: Oxford University Press.

———. 1982a. "The Overseas Chinese and Late Ch'ing Economic Modernization." *Modern Asian Studies* 16, no. 2: 217–32.

———. 1982b. "Overseas Chinese Nationalism in Singapore and Malaya, 1877–1912." *Modern Asian Studies* 16, no. 3: 397–425.

Zhuang Guotu. 1989. *Zhongguo fengjian zhengfu de huaqiao zhengce* (The policies of China's feudal governments toward overseas Chinese). Xiamen: Xiamen Daxue Chubanshe.

Chapter Two

Boundaries and Transgressions: Chinese Enterprise in Eighteenth- and Nineteenth-Century Southeast Asia

Carl A. Trocki

In 1883 the government of Singapore found itself locked in a struggle with a group of Chinese merchants for control of its revenue farms. Legislative council member W. G. Gulland, a prominent Singapore merchant, rose to provide the governor, Sir Frederick Weld, with some background to the problem.

> For the better understanding of this matter in all its bearings we must go back to 1870, when [Tan] Seng Poh and [Cheang] Hong Lim, after a desperate fight, made a long and lasting peace, and founded that great opium syndicate which has ever since played such an important part in the internal workings of this Colony. (Straits Settlements Legislative Council Proceedings 1883, 7)

The "syndicate" Gulland refers to was a Chinese company, or *kongsi*[1], as they were usually called, which had contracted with the colonial government to collect a tax on the sale of opium within Singapore. This concession was known as the "opium farm." It gave the "farmers" the exclusive monopoly over all retail sales of smokable opium in Singapore.

The arrangement was a common one in nineteenth-century Southeast Asia. Virtually all governments, both colonial and indigenous, permitted the sale of opium to all or at least some of their subjects. Most of them farmed out the privilege so as to reduce operating expenses and administrative costs. The farmers got rich and the governments received a reasonably dependable revenue. In Singapore the income from opium was never less than forty percent of the locally collected revenues and at times was nearly sixty percent (Trocki 1990, 96). Other colonial governments were similarly dependent upon opium sales, although none to the same extent as Singapore. Virtually all of these farms, opium and otherwise, were run by Chinese, and many of the consumers were also Chinese.[2] Thus, one can easily understand that a government would want to keep very close watch on any company that had contracted to collect its taxes.

What may seem extraordinary in this case is that the "great opium syndicate" to which Gulland referred controlled the opium and liquor farms for the colony of Singapore together with those for the neighboring Malay state of Johor, the adjacent Straits Settlements colony of Melaka, and also the nearby Dutch possession of Riau in the islands to the south of Singapore (Trocki 1993, 166–82). While it may have seemed tolerable for the Singapore government to allow its subjects to control farms outside of Singapore so long as the farmers and their company were based in the colony, one might question the prudence of such an arrangement for the Dutch in Riau and for the Sultan of Johor. Surely it must have seemed an infringement of their sovereignty.[3] In fact, it was not seen that way; the arrangement was not at all out of the ordinary. Many revenue-farming syndicates in the late nineteenth century crossed state or political boundaries; moreover, the tendency for wealthy Chinese to hold shares in revenue farms all over Southeast Asia, as well as in China, seems to have been quite widespread at this time. The trans-state quality of the farms is something that was, I believe, quite typical of Chinese business enterprise in the era before the appearance of nation-states in the region.

Despite the fact that colonial boundaries were falling into place and creating discrete administrative and economic units, many Chinese economic endeavors paid little heed to these boundaries. Chinese enterprise in the region predated the colonial presence, and thus many of the borders, and even colonialism itself, depended on the Chinese ability to cross the limits that Europeans had set for themselves and their indigenous colonial subjects. Without this mobility colonial governments would have had a far more difficult time collecting their revenues, financing the development of their states, and finding laborers to do the work.

The key organizational structures that characterized Chinese business enterprise during this period were the *kongsis* or shareholding partnerships. Anything larger than a small family-run business was usually formed into some sort of *kongsi*. Larger family businesses and ventures outside the family were almost always organized according to the *kongsi* principle. In Southeast Asia, the *kongsi* developed some unique features not found in China. The most important *kongsis* for purposes of this study, were the revenue-farming syndicates. The aim here is to explore the development of these organizations and the circumstances in which they declined in the early twentieth century.

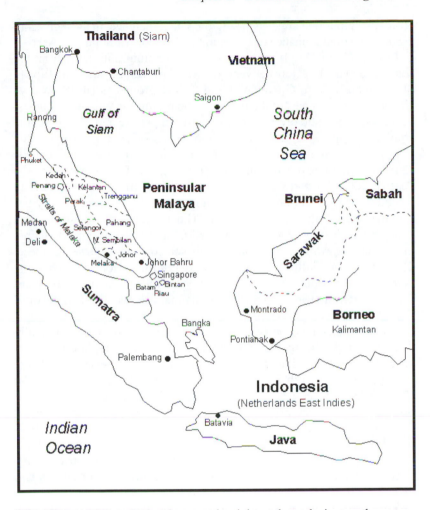

Fig. 1. Area of *kongsi* development in eighteenth- and nineteenth-century Southeast Asia.

The first of the relevant circumstances of the Southeast Asian economies into which Chinese moved in this period was the region's chronic labor shortage. Complementing this was China's growing population and incipient overpopulation. A third circumstance was the existence of a whole range of kinship and pseudo-kinship institutions that formed the basis of village life in southern China. Among these were the *kongsis*, surname organizations, clan groups, mercantile groups, craft guilds, secret societies, and so on. Yet another set of circumstances were the long-term economic trends that affected the region. These included, in the eighteenth century, the predominance of China in the economy of Southeast Asia.

Prior to World War II, virtually all Chinese emigrants came from the southern coastal region between the Gulf of Tonkin and the Taiwan Straits mainly from Guangdong and Fujian provinces (in those days Hainan Island was part of the former). The region has one of the highest degrees of linguistic diversity in China. In Singapore and Malaysia, it is common to speak of the "five kinds of Chinese" as a generality; this refers to the Hakka; the Hokkien, from Fujian province; the Teochew, from the region near Shantou in Guangdong; the Cantonese, from the Pearl River delta and Guangzhou region; and finally the Hainanese, sometimes called Hailam. In China there was a history of enmity between some of these; for example, Hakka against Cantonese, and Teochew against Hokkien. Virtually all Chinese discriminated against the Hainanese, who were frequently not even considered "true" Chinese. These differences often were at the root of conflicts, riots, and other disputes in the various overseas domiciles of these groups. A frequent source of conflict was the tendency to maintain some sort of ethnic division of labor among these groups.

As the nineteenth century opened, China's economic situation rapidly deteriorated. By the middle of the nineteenth century, the European market and its economic initiatives had come to dominate Asia. Despite the great power and wealth that Europeans brought with them, control of the Chinese labor force (the most available and adaptable labor force in Southeast Asia) was usually in the hands of other Chinese, whether through family ties, triad loyalties, debt obligations, or other bonds. It was difficult for Europeans to gain direct access to the labor pool. Finally, the Chinese also had another advantage over the Europeans—they were more mobile under the prevailing technological conditions and they knew the terrain and oceanways more intimately.

These advantages made the Chinese at once valuable and extremely threatening to the Europeans. The Chinese needed Europeans only to supply capital and to protect their property in Southeast Asia, but Europeans needed the Chinese economic infrastructure and Chinese labor if they were to make any money at all from their empire. The Chinese merchants and migrants were operating outside the control of their own government and had already established their own relations with other authorities. They had their own social and economic institutions and they had their own agendas. As I have suggested in my 1990 book *Opium and Empire*, and as Ong and Nonini have suggested in their introduction to this volume, the Chinese were seen as "wild" or at least ungovernable forces, and for Europeans the great trick of empire was to gain control over them.

Chinese Trade in Premodern Southeast Asia

Considering the historical development of Chinese trade in Southeast Asia, the question of transnationalism seems almost irrelevant, for at this time all Chinese economic activity in Southeast Asia was by its very nature international. Prior to the twentieth century, there were no nation-states in Asia. Premodern Southeast Asian states did not have borders in the sense that we understand them; thus the carriage of goods and the delivery of services between political territories was by definition foreign trade.

Beyond this, the contemporary distinction between economic and political spheres did not apply in traditional Southeast Asia. Virtually all trade was conducted by local political leaders as a royal monopoly of sorts. Within states, particularly in the Malay world, royal status meant little more than the right to collect marketable commodities from one's subjects. The ability to conduct foreign trade was one of the principal characteristics of political sovereignty. Foreigners coming to Malay ports invariably traded with the rulers or their agents. On the other hand, Chinese merchants, like most Asian merchants of the era, were private traders. They not only operated without support from their government but also sometimes even acted against its prohibitions. By the sixteenth century it became common to find Chinese acting as agents for Southeast Asian kings (Reid 1988, 1995). This period saw the establishment of more or less permanent settlements of Chinese and other merchants in the port cities of Southeast Asia. In Melaka, for instance, there was a Chinese *shabandar* (head trader) who managed the trading relations of all Chinese merchants as well as others from that part of the world, including Vietnam, Korea, and Japan (Meilink-Roelofsz 1962).

In addition to the trade of private merchants with Southeast Asian rulers, there was also a system of official trade, literally from government to government, which usually functioned as a part of the Chinese tributary system and was initially a ritual exchange (Wolters 1967, 1970). By the eighteenth century, this trade often became indistinguishable from private Chinese trade, as in eighteenth- and early nineteenth-century Siam, where virtually all the foreign trade of the state was conducted by Chinese merchants on behalf of the king. It was this propensity to engage in official economic activities that seems to have brought the Chinese into the business of revenue-farming and other related activities.

With the rise of Melaka after 1400 and the growth of long-distance trading links between Southeast Asia and the rest of the world, private Chinese trade, the "junk trade," came into its own. The goods involved in premodern Chinese commerce included mainly the export of manufactures from China. Some of these were consumed in Southeast Asia and others were trans-shipped to points west. In Southeast Asia, Chinese sought to purchase other luxury manufactures from farther west, in particular Indian cotton goods. From Southeast Asia itself they sought the unique range of forest and maritime products found only in the Asian tropics. By the time Europeans arrived, the Chinese were purchasing significant amounts of pepper and other spices from Southeast Asia as well as gold and tin.

The arrival of Europeans brought a radically different type of trader, one who came on behalf of his own government or a European trading company seeking to enforce their own monopolies and to seize territory. Despite European advances, in the sixteenth and seventeenth centuries Europeans did not significantly alter the earlier systems of commercial relations, as they adapted to local practices and distorted them only for their own purposes in certain specific areas. Their conquest of key port facilities such as Melaka and the construction of fortified "castle" towns there (and later in Manila and Batavia) actually quickened the pace of Chinese commerce in the region. Europeans were major customers for Chinese products, and they usually paid in cash. This was partly because they had nothing else to offer in exchange and partly because they possessed vast supplies of precious metals from the Americas. In the long run prevailing patterns of exchange persisted, and Chinese traders continued to carry goods from China to European bases in Southeast Asia. Traders from Fujian traveled to Manila to meet the silver-laden galleons from Acapulco each year. In the seventeenth and eighteenth centuries, traders from Fujian and Guangdong carried on the China-to-Batavia trade (Blussé 1988). Chinese traders had also come dominate most of the foreign trade of Siam during the same period (Cushman 1993a; Viraphol 1977). Europeans, like Southeast Asian rulers, were content to allow Chinese to collect their taxes and manage many of their economic affairs, particularly those that involved contacts with other Chinese or Southeast Asians.

The Early Modern Transformation of Chinese Economic Activity

By the middle of the eighteenth century a confluence of forces had come to drive Southeast Asian economics. The first was the dynamic impact of Chinese trade, including the increasing demand for local products. The second force was the resultant partnerships between Chinese merchants and indigenous Southeast Asian rulers to enhance production through the import of Chinese labor. A third factor that began to affect the region and this exchange between Southeast Asia and China was the upsurge in the opium trade by English "country traders" from India. These factors were crucial to the formation of the Chinese *kongsi* as it began to take shape in the middle years of the eighteenth century.

These developments can be seen in a number of cases in the island world of Southeast Asia. In Palembang, Sultan Mahmud Badaruddin (r. 1724–1757) married a part-Chinese woman and surrounded himself with a number of local Chinese who had converted to Islam. Together they organized the development of tin mines on the island of Bangka. His Chinese courtiers contracted to import labor from China to Bangka. The island's rich deposits were rapidly brought into production, and it quickly became the major tin field in Southeast Asia (Andaya 1993, 184–94). These relationships seem to contradict the received wisdom about the Chinese migration to Southeast Asia. In the late colonial period and in the early nationalist period in Southeast Asia, both Europeans and Southeast Asian indigenists have often blamed the Chinese migration on the colonial rulers. This is simply not true. First of all, the settlement of Chinese labor was begun with the active encouragement of local rulers, often in opposition to the wishes of the colonial powers.[4] Secondly, it calls into question assumptions about incompatibilities between Chinese and Malays, particularly the willingness of Chinese to convert to Islam. There is evidence that such accommodations were common in all parts of Southeast Asia prior to the nineteenth century.

Similarly close and profitable relations were established between the Buginese-Malay rulers of Riau at about the same time. In the 1760s Daing Kemboja, the Yang-dipertuan Muda (prime minister) of Riau, arranged to have Chinese coolies brought to Bentan Island to pioneer the planting of pepper and gambier (Trocki 1979). Barbara Andaya reports similar relations in Perak. Such arrangements occurred in Pontianak, Sambas (Wang 1977), Trengganu (Hamilton 1930), Brunei (Jesse 1794), Phuket, Chantaburi (Cushman 1993a), and other parts of Southeast Asia.

Several innovations in Chinese economic and social organization characterize this period. First of all, the tendency for Chinese traders to marry into the local society is quite pronounced. This was particularly true in the indigenous capitals. It is probable that this process of assimilation had been going on for quite some time, but we find clear reports of it only at this time. Perhaps one reason it went unreported in earlier days was because it was not seen as an extraordinary phenomenon. The concepts of ethnicity that emerged in the nineteenth century were peculiarly Western and do not seem to have been a part of the consciousness of eighteenth-century Asians. Perceived status and wealth were far more salient social markers than were native language, place of origin, or other ethnic criteria. Large numbers of Chinese assimilated into the upper ranks of Siamese society in Bangkok and into the *mestizo* stratum of Philippine society. Cross-cultural movement was common in the region, particularly in those places where European social, cultural, and racial biases were not given the force of law.

The appearance of large colonies of Chinese laborers in Southeast Asia was a new development. There are no reports of Chinese planters, tin or gold miners, or other such settlements of laborers prior to the eighteenth century. The organization of these enterprises in Palembang and Bangka, in Sambas and Pontianak in western Borneo, and in Riau were typified by these *kongsis* or shareholding partnerships, Chinese-style collaborative operations often including both capitalists and laborers (Horsfield 1848; Trocki 1979).

The Evolution of the *Kongsi* in Nineteenth-Century Southeast Asia

Throughout the nineteenth century, the building block of the Chinese economy continued to be the *kongsi*. Relying on earlier studies such as those by Wang Tai Peng and a few others, it is possible to trace the evolution of the system in Southeast Asia. The *kongsi* changed shape as it came to terms with European capitalism in the nineteenth century, with the Chinese adopting some European business practices; thus the *kongsi* gained a degree of legal status while at the same time maintaining some of their original characteristics.

Among the major changes was the tendency toward the consolidation of *kongsis*. That is, the shares seemed inevitably to fall into the hands of one or two investors. This accelerated in the nineteenth century in larger enterprises. Another trend was the accompanying movement toward social differentiation and class stratification, with wealthy merchants coming to control most of the major *kongsis*. Initially, *kongsis* were dominated by individuals sharing the same surname or kinship link; this was assumed to be part of the social "cement" in the economic enterprise. In fact, it was the fictive kinship ties in the form of sworn brotherhood that gave the *kongsi* its links to secret societies, particularly the Tiandihui. In China, such organizations never became more than marginal groups operating on the fringes of mainstream society. In Southeast Asia, by contrast, such groups very often constituted the mainstream of Chinese society (Trocki 1993). As time passed, ties of brotherhood and kinship were replaced by debtor-creditor relations (Trocki 1979).

As the *kongsis* proliferated, a hierarchy was established, a sort of segmented pyramid with one or two large *kongsis* at the top and many small ones at the bottom. These large *kongsis* seem almost all to have been revenue-farming organizations, the largest of which were the opium farms. They were often connected by chains of indebtedness to the smaller enterprises, which were engaged in primary production. As these connections became more comprehensive, they began to cut across the established ethnic division of labor and ethnic preserves. This often led to conflict and attempts to seek resolution at higher levels. Thus, larger enterprises could be linked together by something like interlocking directorates, with key individuals holding shares in a collection of related *kongsis*. This was the solution embodied in the "great syndicate," which in fact grew out of a struggle between Teochew and Hokkien revenue-farming *kongsis*. Such connections could also be cemented by marriage alliances. Family business patterns merged very compatibly with the *kongsi* structure. By the mid-nineteenth century many of the larger and more prosperous families of Straits-born Chinese were forming family *kongsis*. Finally, the secret societies, or "brotherhood" *kongsis* (which initially may not have been secret at all), began to find themselves marginalized and identified as criminal organizations.

Normally enterprises became *kongsis* when they were broken up into shares that signified investment, and by extension, rights to part of the profits. Workers or coolies could join some *kongsis* provided they got in early, worked hard, and guarded their investments. Even though they might have had no capital, they could gain a share in the profits through their labor. Thus, the *kongsi* structure facilitated the recruitment and retention of a labor force—always a problem in nineteenth-century Southeast Asia. Rather than working simply for wages, the *kongsi* allowed to receive shares in the enterprise. It also meant that capitalists could share losses in risky ventures. Coolies who worked for shares did not receive wages and therefore did not get paid if the enterprise failed to produce. This worked quite well in small mining ventures and probably even for smaller plantations. Toward the end of the nineteenth century these structures were still in common use in the tin fields of Perak (Pasquel 1896). But as these enterprises grew, or in endeavors that were large to begin with, shareholders tended to be major investors and laborers were simply employees. Thus in nineteenth-century Johor, where the *kangchu* rights for pepper- and gambier-producing settlements were divided into shares, the initial partners were generally shopkeepers and other principal investors. As time passed and these rights became valuable as revenue concessions, shareholders were inevitably wealthy merchants in Singapore or Johor Bahru.

In the absence of families and villages, *kongsis* undertook social and political functions in Southeast Asia. As brotherhood organizations, they reaffirmed solidarity through the triad rituals of south China. But unlike secret societies in China, they were the major actors in the economic development of Southeast Asia. The brotherhoods controlled labor and capital and undertook the responsibilities of government for the communities of laborers in the isolated areas where Chinese miners and planters worked. These became secret only when their existence was seen to threaten the colonial states and laws were passed banning them.

Revenue Farms and Global Linkages

The economic benefits stemming from the activities of Chinese settlers had important political consequences. Native rulers not only gained income through their cooperation with the Chinese but in fact expanded their states. Chinese economic activity in this period strengthened and expanded their territorial domains. It is doubtful that the ruler of Palembang had ever exercised regular and consistent powers of government over the Malay inhabitants of Bangka prior to the arrival of the Chinese; Andaya (1993) shows that he was unable to control and tax the Mandarese tin miners who first settled there. But with the arrival of the Chinese laborers and the management of their settlement by Chinese merchants and courtiers in Palembang, the authority of the sultan's court was greatly enhanced. He now had a productive, docile, and taxpaying population settled on land over which he formerly had only nominal control. As both Nonini (1992) and Skinner (1957) have argued, Chinese laborers were important supports for the stability of Southeast Asian states in colonial and precolonial times because they offered rulers additional income that did not require increased reliance upon, or interference with, their own subjects. The same thing happened in nineteenth-century Johor, where the Malay rulers deliberately filled up their underpopulated territories with thousands of Chinese pepper and gambier planters (Trocki 1979). Chinese merchants and laborers were not simply pioneers of the economy; they were also pioneers of state expansion. Since Chinese enterprise frequently moved ahead of the state, there was little precedent for the idea that it ought to remain within given political boundaries. Chinese settlers were key actors in binding open hinterlands to urban centers.

Thus the settlement of the Malay peninsula was carried out by Chinese miners, whose settlements often predated the founding of the British Straits settlements. There were Chinese miners in Perak, Phuket, Kelantan, and Trengganu all before 1780. These settlements rapidly expanded during the improved economic conditions that prevailed during the early nineteenth century, especially following the foundation of the

British colonies.[5] Chinese economic activity became the conduit for the movement of European capital into the Malay states, thus tying them to the colonial urban centers. We could say that the flag followed trade, but in this case it was the British flag that followed the Chinese coolies.

In Kedah, much of the money with which the Chinese had financed the revenue farms was British capital, and the British government in Penang took a keen interest in the security of Kedah (Khoo 1993, 130–31). The impact of the farm was two-sided. On the one hand, Kedah was bound closer to British Penang and thus was more detached from its actual tributary overlord, the King of Siam. On the other hand, the extra income gained by the Sultan of Kedah strengthened his position vis-à-vis his own nobles. Very much the same situation obtained in the state of Johor, where the revenue farms were held by Singapore merchants. In both, the administration of the Malay ruler was enhanced in domestic affairs while he and his state were more closely tied to the colonial state.

As the colonial economies and states grew during the second half of the nineteenth century, the revenue-farming *kongsis* likewise grew. Their expansion can be seen as indicators of the health of the economies. Since farms such as those for opium and spirits taxed what might be seen as luxury consumables, their growth or decline was a direct indicator of the purchasing power of the laboring classes. Moreover, since the tax fell primarily on the workers and not on the capitalists, it was possible to finance the colonial states in Southeast Asia without increasing the cost of doing business. In Singapore opium paid for free trade.

The farms were doubly valuable for capitalists because they were often held by the same financiers who backed mining ventures and lent money to planters. In the early part of the nineteenth century, revenue-farming operations were normally tied to specific industries and localities. Thus in and around Singapore, the opium farmers were also primarily engaged in pepper- and gambier-planting operations. In Penang, the opium farmers generally invested in tin mining in the Malay states. The coolies normally ended up spending much of their wages or pledging their shares to purchase opium or liquor and to gamble in the shops owned by the farmers. This meant that capitalists could count on "recycling" a good portion of the money that was spent on labor. Initially, revenue farms prospered because of their connection with particular productive enterprises such as planting or mining. Their major market was the population of coolies involved in the industry. The revenue farmers co-opted the secret societies in order to defend their interests and intimidate the laborers.

The tendency of revenue farmers to specialize according to industry did not last. In the first instance, the opium farmers naturally tended to diversify their economic interests. Thus in Singapore, the pepper and gambier *taukehs* (or wealthy merchants) such as Tan Seng Poh and Cheang Hong Lim went into shipping. Tan Seng Poh also owned the Alexandra Gunpowder Magazine. Tan Hiok Nee, also a member of the "great syndicate," invested much of his money in real estate in Singapore. Along with this diversification came the internationalization of revenue-farming syndicates.

In addition to the tendency to diversify, the farmers pursued continued growth patterns because of the problems of smuggling. In colonial Southeast Asia, farms were always let for specific territories and specific periods of time, and they were subject to competitive bidding processes. This meant that every time a farm was let, there were always a number of unsuccessful bidders. These individuals could attempt to gain an advantage by purchasing the revenue farms in an adjoining territory and then using that as a base for smuggling.

> Revenue farming was a "trans-national" phenomenon. Although the farms themselves were territorial, the need both to discourage smuggling, which is to say actual competition, was a strong incentive for the formation of transnational alliances without much regard to European colonial boundaries. (Dick 1993, 9)

In the case of the Singapore farms, during the "desperate fight" between Tan Seng Poh and Cheang Hong Lim, a common strategy for the one who lost the Singapore farms in any given year, was to buy the farms for either Riau or Johor. Although these were relatively unimportant as areas for opium sales, the rights often fetched premium prices for the Dutch in Riau and the maharaja in Johor. A buyer could cover his losses by smuggling opium into Singapore and thus get rich while at the same time destroying his competitor. In the long run, if the Singapore farmer was smart, he would offer the smuggler a number of shares in his own *kongsi* in exchange for control over the neighboring farm, and the matter would be settled. By default, the farm had become an international venture. Of course, such arrangements were not always to the advantage of the colonial government, which depended on competition in order to get the highest possible price for its farms. True, cooperation brought stability, but cooperation among revenue farmers meant that the government had to accept a lower rent.

By the 1880s the necessity of controlling both the industry and the revenue farms began to be less important. Growth in urban populations and increasing economic diversity meant that wealthy individuals might attempt to control the farms in areas where they did not actually dominate the local industry. Because of the tendency for local farmers to join forces and hold down the price of the farms, colonial administrators were always looking for someone with enough money and daring to join the competition for their farms and challenge the local interests. What Gulland did not mention in his little speech was that the *kongsi* that had displaced the "great syndicate" in Singapore was a group of Penang merchants who had been invited to bid for the Singapore farms by the governor. The Tan-Cheang syndicate had controlled the Singapore farms for such a long time because they had absorbed all of the competition and were thus able to keep the rent they paid to the government at a very low level. In fact, the government's rent did not increase more than $50,000[6] during the entire decade of the 1870s. In 1870 the great syndicate had gotten the farms for $360,000 annually. In 1879 they paid only a little over $400,000. When Koh Seang Tat and his group of *taukehs* from Penang took the farms in that year, they increased the rent from $400,000 to $600,000 per year, an increase of 50 percent. Hereafter, farm rents began to increase dramatically with every new contract, particularly if there was a new syndicate in the bidding. The *kongsi* that succeeded Koh in 1883 offered $1,020,000 (Trocki 1990, 96, 163).

Events in Singapore illustrate what was happening all over Southeast Asia at this time. If colonial governments found themselves held captive by one group of local Chinese financiers, their alternative was to seek assistance from outside. This could just as easily mean from outside a particular settlement or outside the jurisdiction of that particular colonial power altogether. From the 1870s on we see Chinese capital moving with great fluidity from Singapore, Riau, and Johor on to Batavia, Saigon, and even China. In the 1870s Singapore Chinese owned shares in revenue farms in Hong Kong and Shanghai (Trocki 1990, 178–80). After the tin-mining boom hit the west coast of Malaya, the Penang Chinese began investing in Siam and Sumatra as well as the adjacent Malay states.

There were a number of other reasons for the rather extraordinary mobilization of capital during this period. It appears that conditions finally reached a state where local financial resources were simply inadequate to cover the cost of managing the farms. In the case of Singapore, the rent agreed upon in 1883 was $80,000 per month. It is probable that no other group of Chinese in Singapore would have been able to finance the farms other than the one that already held them. Most of Singapore's Chinese capital had already been mobilized into one syndicate, and the government could not break the unity of that *kongsi*. Thus it was necessary to go offshore. In the case of the British, it is fortunate that they had another wealthy settlement from which to draw capital. For the Dutch and the Siamese, it was necessary for them too to rely on finance capital from the British territories. The plantation area in Sumatra south of Medan was largely financed from Penang and Singapore, particularly by individuals such as Thio Thiau Siat.[7] He controlled massive interests in Sumatra, at one point holding revenue farms all up and down the east coast from Aceh to Riau. He also owned revenue farms in Penang and had extensive investments in China as well. Indeed, it was a part of the global reach of many of the more important Chinese *taukehs* that most eventually tried to go back home to invest at least some of their money.

Revenue farms performed a variety of functions in the Chinese world of Southeast Asia beyond simply supporting colonial governments and squeezing coolies. In an age when European banks often looked askance at Chinese borrowers and when certain lucrative areas of investment were closed to Chinese capital, the revenue farms and the *kongsi* system provided vehicles for Chinese investment and capital accumulation. Perhaps most significant for economic expansion, farms became a source of capital for other ventures. With their large and usually reliable cash flows and their relatively low needs for long-term capital investment, the farms were ready sources of cash. In the absence of a banking system in which Chinese felt confidence, the farms also served as a vehicle for savings and therefore for capital formation. They often doubled as banks. There are reports that farmers often made loans or paid other debts from farm funds.

It is probably no accident that the foundation, management, and expansion of Chinese banks in Southeast Asia were largely the work of opium farmers and former opium farmers. Individuals such as Thio Thiau Siat were instrumental in founding the Deli Bank in 1907. Michael Godley shows that Thio brought together a network of Penang and East Sumatran opium farmers to finance the bank. Elsewhere he was also a prime mover in founding the Chinese Bank of Batavia. One of Thio's partners in the Deli Bank, Khoe Tjin Tek, founded the Hokkien Bank of Medan in 1921 (Godley 1993, 265). In Singapore, the onetime carpenter Wong Ah Fook, a Cantonese who had taken charge of the revenue farms of Johor, founded the first Chinese bank in Singapore, the Kwong Yik Bank, in 1903 (Lim 1993). Also in Singapore, and more successful than Wong Ah Fook, was Low Peng Yam, a major partner in the opium syndicate of 1900. He went on to found the Four Seas Bank (Sze Hai Tong) and was one of its directors and the largest shareholder. This was the major Teochew bank in Singapore and to the present day remains at the core of the extensive Four Seas Group in Singapore. Ian Brown notes that the founders of the Siam Commercial Bank also included a number of Bangkok opium farmers among their membership (Brown 1993, 243). The connection between former opium farmers and banking shows a significant continuity in the institutions and the personnel involved in them. The opium-farming *kongsis* were the pioneering financial institutions of the region and led inexorably to the Chinese banking and financial combines of the twentieth century.

The Demise of the Farming System

The Chinese revenue-farming *kongsis* were among the largest and wealthiest organizations of their time in the region, whether of Chinese or European ownership. They not only mobilized Chinese capital from all over Southeast Asia and provided the financing for most forms of commodity production in the region, but also supported the everyday working of the various colonial states in Southeast Asia as well as the governments of Siam and China. In fact, by the 1880s it was clear to both the Chinese and the colonial governments that the financial well-being of each was intimately connected with the other's. While the relationship was mutually beneficial, it was also one that colonial governments found increasingly uncomfortable. Such incidents as the great opium conspiracy in Singapore, in which the members of the "great syndicate" sought to sabotage Koh Seang Tat and their rivals from Penang and force the government to turn the farms back over to them, were more than an embarrassment: They smelled of treason to colonial governors such as Frederick Weld. Moreover, the farms had become a convenient target for anti-opium forces in both Britain and Malaya, and senior officials in the Colonial Office realized that it would be impossible to ignore public opinion indefinitely. In Britain, this was brought home forcefully when the Society for the Suppression of the Opium Trade gained support from backbenchers in both parties around the turn of the century (Trocki 1990).

Sooner or later all colonial governments began to rethink their dependence upon Chinese merchants. This trend was a part of the larger movement toward the rationalization and standardization of colonial rule. By the 1880s both the Dutch in Java and the French in Indochina had decided to take the farms into their own hands. The rising tide of criminal activity, mostly smuggling, and the additional stress of an economic downturn offered convenient opportunities to turn the farms into state-controlled monopolies (Nankoe 1993; Rush 1990). In the British colonies and in the Dutch colonies outside of Java (the Outer Islands), the farming system remained, largely because Europeans were too thin on the ground to undertake the extensive functions of government necessary to collect their own taxes. It was still easier to let the Chinese do it. The Siamese too found it useful to allow the farming system to persist.

Continuing problems ultimately led the British, the Dutch, and Siamese to take control of their own farms. Beyond the need to constantly manipulate the possible bidders and to be wary of smuggling and conspiracies among farmers, governments found that as the farms grew larger and more valuable, they also became more volatile. While governments could benefit from the increases in revenue that came with intense competition in the bidding, they also discovered that in order to procure the farms, Chinese bidders would offer more than the farms were worth, or at least more than they were willing to pay for them; not long after the farms were taken over, the high-flying syndicate would then petition the government for relief, claiming that they could not meet their obligations. Although the government required farmers to put up security such as title deeds and similar assets, they also realized that if they foreclosed on the farmer, they would still have to look around for another farmer, usually the one who had lost the bid and who had most probably done everything possible to sabotage the syndicate. Thus the farms came to be seen as increasingly unmanageable.

The farms' dependence upon the world economy meant that shifts or price changes in global markets could dramatically affect the local economy. In a place such as Singapore, where the economy was tied to the prices of about four or five major commodities, it did not take much to kick the pins out from under the whole economy. Moreover, the opium farm alone was paying nearly 50 percent of the entire revenue. Global recessions between 1890 and 1910 wreaked havoc with the farms. The 1880s was a period of expansion, and it was followed by a sharp drop in commodity prices in 1890 and 1891. By June 1891 the Penang farm was about a half million dollars in arrears and the Singapore farm had lost over three hundred thousand dollars. In these instances, the government had no alternative but to bail out the farmers and accept a reduced rent.

Increasing attempts by the British in Malaya and by the Dutch in the Outer Islands to bring the local farmers more closely under control continued throughout the 1890s and into the twentieth century. For the first time the colonial governments began to gather pertinent statistical information on the actual details of running the farms. Farmers had always been unwilling to disclose the true profitability of the farms (Trocki 1990), but so long as Chinese capital, labor, and expertise were necessary to provide the products upon which European prosperity depended, the farming system remained. Part of the problem, as far as British official and economic interests were concerned, was the continuing need for Chinese labor. British capitalists were regularly frustrated in their attempts to move beyond the tertiary level of involvement in Southeast

Asian economic activity. They could not independently engage in mining and planting enterprises because they could not control Chinese labor. Chinese labor was tied to Chinese capitalists through the farming system and *kongsi* organization. Opium profits and secret societies were the primary means of labor control in colonial Southeast Asia, and both were out of European hands.

Two new innovations in Southeast Asian economic life changed this system. When rubber became available as a plantation crop (in place of pepper, gambier, sugar, and tapioca), colonial officials found that it was compatible with some sort of quit-rent system whereby the government could actually treat land as a commodity. Planters found that they could import a labor force to Malaya from India (Jackson 1968). The French brought "Tongkinese" (as they called the northern Vietnamese) to their plantations in Cochin-China, and the Dutch sent Javanese to Sumatra. The second innovation was the increasing availability of, and necessity for, steam dredging equipment in tin mining. Wong Lin Ken has suggested that by the 1890s the growing scarcity of easily worked tin deposits in Malaya necessitated techniques that were beyond the technology immediately available to Chinese laborers (Wong 1965). Chinese capitalists could and did continue to compete with British and other colonial economic interests, but they found themselves increasingly at a disadvantage as the administrative and technological revolutions progressed.

By the beginning of the twentieth century, Chinese enterprise faced a further disadvantage in the gradual institutionalization of racist attitudes and, finally, of racist policies by all the colonial governments. Underneath the rhetoric of administrative rationalization by the colonial bureaucrats, the discourse of technological advancement by the businessmen and engineers, and even the humanitarianism of the antiopium lobbyists, one can also read a consistently anti-Chinese message. Chinese were feared, mistrusted, suspected, misunderstood, and resented. Chinese economic success was often seen as a threat to the colonial economy. The waning of free trade and the appearance of neo-mercantilist colonialism at this time supported and justified more rigorous measures to rein in the Chinese. The rigidifying of colonial borders and the poisoning of colonial attitudes laid the foundations for indigenous nation-states and nationalisms. John Butcher has delineated the erection of color bars in colonial legislation and in social practice in British Malaya, noting their anti-Chinese economic policies were less explicit but nevertheless came into force at about this time (Butcher 1979). Thus the moves to shut down the opium revenue farms, although discussed in terms of humanitarianism by the antiopium lobbyists and in terms of economic and administrative rationalism by merchants and bureaucrats, should be seen in this atmosphere of increasing racism.

Jennifer Cushman's account (Cushman 1991) of the rise and fall of the Khaws may perhaps be seen as an example of what befell Chinese who overreached themselves. The Khaw family of Penang, also known as the Na Ranong family of southern Siam, can be seen as the exemplars of late colonial "transgressors." Cushman's study of the rise and decline of this Chinese tin-mining dynasty shows what might be considered as the last stand of the opium farmers. This family in many ways combined the most useful aspects of both European and Chinese systems. They were located in a border area, where they were able to combine a lucrative group of tin-mining concessions in both Malaya and Siam with an extremely intricate network of patronage links with Siamese officialdom at both the local level and in Bangkok. This was buttressed by an extensive network of strategic marriage alliances in both Malaya and Siam. Their placement within a British colony and at the same time under the protection of the Siamese crown gave the Khaws a sort of leverage possessed by few other groups of Chinese.

Cushman has shown how the family financial empire rose to challenge British colonial interests and the imperial corporate affiliates under the management of Khaw Sim Bee. Between about 1890 and the beginning of the First World War, Khaw and his clan built upon the base of their tin-mining and revenue-farming enterprises in the west coast Malay states and southern Siam. By the beginning of the twentieth century, they controlled a vast interlocking conglomerate that included engineering companies, smelters, shipping lines, steam dredging companies, rice mills, banks, insurance companies, and a host of related enterprises in addition to the tin mines and revenue farms that they had originally possessed. Their interests stretched from China to India and from Siam to Australia and New Zealand. Their aim, it seems, was to establish financial and technological independence that would liberate them from the influence of British capital and British political control.

The keys to Khaw's empire were the Eastern Trading Company and the Eastern Shipping Company. The latter was to make it possible for them to break the monopoly enjoyed by the British firm. Cushman notes:

> The Khaw shipping operation [Koe Guan Company] was itself enlarged with the addition of eight vessels from a local Chinese firm in 1902 and further modernised early the next year with the purchase of four steamships in New Zealand. Already owners of the largest shipping firm in Penang with steamers running along the west coast to Rangoon and as far away as China, and in close cooperation with the Singapore-based Wee Bin line, a leading importer of

coolies, the Koe Guan joined forces with several other smaller concerns, including Thio Thiau Siat's pioneering "Ban Joo Hin," to form the Eastern Shipping Company Ltd. in 1907. Registered as a joint stock company with an initial
capital of $1.4 million, it was for some time able to compete against the Straits
Steamship Company. (Cushman and Godley 1993, 269)

One of the directors was Foo Choo Choon, a noted Penang opium
farmer. The interesting aspect of this financial conglomerate is not its
similarity to Western corporate forms of enterprise but rather its hybrid
form, which combined both Western business enterprise with a highly
adapted version of a Malayan Chinese family partnership. In the case of
the latter, Khaw Soo Cheang, and later Sim Bee and two or three key
members of the family, coordinated general corporate and family strategy while each firm or *kongsi* was headed by various members of the kin
group, including those who had been brought in by marriage or others
who had well-established links to the family.

A second element in the Khaw business constellation was their occupation of key official positions within the administrative structure of
Southeast Asian governments. Khaw Sim Bee, while recognized as an
important Penang *taukeh*, was also the governor of Ranong province for
the king of Siam. The family also held positions in Penang, Sumatra, and
Burma. Finally, the family business was likewise buttressed by a network
of opium-farming *kongsis*. Cushman suggests that the Khaws had attempted to finance much of their business empire with the opium-farming profits. The opium farms were abundant producers of cash, and thus
the family may have hoped that the profits from the opium farms would
help them cover contingencies arising from their many new ventures
during the first decade of the twentieth century (Cushman 1986, 76).

Khaw Joo Choe, together with a number of his relatives and others in
the family network, had put together what appears to have been the
largest and most wide-ranging group of opium farms on record. The
Khaws had already been a dominant force in the revenue farms of southern Siam and in the tin-mining states of western Malaya. At the beginning of the twentieth century Khaw Joo Choe was able to organize a
collection of *kongsis* that controlled the opium farms for the region
stretching down the Malay peninsula from Bangkok to Singapore and including all of the Siamese farms and all of the British Malayan ones as
well as some Dutch farms in Sumatra and Riau as well. This, it seems,
was to be the cash cow for the Khaw business empire, embodied in the
Eastern Trading Company and the Eastern Shipping Company.

Unfortunately for the Khaws, their timing was bad. Their network of
companies had been established during the boom period between 1893

and 1904. When the crash came in 1904, much of the entire structure was placed in jeopardy. The family was overextended on every front. In 1903 Khaw Joo Choe had bid $5,040,000 as annual rental for the Singapore farm alone. The entire contract was for over $8.5 million, an increase of 100 percent over the previous contract. No sooner had the ink dried on the contract than the bottom fell out of the economy. The syndicates that Joo Choe formed could not pay their obligations to the various governments and ultimately had to petition for relief. Instead of receiving the agreed-upon $5.6 million, the Singapore government had to settle for $4.2 million in 1904 and even less in 1905 and 1906. Khaw, hoping to recoup his losses, gambled again, taking on the Straits Settlements farms for the period from 1907 to 1910 (the farms were usually let under three-year contracts). But he was doubly unlucky, and even though the second contract was for less money, he failed to meet the terms for that one as well. By 1908 he and some of the major figures in his syndicate were bankrupt.

Meanwhile his *kongsi* in Siam, led by one of his associates from Penang, Cheah Choo Yew, fell afoul of skullduggery by the local revenue farmers in Bangkok. By 1905 the Bangkok farms were in chaos, and the Khaw-Cheah group withdrew from the venture when the government agreed to refund their original investment of 752,800 baht. Thus they made nothing on the Bangkok venture and were forced to take the cash to cover their losses in Malaya.

These difficulties were a disaster for the Khaw dreams of expansion. Eastern Smelting was sold in 1911 for lack of capital to competing British interests at just the time when it began to make a profit. It would have been possible to cover the smelting company's capital needs if the revenue farms had proved viable. On the heels of these events came the murder of the Khaw family patriarch, Khaw Sim Bee, in Trang in 1913. Following this, the entire venture began to unravel. The loss of Sim Bee's influence made it more difficult to activate the informal patronage networks that, together with the revenue farms and the corporate institutions, made up the Khaw-Na Ranong financial empire. While the Khaws continued to hold an important position in the tin industry, their dreams of financial and corporate autonomy, which had driven the formation of the combine, were never realized. Although it remained a viable enterprise until after World War I, Eastern Shipping was already having trouble meeting its commitments as early as 1913, according to Cushman. It is also significant that during these years, the new king of Siam, Vajiravudh (Rama VI), began to raise the first signs of anti-Chinese sentiment within Thai nationalist discourse with his famous essay "The Jews of the East" (Cushman 1991, 88–114).

The financial crises of 1903–1907 were the final straw for the colonial governments concerned with the opium-farming business. It was now seen as irresponsible to allow the state's revenue to be dependent upon the vagaries of the market place and what seemed to be the inherent instability in Chinese business methods and organization. In all fairness, some of the problems really seem to have stemmed from structural adjustments in the overall economy. However, Chinese business methods, such as the *kongsi*, did appear both uncertain and opaque to European and other official observers at the time. Indeed, the very features that made the *kongsi* so successful in economic pioneering—its flexibility, its looseness, and its more or less segmented structure—came to appear as unreliable and even dishonest when the houses of cards collapsed. Moreover, when they were extended—even overextended—into a wide range of ventures all over the world and were held together with little more than handshakes and relationships between brothers-in-law, it became difficult to assign financial responsibility and stabilize the state revenues. This declining confidence in Chinese business practices now led Southeast Asian governments to turn to the expedient of managing their own revenues, and they took steps to abolish the farming system altogether. By 1910 all of the major revenue farms in the western part of Southeast Asia (Siam, Malaya, and the Dutch possessions in Sumatra, Riau, and Borneo) had been taken over by the respective governments and thenceforth run as government monopolies under the management of civil servants. In Indochina the French had already established a monopoly system, and in the Philippines the Americans had not only abandoned the farming system but had banned opium use altogether. Likewise, in 1906 the Chinese government had reached an agreement with the British to systematically reduce opium production with the intention of ending it altogether by 1916. While this aim was frustrated by the Chinese revolution and subsequent emergence of warlordism in China, in 1910 many believed that the end of the farming system was only the first step in the inevitable abolition of opium use altogether.

The collapse of the Khaw revenue-farming syndicates and the subsequent erosion of their financial empire drew a fairly clear line of demarcation between the first era of Chinese internationalism in Southeast Asia and the age of economic nationalism in the region. Although there were not yet any true nation-states in Southeast Asia by 1910, the financial and administrative frameworks for the embryonic nations had been established. These rationalized structures were incompatible with the patterns of Chinese enterprise that had flourished during the nineteenth century.

Chinese businesses, however, were firmly fixed in their international positions. It may have been that revenue farming and other such quasi-administrative concessions were taken out of their hands, but the interests of the large financial combinations the Chinese had established still stretched across the colonial borders and back to China. Chinese, most often former opium farmers, had been successful in founding their own banks, insurance companies, and financial empires. There were still fortunes to be made in rubber, tin, retail sales, and labor contracting, and an increasingly wider range of economic opportunities presented themselves as Europeans began to turn inward and fell to fighting with each other over the spoils of empire.

More important, structures and practices that characterized Chinese businesses during these formative years have proven quite durable. Although there were compromises with Western-style corporate forms, the old *kongsi* structure continued to underlie many Chinese business ventures, particularly the informal ones. This has continued to buttress the family-business relationship. Wealthy Chinese businessmen continue to aspire to the quasi-political sphere in their search for superprofits and work to establish relationships with modern Southeast Asian political leaders.

The *kongsis* have managed to survive. We see their children today in such institutions as the Overseas Chinese Banking Corporation (the OCBC) of Singapore, which is the descendent of the old Hokkien *kongsis* of the town. It is still poised to offset the gains of its rival, the Four Seas Group, the offspring of the major Teochew financial group. Both can probably be traced back to Singapore's great syndicate. Similar linkages between nineteenth-century *kongsis* and the corporate giants of modern Southeast Asia can be found in Kuala Lumpur, Penang, Bangkok, Hong Kong, Jarkarta, Manila, and all the cities on the coast of the South China Sea.

Notes

[1] This term would be pronounced *gongsi* in *putonghua* (Mandarin, or whatever one wishes to call the Chinese national language today). Throughout this paper I will use spellings for this and other terms that are derived from the accepted pronunciations in Teochew, Hokkien, Hakka, Hainanese, or Cantonese. These are the most commonly used Chinese languages in Singapore, Malaysia, and Southeast Asia. This applies to Chinese terms such as *kangchu*, *taukeh*, etc., as well as most Chinese personal names. These usages have already been absorbed into local languages such as Thai and Malay/Indonesian as well as into regional English usage. Even though they are properly Chinese terms and there are ideographs for them, to render them in a *pinyin* orthography based on Mandarin seems a refinement that would only confuse rather than enlighten.

[2] In addition to opium, there were farms for the retail sale of spirits, *baang* (a cannabis preparation), pork, betel nut, and other items as well as for services such as gambling, prostitution, and pawn brokering and for other activities such as the cutting of certain timbers, the collection of birds' nests, the conduct of markets, rice-milling, and so on. With the exception of gambling, none were as lucrative as the opium farm, but colonial rulers often felt gambling to be immoral, and thus not many territories had gambling farms. For a comprehensive view of the farming systems, see Butcher and Dick 1993.

[3] Abu Bakar had been recogized as sultan of Johor by the British government in 1885, but his sovereignty over Johor both prior to this date and until 1912 was also acknowledged. (Thio 1969, 108–9) The revenue farms for Johor and Singapore were, with a few notable exceptions, always held by the same syndicate from 1846 until 1910 (Trocki 1990).

[4] Although the Dutch East India Company (VOC) officials were quite happy to see the tin production of Bangka increase, they were displeased when they discovered that it was impossible for them to monopolize it. A flourishing private trade, supported by the sultan and transported in Chinese junks and English vessels, was carried on throughout the eighteenth century despite Dutch protests.

[5] Penang was taken by the British East India Company in 1786, and a settlement at Singapore was established in 1819. Melaka was first taken by Britain from the Dutch in 1795, during the Napoleonic Wars, and then returned in 1818. The Dutch withdrew from Melaka following the Anglo-Dutch Treaty of 1824, and the settlement was taken by the British.

[6] The Spanish dollar was the common currency throughout colonial Southeast Asia.

[7] Also known as Chang Chao-hsieh and Chang Pi-shih or Chang Chen-hsun (Godley 1993, 262).

References

Andaya, B. W. 1993. *To Live as Brothers: Southeast Sumatra in the Seventeenth and Eighteenth Centuries*. Honolulu: University of Hawaii Press.

Blussé, L. 1988. *Strange Company: Chinese Settlers, Mestizo Women, and the Dutch in VOC Batavia*. Providence: Floris

Brown, I. 1993. "The End of the Opium Farm in Siam, 1905–7." In J. Butcher and H. Dick, eds., *The Rise and Fall of Revenue Farming: Business Elites and the Emergence of the Modern State in Southeast Asia*, pp. 233–45. London: St. Martin's.

Butcher, John. 1979. *The British in Malaya, 1880–1941: The Social History of a European Community in Colonial South-East Asia*. Kuala Lumpur: Oxford University Press.

Butcher, John and Howard Dick, eds. 1993. *The Rise and Fall of Revenue Farming: Business Elites and the Emergence of the Modern State in Southeast Asia*. London: St. Martin's.

Cushman, J. W. 1986. "The Khaw Group: Chinese Business in Early Twentieth-Century Penang." *Journal of Southeast Asian Studies* 17: 58–79.

————. 1991. *Family and State: The Formation of a Sino-Thai Tin-mining Dynasty, 1797–1932*. Singapore: Oxford University Press.

————. 1993. *Fields from the Sea: Chinese Junk Trade with Siam During the Late Eighteenth and Early Nineteenth Centuries*. Ithaca, NY: Southeast Asia Program, Cornell University.

Cushman, J. W. and M. R. Godley. 1993. "The Khaw Concern." In J. Butcher and H. Dick, eds., *The Rise and Fall of Revenue Farming: Business Elites and the Emergence of the Modern State in Southeast Asia*, pp. 267–71. London: St. Martin's.

Dick, H. 1993. "A Fresh Approach to Southeast Asian History". In J. Butcher and H. Dick, eds., *The Rise and Fall of Revenue Farming: Business Elites and the Emergence of the Modern State in Southeast Asia*, pp. 3–18. London: St. Martin's.

Godley, M.R. 1993. "Thio Thiau Siat's Network." In J. Butcher and H. Dick, eds., *The Rise and Fall of Revenue Farming: Business Elites and the Emergence of the Modern State in Southeast Asia*, pp. 262–66. London: St. Martin's.

Hamilton, A. 1930 [1727]. *A New Account of the East Indies*. Edited by William Foster. London: Argonaut.

Horsfield, T. 1848. "Report on the Island of Bangka." *Journal of the Indian Archipelago and Eastern Asia*, vol. 2.: 299–336, 373–427, 705–725, 779–824.

Jackson, James C. 1968. *Planters and Speculators: Chinese and European Agricultural Enterprise in Malaya, 1786–1921*. Singapore; University of Malaya Press.

Jesse, J. 1794. "Substance of a Letter to the Court of Directors from Mr. John Jesse, Dated 20th July 1775 at Borneo Proper." *Oriental Repertory* 2: 1–9.

Khoo Kay Jim. 1993. "Revenue Farming and State Centralisation in Nineteenth-Century Kedah." In J. Butcher and H. Dicks, eds., *The Rise and Fall of Revenue Farming: Business Elites and the Emergence of the Modern State in Southeast Asia*, pp. 125–41. London: St. Martin's.

Lim, P.P.H. 1993. *Immigrant to Patriarch: The Biography of Wong Ah Kook*. Singapore: Institute of Southeast Asian Studies.

Meilink-Roelofsz, M.A.P. 1962. *Asian Trade and European Influence in the Indonesian Archipelago Between 1500 and About 1630*. The Hague: Nijhoff.

Nankoe, H., J.-C. Gerlus, and M. J. Murray. 1993. "The Origins of the Opium Trade and the Opium Regies in Colonial Indochina". In J. Butcher and H. Dick, eds., *The Rise and Fall of Revenue Farming: Business Elites and the Emergence of the Modern State in Southeast Asia*, pp. 182–95. London: St. Martin's.

Nonini, D. M. 1992. *British Colonial Rule and the Resistance of the Malay Peasantry 1900–1957*. New Haven: Center for International and Area Studies, Yale University. Yale Southeast Asia Studies, monograph series no. 38.

Pasquel, J. C. 1896. "Chinese Tin Mining in Selangor". *The Selangor Journal: Jottings Past and Present*, IV (no. 2, Oct. 4; no. 3, Oct. 18; no. 6, Nov. 29; no. 8, Dec. 27; no. 10, Jan. 24.).

Reid, A. 1988. *Southeast Asia in the Age of Commerce, 1450–1680: The Lands Below the Winds*. New Haven: Yale University Press.

————. 1995. "Flows and Seepages in the Long-Term Chinese Interaction with Southeast Asia". In A. Reid, ed., *Sojourners and Settlers: Histories of Southeast Asia and the Chinese*, pp. 48–49. Sydney: Allen and Unwin.

Rush, J. R. 1990. *Opium to Java: Revenue Farming and Chinese Enterprise in Colonial Indonesia, 1800–1910*. Ithaca, NY: Cornell University Press.

Skinner, G. W. (1957) *Chinese Society in Thailand: An Analytical History*. Ithaca, NY: Cornell University Press. Straits Settlements Legislative Council Proceedings. 1883. Singapore: Government Printing Office.

Straits Settlements Legislative Council Proceedings. 1883. Singapore: Government Printing Office.

Thio, E. 1969. *British Policy in the Malay Peninsula, 1880–1910*. Volume 1: *The Southern and Central States*. Singapore: University of Malaya Press.

Trocki, C. A. 1979. *Prince of Pirates: The Temenggongs and the Development of Johor and Singapore, 1784–1885*. Singapore: Singapore University Press.

———. 1990. *Opium and Empire: Chinese Society in Colonial Singapore 1800–1910*. Ithaca, NY: Cornell University Press.

———. 1993. "The Demise of Singapore's Great Opium Syndicate." In J. Butcher and H. Dick, eds., *The Rise and Fall of Revenue Farming; Business Elites and the Emergence of the Modern State in Southeast Asia*, pp. 166–181. New York: St. Martin's.

Viraphol, S. 1977. *Tribute and Profit: Sino-Siamese Trade, 1652–1853*. Cambridge, MA: Harvard University Press.

Wang Tai Peng. 1977. "The Origins of Chinese *Kongsi* with Special Reference to West Borneo". M. A. thesis, Department of History, School of General Studies, Australian National University.

Wolters, O. W. 1967. *Early Indonesian Commerce: A Study in the Origins of Srivijaya*. Ithaca, NY: Cornell University Press.

———. 1970. *The Fall of Srivijaya in Malay History*. London: Lund Humphries.

Wong, L. K. 1965. *The Malayan Tin Industry*. Tuscon, AZ: Association of Asian Studies.

Part 2

Family, *Guanxi*, and Space: Discourses and Practices in the Age of Flexibility

Preface

It is necessary to distinguish family and *guanxi* discourses from family and *guanxi* practices—reflecting the more general contrast made by Bourdieu (1977) between formal structural accounts of exchange and the actual strategies (and their associated tactics) of exchange. Whereas discourse formally describes and prescribes the process of exchange, attention to the unspoken practices central to strategies of exchange points us instead to bodily enactments of meaning, the timing and rhythm of prestations, and the history of prior exchanges. In part 2, this is most clearly set out in the essay by Hsing, who discusses the timing of *guanxi* exchanges, mutual but unstated valuations of gifts exchanged, and hidden, implicit messages conveyed through *guanxi* relations between Taiwanese investors and local officials in Fujian (see also Yang 1994). Hsing's essay makes it clear that the effective deployment of *guanxi* requires much work, in particular the expenditure of sensitively cued emotional labor linked to the giving of material and immaterial gifts.

Chinese transnationalists employ their family and *guanxi* discourses and networks, as we noted in the introduction, to form and operate subcontracting arrangements—a prevailing form of labor and business organization in the period of flexibility—and to cement alliances with members of the new global technocratic and professional elites. Family and *guanxi* practices are characterized by informality combined with the capacity to coordinate dispersed family members, kinfolk, and *guanxi*-linked "friends" across national boundaries and to create strategically important personal ties with bureaucrats in large national and transnational organizations. These practices are thus well suited to the spatial

89

decentralization, complexity, and proliferation of the new markets of global capitalism and to the labile subjectivities it has called into being. Thus in Hsing's essay, Chinese investors employ their *guanxi* networks to penetrate national borders and bureaucracies in southern China and form profitable alliances with local government functionaries. Shaanxi peasants described in Liu's essay deploy—mostly without success—their family, affinal, and native-place *guanxi* networks to extend the spatial scope of their small-scale businesses in China, while the overseas scholars whom Liu also describes take advantage of the *guanxi* they share as sojourners to form successful business ventures spanning the space between Great Britain and China. Lee's essay reports on how supervisors and foremen in a Shenzhen factory are able to mobilize their native-place ties in villages outside the region in order to recruit factory workers at times of peak labor demand.

Beyond part 2, other detailed insights into the tactical adaptability of family and *guanxi* connections among extremely wealthy travelers between Hong Kong and the western coast of the United States and Canada are provided by the essay by Mitchell in part 3, which demonstrates the ways in which dispersed family structures coordinate trans-Pacific capital flows by the transnational elite who have shifted investments to Vancouver, Canada.

References

Bourdieu, Pierre. 1977. *Outline of a Theory of Practice.* Cambridge, England: Cambridge University Press.

Yang, Mayfair Mei-hui. 1994. *Gifts, Favors, and Banquets: The Art of Social Relationships in China.* Ithaca, NY: Cornell University Press.

Chapter Three

Space, Mobility, and Flexibility: Chinese Villagers and Scholars Negotiate Power at Home and Abroad[1]

Xin Liu

In 1987, when traveling on a local bus near Zhenjiang, a small town in Sichuan, I met a group of villagers on board. A friendly farmer in his early forties said to me, "I bet you come from Guangdong."[2] And then he turned to his friends, "From this older brother's (*laoge*)[3] looks and way of speaking, I bet he is from Guangdong!" My gray jacket might have shown some difference from what local people usually wore; nevertheless, I was speaking in Mandarin rather than Cantonese to them. The linguistic difference between these two dialects could not be more apparent. Before I had a chance to explain I came from Beijing, the group of villagers started to talk about Guangdong as a place of wealth. For the villagers in this area, Guangdong and its associated images meant social prestige and economic power. It was meant to be a compliment to associate someone with the image of Guangdong.

In post-reform China there has emerged around the notion of space a complex set of social meanings and practices related to upward and outward mobility. As China becomes unevenly integrated into the global economy,[4] spatial categories as daily experiences have become invested with increasingly differential economic and social values. A significant effect of the economic reforms that began in the late 1970s is that spatial categories have emerged as a primary source for organizing social imagination and action. I argue that manipulations of new social meanings of spaces and transgressions of spatial boundaries have become central to strategies for accumulating economic and symbolic capital (Bourdieu 1990, 112–121), both at home and abroad.

The global capitalism into which coastal China is increasingly integrated is characterized by what David Harvey calls "flexible strategies of accumulation," which have brought into play a new set of spatial-temporal practices. Over the past few decades, innovations in transportation and telecommunication have further overcome traditional spatial boundaries, thus bringing about a new round of "time-space compression" in the flows of capital, people, commerce, and images (Harvey 1990, 284–306; Appadurai 1990; Nonini 1993, 63–65). Fredric Jameson notes that one of the major characteristics of "the cultural logic of late capitalism" is the domination of spatial images and categories in everyday experience (Jameson 1984, 64). Lefebvre further distinguished three interrelated and mutually conditioned aspects of spatial practices—the experienced, the perceived, and the imagined (Lefebvre 1991).[5]

This essay will examine how spatial practices, engendered by globalization and in interaction with Chinese notions of space and power, are experienced by two different groups of people in post-reform China. By comparing the strategies of Shaanxi peasants and the overseas scholars, I argue that mobility and imagination of new social-spatial hierarchies have become important sources in the negotiation of power in everyday life.

It is important to note, however, that the current reordering of social meanings of space is the latest shift in an age-old tradition that associated social power with upward mobility. For centuries in China, upward social mobility often also meant physical movements—traveling within the imperial domains. In order to gain access to commercial opportunities, education, or high office, Chinese people traveled from rural areas to urban centers (Skinner 1977). In particular, after the institutionalization of the national examination system through the Tang (618–907 A.D.) and Song (960–1297 A.D.) periods, scholarship became a possible route for rural elites to climb "the ladder of success" (Ho 1962; see also Johnson 1985). Mobility and traveling were an integral part of the social hierarchy in late imperial China. The closer one moved to the top and the center, the greater one's social power; power and prestige diminished as one moved toward the peripheries. It can be said that this model of stratified, vertical arrangement of space informed the imaginations and strategies of many social groups, such as local elites, merchants, and rebelling peasants (Wakeman 1966, 1985; see also Wakeman and Yeh 1992).

In Maoist China, the "ladder" of space was reordered predominantly around the division between the rural and the urban (see Potter and Potter 1990, 296–312; Cheng and Selden 1994). Despite the Maoist government's emphasis on eliminating the differences between the rural and the urban, for most ordinary people the cities were still thought of as "better" places. In the radical years of the Maoist revolution, the countryside was represented by the government as politically advanced and economically backward at the same time. On the one hand, young people were encouraged to go (or were sent) to the poor rural areas to make revolutionary changes there; on the other hand, disgraced party members such as "rightists" or "capitalist-roaders" and intellectuals were "sent down" (*xiafang*) to the countryside to carry out their "thought reforms" (*sixiang gaizao*). Although the Maoist regime may have intended to reverse the social hierarchy of space by mobilizing city people to settle in the countryside, power could hardly be seen as not emanating from political centers far away from the villages (e.g. Chan, Madsen, and Unger 1992).

Although there may be similarities between the present and the past in terms of the organization of social-spatial hierarchies, the current reordering of social meanings of space is inseparable from a new form of imagination that is closely associated with China's "opening" (*kaifang*) to global capitalism. One crucial difference is that large-scale mobility is no longer directly administered by the state. Instead, many individuals are voluntarily on the move. The possibilities of getting access to the special economic zones or overseas locations of wealth have become one of the central concerns in everyday life. Instead of looking at the actual economic differences between regions both within and outside China, I will examine the way in which new social meanings of space are generated and experienced in daily life.

As a result of the uneven capitalist penetration of China, the shifting economic relations between different regions—both within and outside the country—have become a basis for daily imagination of success and prestige. These include, for instance, the relations between the south and the north, between the coastal areas and the inland areas, between the special economic zones and other areas, between the relatively new special economic zones such as Shanghai and the old ones such as Guangdong, between south China and Southeast Asia (particularly the overseas communities such as Hong Kong, Singapore, and Taiwan), between China and the West. People from different places are likely to provide different or even competing accounts of social-spatial power. However, a general tendency is that the regions mostly affected by the economic reforms and influenced by overseas investments have often been perceived (as well as imagined) as centers of economic and social power.

In particular, overseas traveling has opened up possibilities of access to other social, cultural, and national spaces. Whereas in the Maoist past the strategies of power accumulation were largely directed toward Chinese cities, they are now increasingly oriented toward international cosmopoles such as London, Tokyo, and New York. The images and representations of other social and cultural spaces, which are closely associated with outward mobility, have become one of the most important ingredients for imagining development and modernization. For instance, Mayfair Yang's essay in this volume explores the impacts of transnational mass media in transcending local boundaries and national identities and suggests that the experiences of international traveling, as well as imagination of these experiences, have become part of everyday life in post-Mao China and are the means through which the social reproduction of cultural and national differences and identities is carried out. I maintain that the economic reforms in China have not only brought foreign investments and economic growth but also opened up various kinds of opportunities for traveling and mobility; not only built skyscrapers and highways but also changed the conceptions of space and time; not only brought television and telephones into many households but also reconstituted everyday consciousness of space.

Abroad and Home: Spatial Displacement

A group of Chinese students and professors, about forty in total, arrived at Heathrow Airport one autumn day in the mid-1980s. Before landing, they had agreed to wait for each other at the luggage claim area in order to pass through British customs together, though many had met each other only a few hours earlier. For a significant number of them, this was their first experience of entering another social and cultural space defined by national boundaries. Some waited there as agreed, but others did not. There were complaints among both those who waited and those who did not. The former accused the latter of being inconsiderate or even selfish, while the latter complained about the former's inefficiency and cultural inadequacy. This developed in the following few days into a debate about cultural differences. The core question that was raised concerned whether a cultural (as well as national, in this context) identity should be maintained, given that the traveling subject can no longer be tied to a cultural (national) space that is supposed to be clearly defined or bounded (cf. Clifford 1992). Traveling not only raises questions about integration of and conflict between different social, cultural, and economic spaces but also arranges and rearranges these spaces in certain ways through which social power and cultural knowledge are produced.

Over the past fifteen years, Chinese students and scholars have been sent on an unprecedented scale by the government to Western countries for various kinds of research and study.[6] These "overseas scholars" (*haiwai xueren*) constitute one of the first major groups of international travelers among the mainlanders since 1949. This was part of a governmental strategy of bringing new technologies and scientific knowledge to China. The official discourse in mainland China portrays the overseas scholars as commissioners, rather than travelers, and they are supposed to have a special mission: To help China to catch up with the rest of the world in its technological and scientific development, despite the fact that many scholars have been reluctant to return to the mainland (Zweig and Chen 1995). Nevertheless, their experiences of foreign countries and other cultures have far more than purely academic or scientific significance and have become a focus of social and sociological attention in mainland China.[7]

Within China, traveling across regional boundaries has also become part of everyday experience. Local or regional boundaries are being reworked as the Chinese socialist market economy is penetrated by transnational capital. In recent years many ordinary people have joined the move, traveling from rural areas to cities, from inland to coastal areas, from north to south or vice versa. The physical movements inform representations of space that in turn reorganize social meaning and cultural knowledge about mobility and traveling. There is an increasing tendency for people to employ spatial images in speaking about economic and social differentiation in post-reform China. Social hierarchy has become permeated with the new spatial meanings.

However, not everyone on the mainland has equal access to mobility and traveling. The economic reforms have not only sent Chinese scholars abroad and opened up the Chinese labor market to capitalism but also created new divisions and boundaries of another kind within the country.[8] It is precisely because people cannot benefit equally from "time-space compression" that social-spatial hierarchies construct new inequalities among people. These socioeconomic and political differentiations produce what Doreen Massey (1993) calls "the geometries of power" whereby mobility empowers some while weakening others. Global capitalism does not simply entail homogenization, nor simply brings a new round of "time-space compression;" rather, global capitalism reproduces the geometries of power by producing social, economic, and political differentiations associated with mobility.

> For different social groups and different individuals are placed in very distinct ways in relation to these flows and interconnections. This point concerns not merely the issue of who moves and who doesn't, although that is an important element of it; it is also about power in relation *to* the flows and the movement.

> Different social groups have distinct relationships to this anyway-differenti-
> ated mobility: some are more in charge of it than others; some indicate flows
> and movement, others don't; some are more on the receiving end of it than
> others; some are effectively imprisoned by it. (Massey 1993, 61)

For instance, a group of villagers in northwestern China among whom
I recently conducted fieldwork saw themselves as being "imprisoned"
in a disfavored socioeconomic location. These villagers were aware of
the changing conditions of everyday life brought about by the economic reforms and believed that they were denied equal access to mobility in both the social and the physical senses. Although Chinese
villagers and overseas scholars may have different opportunities regarding travel, I argue that both groups engage in the making or remaking of social-spatial hierarchies that are fundamental to the
reordering of post-Mao society.

Analytically, there are two kinds of strategies for people to use in
dealing with the reordering of spatial meanings. They can be called *spatial extroversion* and *spatial introversion.*[9] Spatial extroversion refers to
practices whereby subjects orient themselves toward people and places
that are supposed to be higher up on social-spatial hierarchies, as well as
to practices that aim at the expansion of social networks beyond one's
own conventional social space. For people in rural China, especially for
those in inland areas, seeking social connections outside their own villages or towns has become one of the dominant concerns. In contrast,
overseas scholars not only expand their networks into other social and
cultural spaces but also tend to reorder internal relations extensively
within their existing social milieu. Such internally oriented practices are
referred to as spatial introversion. I will argue that those who have
moved up to the higher levels of social-spatial hierarchies not only seek
further social mobility through spatial extroversion but also pay a great
deal of attention to the relations within their home space.

Zhao Villagers: Spatial Extroversion

In 1992 I conducted fieldwork in Zhaojiahe, Shaanxi province. In comparison with other parts of China, especially the south and southeast, this
area is considerably short of industrial development. Zhaojiahe, under
the administration of Chengcheng county, is located between Xi'an, the
capital of ancient Chinese dynasties, and Yenan, the Communist base in
the 1930s and 1940s. As elsewhere in rural China, Zhaojiahe went
through the period of people's communes, and household production

was reintroduced to the village in 1981. To the eyes of outsiders, Zhao-jiahe may appear to be a very "traditional" agricultural setting. Electricity became available only a few years ago. There were no telephones in 1992, and there was only one newspaper delivered to the village school twice a week. One can argue that, to a large extent, it is a face-to-face community.

Zhaojiahe is a single-surname village with a population of more than eight hundred people, and a common ancestor can be traced by the village genealogy. On public occasions, Zhao villagers often talked about themselves as people who were reluctant to leave their home village. For instance, an old villager once said to me: "Oh, no! We are not like people in the south. They have nothing to consider, and they do not have a sense of home. If they have money, they spend it on food. If there is a better place, they travel. We are not like that. We consider a lot before we move. We have our property here, our houses." It is true that a relatively large number of Zhao villagers have not traveled beyond the county town, which is about thirty kilometers from the village. A few old women reported that they had never traveled outside the circle of the neighboring villages—a range of five kilometers or so.

However, it is misleading to view Zhao villagers as people who do not *want* to travel. In fact, on many other occasions Zhao villagers made extensive references to spatial categories and employed various kinds of spatial images in representing social status and economic wealth. Spatial representations are always made for particular purposes in order to produce certain effects upon certain groups of people. When I was in the village, Zhao villagers often portrayed themselves as "home-loving" (*lianjia*) people. In my view, this is an indirect expression of their relative immobility. Since the reestablishment of household production in 1981, there has been a sense of crisis among Zhao villagers; for many, the village as a whole has lost almost all its social and economic functions. The villagers can hardly take Zhaojiahe as their collective home any longer. Individual families have begun to show increasing interest in seeking social connections outside the village. By claiming their attachment to home, Zhao villagers are in fact acknowledging their limited ability to travel and protesting their difficulties in benefiting from new economic opportunities located outside their village.

New social meanings of space

The area surrounding Zhaojiahe is cut by several huge dry valleys (although sometimes there are small streams at the bottoms of these valleys) in which both villages and lands are spread. There are also villages sitting on the small plains between these valleys. Two local terms are applied to these two different kinds of living conditions: one is *yuanshang*, which means "up on plain," and the other is *yuanxia*, which means "down in valley." Zhaojiahe is a *yuanxia* village.

Before the 1980s, according to Zhao villagers, the division between *yuanshang* and *yuanxia* had little actual effect on social life in the area. Although *yuanshang* areas were more convenient in terms of transport and access to towns, it was said that *yuanxia* villagers used to be able to produce more grain than their counterparts because the *yuanxia* villages had better access to water. The village groupings had not been organized in any systematic way based on this geographic division. In recent years there has emerged a new social distinction: The *yuanshang* area is now perceived and talked about as a "better-off" place by the villagers in general. The main reason given for this change was that the *yuanshang* area has better access to the market centers. Not all the *yuanshang* villagers are closer to main markets or town centers, but it is true that it is easier for the *yuanshang* villagers to travel by bicycle—the main means of transportation. It is not justifiable to argue that there has already been significant economic differentiation between these two areas. Accessibility to the market centers has emerged as a discourse of social distinction. The villagers started to view this geographic division as a signifier of an unequal socioeconomic relationship. The word *yuanxia* has become an indication of inferior economic status in contrast to that of *yuanshang*. Although the geographic division has long existed, a new social meaning was generated as a result of the market-oriented reforms. The notions of *yuanshang* and *yuanxia* now connote different degrees of social power and prestige.

In the Maoist past, the pattern of bride exchange between *yuanshang* and *yuanxia* villages was not affected by the up/down division in any significant way. A large proportion of women who married into Zhaojiahe before 1980 came from *yuanshang* villages, but since 1980 few brides have been recruited from the *yuanshang* area. When Zhao men talked about young wives in the early 1990s, the focus of discussion was always on the places from which these wives were recruited. When considering a mate choice, Zhao parents would first of all ask *where* the possibility would come from. A shift of focus in the negotiation of marriage has taken place over the past fifteen years: The priority and focus of marriage negotiation has become a question of trying to get one's daughter to a better place.[10] A *yuanshang* girl marrying into Zhaojiahe would be more likely to negotiate a higher bride price than average.[11] To Zhao villagers, mate choice has become part of a new strategy to link up with a more progressive social and economic environment. In other words, family connections became endowed with new spatial meanings, which

were constructed according to either real or imagined economic and social power.

Mobility must have social meanings by which the effects of physical
movements can be cast on others. In order to use spatial categories to divide or differentiate people, places and locations have to be differentiated in the first place. One day when walking around in the village, I saw
three women wearing skirts, which was unusual because Zhao women
always wore trousers. Before I asked any questions, the neighbor of my
host came over and said to me: "That was Xicai's brother's daughter and
her friends from Xi'an.[12] Look at their place [*qiao renjia naxiang*]!" This
comment was rather surprising. Instead of commenting on their dresses,
he commented on the place from which the girls came. In a more general
sense, when talking about their neighbor's guests, Zhao villagers often
referred to the places from which the guests came. Further, it was where
one came from and where one went (in a socioeconomic sense) that determined how one would be treated in the village.

Zhao villagers often talked about different places by referring to
their specific names—Zhaojiahe, Chengcheng, Xi'an, Beijing, and so
on. When talking about other places in general, they used either the
Mandarin term (*na*)*difang* or the local term *naxiang*. In China, it is
conventional to associate different groups of people with their home
places, such as "Beijing *ren* [person or persons]," "Shaanxi *ren*,"
"Chengcheng *ren*," and so forth. However, Zhao villagers are now
talking about "other places" (*difang* or *naxiang*) very selectively. For
instance, when I was in Zhaojiahe, Zhao villagers seldom mentioned
the area of Yenan, to the north of the village, which used to be the
Communist base in the 1930s and 1940s. Although Yenan is slightly
closer to the village than Xi'an, spatial images related to the years of
revolution have almost disappeared. Once I insisted on asking an old
villager about what it was like in the past when the Communists were
fighting with the Kuomintang (nationalist) troops in this area. He said
to me: "Well, the horses that the Kuomintang soldiers rode were really
huge, very tall and very strong. They stayed in Qincheng, the village
up there." According to the local records, there were quite a few villagers traveling to Yenan before 1949, but by the 1990s few Zhao villagers paid attention to what was going on in Yenan. In general, they
paid little attention to places they believed were poorer than theirs.
For Zhao villagers, this notion of place (*difang* or *naxiang*), when
used in a general sense, often meant a paradise somewhere else. When
Zhao villagers said, "Look at that place," they meant social prestige
and economic power associated with that place, which was often beyond their reach.

Kinship as spatial strategies

Let us take family organization as an example to see how the production of space as a major source of social power has had an impact. In Zhaojiahe, many important aspects of conventional kinship that survived the encounter with the Maoist revolution have started to change only in recent years.[13]

To describe the descent group, Zhao villagers use the term *zijiawu*, which is a three-character Chinese word and literally means "people from the same room." It is those (male) people who come from the same "room" who define a descent group. In a broad sense, Zhao villagers take the village as one *zijiawu*, because they share a common ancestor—that is, they all come originally from the same "room." The Maoist revolution did not bring significant changes to the kinship organization, even though Zhaojiahe had become part of a people's commune and had its name changed. For instance, collectivization in the 1950s did not alter the pattern of village exogamy, a practice that was central for maintaining patrilineal descent and virilocal marriage. It has been only in the past fifteen years that this pattern has altered and the conventional locality of bride recruitment has dissolved.[14]

Only in recent years did family connections outside the village gain particular social significance. My host's neighbor, Wanyou, told me a story about how he and his *zijiawu* brother Genwu became hostile to each other recently: "We used to be very good friends, but the relationship soured recently. I have a brother working in Daqing,[15] and his place cannot be compared with ours. I went to visit my brother twice in the past few years, and I brought back a television set the second time. My brother brought a color one, he therefore gave me this black and white one, so what? I used to be much poorer than Genwu, that was why we were fine. But when he saw my brother gave me a television set, he could not bear it. He has four sons, but they all live nearby and no one could give him a television set. This is why he does not like me now."[16]

Wanyou's brother left the village in the early 1950s, and Wanyou had never visited him throughout the whole of the Maoist period. It was only recently that Zhao villagers started to seek economic advantage and social power through travel. In general, social connections outside the village were seen as important social capital. The possibilities of mobility—such as joining the army,[17] moving to the township or the town, going to the university, and so on—have become main sources for negotiating economic and social power among the *zijiawu* brothers. The notion of *zijiawu*, as an important organizer of social relations, seems to have been replaced by a wider concern about achieving economic and social power through various kinds of ties outside the village. The evaluation of social relations relies not only on the kind of relationship established but also on the distance and location from which these relations are made.

Consequently, certain kinds of new categories of relationships have gained social significance as the villagers attempt to seek opportunities outside the village through mobility. Thus friendship, occupational, and neighborhood ties were given more attention than the *zijiawu* bonds. In particular, special attention was paid to those whose relatives, brothers, friends, friends of friends, or relatives of relatives had connections in other places or locations, such as Xi'an or south China. Stories about relatives, friends, or neighbors were often told in terms of the speaker's connections with people in other places. The houses of those who had experiences of travel outside the county often became venues of gossip and conversation. As social spaces were being reorganized through strategies of extroversion, kinship categories such as *zijiawu* have become devalued.

Traveling and "getting rich first"

Socioeconomic differentiation, either imagined or real, is more likely to be represented through spatial categories and images. For instance, Dawa, one of the seven villager groups (*cunmin xiaozu*) in Zhaojiahe, is located slightly away from the main village and thought to be a better-off group by the people in the main village because the proportion of television ownership in Dawa was larger than that of other groups. Dawa was hence nicknamed *Xiao Taiwan* ("Little Taiwan") by other villagers. This metaphor not only captures the emerging socioeconomic difference between the main village and Dawa but also demonstrates a sense of geopolitical division within the village, with the image of capitalist Taiwan and its implications being reworked within a local context.

In everyday experience, Zhao villagers used various opportunities to evaluate different places by comparing their economic conditions. They often raised explicit questions to outsiders about—for instance—their incomes. The day after I arrived in Zhaojiahe, my first host had the following conversation with me at the dining table:

"You from Britain? Is Britain better?"
"Well, fine, not too bad. Britain is fine."
"Better life?"
"The living standard is probably higher."
"Even better than Beijing?"
"Well, yes. The living standard is higher than that of Beijing."
"Really? Better than Beijing?"

"Yeah, sort of."

"Our money does not work there, I am afraid?"

"No, we have to use British pounds."

"Who gives you money, then?"

"It is different and depends on the kind of scolarship a student gets."

"Yours?"

"My living expenses are paid by a government fund."

"How much?"

"About three hundred pounds per month."

"How much is that?"

"About three thousand Chinese yuan."

"It's a hell of a lot."

"Well, things are more expensive over there."

"That is a lot."

"It depends, you know, on how much you have to spend, for instance."

"That is a hell of a lot. Isn't it?"

"Yeah, maybe."

Economic reforms have introduced global space as a source for social imagination. Ideas about foreign currencies were no longer strange even to villagers far away from the big cities or the coastal areas. To a large extent, daily life in the village has been reorganized according to social imagination of "other places," increasingly influenced by images of the overseas locations of wealth. An underlying assumption was re-inforced: Wealth is "out there" and needs to be seized. This assumption, which corresponded to the governmental emphasis on foreign invest-ment and overseas capital as the key source for economic development in recent years, made Zhao villagers see outside forces as the ultimate genesis for social change. It runs counter to the Maoist revolutionary epistemology that stresses hard work (*jianku fendou*) and self-reliance (*zili gengsheng*).

The government slogan says, "Let some people get rich first." Despite the government's effort to insist that the purpose of development is to make a "common prosperity" (*gongtong fuyu*), Zhao villagers did not perceive economic development or the accumulation of wealth as being arranged according to a time schedule; instead, they saw economic op-portunities and wealth as being spatially distributed. To a certain extent, this may have always been so, but the invasion of overseas spaces in daily imagination was largely new. It is also true that for many ordinary villagers, traveling freely has been a new experience. Therefore, mobi-lizing different kinds of possible resources located in "other places" has become an important strategy for "getting rich first."

Famin was my third host in the village and was thirty-two years old in 1992. His family was a big one, five brothers and five (or six) sisters from the same parents. Famin saw his family as powerless in both economic and political terms, because his connection with the outside world was very limited. All Famin's brothers were living in the village, and there was only one sister who had left the area to work—in Urumqi, the Xinjiang Autonomous District in northwest China. In order to make a change, Famin went to Urumqi to look for a job in the winter of 1987 and hoped that his sister and brother-in-law might help. Famin stayed in Urumqi for about half a year, basically working for a construction team. In 1988 Famin returned to the village and remained working on his own "responsibility land" (*zerentian*). Whenever he talked about his experience in Urumqi, Famin always insisted that his family had no useful connections outside the village and that this was why he could not earn extra cash. According to Famin, as well as many other Zhao villagers, the reason that they could not "get rich first" was that they did not have powerful relations outside their own village.

For Zhao villagers and many other people on the mainland, seeking economic opportunities in "other places" has been the main motivation for joining the move. The large-scale mobility in turn produces and reinforces the social imagination of space-place-power. Zhao villagers often see themselves as being "imprisoned" in a "bad" place. They tend to believe that the sources for change lie outside their own social and economic space, which is perceived as being controlled by external agents over which they have no direct control or influence. In this sense, I use the term "spatial extroversion" to describe the strategies often employed by those who see themselves as being "imprisoned" in socioeconomically disfavored locations.

Overseas Scholars: Mobility and Social Power

Once a group of Zhao villagers gathered and talked about the experience of an overseas Chinese student who was a distant relative of someone in a neighboring village. This student was sent to the United States (Meiguo)[18] to take a course in chemistry. The conversation was focused on his experience of working in the university library as a night porter.[19] "He does not need to do anything and just sits there watching, but he makes six dollars an hour," one said. "That is more than fifty yuan."[20] Another villager made the calculation. "Oh, he makes more than three hundred a night!" A middle-aged man then said: "I don't believe it. It can't be that easy to make money in that place [*naxiang*]!"

In respect to economic development in mainland China and its relation to the reordering of capitalist mode of production in the Pacific Rim in particular, Aihwa Ong's essay in this volume distinguishes two types of modernist imaginaries:[21] "a post-Maoist official state project that is tied to the fixed territory of China . . . and a coastal phenomenon that envisions Chinese modernity in transnational terms." These two types of modernist imaginaries can be said to be linked to two types of Chinese subjects—the mainland and the overseas Chinese. As Ong argues, diaspora Chinese may refer to the notion of "Chineseness" in making a cultural identity, but they are by no means constrained by any national boundaries. When discussing the formation of transnational subjectivity of the diaspora Chinese, she speaks about seeking Western citizenship as part of a set of flexible strategies in pursuing economic opportunities in an increasingly integrated global social and political context. The local context is less relevant to the political or cultural identity of the diaspora Chinese, and "their subjectivity is deterritorialized in relation to a particular country, though highly localized in relation to the family" (Ong 1993, 771–72).

Ong's discussion may help us understand the formation of the overseas scholar as a particular type of "traveling subject" (cf. Clifford 1992) whose position has been shaped by these two kinds of modernist imaginaries. For overseas scholars, there is a double process of identity-making. On the one hand, they often tend to borrow the post-Maoist state discourse in articulating a position in relation to the Western capitalist subject, and on the other, they also employ flexible strategies—which are fundamental to the logic of late capitalism—in negotiating power with people back on the mainland. These scholars are not only trying to transgress spatial boundaries in order to gain social power but also reorganizing social meanings and power relations in overseas households and in relation to people on the mainland. In a process of spatial introversion, these scholars are reworking relationships with people back home through overseas travel.

"Traveling to the West"

In *Xiyouji*, the famous tale about the monkey king (Sun Wukong) and his master (Tang Seng) traveling to the west of China for Buddhist truth, there were many dangers and struggles on the road. The stories about overseas scholars traveling to Western countries were also often told in a similar fashion. Difficulty and struggle are important aspects of the story. For those who manage to go abroad, financial struggle is often seen as an immediate and enduring problem. In the case of Britain, where I studied in the early 1990s, the most popular way for Chinese students and scholars to make extra money was to work in Chinese restaurants. Although almost everyone I interviewed complained about the difficulties in managing his or her finances, many bought cars, and some even purchased houses before completing their studies.[22] This seemingly contradictory picture reveals the importance for the overseas scholars of making economic progress, because making money (*zhengqian*) is often seen as the goal of international travel. In the late 1980s, a Chinese official working at the State Bureau of Pricing in Beijing spent six months at the London School of Economics and Political Science as a visiting scholar. After he returned to Beijing, he wrote to his friends in London and told them that the biggest achievement of his trip to England was the money he had made in a Chinese restaurant during the last three months of his visit. His biggest regret, he added, was that he had not spent the first three months of his visit working in that restaurant.

In many ways the traveling scholars share similar spatial assumptions with Zhao villagers. Economic differences are perceived more than ever as differential opportunities associated with travel. To cross national boundaries means to reach the locations of wealth, that is, the Western countries. To many, scholarship is a means for seeking economic and social power. A student in London once said to me, "You can get a Ph.D. here, but many people after you will get their Ph.D.s. It won't be anything special when you go back to China. But if you make some money here and bring it back to China, it will make a great difference." Clearly, travel is a means for them to gain social power by moving to the top of regional or global social-spatial hierarchies.

The crossing of cultural and national boundaries leads to the reorganization of home space, both in the sense of homeland and of the actual homes abroad. For the overseas scholars in London, the family and home are both instruments of "practical management" (Cohen 1992), which provide security and support for individuals and a primary source of power accumulation, allowing cultural capital to be transformed into social power. In the 1980s a typical type of accommodation among the overseas scholars in London was to share a rented house. An ordinary house in London often has two floors with two or three bedrooms, which were supposed to be shared among a few scholars. Within the house, everything was supposed to be Chinese, especially food and language. In the evening housemates took turns using the kitchen while chatting with each other in Chinese. There were usually "family heads" (*jiazhang*) explicitly or implicitly installed in this kind of housing, and these people were supposed to be in charge of calculating telephone or gas bills and collecting checks for rent. Cooperation was needed, for instance, for cleaning the bathroom or the kitchen. When residents completed their studies, they would move out, and others would take their place. While residents often changed, the organization of the house tended to remain stable.

The intrahouse relations were not a simple replication of the age/gender hierarchies that were characteristic of traditional Chinese families (e.g. Baker 1979); rather they were based on discrimination between members with more or less experience overseas. Usually two elements determined the intrahouse hierarchy in London. First, the earlier residents often received more respect (as well as better rooms). Seniority in age itself did not guarantee respect or privilege. Second, those who were close to the landlord or landlady often had more power in making household decisions. In a sense, the domestic hierarchies were built on the degree of experience of British social spaces. If someone has been around for a while, he will often receive more respect. And if one has social connections that could be used to benefit one's housemates—for instance, helping new residents find part-time jobs—one will certainly enjoy a great deal of authority within the house.

An important social function of these London homes is to build cultural walls in order to shut out the outside world. For instance, "foreigners" (*laowai*),—that is, non-Chinese—were not always welcome in households shared by the Chinese scholars. Once when I was invited to a party by a Chinese friend, I asked him whether I could bring a Dutch couple with me. My Chinese friend hesitated on the other end of the phone, discussed the matter with his wife briefly, and replied: "No, it's not convenient to have foreigners. We can't talk freely." For many scholars living in London, their houses were cultural castles that both helped sustain the sense of being Chinese and produced a secure environment for survival in an alien social space.

This practice of spatial introversion through family management was common, in one way or another, among scholars who have moved up along the social-spatial hierarchies. The internal hierarchies were built upon individuals' unequal access to British social spaces, that is, upon experiences outside one's own home circle. In other words, spatial introversion is dialectically activated by the practices of spatial extroversion. Furthermore, the strategies employed in accumulating social power abroad are also the ways to impress people back in the home country. To be overseas enables one to negotiate power and reorganize the fields of social relations back home.

The effects of traveling

Overseas travel has a powerful effect on people back on the mainland. This is because traveling to the West is perceived as the accumulation of social and cultural capital. A widely told story in the late 1980s illustrates this point well. Hoping to get some help and advice, a young provincial woman who loved literature wrote several letters to a few well-known writers in Beijing, but she did not receive a response from any of them. Then she took all of her savings and went to Beijing to visit these writers. Writer A refused to meet her at all; writer B kept saying that he could not afford to waste time talking with her because in one minute he could produce a few hundred words, which would earn him a certain amount of money; when the young woman finally managed to stop writer C at his doorway, he said humorously, "I have no time at any time." With little hope and much anger, the young woman left China for America[23] and later became a naturalized U.S. citizen. A few years later, when she went back to Beijing to visit the same writers who had refused to help her, she received entirely different treatment. Writer A rushed back to Beijing, giving up his vacation in the south, in the hope of meeting her; writer B almost forgot his writing and accompanied her for a whole week touring the city; writer C also changed his tone this time, saying, "I have time at any time whenever you have time."[24] The message is: Where one comes from plays an extremely important role in the renegotiation of social power. Traveling to Western countries not only gives individuals access to wealth (although it may not always be true) but also helps them gain tremendous symbolic capital, to use Bourdieu's terminology.

To obtain foreign residence has thus become an important form of power accumulation in post reform China. In October 1992, after I finished my fieldwork in rural Shaanxi, I went back to Beijing to visit my parents. I was invited to a birthday party held in my friend's house, and his room had been turned into a kind of ballroom with a set of fixed disco lights on the ceiling. After a delicious but hasty meal, the host urged his guests to start dancing. I sat in a corner, enjoying my tea and watching people swirling and waving in the middle of the room, and did not notice that a middle-aged man with a very strong smell of tobacco had approached me. "Have you got a PR?" he asked. I did not understand what he meant. He smiled at me patiently and explained that PR stood for "permanent residence." Before I could answer, he added. "I got one from Canada." I had previously thought PR stood for "public relations." This question was raised again later by another guest whom I did not know either. We had not even introduced ourselves properly before he raised this question. Presumably everyone knew where other people came from, especially those who came back to China from abroad.

Among certain circles of people in Beijing as well as in other big cities such as Shanghai and Guangzhou, topics of conversation have shifted in recent years from discussing how to manage to travel beyond the national boundary to the issue of obtaining permanent residence overseas. The significance of obtaining permanent foreign residence lies in the very possibility for individuals to travel freely. In other words, obtaining foreign residence does not necessarily mean settling down in any single place, but rather acquiring greater flexibility in traveling and accumulating power.

Mobility and flexibility

Overseas scholars are often seen as having moved up to the best places. In order to remain in the West, many of them have to be flexible in seeking job and career opportunities. Scholarship can be used for obtaining opportunities to travel; it can also be used for seeking economic wealth. Many overseas scholars have the experience of changing their majors or even careers in order to seek better opportunities. In her novel, *Go to America! Go to America! (Dao Meiguo qu! Dao Meiguo qu!)*, Zha Jianying (1994) depicts the amazing experiences of a Chinese woman who travels from a small northern Shaanxi town to New York and transforms herself from a (local) government official to an overseas student, from a student of philosophy to a student of commerce, and from a Chinese citizen to a permanent resident in the United States. When writing about the heroine's purpose for returning to school, the author remarks, "The core connotation of the term 'overseas student' lies in traveling and settling 'overseas'; to be a student is secondary, while the subject of study is secondary to the secondary." Because people are supposed to own greater economic power when they go overseas, they are somewhat constrained by such expectations. This is one of the reasons that turning to business has become very popular among the overseas scholars, even if they have to give up their scholarly careers.

Overseas scholars, especially those supported by private sources, tend to turn their attention to profitable fields of study such as applied economics or business management. Although the main task of the government-sponsored scholars is not business, many of them in recent years have started to engage in business activities (Zhang 1989, 10–14). In Britain alone, investment groups, import-export agencies, and other kinds of businesses have become more common among those who are still engaged in research and study.

A couple from Beijing came to Britain in 1987. The husband arrived several months earlier, as a government-sponsored visiting scholar whose major was in communication and mass media. At first they stayed, as arranged by the British Council, at Leeds University, and in 1989 they moved to London. As a visiting scholar, the husband had no assignment of work or research, and while studying he also started to teach *qigong* which he had learned in Beijing. With the help of his wife, whose major was in electronic engineering, his *qigong* classes turned into a very successful business. This, among other things, enabled them to purchase property in one of the prestigious residential areas in London, Highgate Village. At the same time the husband started to practice traditional *qigong* medicine and claimed that he had cured several cancer patients, which may or may not be true, but he was indeed permitted to work in a London hospital, offering alternative treatments for diseases for which Western medicine has not yet developed effective therapies. The couple later combined their *qigong* classes with the *qigong* medical treatment and became a very successful business couple. Traveling around Europe to supervise their classes, they operated a business that they had hardly known a few years before.

When I interviewed this couple, they said that they did not feel uncomfortable about giving up the intellectual careers they had pursued before. This example is one of many cases in which the overseas scholars are seeking different opportunities abroad, which often means giving up what their scholarships had brought them into. Clearly scholarships, job opportunities, business undertakings, cultural identities, and so on are only the means for obtaining social and economic power, which is unequally and unevenly distributed in different geopolitical sites and locations. When necessary, overseas scholars are flexible in the pursuit of opportunities over a range of social and cultural spaces.

Discussion

In recent years there has been a growing literature on the impact of economic reforms on Chinese society, but so far little scholarly attention has been paid to the shifting conceptualization of space and time. Alongside the social, economic, and political changes that have taken place since the late 1970s, spatial categories have emerged—to use Jameson's terminology—as a "cultural dominant" both in the organization of everyday experience and in the negotiation of social power. Especially in China's coastal areas, the experiences of what Harvey calls "time-space compression" are largely dominated by transnational capital and capitalism (see the essays by Lee and Mitchell in this volume). An explosion of spatial images through the mass media in post-reform China has contributed a great deal to the changes in everyday imagination of space/power.

Despite their different social positions, Zhao villagers and the overseas scholars both engaged in what can be called the "geographic production of social relations" (cf. Massey 1993, 60–61), which is reordering post-reform Chinese society. The crucial character of this production is its uneven, hierarchial reorganization of spatial relations among different groups of people, its employment of mobility as a form of social power, and its introduction of flexible strategies for accumulating cultural capital and economic wealth. While Zhao villagers see themselves as being imprisoned by their relative immobility, the overseas scholars are more in charge of the new possibility of travel associated with the market-oriented reforms. These two groups not only have different relations to mobility but also stand at the opposite ends of the same process of geographic production of social relations linked to global capitalism.

Even though people experience differential mobility, a conceptual shift in social imagination about space/power appears to be universal among mainland Chinese. A hierarchical production of space/place characterizes the current fashion of everyday imagining, especially among those who see themselves as being trapped in disfavored geoeconomic locations. Social differentiation is increasingly produced or reproduced by differential access to mobility. In other words, the ways in which people are divided in post-reform China are tied to how different places both within and outside China are imagined and represented. Travel and movement have reordered the power relations between different groups of people, and their identities are reworked according to the shifting images of various kinds of selves and others. The making or remaking of either local or national identities is built upon the social production of spatial divisions such as up-valley/down-valley, rural/urban, inland/coast, north/south, mainland/West, homeland/world (*shijie*). Some of these divisions are relatively new; others are old but endowed with new social meanings.

What are the political implications of this reordering of spatial meanings and practices? The most important foreseeable change will concern the ways in which the state exercises its control and dominance over its population. From a macro perspective, the form of vertical, direct, commanding political control—well known in the later years of the Maoist regime—may have to be modified (cf. Shue 1988) because as the economic reforms continue, different social, economic, political, or cultural spaces—at the local, regional, and international levels—are increasingly penetrating each other, producing different kinds of center-periphery relations associated with different opportunities for development and mobility. Travel within and outside the country can become a mode of resistance to the direct political control of the state. Economic reforms have set the population on the run. Everywhere in China, people are trying to leave various kinds of home spaces in order to "get rich first." From the point of view of ordinary people, travel and its associated imaginings are becoming an important condition of everyday life.

C.L.R. James once wrote, "The relation of classes had to change before I discovered that it's not quality of goods and utility that matter, but movement, not where you are or what you have, but where you come from, where you are going and the rate at which you are getting there" (quoted in Clifford 1992, 96). By transgressing local, regional, or national boundaries on a large scale, Chinese subjects are increasingly set "free," and their differential mobility and social stratification are now tied to the dynamics of global capitalism.

Notes

[1] I wish to thank Aihwa Ong and Donald M. Nonini for their insightful readings of several drafts of this paper. I also thank Kathleen Erwin for her helpful comments.

[2] Guangdong is the first province in which the so-called special economic zones were established by the government in the late 1970s.

[3] A polite way of addressing another male, regardless of his actual age.

[4] For a general discussion of globalization and the world system, see King 1991; for a discussion of the mode of capitalist production with reference to Marx's theory of historical materialism, see Dirlik 1994; for a discussion of transnational economic operations and labor politics as cultural struggles, see Ong 1991.

[5] The experienced spatial practices refer to the physical and material flows and interactions that occur in and across space in a way as to assure production and social reproduction. The perceived spatial practices refer to the representation of space, including all codes and knowledges about spaces, which allow the experienced spatial practices to be understood and articulated. The imagined spatial practices refer to mental inventions that generate new meanings of possible spatial practices, see Lefebvre 1991; cf. Harvey 1990, 218–19.

[6] The *Guangming Daily* (June 8, 1995) reported that the Chinese government has sent more than twenty-two thousand students abroad to study or do research since 1978.

[7] For instance, overseas scholars have been written about since the 1980s. This was followed by the development of a new genre called "literature *of* the overseas scholars" (*liuxuesheng wenxue*), i.e., the overseas scholars write about their own lives abroad. A few popular titles may show the intention: *Traveling around the World; Go to America! Go to America!; A Native of Beijing in New York; Manhattan's Chinese Woman; A Shanghainese in Tokyo*. These novels are not only literary accounts of cultural encounters but also cultural interpretations of the formation of transnational identities and the politics of mobility and traveling.

[8] For a general discussion of the economic stratification in rural China, see Walder 1989 and Lu 1992.

[9] I am grateful to Donald M. Nonini for suggesting these two phrases.

[10] Traditionally it was a central concern for Chinese parents to consider whom their daughters would marry. More specifically, it was social status that concerned the parents. This emphasis in mate choice continued during the Maoist revolution, although what was supposed to be "good" social status changed. For a discussion of how political status replaced the traditional ideas about good families regarding mate choice, see Croll 1981.

[11] In the early 1990s, the average amount of (cash) bride price in this area was about 400 yuan. One needs to note that there are many other elements that are also important in the negotiation of marriage, such as whether the person concerned has abilities other than farming. A carpenter is usually expected to have a better deal. However, the importance is to note that place is the most likely way Zhao villagers will interpret such an event. They would say: "Oh, that family has to entertain the girl better, because she is from *yuanshang*. Otherwise who wants to come to Zhaojiahe?"

[12] The capital of the province.

[13] For a general discussion of changes in family and marriage in post-Mao China, see Davis and Harrell 1993.

[14] Scholars have predicted that, regarding marriage practice in rural China, the process of decollectivization should encourage pre-Communist practices such as village exogamy. See, for instance, Harrell 1992, 323–25. In the case of Zhaojihe, both marriages outside the conventional locality of bride recruitment and marriages within the village (village endogamy) became popular in the past decade.

[15] A city in northeast China, famous among Chinese people for its oil production.

[16] Genwu's story about the same event was different. He said the reason that they became hostile to each other was that Wanyou borrowed a box of fertilizer from him but refused to return it. Wanyou insisted that he had returned Genwu's fertilizer a year ago.

[17] In other parts of rural China, such as some coastal areas in the south, the situation may be different. Due to the pressure of household production and the one-child policy, peasants in other areas may not be willing to join the army.

[18] The villagers could not specify in which state this student was studying.

[19] The Chinese word that the villagers used was *kanmende*, which literally means "someone who watches the door."

[20] The yuan is the primary monetary unit of mainland China. The exchange rate between U.S. dollars and Chinese yuan was about 1:8 in the early 1990s.

[21] For a definition of the notion of social imaginary, see Appadurai 1990, 5.

[22] Among the fifty-two Chinese Ph.D. students (three of whom were female) I interviewed in three London colleges (the London School of Economics, University College, and the School of Oriental and African Studies) from January to

112

March 1994, thirty-one of them owned cars. Seven who owned cars had finished their studies and started to work.

[23] It was said she had an aunt who was living in the United States and helped her move to America.

[24] This story has been told in different places. An original version was told as a true story by Fenkang Sang (1989).

References

Appadurai, A. 1990. "Disjuncture and Difference in the Global Cultural Economy." *Public Culture* 2, no. 2: 1–24.

Baker, H.D.R. 1979. *Chinese Family and Kinship*. London: Macmillan

Bourdieu, P. 1990. *The Logic of Practice*. Cambridge: Polity.

Chan, A., R. Madsen, and J. Unger. 1992. *Chen Village: Under Mao and Deng*. Berkeley: University of California Press.

Cheng, T., and M. Selden. 1994. "The Origin and Social Consequences of China's *Hukou* System." *China Quarterly* 139: 644–68.

Clifford, J. 1992. "Traveling Cultures." In Lawrence Grossberg et al., eds., *Cultural Studies*, pp. 96–116. New York: Routledge.

Cohen, M. 1992. "Family Management and Family Division in Contemporary China." *China Quarterly* 130: 357–77.

Croll, E. 1981. *Politics of Marriage in Contemporary China*. Cambridge: Cambridge University Press.

Davis, D., and S. Harrell, eds. 1993. *Chinese Families in the Post-Mao Era*. Berkeley: University of California Press.

Dirlik, A. 1994. *After the Revolution: Waking to Global Capitalism*. Hanover: Wesleyan University Press.

Harrell, S. 1992. "Aspects of Marriage in Three South-western Villages." *China Quarterly* 130: 323–37.

Harvey, D. 1990. *The Condition of Postmodernity: An Enquiry into the Origin of Cultural Change*. Oxford Basil Blackwell.

Ho, P. 1962. *The Ladder of Success in Imperial China*. New York: Columbia University Press.

Jameson, F. 1984. "Postmodernism, or the Cultural Logic of Late Capitalism." *New Left Review* 146: 53–92.

Johnson, D. 1985. "Communication, Class, and Consciousness in Late Imperial China." In D. Johnson, ed., *Popular Culture in Late Imperial China* pp. 34–72. Berkeley: Unversity of California Press.

King, A. 1991. *Culture, Globalization, and the World System*. London: Macmillan.

Lefebvre, H. 1991. *The Production of Space*. Oxford: Basil Blackwell.

Lu, X., ed. 1992. *Gaige zhong de nongcun yu nongmin* (Villages and peasants during the economic reforms). Beijing: Zhishi.

Massey, D. 1993. "Power-Geometry and a Progressive Sense of Place." In J. Bird et al., eds., *Mapping the Future: Local Cultures, Global Change*, pp. 59–69. New York: Routledge.

Nonini, D. M. 1993. "On the Outs on the Rim: An Ethnographic Grounding of the 'Asia Pacific' Imaginary." In A. Dirlik, ed., *What Is in a Rim?* pp. 161–82. Boulder, Co: Westview.

Ong, A. 1991. "The Gender and Labor Politics of Postmodernity." *Annual Review of Anthropology* 20: 279–309.

———. 1993. "On the Edge of Empires: Flexible Citizenship Among Chinese in Diaspora." *Positions* 1, no. 3: 745–78.

Potter, S. H., and J. M. Potter. 1990. *China's Peasants: The Anthropology of a Revolution.* Berkeley: University of California Press.

Sang Fenkang. 1989. "Fumei huaren luxiang" (An album of Chinese travelling to America). In Z. Li ed., *Bashi niandai zhongguoren zai haiwai* (Chinese abroad in the 1980s), pp. 156–70. Beijing: People's Daily Press.

Shue, V. 1988. *The Reach of the State: Sketches of the Chinese Body Politic.* Stanford: Stanford University Press.

Skinner, W. G., ed. 1977. *The City in Late Imperial China.* Stanford: Stanford University Press.

Wakeman, F., Jr. 1966. *Strangers at the Gate: Social Disorder in South China,* 1839–1861. Berkeley: University of California Press.

———. 1985. *The Great Enterprise: the Manchu Reconstruction of Late Imperial Order in Seventeenth-Century China.* 2 vols. Berkeley: University of California Press.

Wakeman, F., Jr. and W.-h. Yeh. 1992. *Shanghai Sojourners.* China Research Monograph, Berkeley: Institute of East Asian Studies, University of California at Berkeley.

Walder, A. 1989. "Social Change in Post-Revolution China." *Annual Review of Sociology* 15: 405–24.

Zha Jianying. 1994. *Dao Meiguo qu! Dao Meiguo qu!* (Go to America! Go to America!). Shandong: Qingdao Press.

Zhang Jiangwei. 1989. "Meiyou tingbodi: Yiwei liuxuesheng de jingli" (There is no place to rest: The experiences of an overseas student). In Z. Li ed., *Bashi niandai zhongguoren zai haiwai* (Chinese Abroad in the 1980s), pp. 1–33. Beijing: People's Daily Press.

Zweig, D., and Chen C. 1995. *China's Brain Drain to the United States: Views of Overseas Chinese Students and Scholars in the 1990s.* China Research Monograph, Berkeley: Institute of East Asian Studies, University of California at Berkeley.

Chapter Four

Factory Regimes of Chinese Capitalism: Different Cultural Logics in Labor Control[1]

Ching Kwan Lee

I was born with the wrong surname. If only I were one of the Yehs . . .
—Lee Lai-wah, a twenty-year-old woman worker in Shenzhen

We come here, laugh and chat, and a day flies by.
—Chan Yuk-ling, a forty-two-year-old woman worker in Hong Kong

Although both Lee Lai-wah and Chan Yuk-ling were Chinese women working for the same enterprise, their shop-floor comments captured two different worlds of labor found in south China. It was common to see Lai-wah and her coworkers sobbing and being scolded at work, while Yuk-ling exchanged jokes with other workers and the foremen. Based on ethnographic data I gathered while working alongside workers such as Lai-wah and Yuk-ling in both Shenzhen and Hong Kong, this chapter examines how and why Chinese women workers find themselves in vastly different forms of factory politics. The emergence of south China since the late 1980s as one of the most dynamic manufacturing regions of the world has been brought about by the confluence of Hong Kong Chinese capital moving northward into the mainland and massive Chinese labor migrating southward into Guangdong. To churn out the low-cost toys, sport shoes, watches, and clothes that flood consumer markets worldwide, transnational Chinese capitalists have to establish production systems that span space and labor diversities. The central feature of south China's economic growth is the effectiveness of these labor-intensive production systems, particularly their strategies of labor control. Ethnographic data in this essay will show how the same team of managers op-

115

erating two factories on both sides of the Hong Kong-China border have developed different modes of labor regulation that deploy various local, family, and gender identities and interests of the predominantly female labor force. By highlighting the different institutional underpinnings of the two regimes and the respective construction of labor identities in these two factories, I argue that cultural patterns of transnational Chinese capitalism are not fixed endowments that Chinese carry with them anywhere they happen to engage in economic activities. Instead, these cultural patterns are formed under specific historical institutional conditions and with the active participation of Chinese managers and workers as they interact in everyday cooperation and conflict.

The notion of *factory regime* is a useful starting point for conceptualizing modes of labor control. According to Michael Burawoy (1985), it refers to the overall political form of production and encapsulates two political moments at the point of production: the labor process and the political apparatus of production. The political effects of the labor process (the technical and social organization of tasks in production) is shaped by the political apparatus of production (institutions such as the state and the unions, which regulate and shape workplace politics). There are two generic types of regimes: the despotic and the hegemonic. Coercive labor control characterizes a despotic regime, which is founded on workers' dependence on wage employment for their livelihoods; wages are tied to performance in the workplace. On the other hand, consent prevails over coercion in a hegemonic regime, which emerges with state interventions such as state social insurance, compulsory union recognition, and collective bargaining legislation that reduce workers' dependence on wages and circumscribe managerial domination. Thus the notion of factory regime links the micro and macro apparatus of labor regulation.

However, a major pitfall of the concept of factory regime is that it fails to analyze the cultural logics underlying specific forms of domination over labor. Power, whether despotic or hegemonic, works through the cultural agencies of workers and management, their collective subjectivities and practices. In this chapter, I take these cultural processes of the two factory regimes into account and find that management invokes, incorporates, and re-creates workers' extraproduction identities and pre-existing networks in controlling labor. Identities and relations based on gender, family, and localities contribute to class relations in production. The importance of networks, or *guanxi*, in Chinese societies has always been recognized, and much has been written about localistic and familistic networks among Chinese capitalists. What this chapter adds to our understanding of Chinese capitalism is the argument that under different institutional and labor conditions, different types of networks become cardinal to systems of production. I call the two factory regimes in south China *localistic despotism* (in Shenzhen) and *familistic hegemony* (in Hong Kong) to emphasize that managers manipulate, respectively, workers' local and family relations, both of which are gendered—constitutive of and constituted by workers' gender identities.

Mobile Capital and Mobile Labor in South China

The formation of the south China manufacturing region resulted from political economic development in both mainland China and Hong Kong. The massive supply of young migrant workers in south China was largely the result of rural decollectivization since 1979, and the demand for their labor was created by the policy of open-door industrialization in southern provinces, especially in Guangdong. Since the late 1970s, the most fundamental transformation of rural China was the demolition of the commune system and its replacement by the household responsibility system, the implementation of which quickly revealed the massive but hitherto disguised problem of unemployment. By the mid-1980s numerous articles in the Chinese press asserted that some 30 to 40 percent (or 114 million to 152 million) of China's rural labor force was redundant (Taylor 1988). Some of this surplus labor found alternative opportunities in rural nonagricultural employment, including petty retail trade, rural construction, and rural industry. Yet the majority of rural youth resorted to rural-urban migration as a way out of rural unemployment and poverty. From 1983 onward, the Chinese government had also gradually lifted the many regulatory barriers against such migration as stipulated by the 1958 Household Registration Regulations. The result was the emergence of a massive "floating population," which by early 1990 was estimated to be anywhere between sixty million and eighty million (Solinger 1991). In Guangdong in 1990 there were some 3.7 million to 5 million floaters. Most were from the neighboring provinces of Guangxi, Hunan, Hainan, and Jiangxi, although a sizable group came from Sichuan (Li and Siu 1992; Solinger 1991, 10–11). The majority of them ended up in the Pearl River delta region, especially industrial towns in which outprocessing factories concentrated. In Shenzhen City in 1990, out of a total population of 1.67 million, 58.7 percent were floaters (Liang 1991, 47).

Studies on migrant workers in south China revealed the interesting phenomenon that women outnumbered men. In a 1987 survey conducted by the State Statistical Bureau, it was found that 58.3 percent of the migrant workers from within Guangdong and 63.2 percent from outside the province were females. Another survey on factory workers in the Pearl

River delta region found that 70 percent of sampled subjects were females and that the average distance moved for females was greater than
that for males (Li 1989, 50). The largest age group was consistently that
between fifteen and thirty years old (Li and Siu 1992, 21–22). The educational level of migrants was in general low: A hefty 87.3 percent of the
migrants in Guangdong held less than a junior-high degree (Solinger
1991, 21).

The appeal of Guangdong as a migration destination had much to do
with another key aspect of China's economic reform since 1979: an international economic policy that encouraged direct foreign investments. The
door of Guangdong was officially opened in 1980 with the establishment
of special economic zones, extending a broad range of preferential policies for foreign investors to set up factories and enterprises. Then major
coastal cities and towns were declared open areas and competed to attract
foreign investment, much of which came from Hong Kong. From 1979 to
1989 Hong Kong contributed 59 percent of China's total contracted foreign investment, or 80 percent of foreign investment in Guangdong (Sung
1992, 99). By the end of June 1991 there were about twenty thousand
Hong Kong enterprises conducting outprocessing operations employing
more than two million workers in Guangdong (Maruya 1992, 137). The
exodus of Hong Kong manufacturers to Guangdong resulted from en-
dogenous bottlenecks in Hong Kong's economic development since the
1980s. In a nutshell, Hong Kong manufacturers had to respond to the
shortage of labor, the rising cost of production, and growing competition
from manufacturers in Southeast Asia. Given the noninterventionist
policy of the Hong Kong government, local manufacturers, which were
predominantly small enterprises, had a limited capability to pursue technological upgrading compared to their counterparts in Taiwan, South
Korea, and Singapore. Their survival strategy was to take advantage of
the new availability of the massive supply of cheap labor and industrial
land in South China. This allowed Hong Kong manufacturers to continue
to compete on the basis of low-cost, labor-intensive production (Lui and
Chiu 1993). Despite the trend toward deindustrialization in Hong Kong
over the past decade, a sizable manufacturing work force remains, total-
ing 629,200 in 1991 (Labor Department 1992).

Researching the Shop Floor

In 1992 and 1993 I carried out ethnographic research in two factories
owned by the same electronics enterprise, Liton Electronics Limited (all
names used are fictitious). Like many other manufacturing establish-

ments, Liton extended its production lines from Hong Kong into Shenzhen in 1986. Liton made home audio systems marketed under other brand names in the United States and Europe. Established in the 1960s, Liton was one of Hong Kong's oldest locally owned audio manufacturers. After the opening of the Shenzhen plant, the Hong Kong production lines were kept open—despite higher operating costs—to do pilot production and quality-control procedures that particular overseas buyers insisted be done in Hong Kong. Otherwise, the technical procedures involved in producing all models were standardized across the two plants. Work procedure sheets specifying the minute details of tasks for a particular line position were photocopied and hung over exactly the same seats on the assembly lines in the two factories.

I gained access to the enterprise through a friend who was a manager in a local commercial bank from which the enterprise borrowed money. Management and workers in both factories knew I was a graduate student writing a dissertation. I was a full-time assembly worker in the Hong Kong plant, visited workers' homes, and participated in their weekend activities. In Shenzhen, I observed and talked with workers and managers on the shop floor and in the office, but management allowed me to work on the line only occasionally. I lived in factory dormitories together with other Hong Kong managerial staff, but I visited and interviewed workers in their dormitories. I also participated in both workers' and managers' gatherings after work.

At the time of my fieldwork, Liton's Hong Kong factory had fewer than a hundred production workers and several dozen office staff and engineers. All production workers and line leaders were female, while men were employed as repair workers, foremen, or managers. A similar gender hierarchy existed in the Shenzhen plant, which employed some eight hundred workers; again, all assembly-line workers and most line leaders were women, while men occupied positions as repair workers, foremen, or supervisors. In both plants, women made up 80 percent of all production employees. Moreover, in both factories there were regional divisions among workers. In Shenzhen, workers came from fourteen different provinces in mainland China, while women workers in the Hong Kong plant originated from two Chinese provinces. The main difference between the two workforces was that workers in Hong Kong were mostly middle-aged working mothers, while those in China were mostly young single women in their teens or twenties who had recently moved to the city from rural villages. The wage rate in Shenzhen was about one sixteenth that in Hong Kong. The basic wage for a Shenzhen assembly worker as of May 1993 was 6.3 yuan per day, or less than $1 U.S. Overtime work was paid at the rate of 1.4 yuan per hour. On average, a worker earned 200 yuan per month, or $25 U.S., after deductions for rent and utility charges in the dormitory. Three meals per day were provided by the factory. On the other hand, a woman worker in Hong Kong earned a daily wage of $100 HK dollars, or about $12 U.S. There have been few overtime shifts in the Hong Kong plant since the opening of the Shenzhen plant, but Hong Kong workers were paid transportation and meal allowances that amounted to $20 HK per day. The total monthly paycheck was about $3,000 HK, or less than $400 U.S. A team of ten senior managers commuted between the Hong Kong plant and the Shenzhen plant, making daily production decisions for both. Each day about fifty thousand Hong Kong technical and managerial personnel, such as Liton's managers, made frequent border crossings to oversee business establishments on both sides of the border. The many similarities across the two plants offer a unique opportunity for comparative research. If ownership, management, and technology are held constant, two distinctive patterns of production politics emerge—localistic despotism and familistic hegemony. Despotism and hegemony denote two basic modes of domination. The former works through coercion, and the latter works through consent. Localism and familism refer to the mechanisms through which domination is organized, apprehended, and resisted.

The Factory Regime in Shenzhen: Localistic Despotism and Maiden Workers

Localistic despotism

Control in the Shenzhen plant was overt, visible, punishment-oriented, and publicly displayed. The factory grounds were fenced on four sides by high concrete walls, and the main entrance gate was guarded around the clock by security guards carrying batons. Notice boards along the production lines tabulated the daily and hourly output targets, the names of the best and worst workers assessed on a weekly basis, and the daily cleanliness scores of each line. Mottos such as No Spitting, Ask Your Superiors When You Have Problems, and Quality Comes First were painted on the walls in bold Chinese characters. The visible display of rules was only the tip of the regimental iceberg. New recruits were asked to read a ten-page handbook of elaborate regulations. The environment was strikingly similar to the prototypical factory in Karl Marx's time, when "all punishments naturally resolve[d] themselves into fines and deductions from wages" (Burawoy 1985, 88). Liton's handbook, *Factory Regulations*, was filled with despotic codes and penalties proscribing workers' demeanors and attire:

Workers must put on a factory identity card on their uniforms. Violators are fined 5 yuan. Workers who wear slippers at work, spit, or litter are fined 10 yuan. . . . Workers punching cards for others are fined three days' wages. Workers who do not line up for punching time cards, do not change shoes according to rules, do not wear headscarves, have long nails, or wrap up uniforms' sleeves are fined 1 yuan. Workers must apply for a "leave card" when going to the bathroom. Each violation is fined 1 yuan. Workers who refuse overtime shifts are fined 2 yuan for the first time, 4 yuan for the second, 8 yuan for the third, and deduction of all wages for the fourth. . . . Leave of absence without prior permission is fined 30 yuan for the first day and 15 yuan for the second. Leave of absence with prior permission is fined 15 yuan.

In the disciplinary regime of the factory, three aspects inflicted the most pain on women workers: physical controls, timed labor, and the docking of wages. Workers' physical movements were restricted to the floor and the production line where they worked. The office was the most sacrosanct area in the entire plant. The office was a world apart from the shop floor, and workers normally were not allowed in it. Making or receiving phone calls in the air-conditioned office was a privilege reserved for senior line leaders or above. Canteens and dormitories were ranked into A, B, and C categories, serving food of different qualities and quantities for employees of various ranks. Dormitories were distinguished by whether there were electric fans and by the number of bunks in each room. The rigid compartmentalization of the factory property into areas for different ranks of workers contrasted with their former freedom to roam the countryside at will, and new recruits to the factory often staunchly and openly resisted management's transfer instructions. Being moved from one assembly-line seat to another or "being kicked around like a football" was unacceptable to the workers because it was an assault on their personal dignity. Very often compliance was exacted only with the personal appearance of the supervisor or manager on the shop floor.

Closely associated with control over workers' physical movements was the temporal discipline of factory life, which was rigid and uncertain. Fixed working hours were paced by shop-floor bells and punch-card machines. Work began at 7:30 a.m. and lasted until 4:30 p.m., six days a week, with a forty-five-minute lunch break at noon. Overtime was demanded at the discretion of management, which gave only an hour's notice prior to the overtime shift, making it impossible for workers to plan their nonwork hours. On a normal day, two hours of overtime were required. During the peak season—the summer months, when overseas orders were made for Christmas inventory—five hours of overtime on weekdays and all of Sunday were often mandatory. This control over time was experienced as despotic, but the length of the workday and the high temperature of the shop floor were not. As one woman explained:

> It's actually more exhausting at home, with the blazing sun. Here at least we have a shelter above our head. But although tending the field is very busy and hard work, we have a lot of free time. When your work is done, you can play with village friends. Here you have to hold your urine until they give you the permit to the bathroom.

Of all the rules in Liton, the most detested was that of docking wages for all kinds of leaves, even when workers had prior permission or a doctor's notification of their illness. Management insisted on this punitive rule to minimize absenteeism as well as to curtail workers' opportunities for interviews in other factories. This, not the unequal reward system, was in workers' eyes the most "unfair" and "inhumane" practice in "bosses' factories" (a term workers used to distinguish foreign-owned enterprises from the more benign but less profitable state and collective enterprises). One woman complained:

> There is inequality in the villages, too. Some peasant families have larger houses and more land, and some earned more in their sideline trades and production. We who come out to work know managers get higher pay than us workers. But it's really unfair that supervisors will not believe in you when you're really sick. They treat us like we are all liars even when some of us nearly fainted at work.

Objective indications of workers' suffering from despotic discipline were weight loss, a deterioration of what is called "face color," and skin conditions, all indicators of worsening health in Chinese folk medicine:

> You see how terrible my face color has become. I have lost my appetite. They fix the time we have to eat, even though you are not hungry. When you are hungry, they don't allow you to eat. At home, I ate whenever I wanted to, a little at a time. I could eat up to three big bowls of rice. Now all I get is a stomachache. The water in Shenzhen is bad. Many of us get rashes on our skin because of the water.

However, enforcement of despotic rules was tempered by the prevalent pattern of localistic associations among workers.[2] Workers identified each other less by name (many of which were fake) than by their province or county of origin and by the local person who brought them in. When I first appeared on the shop floor, the first thing workers asked was, "Who introduced you here?" Rumor had it that I was the sister of the boss, an identity that I tried in vain to refute during the first two months of fieldwork. Localistic networks, organized according to a worker's native village, county, or province and incorporating different ranks of workers and managerial staff, were easily discernible on the shop floor. On the assembly lines, different dialects could be heard, marking the exclusiveness and the boundaries of localistic communities. Locals also extended various kinds of petty favors to each other: taking along each other's mugs when they got the "leave card" to get water, making signals to alert others about approaching managerial staff, teaching each other work skills, or helping each other to clear piled-up work if they happened to sit close to them. Whenever there was a chance to move around the shop floor, little gestures such as pulling a fellow local's ponytail, a sudden punch in the back, or dropping a little note were used to poke fun and exchange greetings.

Localistic practices by line leaders, foremen, and supervisors abounded and they impinged poignantly on workers' material interests. Hong Kong managers were aware and tolerant of such practices by their junior staff in Shenzhen. In the duration of bathroom visits, the assignment of difficult and easy tasks, applications for home-visit leave, the transmission of skills, promotion opportunities, and the ability to bring in other locals, preference was given to people from one's native place. Membership criteria for locals depended on the interest at stake. The most basic distinction divided all workers into two groups: northerners, who came from provinces north of the Yangtze River, and southerners, who came from south of the river. Each group constructed the other in derogatory terms: Northerners were bumpkinish, silly, rude, and miserly while southerners were cunning, promiscuous, dishonest, and spendthrift. More often, workers made finer distinctions among themselves by county of origin. Petty favoritism was distributed mostly along county lines, while scarcer resources such as promotions or the introduction of locals were limited to people of the same village or kinship group. The plant's organization chart bore the imprint of localism. Under the two Hong Kong managers there were four floor supervisors, all of whom were Hakka men from the county of Longchuan in Guangdong province. Three of them shared the same surname, Yeh, while the fourth one was a Lui. The members of both surname groups were cousins who originated from neighboring villages. Of the nine production foremen under these supervisors, four were also Hakka locals. Ninety percent of the line leaders and repair workers were southerners. Janitors and handymen were older men and women from the northern provinces. Localism was such an entrenched idiom that workers used it to interpret daily life in the fac-

Fig. 1. Three Jiangxi sisters in their dormitory, Shenzhen industrial zone. (Photo by Ching Kwan Lee)

tory. Stories of nepotism were circulated, believed, and written about in complaint letters deposited in the opinion box.

Maiden workers

Management manipulated the gender hierarchy embedded in localistic networks to exert additional control over the majority of the young single women. The notion of "maiden worker" (in Cantonese, women were called *buk mui,* meaning "maidens from the north," or *dagong mui,"* meaning "working maidens") emphasized young women's single status, immaturity, imminent marriage, short-term commitment to factory work in Shenzhen, low job aspirations, and low motivation to learn skills. The social construction of women as maiden workers was not purely ideational; it was embedded in practies as well. It facilitated kin control over women's discipline inside the factory and legitimized management's relegation of women to low-ranked unskilled job positions.

Because supervisors and foremen were usually men, management used the familistic or localistic authority of supervisors or foremen from the same local area over female kin to control women's behavior and ensure their commitment to Liton. A woman worker once arranged for a telegram to be sent to her so that she had an excuse to apply for home leave. Her brother was a technician at Liton as well, and the Hong Kong manager who was responsible for screening leave applications checked with her brother about the content of the telegram. Her brother knew nothing about the telegram and was told to tell his sister that her application was rejected. In another instance, a woman working among ten locals in Liton attempted to quit for a higher-paying factory job, but her effort was vetoed by her uncle, whose wife lived with her in the same dormitory room:

> In the dorm, my aunt, my cousins and I live in the same room. My aunt's bunk is just below mine. Everytime I go out, she'll ask where and with whom I go. Some of my friends left Liton for the factory next door. My uncle and my aunt did not allow me to go. They were afraid that I might learn bad things away from them. They wrote to my parents, who wrote back, insisting that I should not leave Liton.

Because management judged that maiden workers worked only until they had saved enough for their dowries, that they were keener on preparing for marriage than for a career in factory work, only male recruits were groomed to acquire firm-specific technical skills. The promotion track from repair worker to technician, assistant foreman, and then supervisor was denied to women workers. This often led to conflicts between line leaders—mostly women—and male repair workers, who were formally subordinate to line leaders on the assembly lines. Having received a modicum of training in electronics, and possessing the prospect of climbing the organizational ladder, repair workers were contemptuous of women's technical ignorance. Quarrels always erupted when women line leaders complained about repair workers' sluggish responses, and the male repair workers angrily challenged the women to try repairing the lines themselves.

To understand why young women subscribed to the notion of maiden workers and came to terms with localistic, despotic control, their multi-layered subjectivities must be grasped. Many of these young women had fled their home's to evade arranged marriages. Many also had personal goals such as gaining experience, saving for dowries, or financing their educations. Because they intended to marry at some point, factory employment was preferred to other service jobs because of the popular association between factory work and endurance for hardship and disciplined labor, traits deemed desirable for future wives. Thus, entering the factory meant preserving the appropriate femininity of maidens while earning a cash income and enjoying the freedom to explore romantic relationships.

125

Actually, the women's understanding of their maiden status differed from that of management and the male locals. First, their maiden status made dating a legitimate concern. Through localistic networks in Shenzhen, women became acquainted with male locals in other factories or trades whom they would not have known had they not come to Shenzhen. Although inter-provincial dating, especially between northerners and southerners, was stigmatized as "fooling around," there was a consensus among maiden workers that working in Shenzhen gave them more freedom of mate choice and more resources to improve their prospects for desirable husbands.

The second meaning that young women attached to their maiden status was that they should prepare for a future beyond factory work. Instead of a resigned attitude toward gainful employment, as assumed by management, young women saw a future marriage as the beginning of adult responsibilities, both emotional and financial. Their vision of marriage was not of housewifery but rather of partnership in an endeavor to find more important and meaningful work than that in bosses' factories. Therefore, during the slack season, when overtime shifts were less frequent, some women took evening or weekend courses in English, typing, and computers. Others had entrepreneurial ambitions such as opening a small neighborhood restaurant or a small store selling snacks or groceries. In the northern provinces, the initial capital required for such endeavors would be around five thousand to seven thousand yuan, an amount that was within the realm of possibility for women workers who made a conscious effort to save their wages for several years.

In short, under the regime of localistic despotism, coercive domination was exerted through localistic networks and the construction of women as maiden workers. While management used localism as a mode of domination, workers actively manipulated localism to temper managerial despotism. The social construction of women as maiden workers was a gender dimension of the factory regime, although the different parties invested it with different meanings and purposes.

The Factory Regime in Hong Kong: Familistic Hegemony and Matron Workers

Familistic hegemony

Hegemonic labor control in the Hong Kong plant was covert and inconspicuous. Achieved through the internalized discipline of subordinates, who experienced a certain degree of autonomy and legitimacy in their own subjugation, hegemonic domination was conditioned by concessions from the powerful and was therefore always an open and contested process (Thompson 1978; Williams 1977). Factory life in Liton's Hong Kong plant was remarkable for the invisibility of codified rules. An orderly autonomy prevailed among workers, whose attire and demeanor on the shop floor reflected a more liberal regime of production than that in Shenzhen. Most women wore their own clothes, with no headscarves or shoulder strips to distinguish rank. Each day at 8 A.M., women workers began entering the air-conditioned, brightly lit shop floor, punched their time cards, and exchanged greetings with the security guard, who always smiled.

The workday began with breakfast rituals that were the workers' spontaneous creation, rather than a canteen routine imposed by management, as in Shenzhen. Workers took turns bringing breakfast for each other. The food—usually fried noodles, porridge, or freshly baked bread—was bought in their neighborhoods. Others brought newspapers, and nearby workers would each take a page and read or engage in brief conversations until the bell rang at 8:15 A.M. During work hours, women could make or receive phone calls. They were also free to visit the bathroom without a permit. Yet when the flow of work was rapid, they would comment that they needed to go to the bathroom but had no time. Being late for work was not uncommon, given the child-care responsibilities of the women, and the floor manager was lenient enough to turn a blind eye to such tardiness. Because of workers' long tenure with the company, which averaged ten to fifteen years, women usually were aware when a coworker's child was sick or some other emergency at home prevented her from getting to work on time. Line leaders and workers would pitch in for the late or absent worker. Passing and eating snacks, although formally prohibited, were daily practices that foremen, line leaders, and even the production manager knew about, saw, and tolerated. Yet workers ate stealthily, as if to publicly declare that they knew that munching chocolate was forbidden. Foremen and managers would take the initiative and conceal bags of snacks that were accidentally exposed along the assembly lines. In all these demeanors, the bottom line of managerial tolerance or benevolence was that production not suffer. This tacit understanding between workers and management resulted in a self-policed autonomy that benefited both sides.

Daily production routines were also marked by responsible autonomy. Experienced line leaders, based on their intimate knowledge of the work habits of their experienced line girls, were allowed to swap workers' tasks, often in defiance of designs sent down from the engineering department. Two conditions made this autonomy necessary. Changes in product models had become more rapid in recent years, and workers were getting older, causing a slower work pace and leading to deteriorat-

127

ing eyesight in the workers. To keep up with daily production targets, line leaders found it necessary to swap a slow worker's assembly tasks with those of her upstream or downstream neighbors. Line leaders themselves pitched in to help slower workers with more complicated work procedures. Managers and foremen rarely questioned line leaders' initiatives in making these changes. One of them proudly suggested to me that "sometimes when we gave them the wrong materials or made an error in designing the work procedures, they were the ones who pointed that out to us. They were that experienced!"

A distinguishing feature of the hegemonic regime was the prevalence of shop-floor discourses. Donald Roy (1958) noted that daily physical and conversational interplays enabled workers to survive the "beast of monotony." To make the long day pass and to break up the workday, workers developed standardized interplays (what Roy called banana time, window time, fish time, and Coke time) and conversational themes (kidding themes, tales of woe, professor themes, and chatter themes). Group interplay was an example of "consummatory" rather than "instrumental" communication and made the job endurable. At Liton, women also engaged in shop-floor discourses that, I argue, were group processes out of which gender and class relations were socially constructed and collectively apprehended. Seizing these discursive spaces on the shop floor, women workers reaffirmed each other's identities and commitments to family. The cultural emphases of these subordinates were crucial elements in a hegemonic regime because they enabled the dominant power to control and articulate its own interests (Gramsci 1971; Williams 1977; O'Harlon 1988).

Recurrent themes about women's family life dominated shop-floor conversations, which took the form of chatter, gossip, horseplay, and serious discussion. The "children theme" was a daily staple and centered around children's school performances and health conditions. Those with grown-up children either boasted about their children's piety or deplored their newfound independence from parents. On the "relations with men" theme, women exchanged strategies for relating to husbands and offered tips about dating to the few single women workers. Sometimes hearty laughter would develop into woeful stories about divorce, single motherhood, and extramarital affairs. Talk about recipes and best buys were staples during lunch breaks. Sex was another recurrent topic about which women were surprisingly frank. They joked about their own sex lives, mostly about the inconvenience of having sex in public housing complexes where an entire family might live in a studio unit of 150 square feet. When a foreman would walk by in the middle of these vivid banters, women would seize the opportunity to embarass him. In re-

Fig. 2. Playing poker, Sichuan style: factory women at leisure in Shenzhen. (Photo by Ching Kwan Lee)

sponse to the foreman's job instructions, line leaders would say to him something like "I'll do it when I love to," a pun for "I'll make love when I love to" in Cantonese. The foreman would then walk away quietly amidst rowdy laughter among the workers, as if he were a transgressor.

Besides these focused themes, there was also a practice of familistic nicknaming that was not found in the Shenzhen plant and which served to humanize the hierarchical authority among foremen, line leaders, and women workers. For instance, the four line leaders, who were in their forties, were called "mother" by the line "girls," who were in their forties or fifties. Almost everyone had a nickname alluding to one's family situation. For example, "Mrs. Rich" was a woman who was known for having a well-off husband and who put on makeup while on the shop floor. "Fat Mother-in-Law" was the name for a fat woman who had three unmarried daughters. *Pau-pau*, meaning "grandma," referred to an older woman who took care of her grandchildren on weekends. One of the foremen had left his family behind in his hometown on Hainan Island, part of mainland China, and he was nicknamed "Hainan Island." The production manager was referred to as "grandpa" by the workers and the line leaders. The prefix "sister" was added to almost everyone's first name. Because these kinship terms allowed participants to simulate family relationships, the brunt of blame about failures of work performance was made easier for management to deliver and for workers to accept.

The culture of familism (Lee 1993) also existed on the practical level. Although the above discourses were women's own cultural productions and were not engineered by management, managers consciously accommodated women's family-based identities through company policies. An example of familism in practice was management's policy of allowing one to two hours of emergency leave without a deduction of pay. This was in clear contrast to the policy in Shenzhen, where even sick leave with a doctor's notification would result in the deduction of almost three days' wages. In the Hong Kong plant, the production manager would ask the reason for the leave and then sign the worker's timecard so that the personnel section would know it was a legitimate absence. Management considered family problems to be legitimate reasons for emergency leave. If children or elderly in-laws were sick, or if children's teachers asked for a meeting, women could take time off without penalty. Women considered this flexibility a major advantage of working in Liton, and they took care to police themselves and not abuse managerial tolerance. Therefore, when one woman asked for sick leave almost every Friday after her marriage, criticisms developed among other workers. The line leader even suggested to the manager that the woman should not be granted any more leave, as she was obviously exploiting the company.

Matron workers

Si lai, a Cantonese vernacular expression for a domineering and matronly wife and mother in a working-class family, was often invoked by management and workers to explain the behavior and concerns of women workers. To management, *si lai* implied that women workers considered work and pay as secondary to family responsibilities. Women also were concerned about the moral implications of working outside the home and wanted to make sure their own femininity and their families' moral reputations would not be adversely affected. Liton's policies of a five-day work week and leniency regarding emergency leave were designed with this understanding: The important thing was to facilitate women's fulfillment of family responsibilities, not to raise wages or create promotion prospects. Managers' collective portrait of women workers in the Hong Kong plant went like this:

> They [women] work to buy flowers for themselves. If they cared about making more money, they would have left a long time ago. Here, work hours are

stable and work is not too exhausting. Their husbands like the fact that it is a factory, so that no one accuses their wives of exposing their faces in public. Liton is ideal for *si lai*. They get the best of both worlds: They can take care of their kids while avoiding the boredom of staying home.

For foremen, allowing women a degree of shop-floor autonomy meant a better utilization of women's experience for the sake of production. Although foremen and male repair workers were excluded from women's discursive communities and were often subjected to women's banter and teasing, men did not care to entertain these *si lai* women, who were inferior in earnings and rank, both of which were firmly institutionalized in the gendered organizational hierarchy. Acceding to women's domineering demeanor was a way of cajoling them and making a joyful workplace, not a workplace of deference or fear.

However, women's subscription to the *si lai* identity incorporated their own understanding of their organizational subordination to men and their possibilities for resisting management control. On the one hand, women legitimized men's position by recognizing men's role in the family as breadwinners. "They are men of the family. How can they support the family with the little money we earn?" On the other hand, they saw through the facade of official titles and admitted that if they chose, they too could acquire electronics skills that would make them foremen. However, their family responsibilities prevented them from investing time and energy in such training. Women were not hesitant about showing contempt for foremen or repair workers. "Stinking men don't know a thing!" was their comment on the men, whom they often compared with their "mothers," the line leaders, who took care of all daily production routines, from arranging the line to getting the material supplies. The fact that manufacturing was a declining sector in Hong Kong also made women valorize their commitment to families and children more than a foreman's career in a sunset occupation. Thus women saw their male superiors through pitying rather than envious eyes. Finally, women workers realized that their family responsibilities gave them a pretext for circumventing managerial demands. After Liton started production in Shenzhen, line leaders righteously rejected management's assignment of regular instruction visits to the Shenzhen plant. Because these assignments involved cross-border commuting and an overnight stay in Shenzhen, these women cited gender-based inconvenience and then mothering burdens at home to reject this extra workload. Spending the night away from home and their children violated the *si lai* women's family-based femininity so much that management was reluctant to push too hard.

To sum up thus far, two points are clear from the above discussions. First, Chinese managers in the two factories incorporate different identities and networks among women workers as modes of labor control. Even though localistic divisions exist among Hong Kong workers, localism is not a salient theme of shop-floor culture and power relations, as is the case in Shenzhen. The reason for management's invocation of different identities among workers in different factories is related to the macroinstitutional contexts of the two production sites. This will be discussed in the following section. Second, the above discussions of the two regimes show that social construction of women's gender identities contributes to class relations, although in the Shenzhen regime gender identity is constituted in localistic groups while in Hong Kong it is constructed with reference to women's family status and responsibilities. This finding lends support to the suggestion (Wolf 1972; Ong 1988; Barlow 1991) that the Chinese construction of gender is situated within webs of social relations (such as localistic and familistic groups) rather than premised on a notion of an atomistic, individual self outside of or prior to specific social relations.

Institutional Underpinnings of Factory Regimes

The state

What, then, are the institutional determinants shaping these cultural patterns of production regimes? Burawoy's (1985) theory of production politics makes state intervention and regulation the linchpin distinguishing the two generic types of factory regimes. Based on my research, I maintain that the role of the state does not explain all regime differences because Shenzhen and Hong Kong are not in nations where the two theoretically specified consequences of the state were at work. Specifically, neither the clientalist state in Shenzhen nor the minimalist state in Hong Kong circumscribed management's autonomy in labor-control practices. Moreover, neither of the two states provided welfare or social insurance to workers. Under this condition of high managerial autonomy, the deployment of different control strategies was more a response to the organization of the respective labor markets and the corresponding characteristics of workers as perceived by management than a response to constraints imposed by the state.

Clientalist connections, or *guanxi,* have long been considered an institutional characteristic of Chinese socialism (Yang 1993; Walder 1986; Oi 1989). Several features of Shenzhen's open-door industrialization are particularly conducive to the proliferation of clientalism. Decentralization of state power, coupled with competition among localities to grant preferential terms to attract foreign investors, made labor regulations more flexible and negotiable. Most Hong Kong investors established outprocessing factories just outside the special economic zone to evade the regulatory bureaucracy within the zone. Preexisting kinship and place-of-origin ties between Hong Kong investors and mainland Chinese endowed Hong Kong investors with a special kind of symbolic capital that foreign investors elsewhere cannot rival (Smart and Smart 1991; Leung 1993; Hsing, this volume). These ties also became the spawning ground for clientalism: the exchange of gifts and personal favors that benefits both parties.

Liton's managers reiterated that the pivotal factor determining their success in managing factory production in Shenzhen was their relations with the three local state bureaus in charge of taxation, import and export duties, and labor management. Because state officials have the discretion to raise the tax rate on profits, to cause delays at customs checkpoints, or to enforce the prohibition on out-of-province workers, Liton's management took extraordinary care to maintain clientalist relations with these local officials. There were two major ways to maximize enterprise autonomy through clientalist relations. The more direct way was to participate in the gift economy. Sending gifts (from expensive cognacs and dried seafood to imported cigarettes and calendars) during traditional Chinese festivals, hosting dinner banquets and karaoke parties, paying home visits, selling Liton's audio products at the manufacturer's prices to officials, and donating to local school and road construction projects were some of the major gifts. Occasionally preferential consideration was given to officials who introduced children of friends or relatives to work in Liton. These gifts prevented problems from local state bureaus. In the second use of clientalism, management manipulated its clientalist relations with one bureau to counter unwanted encroachment by another bureau. For instance, because of the cozy relationship between Liton and the External Trade Bureau, Liton's management could resist pressure from the Labor Management Bureau to raise wage rates and reform the punitive factory code. Thus clientalism enhanced managerial autonomy in Shenzhen, where no explicit laws specified a minimum wage for workers in outprocessing factories, and no social insurance legislation, compulsory trade union recognition, or collective bargaining existed to protect workers from arbitrary dismissal.

Managerial autonomy in Hong Kong was fostered by minimal state regulation and the provision of social insurance. In their seminal study of Hong Kong's industrial relations, Joe England and John Rear found that before 1967 the "virtual absence of rules imposed from outside the workplace, either by law or by collective bargaining, made it a permissive system which favored those who held power inside the enterprise—the employers" (England and Rear 1981, 361). For industrial workers, there was no minimum wage, no restrictions on daily hours of work, and no statutory provision for maternity leave or severance payments. After the riots and massive work stoppages in 1967, the British colonial government introduced legislative interventions in industrial relations and social welfare. The Employment Ordinance regulated the termination of employment contracts, wage periods, deduction of wages, rest days, and severance pay. Other laws restricted women workers' overtime to two hours per day. The grievance machinery for settling disputes was also established in the 1970s. Finally, in the area of welfare, although Hong Kong developed the world's second-largest public housing system for low-income families, the government's espousal of laissez-faire noninterventionism remained staunch, and there still is no full-fledged social insurance system. Therefore, even with the post-1967 reforms, Hong Kong's industrial relations today remain grossly underdeveloped, not least because of the lack of collective bargaining and the weakness of its unions. Trade union laws in Hong Kong provide unions with "negatively phrased immunities from liabilities for conspiracy at tort and other legal disabilities" but stop short of "granting any positive right of union recognition" (Lethbridge and Ng 1984, 83). Moreover, because unions have never been highly organized in the workplace, there is no developed shop steward system, and collective bargaining is rare in labor dispute resolution (Levin and Chiu 1993, 203). Thus, England and Rear (1981) maintained that since 1967, the application of a British model of voluntary conciliation in Hong Kong has had little or no effect on the realities of workplace relationships, owing to the lack of union pressure on management exerted from the shop floor.

In short, in both Shenzhen and Hong Kong, management enjoys a high degree of autonomy within the enterprise in the organization of production and methods of labor control. Because in both locations the state only weakly constrains management and provides minimal resources for workers' livelihoods outside of paid labor, the role of the state is not as pivotal as Burawoy suggests. Rather, the social organization of the labor market determines workers' dependence and imposes constraints on management and labor.

Labor markets

I link the organization of the labor market with workers' dependence and consequently the constitution of shop-floor interests between management and labor. In Shenzhen's labor market, inexperienced migrant women workers depend on localistic networks for getting jobs and for survival. Management exploits this dependence to legitimatize and facilitate the despotic control that is necessary to exact discipline from a nascent working class. On the other hand, in Hong Kong, women workers' participation in paid work is conditioned by the fulfillment of domestic duties. The women are also financially dependent on other family members' income to support themselves and their children. Management accedes to women's family-based constraints in return for responsible autonomy and self-policed control, which is made possible by the women's long company tenure, their firm-specific experience, and their eagerness to hang on to their jobs in a dwindling manufacturing sector.

Workers in Liton's Shenzhen plant came from fourteen different provinces in the People's Republic of China. Those from Guangdong accounted for only 47.7 percent of the total work force, followed by those from Hubei (21.8 percent), Sichuan (8.7 percent), and Henan (6.1 percent). The rest were from Guangxi, Hunan, Jiangxi, and as far away as Xinjiang. Eighty percent of the work force were women between the ages of sixteen and twenty-five. Management saw in migrant labor's massive numbers, their youth, peasant origin, and lack of industrial work experience the feasibility and necessity for despotism. Although one manager likened women to sheep because both were docile and ignorant, another talked about the need to cultivate consciousness and discipline:

> You don't see workers spitting on the floor in Hong Kong. But here it's their habit to spit even when you stand right next to them. That's how they behave in the countryside. . . . I once saw a new worker putting down her work and rushing back to the dorm when the rain came suddenly. She went to remove the clothes she hung outside. . . . What we offer here may seem meager to you, but it's already a lot for peasant girls. At least they don't have to work under the sun, and we provide three meals and a bed. I'm sure there are many new migrants who will work for free, given these conditions.

Contrary to the fluid image conjured up by the term *floaters,* these peasants made their way into "bosses' factories" through localistic networks. Interviews with workers revealed five major ways in which these localistic networks mediated the labor supply for bosses' factories. First, locals were critical in enabling women to make the initial trip to Shenzhen. Some locals acted as guardians to whom parents entrusted their children. During the annual Chinese New Year holiday, locals who visited their home villages spread information about job opportunities, living standards, and wages, and helped the young to secure parental permission.

Many women who escaped from home depended on locals to finance the first trip and provide initial lodging in a foreign city:

> When we arrived the first night, it was very late. My cousin took me to one of our locals' dormitory. The next day I went to Shajin to join my second sister. I sneaked into the dormitory and hid there for a week until that factory posted a recruitment notice. I got a job there, on the same floor with my sister. Later, when Liton was recruiting, my sister and I left together to join my third sister here.

Second, localistic networks were the channels through which workers could illegally obtain three necessary permits that factories asked for during recruitment: the temporary residence permit, an identity card, and a certificate of marital status. Workers asked locals to find professionals to forge the papers or bribe officials in the local Security Bureau by paying a hundred to two hundred yuan. In many other cases, people simply borrowed the papers of locals whose facial features bore some resemblance to their own. This gave rise to the prevalence of false names among workers. Third, getting and changing jobs and promotions depended on locals' recommendations. Localistic networks spread information about factories that were hiring and recommended locals to good factories—that is, those with higher wages, decent dormitories, a constant supply of water and electricity, and good food:

> If you cannot name the acquaintance who is working there, the guards at the factory gate will not let you in. This is the same in many factories. Sometimes you have to pay the guard, who will then claim you as his acquaintance and take you to the managers. But if you have an acquaintance, even when they are not openly hiring, you'll still get a job.

Fourth, financial assistance was frequently extended among members of localistic networks to deal with late payment of wages or emergencies. The amount involved varied from ten to several hundred yuan. A woman explained two financially needy situations:

> Usually when we send money home, we want to send more because it is troublesome to go to the post office. So we borrow money from several others so that we can send a larger lump sum each time. We usually repay the debt as soon as the next paycheck comes through. . . . There was once when my uncle and four other locals were arrested by the Security Bureau for working without papers. Other natives rushed to tell me and asked me to take twelve hundred yuan to get him released. I immediately went to borrow money from five locals, each of whom lent me some.

Fifth, in times of sickness, workers relied on locals in the factory to do various errands, such as getting food from the canteen, getting buckets of water for bathing, washing clothes, and accompanying them to clinics. Locals were also a major source of emotional support. In all these respects, workers depended on localistic networks for survival. In this situation, management had an interest in incorporating localism into shop-floor practices to facilitate and legitimize control and also to reduce the cost of labor reproduction.

Finally, the impression that women were only short-term workers more interested in marriage than in work was also founded in their short tenure with the company. Yet this high labor mobility was also an effect of the labor market: the mushrooming of new factories in Shenzhen competing for relatively experienced workers and the massive supply of migrant workers competing to get into better factories.

Three differences between the labor markets of Hong Kong and Shenzhen are important for understanding the two regimes. Instead of a massive supply of migrant labor, as in Shenzhen, Hong Kong's labor market was tight and short on experienced workers. Workers who remained in the manufacturing sector held long company tenure, as opposed to Shenzhen worker's high mobility across factories. Finally, Hong Kong workers depended on their families and kin rather than localistic networks for crucial resources not provided by the government or the employer.

Industrialization in Shenzhen since the early 1980s occurred in tandem with deindustrialization in Hong Kong, where the contribution of the manufacturing sector to total employment declined from 47 percent in 1981 to 29.7 percent in 1989. The number of persons engaged in the electronics industry (excluding the manufacture of electronic watches and clocks) also dwindled, from 93,005 in 1980 to 59,341 in 1991, reflecting the trend of plants to relocate to the mainland. Moreover, the graying of the manufacturing work force was apparent, in sharp contrast to the predominance of teenage workers in Shenzhen. In Hong Kong, the percentage of women workers under age twenty-five in the manufacturing sector declined from 50.9 percent in 1971 to 27.7 percent in 1986. Thus, the concentration of married working mothers and grandmothers in Liton reflected Hong Kong's general situation. These married women had an average company tenure of ten to fifteen years, and they were therefore extremely experienced in producing Liton's audio equipment. Owing to the difficulty of recruiting labor in a declining sector and women workers' firm-specific experience, management saw both the necessity and the feasibility for a hegemonic form of control. Yet the familistic character of this hegemonic regime was rooted in the women's dependence on their families, a dependence to which management consciously acceded.

Analyses of the work histories of the women who worked at Liton in Hong Kong indicated two common features that are critical for my analysis. First, many women had experienced intermittent periods when they were dependent on the incomes of their husbands to survive, either because they were full-time mothers without an independent income or because they were piece workers earning less than a living wage. As full-time workers at Liton, these women continued to draw on the resources of the family even as they contributed to the family coffer. Second, the availability of assistance from kin in matters of child care and housework was the critical factor charting the different patterns of their wage employment. One woman recalled how the several stages of her career as a working mother were circumscribed by family circumstances—full-time mothering, piece work, half-day shift work, and full-time work.

> I stayed home after I got married and gave birth to three children. For six years I sewed cotton gloves at home. When my youngest kid entered primary school, I became a part-time worker at Liton. I worked the morning shift. The timing was perfect: My youngest daughter finished her school at one P.M. and I got off from work at twelve-thirty. I went to the market for fresh groceries and then made lunch for both of us. Later, when my youngest daughter began junior high, a full-day school, I began working full-time at Liton.

Similarly, one of her coworkers became a factory worker when family circumstances permitted and necessitated her entry into waged work:

> My eldest son came along one year after I was married. It was 1965. Then I gave birth to one child every year after that. Altogether I have four children. How could I work with four young ones? So the entire family depended on my husband, who was a seamster in a tailor shop. When my youngest daughter went to primary one, we had a very heavy burden to finance their education. My second daughter was old enough to take the youngest one to and from school, so my husband agreed to let me work in factories. . . . For many years, I made them breakfast and lunch before I went to work in the morning. In the evening, I did my market shopping after work and came home to make dinner.

A few women were luckier. With the assistance of kin, they were able to continue working after becoming mothers. A woman who had worked in Liton for twenty-five years had the help of her sister-in-law:

My sister-in-law takes care of my two kids during the week. I take my kids back only during the weekends. Of course, I pay her. But since we are relatives, it's cheaper than finding other babysitters. It costs more than three thousand [HK$] a month for two kids. It'd be doubled if she were an outsider.

Women's family circumstances not only determined when they entered or dropped out of paid work but also attached them to a particular employer who could accommodate their family responsibilities. This led them to forsake job opportunities in other sectors offering higher wages. One may argue that these Hong Kong women workers are subjected to the collusion between domestic patriarchy and workplace patriarchy (Salaff 1992). Yet from the perspective of these women, Liton allowed them to maximize the *balance* of a set of considerations: having an independent income, fulfilling their commitments to their children and families, and maintaining sociability without jeopardizing their femininity. Women workers did not want to maximize any one of these goals; rather, they wished to accommodate potentially competing ones. The location, work hours, system of holidays, and managerial policies at Liton allowed for such integration. This worker's reasoning reflected that of many of her coworkers, who preferred factory work at Liton to higher-paying service jobs:

We mothers are very happy to have Saturdays off. And it's kind of easy to ask for leave, like when you are sick or your kid's teacher wants to see you. . . . Service jobs get off late in the evening, usually around ten o'clock. I could earn more, but I would not have time for my daughter. It would be meaningless to work. A part-time service job is an alternative, but that brings in too little money. So, in terms of work hours and money, Liton is okay.

To recapitulate, the conditions of factory work and the communal resources workers depended on for survival differed between women workers on both sides of the border. Localistic networks in Shenzhen and family and kin in Hong Kong mediated the supply of labor and provided resources that neither the state or employers offered to women. Incorporating localism and familism into the respective factory regimes reduced management's financial burden, legitimized managerial control, and satisfied women workers' mundane interests.

Conclusion

As transnational Chinese capitalists establish production lines in different localities, they deploy different kinds of social networks—networks that exist among workers and those between themselves and state officials. Some of these are preexisting networks, while others have to be spun anew. I have shown how localism, familism, and gender represent different cultural logics, providing the basis for different types of networking crucial to the workings of production regimes. The configuration of institutional factors such as labor market render some of these cultural logics more valid than others and are therefore constitutive of factory regimes. However, if Chinese capitalists have quite successfully drawn on these networks for purposes of labor control, Chinese women workers are not mere victims to these mechanisms of control, since these networks also provide them with the social, material, and emotional support to survive the uncertain conditions of the labor markets in both Hong Kong and Shenzhen.

Notes

[1] This chapter is a different version of an article published in the *American Sociological Review* (Lee 1995). I thank Michael Burawoy for his unfailing support and critical comments throughout the project. Thanks are also due to Aihwa Ong and Donald Nonini for their constructive suggestions on an earlier draft of this chapter.

[2] In Chinese labor historiographies there is abundant evidence of the prevalence of localistic or native-place associations among Chinese workers. See, for instance, Hershatter 1986; Honig 1986, 1992; Perry 1993; Strand 1989; Tsai 1993.

References

Barlow, Tani. 1991. "Theorizing Women: *Funu, Guojia, Jiating." Genders* 10: 132–160.

Burawoy, Michael. 1985. *Politics of Production.* London: Verso.

England, Joe, and John Rear. 1981. *Industrial Relations and Law in Hong Kong.* Hong Kong: Oxford University Press.

Gramsci, Antonio. 1971. *Selections from the Prison Notebooks.* New York: International.

Hershatter, Gail. 1986. *The Workers of Tianjin, 1900–1949.* Stanford: Stanford University Press.

Honig, Emily. 1986. *Sisters and Strangers: Women in the Shanghai Cotton Mills, 1919–1949.* Stanford: Stanford University Press.

———. 1992. *Creating Chinese Ethnicity: Subei People in Shanghai, 1850–1980.* New Haven: Yale University Press.

Labor Department. 1992. *Labor and Employment in Hong Kong.* Hong Kong: Government Printer.

Lee, Ching Kwan. 1993. "Familial Hegemony: Gender and Production Politics on Hong Kong's Electronics Shop Floor." *Gender and Society* 7: 529–47.

————. 1995. "Engendering the Worlds of Labor: Women Wokers, Labor Markets, and Production Politics in the South China Economic Miracle." *American Sociological Review* 60, no. 3: 378–97.

Lethbridge, David, and Sek-hong Ng. 1984. "The Business Environment and Employment." In David Lethbridge, ed., *The Business Environment in Hong Kong,* pp. 70–104. Hong Kong: Oxford University Press.

Leung, Chi Kin. 1993. "Personal Contacts, Subcontracting Linkages, and Development in the Hong Kong-Zhujiang Delta Region." *Annals of the Association of American Geographers* 83: 272–302.

Levin, David, and Stephen Chiu. 1993. "Dependent Capitalism, a Colonial State, and Marginal Unions: The Case of Hong Kong," In Stephen Frenkel, ed., *Organized Labor in the Asia-Pacific Region,* pp. 187–222. Ithaca, New York: ILR Press.

Li, Sieming. 1989. "Labour Mobility, Migration and Urbanization in the Pearl River Delta Areas." *Asian Geographer* 8: 35–60.

Li, Si-ming, and Yat-ming Siu. 1992. "Population Mobility in Guangdong Province." Unpublished manuscript.

Lui, T. L., and S. Chiu. 1993. "Industrial Restructuring and Labor Market Adjustment Under Positive Non-Interventionism." *Environment and Planning A* 25: 63–79.

Maruya, Toyojiro. 1992. "Economic Relations Between Hong Kong and Guangdong Province." In Toyojiro Maruya, ed., *Guangdong,* pp. 126–46. Hong Kong Center of Asian Studies, University of Hong Kong.

O'Harlon, Rosalind. 1988. "Recovering the Subject: Subaltern Studies and Histories of Resistance in Colonial South Asia." *Modern Asian Studies* 22: 189–224.

Oi, Jean. 1989. *State and Pesant in Contemporary China.* Berkeley: University of California Press.

Ong, Aihwa. 1987. *Spirits of Resistance and Capitalist Discipline: Factory Women in Malaysia.* New York: State University of New York Press.

————. 1988. "Colonialism and Modernity: Feminist Re-presentations of Women in Non-Western Societies." *Inscriptions* 3/4: 79–93.

Perry, Elizabeth. 1993. *Shanghai on Strike: The Politics of Chinese Labor.* Stanford: Stanford University Press.

Roy, Donald. 1958. "'Banana Time': Job Satisfaction and Informal Interaction." *Human Organization* 18: 158–68.

Salaff, Janet. 1992. "Women, the Family, and the State in Hong Kong, Taiwan, and Singapore." In Richard P. Appelbaum and Jeffrey Henderson, eds., *States and Development in the Asian Pacific Rim,* pp. 267–88. Newbury Park, CA: Sage.

Smart, Josephine, and Alan Smart. 1991. "Personal Relations and Divergent Economies." *International Journal of Urban and Regional Research,* 15, no. 2: 216–33.

Solinger, Dorothy J. 1991. *China's Transients and the State: A Form of Civil Society?* USC Seminar Series, no. 1. Hong Kong: Hong Kong Institute of Asia-Pacific Studies.

Strand, David. 1989. *Rickshaw Beijing: City People and Politics in the 1920s.* Berkeley: University of California Press.

Sung, Yun-wing. 1992. *Non-institutional Economic Integration Via Cultural Affinity.* Hong Kong: Hong Kong Institute of Asia-Pacific Studies, Occasional Paper No. 13 Chinese University of Hong Kong.

Taylor, Jeffrey R. 1988. "Rural Employment Trends and the Legacy of Surplus Labor, 1978–86." *China Quarterly* 116: 736–66.

Thompson, E. P. 1978. "Eighteenth-Century English Society: Class Struggle Without Class?" *Social History* 3: 133–65.

Tsai, Jung-fang. 1993. *Hong Kong in Chinese History: Community and Social Unrest in the British Colony; 1842–1913.* New York: Columbia University Press.

Walder, Andrew. 1986. *Communist Neo-Traditionalism.* Berkeley: University of California Press.

Williams, Raymond. 1977. *Marxism and Literature.* Oxford: Oxford University Press.

Wolf, Margery. 1972. *Women and the Family in Rural Taiwan.* Stanford: Stanford University Press.

Yang, Mayfair. 1994. *Gifts, Favors, and Banquets: The Art of Social Relationships in China.* Ithaca, NY: Cornell University Press.

Chapter Five

Building *Guanxi* Across the Straits: Taiwanese Capital and Local Chinese Bureaucrats[1]

You-tien Hsing

My very first experience with karaoke was in Mei-jie, a small, semirural town in the Pearl River delta of Guangdong province in south China, in the spring of 1992 as I was conducting my research on Taiwanese manu- facturing investment in south China.[2] In Mei-jie alone, a town of fifty thousand people, there were one karaoke bar, five Taiwanese-style karaoke restaurants, and more than four hundred Taiwanese shoe facto- ries. In the midst of expressive songs about lost love and drifting lives, sung through loudspeakers and under swirling lights, accompanied by seafood and beer, I succeeded in making connections with representa- tives of investing companies and local officials for interviews, just as Taiwanese investors made contact with local Chinese officials.

In 1991 Taiwan surpassed the United States and Japan to become the second-largest investor in China after Hong Kong (Sung 1994, 50). Re- alized direct investment from Taiwan to China totaled $8–10 billion U.S. in 1994, accounting for 20 percent of China's total foreign direct invest- ment. Taiwanese investment provided more than five million jobs in China, of which 70 percent were concentrated in Guangdong and Fujian provinces in the south.[3] Taking advantage of the linguistic and cultural affinity, Taiwanese investors in south China successfully cultivated in- terpersonal relationships (*guanxi*) with local Chinese officials in the re- gion. Using such interpersonal networks, Taiwanese investors have managed to bypass bureaucratic demands on foreign-investment projects and maintain and enhance flexibility in production and marketing.

Indeed, the practice of building *guanxi* between investors and govern- mental officials can be corrupt. For example, the owner of a Taiwanese shoe factory located in a fishing village two hours from Shenzhen told me that he made a deal with the local party secretary that if he helped pay the county's remittance to the provincial government, the county's customs service would not inspect the company's exports and imports too closely, nor would the tax bureau audit its books. To use a Chinese idiom, the officials would "open one eye, with the other closed" (*zhengyi zhiyan biyi zhiyan*) when they visited the factory. Another shoe factory, this one with two thousand workers, managed to maintain good relationships with local customs officials. Once every few months the company would reserve an entire karaoke bar to entertain their friends in the customs service. As a result, the containers of the company's imported materials were never opened and inspected.

However, this kind of relationship-building is not always just corruption. A more intriguing issue involves the way social and business networks are established in a specific cultural and institutional context. One of the most distinctive characteristics of Taiwanese investment in south China is the cultural affinity between the investors and their local partners. The fast growth of "Greater China" and the formation of the Southeast Asian "growth triangle" also suggest that there is a correlation among culture, institutions, history, and the direction of transnational capital flows. While capital flows might be less restricted by national boundaries since the 1980s (Ohmae 1991), they are still confined by institutional and cultural boundaries.

In his analysis of the age of flexible accumulation, David Harvey (1989) has described how local states take initiatives and bypass the central government to link directly with international urban experiences. Peter Evans's (1979) model of triple alliance also deals with the interaction between the multinationals and local societies. However, neither has paid sufficient attention to the question of how local cultural practices have reworked the relations between those who provide capital and those who receive it. Here I adopt Aihwa Ong's view of culture as not just a set of values but also a historically and institutionally situated dynamism (Ong 1987). The next question is, then, how do we understand the interaction between general cultural principles and specific institutional conditions? In the case of Taiwanese investment in south China, how does cultural affinity between Taiwanese investors and local Chinese officials provide the basis for establishing interpersonal networks? And how are such networks shaped by the institutional conditions in south China?

There have been a number of important works concerning the characteristics of "Chinese capitalism" in various countries where Chinese ethnicity is dominant, and especially on Chinese emigrant entrepreneurs in Southeast Asia (Hamilton 1991, 1996; Jesudason 1994; Lim and

Gosling 1983; McVey 1992; Redding 1990; S. Wong 1988). Most writers agree that the foundation of the Chinese style of business organization is familism (which usually includes nepotism, paternalism, and family ownership in firm organization) and interpersonal relationships—*guanxi*, on which a trusting and reciprocal obligatory relationship is built between business partners. The study of interpersonal ties in economic processes has a long tradition in anthropology especially considered as gift exchange (Malinowski 1961; Mauss 1967; Sahlins 1972; Bourdieu 1972; Curtin 1984; Yang 1988, 1989, 1994). Gift exchange is understood as a process of building trusting interpersonal relationships in economic activities. It is established on the basis of reciprocal assistance and enduring indebtedness between the parties involved while practicing the exchange of favors in material and nonmaterial forms.

The historical and institutional context in south China since the economic reform took hold in the early 1980s, especially the increasing fiscal autonomy of local authorities, has shaped the form and content of gift exchange and the way Taiwanese investors establish *guanxi* with local Chinese officials. Encouraged by new policies that allow local governments to retain a major portion of revenue for local use and to grant permission for the investment of foreign capital, local Chinese officials compete with one another to attract foreign investment projects to their areas, offering more generous tax breaks and cheaper land and minimizing bureaucratic holdups.

Local Autonomy and Flexibility in Bureaucracy

China's post-1978 economic reforms have been characterized by the increasing economic autonomy of local authorities at the municipal, city, and county levels and the active role that local officials now play in economic realms. Many commentators have argued that China's current economic system is better understood as a decentralized command economy rather than a full-scale privatization or marketization process in the neoclassical sense (Naughton 1987; Oi 1991; Zweig 1989; Solinger 1987).

This local economic autonomy is characterized by various revenue-sharing schemes that provide incentives to local governments to collect taxes and to engage directly in profit-making activities. For example, most provinces were allowed to retain an average of 80 percent of the commercial and industrial revenues generated in their areas; provincial officials were granted new authority to adjust tax rates and to collect "extra-budgetary funds," such as profits and depreciation funds. In addition, the relaxation of central government controls on bank loans and the granting of loan approval authority to provincial bank branches have given more freedom to local decision makers. At the same time, the central government now permits provinces to engage in foreign trade through local branches of the national foreign trade corporation (Ho and Huenemann 1984; Solinger 1987; Zhang and Zou 1994).

County and municipal governments have also enjoyed the authority to approve foreign-investment projects. For projects under $3 million U.S., the county government has full authority to grant permission; higher-ranking municipal authorities have the ability to approve projects involving as much as $10 million U.S. Municipal and county governments can also issue import-export licenses, set up independent customs services, make grants of industrial and residential land for parcels under a certain size, offer favorable investment conditions for foreign firms, and so on. Many state-owned enterprises have been transformed into collective enterprises, which are owned and run by local governments at different levels.

Compared to other regions in China, Guangdong and Fujian provinces in the south have enjoyed the greatest economic autonomy, largely because of their geographical position in the periphery and their strong social ties with overseas Chinese funding sources. A number of special policies were established to give Guangdong and Fujian the flexibility to take advantage of their spatial and sociocultural proximity to the outside world. The two provinces were among the first in China to remit a fixed lump sum, rather than a certain percentage of their tax revenues, to Beijing each year, retaining the rest. It means that the more they earn, the more they get to keep within the region. Guangdong and Fujian can also retain a large portion of the foreign exchange they earn from exports and tourism as well as a share of the remittances they receive from abroad. They were also the first two provinces allowed to borrow directly from abroad. Many Guangdong branches of national trading companies were allowed to split off and become independent (C. Wong 1992, 208; Vogel 1989, 89). In terms of distribution of raw materials, management of commercial activities, wage determination, and commodity price setting, the southern provinces have also enjoyed greater decision-making authority.

This increasing fiscal autonomy was accompanied by a shift of financial responsibility onto local authorities. Indeed, many local bureaucrats have been highly motivated to exploit for their personal gain the new opportunities provided by fiscal reform. Yet the motivation comes also from the greater financial responsibility now required of local governments, which are required to be self-sufficient financially and to seek

146

additional revenues to fund the increasing local share of expenditures on infrastructure, education, public health, and other items. According to the vice governor and the party secretary of a small town in the greater Guangzhou area, the township enterprises—many of them joint ventures with Taiwanese and Hong Kong companies—contributed 70 to 75 percent of the total revenue of the town in 1992. The municipal government of Guangzhou paid for only the basic salaries of the party cadres and schoolteachers in town. As a result, land sales have become one of the major sources of revenue for local governments and a main channel for attracting foreign investment to the region. Large areas of agricultural land have been transferred to industrial parks and commercial housing projects. The revenue generated from the sale of land leases in the coastal cities of south China accounts for more than 35 percent of the total annual revenue of these cities. In the cities of Shenzhen and Zhuhai, where special economic zones are located, the figure can be as high as 50 percent.[4] In Haikou, the capital city of Hainan Island, investment in property constitutes half of the fixed social investment and contributes 23 percent of the total revenue of the city.[5]

Local officials with newly gained economic authority have become the most important agents for Taiwanese investment in south China. They tend to be more flexible about regulations than provincial or central authorities and are more willing to cooperate with overseas investors. Many Taiwanese and Hong Kong investors I interviewed agreed that it is faster and simpler to deal with local officials than to struggle with bureaucracies at higher levels.[6] For export-oriented manufacturing, which is what most of the overseas investors were engaged in[7], speedy production and delivery are the most important factors allowing them to be competitive in the world market. Delayed deliveries often result in reduction of payment or the cancellation of orders. The need to bypass formal bureaucratic procedures in order to keep production and delivery moving as quickly as possible is important, particularly for small- and medium-sized producers with limited operational capital. Lower-level officials at the county and city levels, motivated by the new fiscal schemes, are more willing to accommodate overseas investors' needs to speed up the application process for investment projects and to make flexible arrangements with individual investors. These include more favorable tax policies; cheaper land, power, and water in the initial stages; relaxed customs inspection of imported materials and export-ready products; halfhearted implementation of environmental and labor regulations; permission to sell a greater percentage of products in the domestic Chinese market; quick approval of factory expansion plans, and so on. In one of my interviews, when I asked about the effects of the nationwide policy of three-year tax holidays for foreign investors, a Taiwanese electronics company owner told me that these policies are "made for fools" and that more-advantageous policy breaks can be tailor-made through individual arrangements with the local officials.

The ability to make flexible deals with low-level Chinese officials has been a major attraction for small- and medium-sized investors from Taiwan. Some medium- to large-sized investors would even split their investment into a number of smaller projects so to avoid the involvement of higher-level governments. For instance, one Taiwanese shoe company has built six establishments in different towns in the Pearl River delta region, hiring more than four thousand workers altogether. Yet each establishment was kept small enough, in terms of the total amount of capital, the number of employees, and the amount of land used for factory buildings, to qualify as a small project that could be approved by the county government.

Even large projects that require approval by provincial, municipal, or central government need full cooperation at the local level, where production is actually carried out. Bureaucratic holdups can happen in any stage of the investment process, such as leasing land, establishing electricity, water, and telephone service, obtaining permits, recruiting workers, meeting environmental protection requirements, and so on. As a result, the success of investment in China has come to depend largely on the relationship the investors have cultivated with local-level bureaucrats. Investors have to cultivate good relations with local officials of various agencies such as the public security bureau, the customs service, the public health department, the tax bureau, the Committee of Foreign Economics and Trade, the labor department, local banks, and the electricity, water, and telephone companies. The definition of efficiency in this case is the level of cooperativeness of the local officials. For local officials, it is to their benefit to attract foreign investors so as to strengthen the economic base of their localities. They also gain personal benefits, such as a large raise in their salaries or bonuses based on profits of the joint ventures and collective enterprises. In fact, the income levels of government officials in south China have been a good indicator of towns' success in joint-venture arrangements with overseas investors.[8]

Blood Is Thicker than Water

Many Taiwanese investors I interviewed agreed that compared to other overseas production sites, China is more attractive because of the cultural and linguistic affinity between Taiwanese and Chinese (see figure

**Fig. 1. Taiwanese direct investment in China
and ASEAN Countries**

(in millions of U.S. $)

	1988	1989	1990 (Jan.-Jun.)
Mainland China	420	517	661
Thailand	842	871	313
Malaysia	313	815	712
Philippines	109	149	139
Indonesia	916	158	377

Source: Kao et al. 1992, 26.

1).[9] Such cultural affinity has facilitated the establishment of interpersonal relationships between Taiwanese investors and local officials.

Cultural understanding between investors and local agents does not guarantee the success of the investment projects, however, and it is very difficult to measure how critical cultural understanding and interpersonal networks are to the formation and operation of the enterprises. In addition, the significance of interpersonal relationships is by no means unique to Taiwanese investment in China. Nevertheless, we cannot afford to ignore cultural factors, for they were mentioned frequently in the interviews I conducted with Taiwanese investors in China. The question is, if interpersonal relationships are a key factor in the success of Taiwanese investment in south China, and the cultural affinity between the investors and their local agents is crucial for the establishment of such relationships, how do cultural connections affect the establishment of interpersonal networks in specific institutional conditions? What are the culturally embedded principles that facilitate the establishment of these interpersonal networks?

In their study of Hong Kong investors in Guangdong, Josephine Smart and Alan Smart (1991) found that for Hong Kong investors, gift exchange is a way of bridging the socialist and capitalist economic systems. Participation in the system of gift exchange with local Chinese officials helps the Hong Kong investors to "facilitate the speedy establishment of small-scale, socially mediated investment." Smart and Smart reported that personal relationships act as a catalyst to facilitate an investor's ease in establishing enterprises in China: "Paperwork can be speeded up, and negotiations are less detailed than in larger, bureaucratically mediated investments." The gift may be either in material form or a piece of information concerning whom one should talk to in order to get certain requests accepted or to ensure greater cooperation from local bureaucrats regarding production and management issues (Smart and Smart 1991, 227–28). As a comparison, Phyllis Andors's research on Shenzhen showed Japanese managers' frustration over their lack of *guanxi* with local Chinese officials and their disadvantage in obtaining special privileges when compared with their Hong Kong Chinese counterparts (Andors 1988, 35).

Flexible interpretation and implementation of laws

As suggested before, increasing local economic autonomy has provided the institutional basis for flexible arrangements between Taiwanese investors and Chinese officials at the macro level. At the micro level, the Chinese bureaucratic tradition of flexible interpretation and implementation of law has been another important element that affects the extent and form of the networks established between business and the state. The tension between the central state and local authority has a long history in China, and Chinese local bureaucrats have a tradition of avoiding the scrutiny of the central government while not creating direct conflicts with it (Min 1989). Local bureaucrats have developed the skill of making decisions based on what higher-level officials would not oppose rather than what they would allow. In Chinese it is called "looking for holes" (*zuan kongzi*), the philosophy being that "if something is not explicitly prohibited, then move ahead; if something is allowed, then use it to the hilt" (Vogel 1989). The application of such a philosophy in the local decision-making process is demonstrated by local officials' flexible interpretation and implementation of regulations imposed by the higher-level governments. There is a Chinese idiom that well reflects such superficial compliance with top-down policies and the tension between the high- and low-level authorities: "policies from the top, counter-strategies at the bottom" (*shang you zhengce xia you duice*). It means that whatever the policies from the top may be, there is always a way to implement them to the benefit of the locals.

The degree of local officials' autonomy and the width of the gap between written regulations and actual practices depends on how well such a culture of superficial compliance is developed and how fiscally independent the local government in question is. An official in charge of foreign trade and investment in Xiamen, Fujian province, explained to me why Guangdong has been one step ahead of Fujian in economic reform: "Leaders in Guangdong have been more willing and daring to push the limits of policies imposed by the central government. They are also readier to try out new strategies before they receive clear signals from Beijing." Facing the problem of a rapid decline in the tax revenues remitted to the central government,[10] Beijing began to tighten up its control of loans and project approvals in the early 1990s. However, in a city district of Guangzhou, an officer of the land bureau told me that since the central government imposed austerity policies in 1993 and increased restrictions on the size of lots that the district government can lease to developers, they had adopted the strategy of "small is beautiful," dividing the lot for one project into several smaller lots and granting land-use permission individually in order to avoid the involvement and scrutiny of higher government units. Such a strategy is but one of the many examples of how local Chinese officials, influenced by the tradition of central-local tension in Chinese history, take advantage of newly gained economic resources at the local level. The culture of *shang you zhengce xia you duice* is therefore rooted in the bureaucratic tradition in China and has blossomed in the current institutional context.

Taiwanese investors obtained favorable investment conditions from local officials on the basis of their understanding of such flexibility in the interpretation and implementation of regulations. A Taiwanese investor commented that the way he dealt with mainland Chinese officials was very similar to the way he had dealt with Taiwanese officials before.[11] Given the loose control of the Beijing central government on small businesses and the negotiable policy implementation in Taiwan, Taiwanese investors have found few cultural barriers to "finding the holes" in south China. The degree of flexibility tends to increase as one moves down through the levels of government bureaucracy.

Tax relief has been one of the most critical investment conditions. The standard enterprise income tax rate on foreign-funded joint ventures is 33 percent. Such ventures are totally exempt from this tax for the first two to three profitable years. For the following three to four years, only half of the tax is imposed; in many cases the tax-free period is extended, or tax rates kept at 15 percent, even after the official tax-free period was over. Other favorable investment conditions that local governments have the authority to grant to foreign ventures involved the transfer of profits out of China, relaxation of the rules on foreign exchange balance, reduction of power and water fees and land prices for factory buildings, exemption from import license requirements, provision of cheap loans, relaxation of restrictions on hiring nonlocal workers, exemption from social welfare contributions, and so on.[12] In addition, local banks have enjoyed a high degree of flexibility in granting loans: There are no upper limits on the size of loans to be granted to enterprises, nor are there any clearly stated policies on the criteria for loan approval. Underneath the stated policies, which are supposed to be applicable universally, the actual investment arrangements are mostly tailor-made for individual enterprises and investors, and the profitability of the investment package is

mostly dependent upon the relationship between the investor and the local officials. As one Taiwanese investor forthrightly put it, "No favorable
investment policies issued by the government can be as favorable as the
special deals I made with the local officials."

The increasing economic autonomy of Chinese local governments,
combined with the culture of Chinese local bureaucracy in their flexible
interpretation and implementation of centrally imposed laws, has provided an institutional framework in which the actual practices of gift exchange are carried out. Generally speaking, gift exchange differs from
market exchange in that it is highly personalized, embedded in ongoing
personal relations. The meaning and the effect of the gift depends on
who gives and who receives, and on what their relation is and will be.
Unlike market exchange, the value of the gift is not always measurable
in monetary terms, and gifts have a utility independent of their monetary
value (Sahlins 1972, 12). Meeting the expectations of reciprocity and
fair return is crucial in sustaining the exchange relationship. The timing
of returning the gift is not as fixed; a gift does not require immediate return. In fact, an exchange relationship does not come to a clear end after
one transaction; it is an indefinite indebtness between the participants
(Sahlins 1972; Malinowski 1961; Yang 1994). These general rules of gift
exchange are similar to those found in China (Tsao and Zhang 1992).

In the following sections I will examine the ways in which the principles of gift exchange in Chinese societies were applied in actual practice
between Taiwanese investors and local officials in south China. I have
identified three cultural-institutional elements that have shaped the practice of gift exchange: ways of assessing the value of a gift; the sense of
time in Chinese culture, which includes the meaning of efficiency, the
timelessness of the exchange relationship, and the importance of timing
in giving gifts; and the sense of space in Chinese culture, especially the
vague boundaries between the public and private domains. In addition,
linguistic commonality as a tool of communication between gift givers
and receivers, especially the understanding of the hidden messages underneath the spoken words, plays a crucial role in the establishment of
guanxi through gift exchanges.

Assessing the value of a gift

Gift exchange is not always an equal exchange in quantitative terms, and
the exchanged gift is not necessarily in material form. In fact, the art of
gift exchange is to maintain the balance between offering material favors
and expressing friendship and loyalty to each other as the basis of mutual
trust, which goes beyond immediate material benefits. Although mutual
benefit between gift givers and receivers is the ultimate principle, the

way to achieve it is more intricate; it is hardly as straightforward as buying privileges with cash. It takes cultural understanding to perceive where the balance point is and to assess the value of a gift in nonmonetary terms. In many cases the nonmaterial gift is even more valuable than the material gift if the former expresses a greater degree of loyalty. For example, a Chinese official might ask an overseas investor to be the sponsor of his or her child, who wishes to attend a U.S. university. The overseas investor might or might not have to take financial responsibility for the child, but being a sponsor involves greater risks than simply offering some luxurious gifts or cash. A favor that requires a certain degree of risk is far more effective in winning the trust of the other, and it paves a smoother path for future collaboration.

What matters is not just the gift itself but also the message carried by the gift-giving. A rare but not necessarily expensive gift that cannot be bought "just because one has the money" sometimes demonstrates greater sincerity and respect for the gift recipient. A Taiwanese businessman once brought a box of Chinese herbal medicine to a friend who was the vice director of the land bureau in a town where the Taiwanese planned to expand his factory. Found only deep in the mountains in the northeast of China, the medicine was rare and required special efforts and connections to obtain. The Taiwanese had learned that the medicine was just what the mother of the vice director needed. The gift was much appreciated, because it showed how much the Taiwanese was concerned with the well-being of the vice director's family, something very close to the heart of Chinese people. The return of the favor was a very generous condition in leasing an additional piece of land to the factory.[13]

Sense of time: Efficiency, timelessness, and timing

In market exchange, the object to be exchanged is detached from the persons involved in the exchange; therefore the exchange can take place between strangers. In gift exchange, the persons who are engaged in the exchange relationship determine the nature of the exchange. Unlike market exchange, gift exchange cannot happen between strangers. It happens only between those who have a certain type of preexisting interpersonal relationship, such as classmates, people from the same native place, relatives, colleagues, or those who were sent down to the rural areas together during the 1960s and 1970s. When such a preexisting social connection is absent, a potential participant is linked up with others through a mutual acquaintance and must establish a basis of familiarity before any of the parties can move further in the exchange relationship.

Although good interpersonal relationships facilitate the investment process and help move things along quickly and more efficiently, it takes time to build such relationships. When an investor boasts that he or she can solve any problem immediately by making a phone call to the governor of the town or the chief officer of the customs service, it means that a vast amount of time and energy has been invested in advance in order to reach such a level of "efficiency." Efficiency requires the patience to allow a trusting relationship to grow gradually over time. It is not just a matter of getting things done in the shortest possible time, but of establishing an effective interpersonal network that can facilitate the process of investment at critical moments.

Gift exchange is also a continuous practice. Unlike market exchange, the relationship between the participants in gift exchange does not end immediately after the exchange is completed. One is expected to return the favor that is given, which is seen as repaying the "debt" of favor. On the other hand, those who give others a favor see it as a form of saving. Eventually the one who has received the favour will have to repay the "debt" of favor, with interest. It is important to pay back more than what one has received, as a Chinese idiom says: "When given a foot, give back a yard." Since gift exchange is not always an equal exchange in quantitative terms, the "favor debts" rarely get cleared in one transaction. As a result, favors are accumulated and interpersonal relationships thickened as the exchanges of gifts and favours continue.

According to a Taiwanese investor, the least effective way of making friends with local officials is to shower them with cash or luxurious gifts right in the beginning or to present the gift in a once-and-for-all fashion. Instead, a "constant drizzle" will facilitate a more stable and lasting relationship. He explained that each time he visits his factory in China, he brings with him a couple of books of Chinese poems for a local official who enjoys literature very much. Sometimes the gift would be, for example, an out-of-print novel written in the 1920s. The gifts have never been extraordinary, yet they were given constantly to remind the receiver of the friendship of the giver and the favor he owed to the latter. Eventually the Taiwanese won the trust of the official and was seen as a reliable man to work with. He could now go see the chief of the public security bureau in town directly, without having to file his case through the bureaucratic jungle, when he needed help.[14]

It is also important to present the gift in advance, before asking for favours. A joint venture that has a number of trucks frequently delivering materials and finished products had managed to maintain a good relationship with the traffic policemen in town. Three times a year, before each of the three major Chinese festivals—the Dragon Boat Festival, Midautumn Day, and the Chinese New Year—the company presented imported liquor or other gifts to the public security bureau. One Chinese

154

New Year, the company did not send the gifts. As a result, right after the New Year, their trucks started getting speeding tickets. The company got the message and brought the gifts to the bureau. But the gifts were returned. The policemen told the company that they could not accept the gifts because "it is obvious that you are trying to bribe us."

Sense of space: Vague boundaries between the public and private domains

It is often argued that Chinese do not see the public (*gong*) and the private (*si*) domains as polar opposites.[15] Instead, the public and the private are seen as being on a continuous spectrum (Yuzo 1994) or as being concentric circles. *Gong* is a congregation of private, individual entities, and there are different levels of publicness. Therefore, the expansion of *si* is not always considered as an invasion of *gong*, but rather as an adjustment of the level of publicness (or privateness) in different situations. Such statements can be overly generalized, but the way Chinese local officials deal with overseas Chinese investors reveals the validity of the general observation. As China continues to move away from a socialist system in which the public sector is pervasive, and while a clear legal framework redefining the private has yet to be built, border crossing between *gong* and *si* has been a matter that mixes legal considerations with culturally informed interpersonal relations.

In the negotiation process between Taiwanese investors and local Chinese officials, the benefit that an official acquires from offering a favor to an investor does not have to be seen as an act entirely for personal gain nor a violation of the public interest, if it is performed properly. For an investor, the art of offering favors to an individual official involves not putting him or her on the spot. It is important to take care of the latter's colleagues and not to embarrass any particular person. On the other hand, the investor needs some special friends on whom he or she can count when the need arises. The key is to maintain a good relationship with everyone in a bureaucratic unit while at the same time making a special effort to build stronger relationships with selected ones.

Gong and *si* are often intertwined, and private and public interests are not always in conflict. A Taiwanese investor commented that the best way to maintain a relationship with an official is to offer him or her the opportunity to gain personal benefit while at the same time benefiting his or her organization. For example, a broker trying to sell machinery to a state-owned factory would find it easier to get the contract if he or she can arrange a trip for the relevant government decision makers to visit the foreign equipment supplier. Those who get to represent the factory on the trip gain the direct personal benefit of a free trip abroad, and therefore owe a favor to the broker, while at the same time the entire organization benefits from getting more information about the new equipment. In fact, a U.S. equipment supplier told me that a free trip to visit suppliers abroad has routinely been part of the deal in his negotiations with his Chinese customers. In the typical one- to two-week visit to the United States, one day was spent visiting the supplier's factory, and the rest of the trip usually included visits to Las Vegas, New York, Los Angeles, and so on.

As the benefits are shared by the group, so is the responsibility. One of the most widely used terms in the government is "collective discussion." The official in charge of granting import licenses might tell the applicant, who wishes to receive more-generous tax breaks on imported materials, that the case needs to be discussed collectively with his or her colleagues in the department. This means that the favor expected from the applicant will be shared by a group of officials at different ranks, as will the risks involved in granting a special tax break to the applicant.

Hidden messages in the language

As mentioned before, when asked about the major advantage of investing in China compared to other overseas production sites in Southeast Asia, most Taiwanese investors' answer was the common language they share with local Chinese. In gift exchange relations, participants need to express their expectations explicitly enough in order to obtain satisfactory results. Yet it is also important to demonstrate that the exchange relationship is based not just on the immediate material benefits but also on a long-term friendship. One should not expect anything in return when offering a gift or favor to a true friend. Therefore, the expectation of the gift giver cannot be too explicit if it is to look sincere, respectful, and not too pressing. On the other hand, the gift receiver is expected to understand what is expected of him or her, without explicit explanations, if he or she is a true friend of the gift giver. To reach such a subtle balance between explicitness and implicitness requires effective communication between the participants.

Taiwanese speak Hokkien, a dialect they share with the people of southern Fujian. They also speak Mandarin, the official language in both Taiwan and mainland China. The linguistic connection has been an effective tool for communication between overseas investors and their local agents. Although it is not the only tool with which to build trusting relationships, doors open more quickly when knocked on by someone speaking a familiar language. Sharing a common language does not mean simply effective communication in technical terms. More important is the understanding of hidden messages, which determines the effectiveness of the communication. On many occasions, what is spoken is not as impor-

Fig. 2. Mainland Chinese officials entertaining Taiwanese capitalists in a karaoke restaurant. Note the TV
monitor in the top right-hand corner. (Photo by You-tien
Hsing)

tant as what is unspoken. Therefore, it takes both technical understanding
of the spoken words and cultural understanding of the hidden meaning to
fully grasp the expectations of the participants in gift exchange.

For example, when an investor asks for a greater allowance of products to be sold in local markets, the official in charge might tell the investor, "Let me *yanjiu yanjiu* about it." Literally, *yanjiu* means "do
research" or "look into the matter carefully." Yet the conclusion of the
"research" often depends on the favor that the applicant is willing to offer to the official. Since the pronunciation of *yanjiu* is close to that of the
Mandarin words meaning "cigarettes and liquor," in earlier days *yanjiu*

literally implied a demand for cigarettes and liquor as gifts.[16] The three elements described earlier—that is, the type (and therefore the monetary and use value) of gift, the timing of the gift, and the occasion on which the gift is presented and received—are parts of the hidden message. If the cigarettes offered by the applicant are not good enough, the official may reject the gift and at the same time offer a different kind of cigarette (usually the most expensive brand) to the applicant as a way to show the latter the type of cigarette that is preferred. If the official gives the applicant her or his home address and invites the applicant to have a cup of tea with him or her at home, it usually implies that the gift should be presented and the negotiation made at the official's residence rather than at the office. Furthermore, whether the official accepts the gift or not indicates the chances that the favor will be granted to the applicant. If the official feels the favor asked by the applicant is too unrealistic or beyond his or her realm of influence, the former will not accept the gift as a way to tell the latter that he or she is unable to help.

Conclusions

The concentration and the rapid growth of Taiwanese capital in south China since the late 1980s suggests that transnational capital does not flow across this space without constraints. National borders might be threatened in the age of globalization, yet cultural-institutional maps still dictate the direction and the way in which transnational capital expands and is accumulated. Based on shared cultural codes in gift exchange and shaped by increasing local autonomy in China, Taiwanese investors have successfully established interpersonal relationships with local Chinese officials, and these relationships in turn have consolidated their business partnerships.

Gift exchange may be seen as a general principle of the establishment of interpersonal relationships in Chinese societies. It might also be safe to argue that Chinese tend to rely on gift-exchange-based interpersonal relationships more than some other peoples (Ruan 1993). Yet the importance of interpersonal ties is not unique to Chinese societies, nor is gift exchange a principle of establishing intepersonal relations adopted only by Chinese. What we can be more certain about is that the practice and form of gift exchange vary between societies depending on the specific historical and institutional context. The culturally available tools that facilitate the practice of gift exchange and hence the establishment of interpersonal networks between Taiwanese investors and local Chinese officials include the linguistic connection, the understanding of the non-market value of gifts, and the sense of time and space in Chinese culture.

The principle is applied and the tools are used in an institutional context characterized by the increasing autonomy of local Chinese officials and their tradition of flexible intepretation and implementation of the regulations imposed by the central government.

This is far from a complete picture of the negotiation between local culture and transnational capital. The cultural and linguistic affinity between Taiwanese investors and local Chinese officials might be necessary in establishing the social networks, yet it is not sufficient to guarantee a successful business operation in south China. Moreover, this cultural and linguistic affinity, which is suggested by Taiwanese investors themselves as one of the most important reasons for their interest in investment in south China, needs to be problematized. Cultural affinity does not always come naturally simply because both Chinese and Taiwanese are "descendants of the Yellow Emperor" (*huangdi zisun*). The establishment of *guanxi* is conditioned by other principles of social organization, such as kinship, place of origin, and regional dialect. Most Taiwanese have ancestors who migrated from southern Fujian province three or four hundred years ago, and as a result they speak Hokkien, the dialect of southern Fujian. Many of them choose to invest in their ancestral hometowns for both sentimental and pragmatic reasons. In one's hometown, among people of one's own dialect group, one finds friends and reestablishes social networks more quickly. But cultural affinity does not always produce positive results in business operations, either. After more than forty years of rivalry between the regimes in mainland China and Taiwan and the social separation between the two territories, the opening of the border in 1987 did not automatically heal the old wounds. Tension and distrust between Taiwanese and their local Chinese partners and employees is not unheard of. More often than not, legal disputes over business arrangements, labor relations, and personal affairs make the headlines. A Chinese official even commented that "Taiwanese know too much of the dark side of the Chinese."[17]

Finally, my analysis of the autonomy of China's local governments is not to be understood in terms of a dichotomy between state and society. The dynamism of development comes from the interaction among national government, local government, foreign capital, and new social forces that are generated from such interactions. As Yang (1994, 45) has pointed out, although interpersonal relations are usually regarded as being in line with bureaucratic power, whether as official corruption or as patron-client ties,[18] they are also a force working against state power. The establishment of interpersonal ties between Taiwanese investors and Chinese local officials should be seen as a way for local bureaucrats to bypass the control of the central state and link up directly with the outside world.

Acknowledgment

I would like to thank Aihwa Ong and Donald Nonini for their insightful and detailed comments on an earlier version of this paper. I also benefited from the criticisms of Manuel Castells, Li Yih-yuan, Wong Siu-lun, Shirley S.-Y. Liu, Michael Watts, Dick Walker, Gillian Hart, Hsia Chu-joe, Schive Chi, Mayfair Yang, Zhu Yung-han, Chu-Chia Steve Lin, Gary Hamilton, Annalee Saxenian, and Peter Hall at different stages of this research.

Notes

[1] This is a revised version of an essay to be published in a forthcoming issue of *Environment and Planning A* entitled "Blood, Thicker than Water: Interpersonal Relations and Taiwanese Investment in Southern China."

[2] Meijie is not the real name of the town. The analysis in this paper is based on interviews conducted in Taiwan, Hong Kong, Guangdong (the Pearl River delta), Fujian (Xiamen Special Economic Zone), and Shanghai between 1991 and 1994. I conducted interviews with 54 local Chinese officials and 134 Taiwanese and Hong Kong investors and factory managers and Chinese managers, staff, and workers in the factories. I have focused my factory interviews on the export fashion shoe industry, and I stayed in two Taiwanese-financed fashion shoe factories in the Pearl River delta for one month.

[3] The government of the People's Republic of China announced that the pledged Taiwanese investment in China was $20 billion U.S.; the realized investment can be around $10 billion U.S. (Kao et al. 1995, 55).

[4] *China Times Weekly* 36, September 1992.

[5] *World Journal*, December 23, 1992. This phenomenon of land sales as the major revenue source also occurred in some inland regions, such as Sichuan province.

[6] China Interview A-1, A-2, E-1, F-1.

[7] According to a survey of 319 Taiwanese firms in China in 1991, 68 percent of the products were sold in the markets outside Taiwan and China (Kao et al. 1992, 132). This has changed since the early 1990s. An increasing number of overseas investors from Taiwan and Hong Kong have begun to explore the domestic market in China, which is in fact one of the main reasons for their investment in China.

[8] China interview O-1.

[9] China interviews A-1, A-2, A-3, B-2, C-1, D-4, F-1, G-2, G-3, H-3. This finding is confirmed by a survey cited in Lee-in Chen Chiu and Chung Chin (1992). Among 97 surveyed Taiwanese investors in China, 82 percent saw similar language and culture to be important factors in their move to China, second only to

the low cost of wage labor. The low cost of wage labor here included the wages of both operators and managers. Further, Taiwanese investment in China has grown faster than that in the ASEAN countries since the late 1980s (see figure 1). Although other investment conditions have played an important role, language was one of the major problems for Taiwanese investors in the ASEAN countries. What should be noted here is that the figures in the table show only the registered projects. The real figures may be five times higher (in millions of U.S.$).

[10] At the beginning of the reform, the central government received more than 80 percent of the nation's total tax revenue. By 1994 its share had dropped to 28 percent. (*Zhongshi Zhoukan*, January 1, 1995).

[11] China interview E-1.

[12] *China Market*, July 1992.

[13] China interview C-2.

[14] China interview E-2.

[15] Here the use of *public domain* and *private domain* is different from what Habermas (1989) has referred to in his discussion of Western democracies.

[16] In recent years, a favorable conclusion of *yanjiu* requires gifts that are more valuable than cigarettes and liquor.

[17] China interview 0-3.

[18] This is the view held by Walder (1986). In his study of the labor-management relationship in Chinese industry, Walder suggested that the gift-exchange-based interpersonal relationship (or to use his term, "networks of instrumental-personal ties") is a substitute for the "impersonal market transaction in a setting where such markets are restricted and scarcity prevails" (Walder 1986, 26). The relations are wielded by party cadres and officials to control their dependants.

References

Andors, Phyllis. 1988. "Women and Work in Shenzhen." *Bulletin of Concerned Asian Scholars* 20, no. 3: 22–41.

Bourdieu, Pierre. 1972. *Outline of a Theory of Practice*. Cambridge: Cambridge University Press.

Chiu, Lee-in Chen and Chin Chung. An assessment of Taiwan's indirect investment toward Mainland China. Taipei, Taiwan, Republic of China: Chung-Hua Institution for Economic Research [1992]. Series title: Occasional paper series (Chung-hua ching chi yen chiu yuan); no. 9201.

Curtin, Philip. 1984. *Cross-Cultural Trade in World History*. New York: Cambridge University Press.

Evans, Peter. 1979. *Dependent Development: The Alliance of Multinational, State, and Local Capital in Brazil*. Princeton: Princeton University Press.

Habermas, Jurgen. 1989. *The Structural Transformation of the Public Sphere: An Inquiry into the Category of Bourgeois Society.* Translated by Thomas Burger with the assistance of Frederick Lawrence. Cambridge, MA.: MIT Press. Series title: Studies in contemporary German social thought.

Hamilton, Gary, ed. 1991. *Business Networks and Economic Development in East and Southeast Asia.* [Hong Kong]: Centre of Asian Studies, University of Hong Kong. Series title: Centre of Asian Studies occasional papers and monographs; no. 99.

———. 1996. "Overseas Chinese Capitalism." In Tu Wei-Ming, ed., *The Confucian Dimensions of Industrial East Asia*, pp. 1–23. Cambridge, MA: Harvard University Press.

Harvey, David. 1989. *The Condition of Postmodernity: An Enquiry into the Origins of Cultural Change.* Oxford [England]; Cambridge, MA: Blackwell.

Ho, Samuel P.-S., and Ralph W. Huenemann. 1984. *China's Open Door Policy: The Quest for Foreign Technology and Capital.* Vancouver: University of British Columbia Press.

Jesudason, James V. 1994. "The Changing Logic of Chinese Business in Malaysia: National and Traditional Dimensions." Paper presented at the Conference on Transnationalization of Overseas Chinese Capitalism: Networks, Nation-States, and Imagined Communities, University of Singapore, August 8–13.

Kao, Charles H.-C., Chu-Chia Steve Lin, Cher Hsu, and Wennie Lin. 1995. *The Taiwan Investment Experience in Mainland China: A Firsthand Report* [in Chinese]. Taipei: Commonwealth.

Kao, Charles H.-C., Joseph S. Lee, and Chu-Chia Steve Lin. 1992. *An Empirical Study of Taiwan Investment on Mainland China* [in Chinese]. Taipei: Commonwealth.

Lim, Linda Y.-C., and L. A. Peter Gosling, eds. 1983. *The Chinese in Southeast Asia.* 2 vols. Ann Arbor: Center for South and Southeast Asian Studies, University of Michigan.

Malinowski, Bronislaw. 1961. *Argonauts of the Western Pacific: An Account of Native Enterprise and Adventure in the Archipelagoes of Melanesian New Guinea.* Preface by Sir James George Frazer. New York: E.P. Dutton & Co. Series title: Studies in economics and political science.

Mauss, Marcel. 1967. *The Gift: Forms and Functions of Exchange in Archaic Societies.* Translated by Ian Cunnison. With an introduction by E.E. Evans-Pritchard. New York: Norton.

McVey, Ruth, ed. 1992. *Southeast Asian Capitalists.* Ithaca, NY: Cornell University Press.

Min, Tu-ki. 1989. *National Polity and Local Power: The Transformation of Late Imperial China.* Edited by Philip Kuhn and Timothy Brook. Cambridge, MA: Council on East Asian Studies, Harvard University.

Naughton, Barry. 1987. "The Decline of Central Control over Investment in Post-Mao China." In D. Lampton, ed., *Policy Implementation in Post-Mao China*, pp. 51–80. Berkeley: University of California Press.

Ohmae, K. 1991. *The Borderless World: Power and Strategy in the Interlinked Economy*. London: Fontana.

Oi, Jean C. 1991. "The Shifting Balance of Power in Central-Local Relations: Local Government Response to Fiscal Austerity in Rural China." Paper presented at the China Faculty Seminar, University of California at Berkeley, April 18.

Ong, Aihwa. 1987. *Spirits of Resistance and Capitalist Discipline: Factory Women in Malaysia*. Albany: State University of New York Press.

Redding, S. G. 1990. *The Spirit of Chinese Capitalism*. Berlin: Walter De Gruyter.

Ruan, Danching. 1993. "Interpersonal Networks and Workplace Controls in Urban China." *Australian Journal of Chinese Affairs* 20: 89–105.

Sahlins, Marshall. 1972. *Stone Age Economics*. Chicago: Aldine.

Smart, Josephine, and Alan Smart. 1991. "Personal Relations and Divergent Economies: A Case Study of Hong Kong Investment in South China." *International Journal of Urban and Regional Research* 15, no. 2: 216–33.

Solinger, Dorothy J. 1987. "Uncertain Paternalism: Tensions in Recent Regional Restructuring in China." *International Regional Science Review* 11, no. 1: 23–42.

Sung, Yun-wing. 1994. "Hong Kong and the Economic Integration of the China Circle." Paper presented at the China Circle Conference, Hong Kong, December 8–11.

Tsao, Jin-ching, and Zhang Le-tian. 1992. "The Social and Cultural Characteristics of Traditional Villages: '*Renching*' and Network of *Guanxi*—A Village in the North of Zhejiang." *Tansuo yu zhengming* 2: 51–59.

Tu, Wei-ming, ed. 1996. *Confucian Traditions in East Asian Modernity: Moral Education and Economic Culture in Japan and the Four Mini-dragons*. Cambridge, MA.: Harvard University Press.

Vogel, Ezra. 1989. *One Step Ahead in China: Guangdong Under Reform*. Cambridge, MA: Harvard University Press.

Walder, Andrew G. 1986. *Communist Neo-Traditionalism: Work and Authority in Chinese Industry*. Berkeley: University of California Press.

Wong, Christine P.-W. 1992. "Fiscal Reform and Local Industrialization: The Problematic Sequencing of Reform in Post-Mao China." *Modern China* 18, no. 2: 197–227.

Wong, Siu-lun. 1988. *Emigrant Entrepreneurs: Shanghai Industrialists in Hong Kong*. Oxford: Oxford University Press.

———. 1992. "Business Networks, Cultural Values, and the State in Hong Kong and Singapore." Paper presented at the Third Soka University Pacific Basin Symposium, September 14–16.

Yang, Mayfair Mei-hui. 1988. "The Modernity of Power in the Chinese Socialist Order." *Cultural Anthropology* 3: 408–27.

———. 1989. "The Gift Economy and State Power in China." *Comparative Studies in Society and History* 31: 25–54.

———. 1994. *Gifts, Favors, and Banquets: The Art of Social Relationships in China*. Ithaca, NY: Cornell University Press.

Yuzo, Mizoguchi. 1994. "A Comparison of the Concept of Public and Private in China and Japan" [in Chinese]. *The Twenty-first Century Bimonthly* 21: 86–97.

Zhang Amei and Zou Gang. 1994. "Foreign Trade Decentralization and Its Impact on Central-Local Relations." In Jia H. and Lin Z., eds., *Changing Central-Local Relations in China: Reform and State Capacity*, pp. 153–80. Boulder: Westview.

Zweig, David. 1989. "Internationalizing China's Countryside: The Domestic Politics of Rural Exports." Paper presented at the Nineteenth Sino-American Conference on Mainland China, Taipei, June 12–14.

Part 3

Transnational Identities and Nation-State Regimes of Truth and Power

Preface

In her essay in this part, Ong discusses the ways in which new alternative narratives of modernity that reinforce the localizations of citizen-subjects by nation-state regimes are being worked up by Asian economic and political elites. These narratives may either enter directly into "state projects of modernity" or paradoxically take the form of declaration of transnational Chinese solidarity—the "glow of Chinese fraternity" and the idea of "Greater China"—but presuppose the disciplining of citizens by nation-states: "Chinese culture," as that which presumes to order harmoniously the three regimes of nation-state, family, and capitalist workplace, is but a metaphor for the stern hand of state discipline, regulation, and control. Much of the discourse promoting "Confucianism" by these elites—in China, Taiwan, Singapore, and elsewhere—appears due to their belief that Confucianism effects just such a metaphorical reduction.

By way of contrast, the other essays in part 3 address in various ways the theme of Chinese transnational strategies of capital accumulation vis-à-vis the localizing operations of nation-state, workplace, and familistic regimes of truth and power. Nonini writes of the ways in which working-class men from Malaysia travel to work for labor contractors in Japan in order to avoid being confined to the Malaysian labor market in their pursuit of economic capital and being stigmatized as "Chinese" by Malaysian state functionaries. These men take advantage of the relative immobility of the women with whom they have relations in Malaysia—their mothers and wives—who care for their children and maintain their households while they are overseas. At the same time, as undocumented laborers, they must evade the Japanese state's regime of regulation.

Fig. 1. A Chinese "astronaut" floating in space with lifelines to Hong Kong, Australia, and Canada. (Reprinted with permission from the *South China Morning Post*, March 20, 1989)

In contrast, wealthy Hong Kong entrepreneurs in Vancouver, Canada, studied by Mitchell, are able to elude the localizations imposed on immigrants by the Canadian nation-state by qualifying for its "business immigration program" through their investments and by directly becoming citizens. They simultaneously accumulate economic and social capital and discipline both middle-class Hong Kong emigrants, who fear being denied entry or permanent residence in Canada, and racially antagonistic Anglo Canadians who are anxious they may disinvest from Canada. The intimate connection between gender, age, and family regime for the elite Hong Kong entrepreneurs who ride the trans-Pacific shuttles between Hong Kong and the west coast of North America is encapsulated in the cartoon of the patriarch "astronaut" (see figure 1): He vaults the Pacific while other family members remain "in their place." (Ong 1993).

Outside of part 3, Liu's essay in part 1 discusses sojourning Chinese scholars in London who seek to obtain both educational capital—degrees and certificates—and economic capital by escaping the confines of China on government fellowships, but who then reconstitute a family like hierarchy privileging seniority in residence in their domestic arrangements in Great Britian.

References

Ong, Aihwa. 1993. "On the Edge of Empires: Flexible Citizenship Among Chinese in Diaspora." *positions* 1, 3: 745–78.

Chapter Six

Chinese Modernities: Narratives of Nation and of Capitalism

Aihwa Ong

Modern China is the product of the conjoining of modernist discourses origi-nating in the West and native institutions . . ., historical social conditions . . ., and native reaction-formation. . . . Therefore, any diagnosis of power in con-temporary China is a critique neither simply of the West nor of China's tradi-tion, but of their offspring: China's modernity.

Mayfair M.-h. Yang

The destiny of Singapore remains very much a rewriting and a re-imagining by each generation of what is possible. . . . How can it be otherwise for a na-tion that was born of imagination, erected on dreams and has created a net-work of internal, unseen information to reach beyond herself?

Ban Kah Choon

This essay explores how, in contemporary Asia, "Chinese culture" be-comes the raw material in imaginaries of modernity. Social imaginaries have been called the "constructed landscapes of collective aspirations . . . now mediated through the complex prism of modern media" (Ap-padurai 1990, 2). I take modernity as an evolving process of imagination and practice in particular historically situated formations. Metanarra-tives with different claims to truth—about culture, the people, their as-pirations—are knowledge-power systems (Foucault 1979, 1982, 1991) that construct "imagined communities" (Anderson 1982) of belonging in the modern world. Scholars have tended to study such imaginaries as the work of nation-states (Anderson 1982; Bhabha 1992; Yang 1994), but

transnational imaginaries must be taken into account as important formations in late capitalism (see Gupta 1992).

In Asia, contending sites of power—nation-states, capitalist centers—
articulate different visions of modernity that are in tension and complicity
with each other. I use the term "imagined community" for both the imaginary work of a single nation-state as well as the imaginaries of other kinds
of collectivities—for example, those brought together by the reconfigurations of global capitalism. In this essay I will discuss how Chinese culture
is variously reified and deployed in two competing discursive systems: the
modernist imaginary of the nation-state (emphasizing essentialism, terri-
toriality, and fixity) in tension with the modernist imaging of entrepreneurial capitalism (celebrating hybridity, deterritorialization, and fluidity).

In recent decades, scholars have dealt with the issue of modernity in
two ways. Scholars such as Mayfair Yang (1994; see also Corrigan and
Sayer 1988) view modernity as a state project, drawing on Michel Foucault's concept of modern power as the multidimensional interplay between technologies of power and embodied practices. Calling this modern
power "biopolitics," Foucault (1979, 1991) notes that the modern state is
characterized by its productive and creative capacity to develop rules and
rituals that increase the surveillance and control of the population in order
to ensure its health, productivity, and security, and thus those of the state as
well. While Foucault was deeply troubled by state rationality, he focused
on ruling through consent and ignored state repression. A larger view of
the disciplinary constitution of state power should include the coercive elements—those instrumentalities that are both productive and repressive,
and which must be ideologically justified in cultural terms.[1]

In contrast to the notion of modernity as a state project, other scholars have paid increasing attention to the modernities that are produced
out of the articulations, productions, and struggles between capitalist
forces and local communities in different parts of the world (Ong 1987,
1991, 1996; Nonini 1993; Friedman 1992; Hannerz 1989). Allan Pred
and Michael Watts (1993) refer to the confrontations between local cultural forms and the global forces associated with capitalism as the reworking of "multiple modernities." Their approach seems to suggest that
modernities in non-Western countries are only reactive formations or resistances to Western capitalism.

Shifting from that Western vantage point, I consider modernist projects as knowledge-power processes that arise out of tensions between
local and regional forces, and not merely in reaction to the West. I reject
the simplistic binary opposition of the West and the non-West in accounting for emerging multiple modernities. Alternative visions of
modernity may exist within a single country or a single region of the

172

world; their configurations are to a large extent conditioned by geopolitics and the dynamism of global capitalism. For instance, up until recently, nationalist views in Asia posed an opposition between socialist and capitalist visions of modernity.[2] Furthermore, there are alternative modernities expressed by subalterns that are marginalized or even suppressed by the dominant forms (see Scott 1985; Ong 1987; Nonini 1993). Here I wish to attend to dominant imaginaries about the nation and about capitalism and their regulatory influences over transnational publics associated with Asian capitalism.

In Asia today, state projects of modernity are engaged in the production of national subjects, whereas alternative modernities associated with flexible accumulation celebrate self-propelling subjects. Major themes in this negotiation of modernity are the tension between the nation and its subjects and the tension between Asianness and the West (see also Duara 1995). There is a double "cultural liminality" constructed through ideological struggles between the nation and marginalized subjects (Bhabha 1990, 299) as well as through the dialectic construction of difference across political borders. National discourses of modernity are ideological productions of appropriate national subjects who are culturally homogenized, biopoliticized, and localized within the national territory, while capitalist narratives of modernity—such as those about "Greater China" (an overseas Chinese capitalist zone)—celebrate subjects in diaspora and the ways their hybridity and flexibility suggest transnational solidarities. These rival imaginaries invoke Chineseness—one in terms of the fixity of the nation and culture, the other in terms of the fluidity of triumphalist capitalism—in unstable and fluid discourses that, as a discursive matrix, can at strategic moments claim a unified vision of Asia-Pacific modernity.

Government officials, academics, and business leaders are the key formulators of triumphalist Chinese capitalism. By virtue of the high regard in which most Asians hold their leaders, ideas articulated by them acquire a special truth claim, and they influence national consciousness and popular understanding of changing relations between state and subject and between culture and capitalism. I will discuss how these discourses variously constuct modernity as a state project in China and in Singapore, how modernity can be seen as the ideological construction of transnational Chinese capitalism, and the ways these narratives intervene in the moral economies of nations. While visions of mobile Chinese capitalism may threaten the integrity of the nation-state, modern regimes of power can also claim the fixity of Chinese cultural traditions for their own nation-building purposes. Tensions between constructions of fixed and fluid Chinese subjectivities are played out in the shifting dynamics involved in the renegotiation of relations between national regimes and diasporic capitalism and in the reenvisioning of a new geosymbolic space in this region of the world.

Chinese Modernity as a State Project

The nationalism question in post-Mao China has been broached in terms of the differences between the majority Han and minority groups (Schein 1992) as well as the ideological struggles among the Han themselves (Yang 1994; Rofel 1994). There are growing tensions between those who see in market reforms the route to China's future and members of the Communist Party who still adhere to the view of a socialist future with the state maintaining central control over the economy and society.

Up until the late 1970s, official Chinese national identity was firmly determined by socialism and clearly defined by the territorial boundedness of the mainland. Chinese in Macao, Hong Kong, and Taiwan, as well as Chinese citizens living in other countries (*huaqiao*) were alternately protected and neglected (Fitzgerald 1972) as China tried to establish relations with newly independent Southeast Asian countries. China's isolation from the world community allowed it to secure its identity as a Communist giant that claimed leadership of the struggling third world.

This national identity, which was located in a particular territory (the mainland) and in a specific history (that of the People's Republic), came under pressure when China opened its doors to global capitalism in the early 1980s. An immediate influx of investments by Hong Kong and overseas Chinese soon made the Pearl River delta, centered in Guangzhou (Canton), Guangdong Province, the world's largest manufacturing center. A Hong Kong banker claims that "Hong Kong is the prime driver of the greatest economic takeoff in history."[3] Indeed, undeterred by the 1989 Tiananmen crackdown, Hong Kong investors led other Chinese capitalists from Taiwan, Singapore, Malaysia, Thailand, and elsewhere in pouring over $2 billion U.S. into Guangdong Province and in employing some three million mainland workers by 1991.[4] Today, ethnic Chinese from outside China are the major investors and manufacturers in south China's development.

The integration of this coastal strip with second-tier cities (Sassen 1994) such as Hong Kong, Singapore, Taipei, Bangkok, Kuala Lumpur, and Jakarta produced an influx of overseas Chinese people, capital, and Western investments, in addition to uncontrollable flows of information and media images. Increased trade, traffic, and interaction stimulated rising demands for foreign goods, ideas, and cultures as well as the desire to travel to other countries, called "leave-the-country fever" (see Liu's and

Yang's essays in this volume). In particular, the presence and activities of Chinese from overseas (*haiwai huaren*), mainly Southeast Asia, created all kinds of border-crossing networks that seem to suboridinate political differences to trade interests. Overseas Chinese are viewed as bridge builders who, especially after the Tiananmen crackdown, emerged as a critical group in providing the capital and expertise to fuel China's economic takeoff. They are lauded in the press for, among other things, "adding wings to the [China] tiger" (Ong 1996). These cross-cutting ties between mainland and oveseas Chinese, between mainlanders and foreign investors, and between Chinese socialism and foreign capitalism all help to disrupt the political borders of the nation.

Thus globalization, with its transnational flows and networks, can weaken a sense of national integrity. Stuart Hall notes that England, suffering from economic decline, has regressed to a defensive and dangerous form of national identity, which is driven in part by reliving the past through myth and in part by racism (Hall 1991; 25–26). Paradoxically, China, which in the 1980s embarked upon a buoyant wave of global capitalism, is also now experiencing a crisis of cultural identity, brought about by the influx of foreign capital, overseas Chinese, new commodities, images, and desires that bypass government rules and generally challenge the image of the socialist state.

When market reforms were first launched by Deng Xiaoping, the regime was careful to define Chinese modernity in a fixed territorial position vis-à-vis other nation-states in the world. Despite Deng's call to mimic Hong Kong, "socialism with Chinese characteristics" represents an attempt to domesticate freewheeling capitalism through state control and to drive home the Deng logic that socialism will use capitalism for increasing the power of the Chinese nation-state ("It doesn't matter whether the cat is black or white as long as it catches mice"). The goal was to raise the overall standard of living within a hundred years so that China can escape its status as a developing country, thus strengthening its global position in regard to other countries. The challenge for the state is to balance its political and territorial interests against the promiscuous opportunism of overseas Chinese capitalism. While China welcomes offshore Chinese investments, mainland officials remain ambivalent and suspicious of capitalism, and of overseas Chinese who appear to have little sentiment for the motherland.

Indeed, nationalist fears have been fueled by an alternative vision that challenges state control of what constitutes Chinese modernity. This is the trope of "Greater China" (*da Zhonghua*), a term coined by overseas economists to describe the increasing economic integration among China, Hong Kong, and Taiwan produced by globalization. The combined foreign currency reserves of Taiwan, Hong Kong, and Singapore, together with those of China, it is claimed, would place the Chinese bloc way ahead of Japan as Asia's first-rank economic giant (Kotkin 1992, 197). Indeed, Greater China as a zone founded on overseas Chinese capital challenges the modernist project of the Chinese state. Some writers have gone so far as to claim that overseas Chinese, not the nation-state, are "the mother of China's [economic] revolution" (cited in Chen 1994). While this view may be more popular in the southern provinces, such as Guangdong and Fujian, that have benefited most from overseas Chinese investments, it is strongly rejected by mainland officials, who feel intense tension over capitalism and worry about the erosion of state control.

This position echoes the earlier message of Meiji Japan, the first Asian country to undertake capitalism for state-strengthening. It also resonates with the ideological positions of China's capitalist neighbors, countries such as Singapore, Malaysia, and Indonesia, which are represented by the Association of Southeast Asian Nations (ASEAN). Indeed, ASEAN countries have been proponents of the strong bureaucratic state and the belief that the alliance of state and private (mainly ethnic Chinese) capital should remain under state control (Higgot and Robison 1985). Thus although Southeast Asia states are, unlike China, unambivalent about capitalism, they are also heavily invested in retaining state control over capital. Any hopes for converting Greater China into a political entity are dashed against the strong Southeast Asian states and the implacable resistance of China herself (see Uhalley 1994).

On the mainland, patriotic scholars are quick to reject Greater China as a bankers' fantasy, an illusion of outsiders greedy to cash in on China's booming economy. They fear that any ideological recognition of a Chinese transnational capitalist zone will undermine China as a territorially based political entity. In the fall of 1993 I visited China's leading special economic zones in Shenzhen, Xiamen, Shantou, and Guangzhou/Canton, all in south China, to discover local reactions to overseas Chinese capital. At a conference at Shantou University, Professor Huang Kunzhang asserted:

> From the national perspective, we reject the concept of Greater China. From the the legal perspective, we cannot mix up different nationals [simply] because of their having the same culture and language as we do. . . . [Similarly,] most Southeast Asian Chinese reject this concept.
>
> [But] Taiwan likes this view of Greater China. It is a business concept to capitalize on China's development. Western scholars see a stronger China and project their own model of a larger China by exaggerating data on overseas Chinese development.
>
> This problem must be seen at the level of government-to-government relations. We see things as a business matter. Overseas Chinese come not because

they are patriotic but because of investment benefits. We need to clearly differentiate among different kinds of Chinese—those who are nationals, and those who are from overseas.

Professor Huang's contrast of profits and patriotism has been picked up by other scholars who elaborated on the differences between the mainland and Chinese from other countries. Foreign Chinese nationals invest in China primarily for profits, not because they were loyal to the Chinese nation-state. They are opportunists and parvenus eager to enrich themselves while incidentally benefitting China. Others acknowledge that overseas Chinese have different degrees of attachment to the ancestral homeland and that mainlanders cannot assume that they all have China's real interests at heart. This view was reiterated for me in Guangzhou by the director of overseas Chinese affairs.

> Overseas Chinese emigrants must be distinguished by generations. The first generation has sentiments for China. The second generation, educated in the West, has not given up the concept of ancestral home but their affection is not as deep. Only their parents have deep feelings; they want to do business and develop China quickly. We welcome them and their technical knowledge— that is, people with yellow skin [*you huang pifu de ren*].

Despite the tantalizing appeal of "our kind of people" and the racialist construct of overseas Chinese, the official view is that in practice one cannot count on the loyalty of overseas Chinese, only on their desire to make a profit off China (see Hsing's essay in this volume).

Pro-official narratives clearly differentiate the mainland "socialism with Chinese characteristics" from the Greater China idea of Chineseness with capitalist characteristics. Chen Xiyu of Xiamen University warns that "constructing an economic zone based solely on race is theoretically weak and inconsistent with objective political and economic conditions." He insists that despite the free flow of overseas Chinese capital into China, the integrity of the nation-state must be defended.

This fear of the erosion of the nation-state by mobile capitalism is shared by countries in Southeast Asia. They worry that capital flight to China will weaken national economies; however, Southeast Asian regimes are also sending official delegations backed by *huaqiao* capital to cash in on China's boom. The fear remains that an economically powerful China will exert direct political domination over the region, thus weakening their existence as independent nation-states. China's 1974 seizure of the Paracel Islands and its more recent claim on the Spratly Islands raised fears, as expressed by a Malaysian official, that China's resurgence will "turn the South China Sea into a Chinese lake."[5] The Singapore government, in a rare expression of its dependence on the United States' presence in Southeast Asia, notes that "when China becomes powerful in twenty or thirty years' time . . . that's our worry; China may want to flex its muscles, and then it will be a very troublesome world."[6]

Indeed, there is a pervasive fear that ethnic Chinese investments in China may represent a reemergence of this group's putative prewar political support for the mainland.[7] Academic *huaqiao* spokesmen have stepped in to soothe fears that ethnic Chinese will become political turncoats for China: "They are doing it for profit. They aren't doing it for patriotic or sentimental reasons."[8] But protests against Chinese capital flight have been expressed in the Philippines (Lim 1993) and dramatically enacted in the recent anti-Chinese rioting over a bank collapse in Medan, Indonesia. Local scholars shun using the term diaspora in order to avoid the implication that ethnic Chinese are disloyal citizens, still bound by sentiments to China. Capital-bearing, profit-seeking Chinese pursuing their flexible strategies have reinforced old fears that already consider them suspect citizens in their home countries.[9]

On the mainland, the effort to strengthen state control over Chinese identity has also taken a moralistic, culturally specific turn. Since the 1980s there has been a hiatus in official campaigns against "spiritual pollution" from the West. But whereas state regulation in the Maoist period focused on policing "bad" classes and "deviant" sexual subjects to construct the national identity,[10] in this era of market reforms the state has turned its attention to problematic economic and political behavior. This is not surprising given the emergence of important new categories of people such as investors, professionals, sex workers, tourists, and urban consumers in the coastal cities and border zones, people who are particularly disruptive of a unified nation. However, these new subjects are critical to the booming Chinese economy as both producers and consumers, and the loosening of sexual mores is considered part of a general liberation from the oppressive past and an aspect of the economic "opening" (*kaifang*). The proliferation of karaoke bars has prompted me to use the term "karaokeization" to symbolize the transnational publics of coastal cities, which have an increasingly large population of overseas Chinese and other foreign businessmen and travelers (Ong 1996). In Shenzhen, the foremost capitalist dreamland where overseas Chinese and newly rich peasants spend freely and carouse exuberantly amidst images of naked female torsos displayed in hotels, restaurants, and airports, an official expressed the new state attitude toward the commodified "culture market" (*wenhua shichang*): "Let them [young people] have their desires! If they have money, they can do what they want. Just no more Tiananmens!"

Policing political ideas and economic norms, not sexual freedom, is the focus of state concern as the new transnationalized spaces within the body politic destabilize a coherent national imaginary.

From the Beijing perspective, then, official critiques express a strong ambivalence over capitalism, which is viewed as both necessary for strengthening the country but also corrosive of state control and Communist ideals. Attempts at ideological regulation resurrected Confucius, recently vilified as representing the "four olds" of Chinese feudalism but now cast as a thoroughly Chinese guide to "patriotic education" in the age of flexible accumulation. Recently, academics in Beijing called for a "Confucian renaissance" to combat the "money worship" associated with Western capitalism. "The Confucian school [*Rujia xuepai*] does not oppose profiting through merchandise and money but advocates fairness in buying and selling, and neither is it opposed to making money and wealth but advocates that such practices be guided by morality." The official message is that there is a venerable Chinese way of making money that is specific to the historical and cultural boundedness of the nation: "The traditional culture of China's Confucian school has a two-thousand-year history, with a wealth of ancient books and records, and an abundant system that can serve as a single source for building a new culture."[11] Such ideological work to define Chineseness narrowly as a singular cultural formation deeply rooted in the heartland and history of the continent, seeks to tame those overseas Chinese, and the mainlanders they influence, whose self-interested pursuits threaten the state's control of social and territorial integrity. Thus while capitalism increases state power, the latter must also rein in capitalism's corrosion of the state. This dynamic also underlies modernist discourses in Southeast Asia, where strong states talk to other strong states about pan-Asianism while securely tightening their grip on national and territorial interests.

"The Glow of Chinese Fraternity"

Greater China, an idea of an open-ended space of Chinese capitalism, resonates with other images that emphasize Chinese diasporic networks bridging countries and regions. The key role of ethnic Chinese in flexible accumulation across the region and into China has revived old images of historical ties between south China and the *huaqiao* and stimulated new visions of a far-flung Chinese world whose reach is limited only by its mobile capitalism. Lee Kuan Yew, the former premier of Singapore and the chief spokesman for overseas Chinese, refers to "the glow of Chinese fraternity" cast by modern Chinese transnationalism.

The symbolic reworking of things Chinese retains its masculinist bias in celebrating common racial origins, ethnic traditions, and shared values expressed in the joint activities of kinsmen. A summary statement at the Guangdong conference on ethnic Chinese economy asserts that

> the big question is not Greater China but that there are Chinese people inside and outside China [in Southeast Asia]. Overseas Chinese have the same language and same ancestral stock [*tongwen tongzhu*] as we do; they are like the married-out daughter [*jia chuqu de nuer*] who still has feelings [*ganqing*] for home. They are the same kind of people [*tongzhong*].

While mainland scholars use the diminuitive feminine signifier to describe overseas Chinese, their focus is on the sentimental ties that can develop informally even with "married-out daughter" communities. Thus the message is that ethnic Chinese in Southeast Asia and mainland Chinese are, beneath their current political differences, essentially the same kind of people.

Although the tension remains between wishing to distinguish between the People's Republic of China and overseas Chinese, this insistence on cultural continuity makes Chinese everywhere the same; if they are not part of the mainland society, they are still an extension of China, as civilization (*wenhua*). The historical linkages between south China and Hong Kong, Taiwan, and Southeast Asia have always lain at the bottom of overseas Chinese consciousness (Ong 1996). In the early days of the Chinese republic, Sun Yat-sen called on overseas Chinese—then referred to as *Nanyang* ("Southern Ocean") Chinese—to support the Republican struggle (see Duara's essay in this volume). Later appeals for help came when the mainland was invaded by the Japanese. Intellectuals, students, *amahs* (domestic servants), laborers, housewives, teachers, and businessmen contributed hard-earned dollars to "save the motherland." This prewar loyalty to the mainland is now tapped as Cantonese scholars urge that, with the help of overseas Chinese, "Guangzhou should be the cradle of China's new culture" (White and Li 1993, 164). In this century, overseas Chinese sentiments have been drawn on and revived for purposes ranging from saving the motherland to constructing a regional market economy linking Guangdong to Hong Kong, Taiwan, and Southeast Asian centers.

Implicit in these narratives invoking durable bonds between the mainland and emigrant Chinese communities is the recognition of a new stage in East-West trade competition. For some mainland and overseas Chinese leaders, June 6, 1989, was memorable not so much for the Tiananmen crackdown as for marking the date when Japanese and American investors abandoned China. Overseas Chinese stepped up their investments in the mainland, helping to raise China's annual growth rates to double-digit figures. Lee Kuan Yew put it this way:

> What ethnic Chinese from Hong Kong, Macau, and Taiwan did was to demonstrate to a skeptical world that *guanxi* connections through the same language and culture can make up for a lack in the rule of law and transparency in rules and regulations.

His statements sketch a vision of a larger reality underlying transnational Chinese cooperation:

> People feel a natural empathy with those who share their physical attributes. This sense of closeness is reinforced when they also share basic culture and language. It makes for easy rapport and the trust that is the foundation of all business relations.[12]

Lee's remarks were made at a 1993 Hong Kong conference limited to entrepreneurs of Chinese ancestry from all corners of the world. The opening speech by the leader of the Hong Kong Chinese Chamber of Commerce hailed the guests as "belong[ing] ultimately to one big family." This meeting was an unrestrained celebration of a transnational Chinese solidarity based on common racial origin, ethnic traditions, and alliances and transcend ideological and cultural differences.

It is important to note that key terms such as *guanxi* (interpersonal relations), *networks, neo-Confucianism, tribes,* and *multiculturalism* have been constructed by Western academics to define Chinese culture and are now being reissued by American business schools to "explain" the "East Asian miracle." American business academics such as John Kao and Joel Kotkin mediate between business-speak, or what Bruce Cumings calls "Rimspeak" (Cumings 1993) and the self-Orientalizing discourses (Ong 1993) of ethnic Chinese spokesmen in Southeast Asia. Lee Kuan Yew cites Joel Kotkin's book *Tribes* (Kotkin 1992) to claim that "networking between people of the same race has always existed," thus gaining a scientific gloss from an essentialist construction of culture. Kotkin in turn cities Taipei attorney Paul Hsu, who "sees a new transnational 'Chinese-based economy' based on ties of common ethnic origin, language, and culture." Hsu asserts that "this is something new, a pioneering effort. . . . The old government ideology of nation-states will be outmoded. The government won't lead this effort" (Kotkin 1993, 20–21).

It is precisely this continual invocation of Chinese cultural affinity and racial exclusivity that has disturbed some Western observers, who are struck by the increasing number of regional business meetings restricted only to entrepreneurs of Chinese ancestry. The idea of a Greater China is often implicitly invoked by overseas Chinese leaders, who suggest that only fraternal networks can provide access into Chinese-dominated arenas. John Kao (1993) refers to the "open architecture" of Chinese *guanxi* networks, suggesting that there are openings for Westerners. Hong Kong businessmen claim that by associating with *guanxi* networks, non-Chinese entrepreneurs can "both tap and create the opportunities" for access to local resources and contacts in China.[13] The open architecture of networks has engendered a "symbiotic relationship" between U.S. and Chinese business partners (Kao 1993, 31), who, it is suggested, are more culturally adroit and multicultural than the Japanese in helping Westerners tap into the Asia Pacific markets.

Such triumphalist capitalist narratives (see Nonini's essay in this volume) ultimately draw symbolic power from claims that overseas Chinese, undisturbed by Communist rule, have preserved "Confucian" culture outside China and that it is the genuis of Confucian values that accounts for their success in different areas of life. Some Asian scholars, concerned about the backlash in Southeast Asia over claims of such irreducible cultural difference, emphasize the importance of "Western education." Thus Wang Gungwu comments, rather equivocally, "I am not convinced that Confucianism itself contributed to entrepreneurship. . . . While Confucian values make us what we are, what makes a good entrepreneur depends on many factors which are not peculiar to Chinese entrepreneurs." He mentions their acquired skills in the English language and Western business practice.[14] Multicultural experiences are also mentioned by Lee Kuan Yew, but in a way that seems to reify Chinese cultural distinctiveness. In his earlier speech, Lee notes that overseas Chinese can teach the mainland "the economic value of multiculturalism, derived from coexisting with and absorbing the good points of other cultures."[15] The implication is that although ethnic Chinese have lived among other cultural groups, they have remained Chinese in a basic, unchanging way, since cross-cultural learning is significant only for Chinese economic advancement. In effect, cultural hybridity has been employed to highlight the economic peculiarity of the Chinese.

Such discourses, produced in a circuit that migrates from political centers to entrepreneurs' circles, constitute a new regime of truth about a distinctive Chinese capitalism. The power of such an East Asian narrative derives in part from defining Chinese business activities as a kind of moral economy based on Confucian ideals, in contrast to the Western liberalism said to prevail in less successful Asian countries, such as the Philippines. As we shall see, this transnational Chinese imaginary is also a narrative that constructs a moral economic hierarchy in Southeast Asia.

Hierarchical Moral Economies:
Hard Versus Soft Societies

Besides his discourse on fraternal business networks, Lee Kuan Yew has also elaborated a thesis on how cultural differences between societies are reflected in their capitalist performance. Lee has long formulated a theory of "hard" versus "soft" societies by reworking older colonialist themes that deployed terms such as *Asiatic, Oriental,* and *Mohammedan* as evaluative racial categories in relation to modern society. The British and other Europeans had defined Malays as "indolent" and "lazy" while celebrating the "softness" of their culture in contrast to the "hardworking," "acquisitive," and "brutish" Chinese immigrants (Alatas 1977).[16] In the 1960s and 1970s, as prime minister, Lee began a campaign to build a "rugged society" in Singapore, both to forestall hostile forces in the surrounding Malay world and inculcate behavior and norms that would make Singapore a modern capitalist society. This instance of what Don Nonini calls "reflex modernity," or the techniques whereby a postcolonial state reworks old colonialist themes to its own benefit, is also conspicuous for its gendered imagery of hard virility versus soft femininty (see Heng and Devan 1995; Ong 1995). Lee's rugged society model contrasted a disciplined, achievement-oriented work ethic compared to the "soft" society of the Malays. Lee remade the colonial image of ethnic Chinese into a positive one based on Confucian values of hard work and frugality that were on a par with Western concepts of individual striving and meritocracy ("rugged individualism"). Such a postcolonial reconstruction arose in part from a subaltern opposition to colonial racism. By the 1970s there was an element of righteous vindication when Lee visited Cambridge University, his alma mater, and chided the British for their decline in productivity and civility. Indeed, the Singapore vision of modernity soon dropped the Western value of individualism and focused more explicitly on the assumed links between Confucian values and the rise of Asian industrialization.

Singapore's national identity since the 1980s has been geared toward promoting the development of a well-disciplined "Confucian" capitalist society. In an effort to create an authentic Chineseness among the culturally heterogeneous and Westernized population, the state employed Harvard professor Tu Wei-ming to oversee programs sponsoring instruction and research in Confucian ethics and philosophies. Ideological regulation through the educational system, and the reification of Singaporean culture as "Confucian," are disciplinary schemes to shape and control a workforce geared to state-managed economic development and "state-fathering" (Heng and Devan 1995) of the social body. State patriarchy is central to the form of state-sponsored export-oriented capitalism in Singapore.[17]

The biopolitical force is most apparent in innumerable campaigns to improve the labor force—language skills, academic performance, health practices, saving rates—and to ensure the "quality" of its reproduction, as in government drives to promote marriage and childbirth among female university graduates, who are mostly Chinese (Heng and Devan 1995). Such disciplinary schemes are represented within a moral economy of asymmetrical obligations between subjects and the state.

In his study of peasants in Southeast Asia, James C. Scott (1976) constructs a model of patron-client exchanges that is morally acceptable to villagers because it is based on the assumption that their patron will guarantee their collective security in times of trouble. Following Scott's line of reasoning, one can say that in Singapore's political culture, a moral economy is elaborated on the basis of "Confucian," or more recently "Asian," values that uphold strong government control in every area of life in exchange for the state guarantee of collective well-being. For instance, the near-universal state provision of low-cost housing so that every family can be guaranteed access to a home is a formidable structure for producing control as well as building social consent. Indeed, this provision of collective well-being secures ideological justification for the elements of repression (Chua 1991). Such architectural morality—the preservation of families—at home is reinforced by the official evaluation of less morally justifiable regimes elsewhere in Asia.

In recent years Lee, now acting as a elder Asian statesman-at-large, has begun to pronounce on the relative economic performances of Southeast Asian countries. He assesses them not by comparing socialist with capitalist regimes, as was the case in the past, but by contrasting those assumed to possess Confucian values with those that do not. Invited to Manila, Lee declared:

> Contrary to what American commentators say, I do not believe that democracy necessarily leads to development. I believe that what a country needs to develop is discipline more than democracy. The exuberance of democracy leads to undisciplined and disorderly conditions which are inimical to development.

In Lee's view, the Philippines is handicapped by both its American-style constitution, which undermines social discipline and stability, and its lack of Confucian values; both factors account for the country's being less successful than other developing Asian countries.

> The ultimate test of the value of a political system is whether it helps that society to establish conditions which improve the standard of living for the ma-

jority of its people, plus enabling the maximum of personal freedoms compatible with the freedoms of others in society.[18]

This manifesto of an Asian political system that balances collective security against individual rights is elaborated by another Singapore official, George Yeo. Speaking to a European audience, Yeo, the minister for information and the arts, also criticizes Western-style democracy:

No democracy can function without strong moral underpinnings supported by the entire communities. Democracies which see only rights without obligations eventually destroy themselves.[19]

He offers Singapore as an experiment in which both democracy and socialism "must become smaller. . . . In Singapore, we deliberately work our welfare policies through the family. The objective is to strengthen the family net, not weaken it."[20] An Asian form of democracy, then, is one with limits on both democracy and socialism—that is, limits on the expansion of individual rights and on claims on the state. Through the provision of support systems such as near-universal home ownership and other social services, the state gains moral legitimacy from the population (Chua 1991). Furthermore, by presenting itself as pro-family, the state places pressures on the family as the basic unit of responsibility. The moral economy of the state is thus aligned with the moral economy of the family. Yeo continues, "for many East Asian societies, it is not only the family that is socialist, it is the extended family and sometimes the entire clan." Thus Confucian rhetoric, despite the rising rate of divorce and the growing number of women who are not married, helps the state to reframe the paternal order as a response to the social changes engendered by capitalism.

This invention and reinvention of official morality focuses on the Asian family as the nexus and vehicle of state power. It is the first of many levels of moral defense against individual interests. By attributing the economic success of Asian countries to smaller, more flexible Asian forms of democracy, Singapore's leaders reinforce their regime of truth, and by invoking Confucian values, they tap into the unconscious desires and nostalgia of the diasporic Chinese population. Such moral management is especially successful when comparisons are made across countries in terms of their assumed possession or nonpossession of Confucian culture. In Lee's view, the Philippines will soon be overtaken economically by a war-ravaged but "Confucian" country such as Vietnam.

Lee makes this point in an interview with The *Asian Wall Street Journal*: "[Vietnam] is a different society, differently geared [than the Philippines]. It is a high-compression engine, not a low-compression engine. It's hard-driving." He points to the Confucian intangibles—the coherence of a society and its commitment to common ideals, goals, and values such as belief in hard work, thrift, filial piety, and national pride—as key factors in economic advancement. The journalist notes that "by implication, the Philippines is a *softer* place, not so *naturally* industrious and serious, with a doubtful ability to pull together in collective endeavor" (emphasis added).[21] These remarks about differences in cultural values become essentialized as concrete, biopolitical differences as well. After that come the usual Orientalizing questions: "Why do Asians study harder? Why do they work harder? Why do they save more?"—excepting, of course, the Philippines, which was called a "celebrated failure." Such narratives on the moral bases of development do not mention how capitalism as an ideology of endless desires and as a system of exploitation, in combination with both biopolitical and oppressive state measures, may have played a role in the economic behavior of Asian subjects.

Citizens, workers, and their masters are shifted around in relation to particular discourses about moral value and economic performance. The academic world furnishes studies that support this construction of the "good" Chinese. For instance, a book based on the life histories of Singaporean Chinese merchants (Chan and Chiang 1993) develops the concept of the "Confucianist merchant" (in the nineteenth-century Confucian world view, this would have been an oxymoron). Although the individuals represented were highly commercial and narrowly concerned with material needs and the survival of their families, as was common in immigrant families, the authors use the Confucian imprimature to sanitize the image of the merchant and money-lender. Recast as Confucianist merchants, these rags-to-riches immigrants gain moral stature as solid Singapore citizens.

The floating of such symbolic icons and the narratives tying Chinese cultural values to worldly success are processes engaged in a struggle to stitch together the inherently divergent tendencies of the state and market logics, and the tensions between an organic conservatism and individual desires (Hall 1988, 53–54). As constituted regimes of truth, narratives of moral economies express a "contradictory unity" whereby the state attempts to balance its political needs for social control and stability against the dynamic and diasporic tendencies of capitalism. Observers have noted that the Singapore state maintains power through orchestrating crises—declining (Chinese) marriage and birth rates (Heng and Devan 1995); a "Marxist conspiracy" to subvert the government (see Seow 1994); the furor over the Michael Fay incident (see below)—that become opportunities for the government to identify "threats" to state security, to marginalize potentially dissenting groups, and to instill self-surveillance in a population induced to feel continually under siege. The basic tension between the state's desire for stability and the anarchic reign of the marketplace compels continual adjustment in relations between the nation and its subjects. What if, despite the orchestrated debates and educative processes, profits prevail over patriotism in the subjects' self-image?

The ranking of Confucian over non-Confucian countries installs a new status hierarchy whereby the former are held up as models of Eastern capitalist modernity while those that follow American liberal democracy are at the bottom. This grid of cultural difference between countries also constructs those less successful, or "soft" subjects—women, Muslims, Malays—as Asian Others who exist outside as well as within one's nation-state borders. When the narratives about Chinese cultural networks, smaller Asian democracy, hard versus soft societies, and Confucian icons are viewed as the cultural products of Asian economic development, we see that despite their having arisen from different sites, their discontinuities, and their tensions, they are nevertheless, at a higher level, renegotiating relations with the West.

Modernity and Orientalism: Spiritual Difference from the West

Although American interests continue to dominate the Asia Pacific, recently local leaders have began to proclaim that newly industrializing Asian countries are caught up in an "Asian renaissance." This cultural ferment means, in the words of an official, "We're not saying that we're culturally superior. We're just saying we're not inferior."[22] As in earlier anticolonial movements, the current Asian cultural renaissance is based on nationalistic claims of an indigeneous spiritual domain that is independent of Western domination (Chatterjee 1993). Statements of Asian cultural difference from the West have been building for more than a decade; they arise from different circumstances than those that gave birth to the Greater China imagery, but both sets of narratives are rooted in the spread of the subcontracting mode of capitalism in Asia.

The romanticization of Chinese business empires was first stimulated by the rise of Hong Kong tycoons in the 1970s. Shipping magnate Li Kung Pao, Asia-Pacific real estate developer Li Ka-shing, Y.-C. Wang (Taiwan), "sugar king" Liem Sioe Liong (Indonesia), "merchant mandarin" Robert Kuok and his brothers (Malaysia), and Bangkok Bank's Chin Sophonpanich (Thailand) not only have been written up in regional business magazines but also have been celebrated in a recent issue of

Forbes devoted to the five hundred biggest non-American firms. Besides many articles describing the vast and intricate networks of these empires, The *Far Eastern Economic Review* lovingly documents the mythological rise-from-poor-immigrant-boy-to-rich-entrepreneur stories of these capitalists. Although many of the business leaders (or their fathers) came from poor peasant backgrounds and were barely educated, the business magazines laud them as "Confucian gentlemen" (*junzi*). Robert Kuok, the commodities and property tycoon, is described as "discreet to the point of invisibility. He has also been wise in his dispensation of succour to politicians, and benevolent, until recently, in his treatment of shareholders."[23] This picture of Chinese capitalists as embodying Confucian nobility is also elaborated by *Forbes* magazine: "The overseas Chinese display strong self-reliance and the Confucian virtues of thrift, discipline, industriousness, family cohesion, and reverence for education. . . . Wealthy Chinese . . . demonstrate Confucian respect for familial and clan ties by an act of benevolence, such as building a school or hospital [in their ancestral villages]."[24] That *Forbes*, the West's leading capitalist magazine, has embraced the myth of the return of a Confucian nobility whose intelligence, noble values, and benevolence are qualities for capitalist success further fuels the region's pride and confidence in itself, lending legitimacy to Asian leaders' claims about an imagined community among the Asian tigers, which are linked together by such Chinese business empires.

The earliest seeds of an Asian postcolonial turning-away from Western capitalist blueprints can be found in the launching of the Malaysian industrialization program. The prime minister proposed a "look East" policy, urging his subjects to emulate Japan—despite fresh memories of the Japanese wartime occupation of the country and much of Southeast Asia—as a model for economic development. The Japanese managerial philosophy, he noted, emphasized a strong work ethic and concern for the welfare of the workers, values that did not contravene Islamic religion (Ong 1987, 149–50). Japan soon became the major investor in Malaysia, Thailand, and Indonesia, helping to build the base of their industrial programs (Steven 1990). By the end of the decade, Japan's rising economic power and moral prestige in Southeast Asia encouraged efforts to stand up to American domination, as in the publication of the book *The Japan that Can Say No* (Ishihara 1990), a tract widely interpreted on the other side of the Pacific as "America-bashing."

With the economic emergence of China, however, most recent representations of Asian cultural difference are associated with China and the overseas Chinese and with a more broadly based notion of Asian values. Narratives insisting on a spiritual difference from the West often boil down to the reified Confucian values already popular with business leaders and the media (see Blanc's essay in this volume). As often enunciated by Malaysian and Singaporean leaders, these values consist of "the family, education, high savings, hard work, home ownership, and clean living,"[25] a list of attributes that Western scholars would associate with Thatcherite and Reaganite formulations for dealing with excessive economic individualism and insecurities generated by globalization (Harvey 1989, 168). Indeed, through much of this century Western scholars have identified these features among the univeralistic norms of modernity. Now appropriated and dressed up in timeless Orientalist guise by Southeast Asian regimes, they operate as normalizing truth-claims to regulate the newly affluent populations. Furthermore, the rise of the entrepreneurial state associated with peripheral Fordism in Asia has created its own ideological doctrine of "the Asian Way," defined as "an intricate ideology . . . to justify why it is no longer possible to compete with Asians under the old rules."[26]

This new interest in collectively defending Asian free trade is also reflected in the redefinition of "East Asia." The term has been expanded beyond its cold war boundaries to include China, Japan, Korea, Taiwan, and Hong Kong as well as Southeast Asian nation-states—a region whose combined gross domestic product is expected to be 33 percent of the world economy by 2010.[27] That the concept of Asian values is deeply invested in market competition was dramatically highlighted by the reactions to the American threat to withdraw 'most-favored-nation' status from China in retaliation for alleged human-rights violations.

Human rights have become the core issue in articulations of Asian cultural difference from the West. Global debates about human rights in Asia allow local leaders to publicly resolve the contradictions between the community and the state, between spiritual and material interests, and between the unfettered individualism associated with the West and the self-censuring political culture in Asia.

A year after the world conference on human rights in 1993, Chinese premier Li Peng instructed the visiting Australian foreign minister:

There is not only one model of human rights. The Vienna statement includes the basic views and demands of many developing countries on the issue of human rights. It expressly points out that "the right of developing countries to develop [*fazhan quan*] is part of and inseparable from human rights."

While emphasizing general human rights, we cannot neglect the characteristics of the country and region and the importance of historical, cultural, and religious backgrounds. We cannot neglect each country's conditions and cannot demand a singular model of human rights.[28]

This view that economic development—nay, capitalism—is a fundamental human right is echoed by Southeast Asian governments, which
claim that economic development is "the only force that can liberate the
third world.[29] In a novel reworking of older anti-imperialist rhetoric,
postcolonial leaders see themselves as continuing to resist Western domination through capitalist development. Furthermore, their rejection of
the Western human-rights campaign as a trade weapon also implicitly
criticizes the new Western evil Other—that is, the privileged and lazy
working classes that are demanding all kinds of protectionism at the expense of Asian development.[30]

Thus from Beijing to Singapore there is a chorus of voices asserting
that capitalism is a human right, while the U.S. human-rights campaign
is denounced as "an instrument to perform power politics" that force less
powerful countries to accept an imposed Western standard (Fan 1994).
For the first time, a group of Asian leaders spoke out against American
"arrogance": The Malaysian finance minister called efforts to link
change in human rights or labor policy to U.S. market access as "conde-
scending and even arrogant," while others claimed in international fo-
rums that Asian economic ascendency owes little to the "arrogant West."
Even among the normally tactful Japanese, resigning Japanese prime
minister Hosokawa issued a parting shot: "It is not proper to force West-
ern- or European-type democracy onto others."[31] These voices raised in
righteous anger are not only contesting Western notions about human
rights and democracy but also expressing fears that the West's continuing domination will derail Asian capitalism, which has become, in their
narrations, synonymous with Asian modernity.

Furthermore, to prevent the West from capturing the moral high
ground, Asian scholars claim that indigenous humanistic traditions actually inform Asian capitalism. In the *Beijing Review*, an official publication of the Chinese government, Dong Yunhu defines an alternative
notion of human rights rooted in Asian civilizations:

> Although the human rights concept centering on individuals originated in the
> West, the humanitarian spirit, such as the value of human dignity in India, and
> Confucian humanism in China, has long been a part of Asia's cultural tradi-
> tion. In these humanitarian traditions, humanism and kindheartedness were
> regarded as the natural features of man. The idea that "the aged should be well
> supported, children should be brought up, the able-bodied should be given an
> opportunity to bring his ability into full play, and the disabled should be
> helped" also encouraged people to be concerned about society and others be-
> fore themselves. (Dong 1993, 11)

He goes on to link these spiritual traditions to the rights of the modern nation-state:

> The cultural tradition of respect for individual rights while *guaranteeing* the state, social, family, and other collective rights has played an important role in promoting economic and social progress in the region and will continue to promote its further revitalization. (Dong 1993, 12; emphasis added)

Dong is confident that Southeast Asian leaders would agree with him that a balance between individual human rights and collective socioeconomic rights is the Asian model of development: "This collective humanitarian tradition is helpful for Asia and has promoted a high economic growth rate and the improvement of living standards" (Dong 1993, 12).

There is thus a move beyond the simple reiteration of Chinese (Confucian) values to the articulation of a pan-Asian humanitarian model that is based on ahistorical and homogenizing descriptions of Asian cultures to legitimize overall state policies of capital accumulation, labor control, and social control. The invocation of Asian values often becomes a *carte blanche* to legitimize any action of ruling regimes. Some discourses come close to Orientalizing Asian traditions as timeless and irrefutably embodied in all Asians. The incantation of strong families, loyalty to elders, discipline, frugality, work ethic, and so on are also pointed critiques of the West.

The brightest voice in such cultural criticisms belongs to Kishore Mahbubani, the Harvard-educated permanent secretary of the Ministry of Foreign Affairs in Singapore. He has published articles in America entitled, "The Dangers of Decadence: What the Rest Can Teach the West" (Mahbubani 1993) and "The United States: 'Go East, Young Man' " (Mahbubani 1994). Another Singaporean who lectures to the West is Tommy Koh, a former ambassador to the United States who enunciated "alternative values" that helped make Asian countries "successful and [which] could possibly be of use to others."[32] Mahbubani insists that an America suffering from "unfettered individual freedom" and its resulting "massive social decay" ought to learn about social values from its Asian neighbors. Mahbubani makes valuable observations about American society from an Asian perspective. Nevertheless, although he talks about the recent historical upheavals that have compelled Asian societies to break with past "mental ossification" (Mahbubani 1994, 18), he also invokes a sixth-century Confucian vision of a well-ordered, unbashedly patriarchal society as a guide to contemporary Asian societies and even the United States (Mahbubani 1994, 20). Here we are reminded again of the biopolitical concerns of state-sponsored capitalism, which underlines the rhetoric of Confucianist discourse.

Stitching Together Disjunctures at Home

These imaginaries—of the nation-state, of Greater China, and of Asian values—are produced from different sites, and they are in varying degrees of tension with each other; they also ultimately have points of application "at home." How do claims of the Asian way and a moral unity against the West engage the interests of subordinate groups in their own countries? In what ways do they set the terms of thinking and talking about Asian capitalism and cultural difference? How do regimes of truth "stitch together" the disjunctures between market logics, individual interests, and the biopolitical needs of the state (Hall 1988, 53)?

One way triumphalist narratives of nation and capital deal with contradictory forces is to remain silent about such realities as social upheavals, the historical and ongoing exploitation of Asian labor, women, and children, rampant consumerism, public incivility, cutthroat individualist competition, rising divorce rates, and the cultural hollowness that flourishes in south China and the Asian tigers as much as in other places undergoing rapid capitalist development. One may ask how Confucian, indeed, are the everyday practices of the majority of overseas Chinese, if we go beyond the narrow definitions of discipline and diligence and remember that Confucianism also means a turning-away from materialism and narrow concerns with the family. The majority in English-speaking Chinese in Southeast Asian communities have never read Confucius; their beliefs and practices are a heterogeneous mix of interacting Chinese elements, other cultures, and state definitions of national culture from above (see Heng and Devan 1995; Chun 1994). Furthermore, the purported welfare-oriented model of Asian business entails not just paternalism but also exploitation of indebted workers (Chun 1989). In both state-sponsored capitalist ventures and in family firm operations, the exploitation of young female workers and children is pervasive and in some cases has been intensified by flexible accumulation (Ong 1987, 1988, 1991; Liu 1990; Cheng and Hsiung 1992; Wolf 1992; Nonini 1993; Lee 1994; Greenhalgh 1994; Ong and Peletz 1995, Hsiung 1996). These subaltern groups who bear the main burden of Asian capitalist success are almost never mentioned in dominant discourses of the Asian way. Though indispensable to capitalist success in the region, they are rendered invisible and speechless, an effect of the symbolic violence (Bourdieu 1977) of triumphalist Chinese modernity.

Another way hegemonic discourses weave around problematic areas is by attaching their regimes of truth to certain political positions, such as the overwhelming importance of national stakes. For instance, in late 1993 there was a major fire in a Shenzhen factory owned by a Hong

Kong subcontractor. The fire killed eighty-four female workers who were trapped by barred windows and sealed doors. Human-rights groups contend that 90 percent of foreign joint ventures in China flouted safety rules with the help of corrupt local officials. Their victims are usually young female workers who have migrated from poor inland provinces. Because most have no residence permits, their illegal status is used by employers to discipline them by threats of exposure and expulsion (see Lee's essay in this volume).[33] When I was in Guangzhou a couple of months after the Shenzhen fire, TV talk shows and the media appeared to be mainly concerned with defending the state and foreign investors. Journalists and officials noted that there were adequate laws protecting workers' safety, and that it was the failure to implement the rules that caused the tragedy. Others shielded foreign companies from blame, noting that doors and gates were welded shut to prevent workers from stealing products. There was hardly any mention of the youth and gender of the workers, who were referred to as "migrants," a stigmatized term in coastal China. Many of the fire victims could not be identified because their names were not on record. There were no demands by local women's groups to defend their interests. Although young women are the paradigmatic workers of China's industrial boom, they are rendered faceless even when sacrificed to the greed of officials and investors. Elite pronouncements are often taken as disinterested statements protecting Asian cultures when in fact their effects has been to reinforce state power in legitimizing official policies and in suppressing dissent.

Singapore has emerged as the chief English-language articulator of a Chinese modernity. The international coverage of the caning of the American teenager Michael Fay in Singapore for vandalism has made tiny Singapore representative of what the West thinks Confucian discipline and efficient capitalism are all about. In Singapore, the Fay case was skillfully handled by political leaders and writers as an educative process highlighting the difference between the soft, decadent West and the strong East. The standoff with the United States over an appropriate means of punishment for vandalism was cast as a David-and-Goliath contest: "a small state stood up to the bullying of a superpower whose media was largely blinded by an avowal of individualism."[34] Although a 1986 study showed that just over one quarter of those Singaporeans surveyed supported caning as an appropriate punishment for vandalism, this figure rose to 79 percent in a recent poll, "probably because Singaporeans felt affronted by the bully-boy tactics adopted by the U.S. media over the caning of Fay."[35] Differences over crime and punishment were orchestrated into a lesson about deep cultural differences toward individualism, social order, and the symbolic domination of the West. The government's handling of the incident "focused minds on the issue of law and order" and convinced the majority of Singaporeans that their interests lay with those of the ruling party. The press allowed one timid dissenting voice to slip in: "We say . . . 'Ya, ya, he deserves it . . .,' but deep inside wonder about the direction of punishment-versus-crime here."[36] Lists of differences from America filled the papers: Singaporeans were more "compassionate," lacked "cynicism toward authority," and needed to maintain the "moral authority of the government"; in Singapore, "families of criminals are more likely to feel they have been shamed before society, rather than blame it." All these perceived differences reinforce the cultural rightness of state policy.

In sum, both the Shenzhen fire in China and the Michael Fay incident in Singapore were local occasions that allowed national disciplinary hegemonies to conjoin discursively coincidental interests between subordinate groups and the nation-state. In both cases, national discourses of the difference in Asian capitalism have mobilized wide public support and increased the demand for parity and respect from the Americans in a way that postwar Japan never attempted. This shifting, multinational cultural representation of the emerging Asian way has caused *Asiaweek*, a news magazine, to trumpet, "Asiamerica! The next century's super-culture."[37]

Conclusion: A Momentary Glow of Fraternity

The many modernist visions—of the Chinese nation, of overseas Chinese capitalism, of Asian spiritual difference—emanate from sites of unequal power in the Asia Pacific. Separately and collectively, these circuits of symbolic power are claiming the region to be no longer an unchallenged domain of American capitalism but the eastern frontier of Asian expansion. The varied ideological work of imagining heterogenous and complex Asian experiences into a stable and coherent set of collective values and goals is defining a modernity alternative to that of the West.

I use the term *alternative* not to suggest that these ideological positions represent an absolute moral or epistemological difference from ones held in the West.[38] Asian modernist imaginations that insist upon their cultural and spiritual distinctiveness are contradictory, self-Orientalizing moves. A common ethnographic assumption holds that speaking subjects are unproblematic representers of their own culture, whereas I argue that their truth claims, like those of ethnographers, are articulated in webs of power. Indeed, the question of "ownership of culture" and articulating its particular truths is an open-ended, contested process. *Alternative*, then, is used here to refer a dynamic that is oppositional to existing hegemonies, a counterforce arising from other sites that are not without their own particular mix of expansive and repressive technologies.

Indeed, in a world of Western hegemony, Asian voices are unavoidably inflected by Orientalist essentialisms that infiltrate all kinds of public exchanges about culture. I use the term *self-orientalization* in recognition not just of such predicaments but also of the agency to manueuver and manipulate meanings within different power domains. Statements about Chinese modernity are an amalgam of indigenous ideas, Western concepts, and self-Orientalizing representations by Asian leaders. Such formulations of modernity should not come as a surprise, since the Asia-Pacific region as a geopolitical entity was constructed by European-American imperialism and capitalism (Dirlik 1993).

Early in the twentieth century, Enlightenment concepts of liberty and progress, as well as social Darwinist views of inequality among nations, informed the thinking of many intellectuals in China and Southeast Asia. Currently, what are claimed to be Chinese or Asian values or the Asian form of democracy are derived from Western notions of progress. The standard postwar tract on modernization—in the sense of belief in progressive evolutionary development, rationality, property ownership, family stability, and social order—owes much to an American reformulation of Western bourgeois thought. Many of its statements—such as the imperative of economic development, scientific and technological progress, and the rational management of society—can be found in books such as W. W. Rostow's *Stages of Economic Growth: A Non-Communist Manifesto* (1960) or repackaged in Margaret Thatcher's and Ronald Reagan's speeches. Furthermore, claims that Chinese and Asian modernity is based on cultural difference disguise the fact that although indigenous societies have their own essentializing notions about culture, many of the remarks are self-Orientalizing in that they reify Western concepts of Chineseness, *guanxi* networks, neo-Confucianism, and the like. Thus the narrations of Asian modernity contain many of the elements in Western discourses, since they have been informed and are continually produced in negotiation against Western domination in the world (cf. Yang 1994).

I therefore use the term *alternative modernities* to denote not so much the difference in content from Western ones as the new self-confident political reenvisioning of futures that challenge the fundamental assumption of inevitable Western domination. *Modernity* is a polysemic term in Asia, as elsewhere, and I have merely touched upon a small set of imagined modernities linked to a range of Chinese societies and their increasing interactions. In Asia, state narratives insist that their modernity is an alternative to the West because from the viewpoint of Asian states, capitalism should strengthen state control, not undermine it. The major difference from modernities in the West thus lies in the way state biopolitics and economic competition are routinely recast as timeless cultural practices and values, and in the way events generated by the breaking down of national borders are managed through the institution-alization of Confucian moral economies, set off against Western liberal democracies. These hegemonic moves seek to instill cultural solidarity and control in the diverse populations while deflecting Western domina-tion in the economic and political realms. A Hong Kong writer asserts that despite national borders, concrete trade interests that allow profits and trust to grow between countries within Greater China's "community of Chinese" (*Zhongguoren gongtong di*) is "a system that would restore something like the offering of imperial tribute, so that China maintains the regional order of the Asia-Pacific area" (cited in White and Li 1993, 191).[39]

These discourses—both state- and capitalist-borne—intersect in pro-nouncing the cultural logic of Asian capitalism a fraternal solidarity that strengthens morality and the nation-state (as opposed to individual frag-mentation and displacement in the West; see Jameson 1991). This hege-monic moment is attained when leaders of different countries find in the master Chinese symbols certain "points of articulation" (Hall 1988, 60) between various locales in Asia. As the ever astute Lee Kuan Yew notes, this *"momentary* glow of fraternity" (emphasis added) may not outlast China's emergence as a superpower.[40] Nevertheless, such a hegemonic moment describes an alternative map of symbolic power, inscribing the "hard" masculinist surfaces of triumphalist Chinese capitalism and cul-tural chauvinism across the Asia Pacific. What we have, then, is a para-digm change in capitalism as the West knows it. Heretofore the world-systems model has posited the West (and Japan) as the center and the non-West as the periphery. More recently, the Western capitalist con-cept of globalization has come to denote a world dominated by transna-tional capitalist operations regardless of geopolitical differences. It is a historical irony that at a point when a new Asian hegemony is emerging out of the particular imbrications of state and capital in the Asia-Pacific region, so much Western academic attention remains riveted on the West itself or mesmerized by its own colonial past and present in "the per-ipheries." Chinese modernities are new imaginaries and regimes of dom-ination decentering Western hegemony in the new era. A synergy of political, economic, and ideological processes is producing a geopoliti-cal center in East Asia. Will the momentary glow of fraternity forged in alternative Chinese modernities, and in renegotiating American global domination, become the Asia-Pacific hegemony of the new century?

Notes

I am grateful to Donald Nonini for his close reading and insightful comments. Mayfair M.-h. Yang, Katharyne Mitchell, and Prasenjit Duara also made helpful suggestions.

[1] I thank Don Nonini for discussing this distinction with me.

[2] A conventional understanding of modernity is the assumption of a progressive evolutionist development of individuals, institutions, and society governed by rational thinking and science. See, for example, Rostow 1960, which unintentionally makes clear that there is substantial overlap in the capitalist and teleological communist goals of modernization, if not in the means to get there.

[3] *New York Times*, April 19, 1992, 1.

[4] See Hong Kong Trade Development Council, 1991.

[5] *International Herald Tribune*, November 23, 1993, 8.

[6] *San Francisco Chronicle*, May 29, 1994, A-8. For instance, at a speech before an assembly of Chinese entrepreneurs, the former prime minister of Singapore, Lee Kuan Yew, after lauding Chinese networks in promoting China's economic development, warned ethnic Chinese to guard against "Chinese chauvinism": "But we must be honest and recognize that at the end of the day our fundamental loyalties are to our home country, not to China (*International Herald Tribune*, November 23, 1993, 4).

[7] Before World War I, ethnic Chinese in Southeast Asia were a major source of economic support for Sun Yat-sen's revolutionary activities in China, and later for the mainland resistance to Japanese occupational forces. During the struggle for independence in Southeast Asia, ethnic Chinese were often represented as a pro-Communist "third China" that threatened the fragile new nation-states. Thus contemporary Chinese in Southeast Asia fear that their investments in China would revive such perceptions among the indigenous population.

[8] *Asian Wall Street Journal*, December 10–11, 1993, 8.

[9] The political construction of ethnic Chinese in Southeast Asian has a long tradition stemming from the colonial era. See, for instance, Freedman 1969.

[10] That is those whose class background fell under the "five black categories" of landlord, rich peasant, bad element, counterrevolutionary, and rightist (see Yang 1994, 186–87; Hinton 1966; Chan, Madsen, and Unger 1984). The sexually deviant included those who celebrated romantic love, the sexually permissive, prostitutes, and homosexuals (see Honig and Hershatter 1988).

[11] *China News Digest*, September 20, 1994, 40.

[12] *International Herald Tribune*, Nov. 23, 1993, 4.

[13] *South China Morning Post,* November 25, 1993.

[14] *South China Morning Post*, November 23, 1993, Bus. 1.

[15] *International Herald Tribune*, November 23, 1993, 4.

[16] For another example of how these colonialist discourses were reworked in postcolonial business contexts, see Ong 1987.

[17] David Harvey, following Alain Lipietz, calls such state-sponsored mass-production industrialization and its labor organization "peripheral Fordism," i.e., regimes that are conductive to strong patriarchal control in shaping gender relations Harvey (1989 155, 165). For an ethnographic example, see Ong 1987.

[18] *Far Eastern Economic Review,* December 10, 1992.

[19] Ibid.

[20] *International Herald Tribune*, June 22, 1994, 4. Although Yeo claims that what he calls "smaller democracy" has evolved out of Asian experience, his views echo those of American conservatives who have for decades called for smaller government.

[21] *Asian Wall Street Journal*, December 3–4, 1993, 8.

[22] *Wall Street Journal*, April 13, 1994, A1.

[23] *Far Eastern Economic Review*, February 7, 1991, 46.

[24] *Forbes*, July 18, 1994, 140–43.

[25] *The Economist*, May 28, 1994, 13. Ironically, while the Taiwan regime is trying to maintain its political independence from mainland China, it participates in the Confucian discourse by claiming possession of a more "authentic" Confucian cultural heritage (Chun 1994), emphasizing its "progressive cultural alienation from a country that is increasingly seen as brutal, lawless, corrupt, and irrelevant to Taiwan's future" (*New York Times*, June 26, 1994, A6). Indeed, one may add that many in Southeast Asia also view China in this light, but hegemonic discourses about Greater China or the Asian way gloss over them in order to enforce a sense of regional cultural solidarity.

[26] *The Economist*, November 5, 1994, 18.

[27] *San Francisco Examiner*, May 29, 1994, A8.

[28] *Renmin Ribao*, April 4, 1994, 1 (my translation).

[29] *Far Eastern Economic Review*, June 17, 1993, 26.

[30] I appreciate Don Nonini's reminding me of this point.

[31] *Wall Street Journal*, April 13, 1994, A6

[32] *Asiaweek*, January 5, 1994, 18.

[33] *China News Digest*, October 16, 1994.

[34] *Straits Times* (Singapore), August 23, 1994, 19.

[35] *Straits Times*, May 29, 1994, 6.

[36] *Straits Times*, April 29, 1994, 17.

[37] *Asiaweek*, December 1, 1993, 20–25.

[38] I thank Prasenjit Duara for helping me to clarify this point. See Duara 1995.

[39] This claim is extremely significant in the recent Japanese revisionist history that considers the Chinese tributary system, rather than the coming of the Europeans, as the source of Japanese and Chinese modernity (Hamashita 1988).

[40] *Business Week*, November 29, 1993.

References

Alatas, Syed Hussein. 1977. *The Myth of the Lazy Native*. London: Frank Cass.

Anderson, Benedict. 1982. *Imagined Communities: Reflections on the Origin and Spread of Nationalism* 2nd ed. London: Verso.

Appadurai, Arjun. 1990. "Disjuncture and Difference in the Global Cultural Economy." *Public Culture* 2, no. 2: 1–24.

Ban, Kah Choon. 1992. "Narrating Imagination." In Ban K.C., A Pakir, and Tong C.K., eds., *Imagining Singapore*, pp. 9–25 Singapore: Times Academic Press.

Bhabha, Homi K. 1990. "DissemiNation: Time, Narrative, and the Margins of the Modern Nation." In Homi K. Bhabha, ed., *Nation and Narration*, pp. 291–322. London: Routledge.

Bourdieu, Pierre. 1977. *Outline of a Theory of Practice*. Cambridge: Cambridge University Press.

Chan, Anita, Richard Madsen, and Jonathan Unger. 1984. *Chen Village: The Recent History of a Peasant Community in Mao's China*. Berkeley: University of California Press.

Chan, Kwok Bun and Claire Chiang. 1993. *Stepping Out: The Making of Chinese Entrepreneurs*. Singapore: Simon and Schuster.

Chatterjee, Partha. 1993. *The Nation and Its Fragments: Colonial and Postcolonial Histories*. Princeton: Princeton University Press.

Chen, Xiyu. 1994. "Research Note on the 'Chinese Economic Zone,'" ISSCO Bulletin 2, no.2: 3–4.

Cheng, Lucie and Ping-chun Hsiung. 1992. "Women, Export-Oriented Growth, and the State: The Case of Taiwan." In J. Henderson and R. P. Appelbaum, eds., *States and Development in the Asian Pacific Rim*. Newbury Park, CA: Sage.

Chua, Beng-Huat. 1991. "Depoliticized but Ideologically Successful: The Public Housing Programme in Singapore." *International Journal of Urban and Regional Research* 15, no.1: 24–41.

Chun, Allen. 1989. "Pariah Capitalism and the Overseas Chinese of Southeast Asia: Problems in the Definition of the Problem." *Ethnic and Racial Studies* 12, no. 2: 233–56.

———. 1994. "From Nationalism to Nationalizing: Cultural Imagination and State Formation in Postwar Taiwan." *Australian Journal of Chinese Affairs* 31: 49–72.

Corrigan, Philip, and Derek Sayer. 1985. *The Great Arch: English State Forma-tion as Cultural Revolution*. London: Basil Blackwell.

Cumings, Bruce. 1993. "Rimspeak." In A. Dirlik, ed., *What Is in a Rim? Critical Perspectives on the Pacific Region Idea*, pp. 29–47. Boulder: Westview.

Dirlik, Arif. 1993. "The Asia-Pacific in Asian-American Perspective." In A. Dir-lik, ed., *What Is in a Rim? Critical Perspectives on the Pacific Region Idea*, pp. 305–29. Boulder: Westview.

Dong Yunhu. 1993. "Fine Traditions of Human Rights in Asia." *Beijing Review*, June 28–July 4, 11–12.

Duara, Prasenjit. 1995. *Rescuing History from the Nation: Questioning Narra-tives of Modern China*. Chicago: University of Chicago Press.

Fan Guoxiang. 1994. "A Reasonable and Practical Choice." *Beijing Review*, March 14–20.

Fitzgerald, Stephen. 1972. *China and the Overseas Chinese: A Study of Peking's Changing Policy, 1949–1970*. Cambridge: Cambridge Univer-sity Press.

Foucault, Michel. 1979. *The History of Sexuality. Volume I: An Introduction*. New York: Vintage.

———. 1982. "The Subject and Power." In P. Rabinow and R. Dreyfus, eds, *Michel Foucault: Beyond Structuralism and Hermeneutics*, pp. 208–28. Chicago: University of Chicago Press.

———. 1991. "Governmentality." In G. Burchell, C. Gordon, and P. Miller, eds., *The Foucault Effect: Studies in Governmentality*, pp. 87–104. Chicago: University of Chicago Press.

Freedman, Maurice. 1969. "The Chinese in Southeast Asia: a Longer View." In R. O. Tilman, ed., *Man, State, and Society in Contemporary Southeast Asia*, pp. 31–99. New York: Praeger.

Friedman, Jonathan. 1992. "Narcissism and the Roots of Postmodernity." In J. Freidman and S. Lash, eds., *Modernity and Identity*. Oxford: Basil Black-well.

Greenhalgh, Susan. 1994. "De-Orientalizing the Chinese Family Firm," *Ameri-can Ethnologist* 21, no. 4: 746–75.

Gupta, Akhil. 1992. "The Song of the Non-Aligned World: Transnational Iden-tities and the Reinscription of Space in Late Capitalism." *Cultural An-thropology* 7, no. 1: 63–79.

Hall, Stuart. 1988. "The Toad in the Garden: Thatcherism Among the Theorists." In C. Nelson and L. Grossberg, eds. *Marxism and the Interpretation of Culture*, pp. 35–73. Urbana: University of Illinois Press.

———. 1991. "The Local and the Global: Globalization and Ethnicity." In A. King, ed., *Culture, Globalization, and the World System*, pp. 19–39. Lon-don: Macmillan.

Hamashita, Takeshi. 1988. "The Tribute Trade System and Modern Asia." *Tokyo: Memoirs of the Research Department of the Toyo Bunko*, no. 46.

Hannerz, Ulf. 1989. "Culture Between Center and Peiphery: Towards a Macroanthropology." *Ethnos* 54: III–IV.

Harvey, David. 1989. *The Condition of Postmodernity: An Inquiry into the Origins of Cultural Change*. Oxford: Basil Blackwell.

Heng, Geraldine, and Janadas Devan. 1995. "State Fatherhood: The Politics of Nationalism, Sexuality, and Race in Singapore." In A. Ong and M. Peletz, eds., *Bewitching Women, Pious Men: Gender and Body Politics in Southeast Asia*, pp. 195–215. Berkeley: University of California Press.

Higgot, Richard, and Richard Robinson, eds. 1985. *Southeast Asia: Essays in the Political Economy of Structural Change*. London: Routledge and Kegan Paul.

Hinton, William. 1966. *Fanshen: A Documentary of Revolution in a Chinese Village*. New York: Vintage.

Hong Kong Trade Development Council. 1991. *Recent Investment Environments of Guangdong, Fujian, and Hainan* (second edition). Hong Kong: Hong Kong Trade Development Council, Research Department.

Honig, Emily, and Gail Hershatter. 1988. *Personal Voices: Chinese Women in the 1980s*. Stanford: Standford University Press.

Hsiung, Ping-Chun. 1996. *Living Rooms as Factories: Class, Gender, and the Satellite Factory System in Taiwan*. Philadelphia: Temple University Press.

Ishihara, Shintaro. 1990. *The Japan that Can Say No*. New York: Simon and Schuster.

Jameson, Frederic. 1991. *Postmodernism, or the Cultural Logic of Late Capitalism*. Durham: Duke University Press.

Kao, John. 1993. "The Worldwide Web of Chinese Business." *Harvard Business Review*, March-April 1993: 24–37.

Kotkin, Joel. 1992. *Tribes: How Race, Religion, and Identity Determine Success in the New Global Economy*. New York: Random House.

———. 1993. "Family Ties in the New Global Economy." *Los Angeles Times Magazine*, January 17.

Lee, Ching Kwan. 1994. "Women Workers and Manufacturing Miracle: Gender, Labor Markets, and Production in South China." Ph.D. dissertation, University of California, Berkeley.

Lim, Willy Laohoo. 1993. "Filipino Reactions to Philippine Chinese Investments in China." *China Currents* 4, no. 4: 3–9.

Liu Tai-luk. 1990. "The Social Organization of Outwork: The Case of Hong Kong." Ph.D. dissertation, Oxford University.

Mahbubani, Kishore. 1993. "The Dangers of Decadence: What the Rest Can Teach the West." *Foreign Affairs* 73, no. 4: 10–15.

———. 1994. "The United States: 'Go East, Young Man." *Washington Quarterly* 17, no. 2: 5–23.

Nonini, Donald M. 1993. "On the Outs on the Rim: An Ethnographic Grounding of the 'Asia-Pacific' Imaginary" In A. Dirlik, ed., *What Is in a Rim? Critical Perspectives on the Perspectives on the Pacific Region Idea*, pp. 161–82. Boulder: Westview.

Ong, Aihwa. 1987. *Spirits of Resistance and Capitalist Discipline: Factory Women in Malaysia*. Albany: State University of New York Press.

————. 1988. "The Production of Possession: Spirits and the Multinational Corporation in Malaysia." *American Ethnologist* 15, no.1: 28–42.

————. 1991. "The Gender and Labor Politics of Postmodernity." *Annual Review of Anthropology* 20: 279–309.

————. 1993. "On the Edge of Empires: Flexible Citizenship Among Chinese in Diaspora." *Positions* 1, no. 3: 745–78.

————. 1995. "State Versus Islam: Malay Families, Women's Bodies, and the Body Politic in West Malaysia." In A. Ong and M. Peletz, eds., *Bewitching Women, Pious Men: Gender and Body Politics in Southeast Asia.* pp. 159–194. Berkeley: University of California Press.

————. 1996. "Anthropology, China, Modernities: The Geopolitics of Cultural Knowledge." In Henrietta Moore, ed., *The Future of Anthropological Knowledge.* pp. 60–92. New York: Routledge.

Ong, Aihwa, and Michael Peletz, eds. 1995. *Bewitching Women, Pious Men: Gender and Body Politics in Southeast Asia.* Berkeley: University of California Press.

Pred, A., and M. Watts. 1993. *Reworking Modernity: Capitalisms and Symbolic Discontent.* New Brunswick, N.J.: Rutgers University Press.

Rofel, Lisa B. 1994. "Yearnings: Televisual Love and Melodramatic Politics in Contemporary China." *American Ethnologist* 21, no. 4: 700–22.

Rostow, W. W. 1960. *Stages of Economic Growth: A Non-Communist Manifesto.* Cambridge, MA: MIT Press.

Sassen, Saskia. 1994. *Cities in a World Economy.* Thousand Oaks, CA: Pine Forge Press.

Schein, Louisa. 1993. "Popular Culture and the Production of Difference: The Miao and China," Ph.D. dissertation, Dept. of Anthropology, UC Berkeley.

Scott, James C. 1976. *The Moral Economy of the Peasant.* New Haven: Yale University Press.

————. 1985. *Weapons of the Weak.* New Haven: Yale University Press.

Seow, Francis T. 1994. *To Catch a Tartar: A Dissident in Lee Kuan Yew's Prison.* Southeast Asian Studies Monograph no. 42, New Haven: Yale Center for International Area Studies.

Steven, Rob. 1990. *Japan's New Imperialism.* Armonk, N.Y.: M. E. Sharpe.

Uhalley Stephen Jr. 1994. 'Greater China': The Contest of a Term." *Positions* 2, no. 2: 274–93.

White, Lynn, and Li Cheng. 1993. "China's Coast Identities: Regional, National, and Global." In Lowell Dittmer and Samuel S. Kim, eds., *China's Quest for National Identity*, pp. 154–93. Ithaca, NY: Cornell University Press.

Wolf, Diane L. 1992. *Factory Daughters: Gender, Household Dynamics, and Rural Industrialization in Java.* Berkeley: University of California Press.

Yang, Mayfair M.-H. 1994. *Gifts, Favors, and Banquets: The Art of Social Relationships in China.* Ithaca, NY: Cornell University Press.

Chapter Seven

Shifting Identities, Positioned Imaginaries: Transnational Traversals and Reversals by Malaysian Chinese[1]

Donald M. Nonini

The high romances of transnational Chinese capitalism—the triumphant narratives of the founding and growth of family business empires throughout the Asia Pacific—are compelling for many reasons, not least of which is that they register major shifts in economic dominance between regions of the global economy toward an emerging Asia Pacific capitalist center as the preexisting industrial centers of North America and Europe enter into a protracted period of decline and stagnation in the contemporary period of flexible accumulation (Harvey 1989; Nonini 1993). Stories of the dynastic histories of Liem Sioe Liong, Li Ka-Shing, Li Kung Pao, and other Asia-Pacific entrepreneurs have become emblematic of the economic success of "overseas Chinese" and the prominence of this success in the new global order (see Ong's essay in this volume). These narratives herald in congratulatory prose the arrival of a small elite of extraordinarily wealthy Chinese transnational businessmen, casting this as the emergence of a group of new entrepreneurial heroes on the deterritorialized stage of late capitalism (see, for example, Kao 1993). In their telling, such narratives celebrate putatively primal features of Chinese culture—thrift, family, commercial acumen, networks, connections, Confucian hierarchy. They also index new cultural shifts and the emergence of "alternative modernities," as Aihwa Ong argues in this volume.

   In this essay, I resituate this discourse of economic success by seeking to locate what it brackets, backgrounds, or negates by way of *difference.* That is, I take seriously recent theoretical work in the studies of diasporas (Clifford 1994; Gilroy 1987, 1994) and transnational projects (Basch,

Glick Schiller, and Szanton Blanc 1994; Glick Schiller, Basch, and Szanton Blanc 1992) to argue that the transnationalization of what has been called overseas Chinese capitalism can be understood only relative to the strategic bricolage of transnational practices by those nonelite diasporic Chinese who do not enter into these narratives, except by way of backgrounded contrast, because they are not "successful" (cf. Pan 1994). They do not form the heroic subjects of such "Rimspeak" (Cumings 1993) and "Rimwrite" narratives; at most they form a middle- and working-class audience for the enactment and codification of these narratives. Nonetheless, they engage in transnational practices of great consequence to the reorganization of flexible capitalism across the Asia Pacific. Their obliteration (or negation) in these narratives represents only the most superficial level in a multilayered cascade of symbolic violence (Bourdieu 1977) in which they act as both agents and victims.[2]

My argument is based on ethnographic and historical research carried out over the last five years in one urban Chinese community in northwestern Peninsular Malaysia. What my findings suggest is that we must guard against the reification of transnational overseas Chinese capitalism by making a double theoretical move. On the one hand, we need to examine the interplay among practices that articulate the local with the translocal or cosmopolitan (Hannerz 1990) and the national with the transnational in the construction of identities. On the other, we must consider the constitution of such practices out of those interconnected class, national, and gender regimes of truth and power to which diasporic Chinese are subject. Transnational practices of modern Chinese persons cannot be understood separately from the cultural politics of identities inscribed on them by such regimes in the spaces they traverse and reside in. Yet, through their strategic mobilities fueled by imaginaries of power and desire, they themselves seek to transcend these regimes, while working through these regimes to discipline others.

For nonelite Malaysian Chinese, mobility that crosses national boundaries represents a form of power vis-à-vis late modern regimes of power-knowledge (on the latter, see Foucault 1978, 1979, 1980, 1991). Of relevance here are the regimes of power-knowledge focused on three loci: families, capitalist worksites, and nation-states. These regimes take a variety of forms and are expressed through various modalities that overlap with and interpenetrate one another, yet all require the *localization of disciplinable subjects*. For Chinese families, familistic regimes dominated by men and the elderly not only regulate and exploit the labor power (whether compensated by wages or not) and reproductive power of family women, younger men, and children. These regimes also constitute subjects such as the ideal Chinese daughter through the discourse of *xiao*, "filial piety," and discipline them through forms of violence (see Ong 1991, 1993). Disciplining those who rebel or act abnormally extends even to the supernatural, as in the case of gods in the Taoist/Buddhist pantheon who, when children show insufficient deference before their altars, take retribution against them by making them sick, crippled, or insane. Familistic regimes are buttressed by state institutions—schools, police, courts of law—that instill deference to male and elder authority. For their effects, familistic regimes require the localization of subjects within certain determinate spaces—for example, unmarried women are expected to be at home, close to it, or in other spaces (such as factories and schools) locatable in relation to home, although—and this is central to contemporary Chinese transnationalism—there need be no congruity between these familistic spaces and specific nation-state territories.

In businesses, regimes of management not only regulate the labor of Chinese laborers but also inscribe certain disciplines in and on their bodies, through state police powers and violence, normalizing discourses about deference, bodily control, and families,[3] and by the operation of what Marx called the "dull compulsion" of everyday economic life. These discourses lead the working-class Chinese men I study to describe themselves as, "having no position" (*meiyou diwei*), that is, as being in no position to position others relative to themselves. Where businesses are operated by Chinese owners, managerial and familistic regimes overlap and compound each other's effects. Here too, these effects require that subordinate subjects be locatable and confinable to certain spaces. And, as Ong (1990) notes, modern nation-states show a governmentality (Foucault 1991) preoccupied with the biopower of their populations, which takes the form of disciplines and associated discourses of nationality and citizenship that police their subjects. But again, these regimes derive their effects by being specific and limited to national sovereign spaces, that is, territories (see Mitchell's essay in this volume on the making of the good Canadian citizen-subject).

The operations of these regimes are thus spatially delimited. Chinese transnationalists engage in practices that seek to *resist the localizations these overlapping regimes require of them as disciplinable subjects, while appropriating for their own uses the effects of the localizations these regimes have upon other disciplinable subjects*. These strategic practices are informed by imaginaries of power and desire. Here I follow Deleuze and Guattari's (1983) emphasis on desire to posit the existence of collective imaginaries, or utopian fantasy-scripts for repertoires of practices: products of the imagination that transcend delimited spaces and the localizations of bodies by regimes of truth and power associated with these spaces. Imaginaries are thus generative schema for new habitus (Bourdieu 1977) of power. So, for example, elder Chinese men, who own small-scale capitalist enterprises, act out transnational imaginaries to escape the stigma associated with their minority status within the Malaysian nation-state; at the same time, they seek to localize their grown sons and daughters in other national spaces as their subordinates. And adult working-class Chinese men imagine transnational ventures of labor migration to Japan in order to bypass regimes of control directed at them by state functionaries and employers in Malaysia, while depending on the labor of the wives, sisters, and children who are localized within working-class domestic spaces in Malaysia and await their return.

The Cultural Politics of the Chinese Diaspora in Malaysia

Recent literature on the concept of diaspora suggests the flexible, multiply inflected potentials of diaspora as a concept for indexing the experiences of dispersed persons and populations of displacement, border-crossing, border violation, transculturation and hybridization (Clifford 1994; Gilroy 1987, 1994). Clifford argues that diasporas can best be defined diacritically within a discursive field: They are defined in contrast to the territorially based norms of nation-states and to indigenous, especially autochthonous, claims made by tribal and other long-residing peoples (Clifford 1994; 307).

If we follow out Clifford's suggestion, diasporic Chinese identities (in Southeast Asia or elsewhere) can be seen only contrastively vis-à-vis alternative and opposed positions of citizenship and indigenousness, fixed by the regimes of truth and power of nation-states in the Asia Pacific. These identities become a cross between the officialized identifications ("race," "citizen," "Chinese," "native") constituted by these regimes and the flexible strategies of Chinese to escape just such identifications.

The cultural politics of Chinese urban communities within Malaysia since the 1960s can be understood only relative to the project by the modernizing postcolonial Malaysian state of instituting a regime of governmentality regulating the biopower of its citizen population, particularly in the realms of culture and economy. Contested issues arising over "Malaysian culture" in contrast to "Chinese culture" have included the government's periodic prohibition of the right of Chinese to perform the lion dance in public festivals and its limitation on the use of Mandarin Chinese in secondary schools and universities. Malaysian Chinese have questioned the Malaysian government's installation of the national language, Bahasa Malaysia, instead of English as *the* language of university instruction, and have shown great resentment about the setting of ethnic quotas in Malaysian university admissions that overrepresent and "favor" Malays or *bumiputras* ("sons of the soil," that is, indigenes) over Chinese.

In the realm of the economy, Malaysian Chinese are also aware that for more than two decades the Malaysian state has implemented ethnic quotas favoring *bumiputras* for employment in the government sector and in private corporate enterprises, for stock ownership in corporations, and for government contracts. Government policies privileging small-scale (and often inefficient and poorly run) Malay contractors have particularly incensed Chinese owners of family firms, who are not allowed to bid on lucrative contracts for construction and services. In all such practices, the Malaysian state displays a modern governmentality that in aggregate discriminates against citizens of Chinese descent.

Since the 1970s, Chinese political parties, community organizations, and interest groups have proven largely ineffective in preventing these changes from being implemented by a powerful modernizing Malay state elite, whose primary base of electoral support has been among Malays antagonistic to Chinese cultural and economic rights. Since the late 1980s, firmly ensconced in power, this state elite has yielded somewhat on minor cultural issues, such as the public performance of the lion dance, and has also begun to allow the founding of private universities and colleges. Nonetheless, the basic contours of indigenist policies favoring special rights for *bumiputras* have remained in effect. State language and culture policies have had the tendentious effect of provincializing Chinese, of putting them "in their place." Chinese realize this and have been deeply angry about it.

The convergence of state biopower (Foucault 1978, 140–44) and Malay indigenist discourses acts to discipline, register, and locate Chinese as questionable and problematic citizens, for while residing in Malaysia, they are positioned within Malaysian space yet are not identified as being of Malaysian society or history. The photograph and name of the citizen on the "I.C."—identity card—mark the "race" of its holder; as of the 1990s the I.C. itself has become the source of data for the state about the location and nature of the body of its holder by means of a recently implemented computerized data base containing files on all citizens.

The complex interplay between the adverse civil identifications imposed on Chinese by this official indigenism and the strategies undertaken at many levels by nonelite Chinese to nullify or transcend these identifications has constituted a diasporic Malaysian Chinese identity,

Malaixiya huaren. Chinese have enunciated new discourses about "culture" and "belonging to" Malaysia, although such speech and writing are discreet, given the presence of sedition laws aimed at suppressing discussion of sensitive topics such as Malay "special rights," *tequan.* Thus there has been much discussion among Chinese about the definition of Chinese culture. Counterposed to the state-imposed and -sanctioned national culture which is celebrated for being formed out of Malay culture, Chinese culture is characterized by its proponents as simultaneously properly Malaysian and traditionally Chinese, as in the commonly cited phrase "culture derived from five thousand years of tradition"—*wuquiannian quantongxialai de wenhua*, that is, coming from China—which I heard used in banquet speeches made by Chinese leaders. A compensatory oppositional discourse on the part of Chinese seeking to affirm local identities and authentic national Malaysianness has also come into existence. Informants often complained of being treated as second-class citizens, *dierdeng gongming*; were they not, they exclaimed angrily, as Malaysian as *bumiputras*, and shouldn't they have the same rights?

Chinese have also adopted instrumental strategems employing extralegal means and public deception, which play in ironic ways into the accumulation needs of state functionaries and *bumiputra* petty property owners. There have been the ubiquitous payments of "coffee money" to clerks, police, inspectors, and others in order to obtain permits, licenses, and free passage. In certain lines of business, such as truck transport, the "Ali Baba" arrangement has become common, in which a Chinese "Baba" rents for a fee from a *bumiputra* "Ali" the rights to use a permit or license issued to Ali by a government bureau, or, in a more sophisticated arrangement, brings in an Ali as his business partner.[4] Many such transactions become routinized and familiarized as long-standing friendship relations—a flexible, if limited, extension of *guanxi* practices across ethnic lines (see the introduction to this book and the preface to part 2). Such instrumental strategems become the basis for a labile and shifting public identity, one reinforced by jokes and narratives of successful trickery and deception that affirm from the Chinese side an interpersonal ethnic boundary between Chinese and *bumiputras*.

For middle-class Chinese, above all else it has been the state discursive control and disciplining of young Chinese that has called forth new eluding practices, for the two represent moves in a larger strategic game of class reproduction situated within a politics of antagonistic ethnic groups. For instance, protestations by Chinese over both ethnic quotas in university admissions and the use of Bahasa Malaysia as the language of school instruction have been particularly bitter. Chinese frequently argued to me on behalf of being allowed to learn and use their "mother tongue," *muyu* (that is, Mandarin), yet this is a language that relatively few speak on a daily basis. Others, fluent in Mandarin but having no or little English capability, eagerly extolled the virtues of university instruction in English, saying, "Malay language—it's useless in universities, since so many of the books are in English, and where else can you speak it except here [Malaysia] and Indonesia? English you can speak anywhere!"

Despite their unequal positionings within the familistic regime, members of middle-class Chinese families are committed to strategies for accumulating various forms of capital, requiring the conversion of family economic capital into other forms of deployable capital—educational, cultural, social—that allow family members broadly similar life chances (Bourdieu 1984, 1986; see also the introduction to this volume). For members of middle-class families, the potentials for finding new sources of capital and making new conversions of family capital have come increasingly to be set by the economic opportunities for Chinese made possible by flexible accumulation throughout the Asia Pacific—new possibilities for investment, gaining trade and market share, subcontracting, and professional employment, whether in Kuala Lumpur, Los Angeles, Hong Kong, or elsewhere. To take advantage of these possibilities has required new transnational practices.

It is in terms of these transnational practices that the profound antagonism on the part of Chinese toward Malaysian state indigenist discourses and practices surrounding culture makes sense. Mandarin Chinese and English are, in different but overlapping spheres of business in the Asia Pacific, cosmopolitan languages whose uses span national borders. Policies that disadvantage Malaysian Chinese children and adolescents in their mastery of these languages cut to the quick of strategies of Chinese middle-class reproduction. Similarly, government admissions quotas for Malaysian universities impede the acquisition by Chinese young men and women of a "degree" (*wenping*), which is viewed as the essential "qualfication" (*zige*) for finding high-paying employment not only within the rapidly expanding high-tech sector of the Malaysian export-oriented economy but also beyond Malaysia in the corporate sectors of the Asia Pacific at large—in Singapore, Australia, Canada, Hong Kong, New Zealand, the United States, Taiwan, and, by extension, Great Britain. Government quotas favoring the hiring of *bumiputras* over Chinese within the corporate sector in Malaysia—and within government service—are seen as having similar harmful effects. According to many informants, when it comes to hiring, "it is *kulit-fications* and not qualifications that matter"—*kulit* being the Malay word for "skin."

Middling Transnational Traversals: "Walking on Two Roads, Not One"

It is within the contrastive national field of contested diasporic Chinese identities described above that the transnational traversals of most middle-income urban Chinese take place. I start with the stories provided by older, petty-property-holding Chinese men because they made up most of my informants, not because their points of view are to be privileged as "true." The familistic regime inscribes older male claims with hegemonic facticity within the setting of the family. Other perspectives— those of women, children, younger grown sons—are equally "true" and valuable for the understanding of Chinese transnational strategies; although these were usually not directly accessible to me, I try to suggest what they might be.

Transnational traversals by middle-class Chinese of/from/in Malaysia characteristically begin by men sending their grown children overseas to acquire a university degree. In terms of their chances of being sent, adult sons tend to be favored over adult daughters, but not by much.[5] For even small-scale businessmen, sending their adult children—particularly their sons—for degree courses in universities in anglophone nation-states is the first step in a *potentially* permanent transnational movement and relocation. It is precisely the potential rather than the unconditional necessity for such a move that makes this option so attractive to elder men controlling family property, particularly since a family may have two or more sons and/or daughters overseas in more than one country simultaneously.

In 1991 I met Mr. Ang, the former owner of a truck transport company in Penang state:

> Ang drives us (his wife, Xiujin, and I) to Kulim. He says his reason for doing this was that it is his old home, where he grew up. His family included thirteen children and was very poor, and his father died when Ang was about eight years old—whereupon he began working.
>
> Ang says that he now lives with his family on the outskirts of Auckland, New Zealand, about thirty kilometers from the city itself. Of his three children, all three are in New Zealand, and two are studying at a university there. He is presently not engaged in any business; I ask whether he is planning on opening a business in New Zealand and he says no, not at present, since the economy there is currently not doing well. He will be in Malaysia, most of

that time in Kuala Lumpur, until the end of August, looking after some property he owns there.

He has permanent residence in New Zealand, but has not given up his Malaysian citizenship. He and his family only moved to New Zealand late in 1990. When I ask him later about this, he says, "Why should a person who can walk on either of two roads cut himself off from one—and leave only one? What if that single one is cut off as well?"

I ask him why, if the New Zealand economy is so bad, he emigrated there. He replies that he did this in order to give his children the opportunity to study in New Zealand universities, where they would learn English. He hopes later to send his eldest child, a son, who has been studying computer science in New Zealand, to America for graduate study in computer science, where it is most advanced (*xianjin*). His second child, a daughter, also studies at the university, in commercial studies. It is to give them an opportunity that he has not had himself, to help them make a life for themselves. He has told all his children that they will not inherit any property from him—that their educations represent his capital, *benqian*, given to them. He has done this in order to avoid the common situation in which the children of a Chinese man with money spend it freely and thoughtlessly, not realizing how hard it had been to earn. "I earned my money a penny and a penny at a time."

Sending an adult son for education overseas is a gendered and classed strategy that achieves several goals associated with transnational repositioning. First, the son acquires transferable cultural capital (Bourdieu 1984) in the form of an English-language university education, most preferably in a technical academic field—electronic engineering is a favorite—or in business studies. A university degree provides certifiable eligibility for technical or professional employment, at the very least within the country where the degree is awarded, and usually beyond it in other countries, including Malaysia. Expatriated economic capital has been converted successfully into educational capital.

Second, the son demonstrates to the host country's government that he is a potentially desirable immigrant whose skills are locally in short supply. This is the first step toward permanent residency, and later citizenship, for not only the son but also other family members, particularly when the older man invests economic capital as well, or has his son act as its conduit, in the host country. This has been particularly effective in anglophone countries—the United States, Canada, Australia, New Zealand—whose nation-states, facing economic stagnation from the 1980s onward, have passed new legislation allowing immigrants with investible wealth and technical expertise to become citizens more readily (see Mitchell's essay in this volume). Thus, the older men of the family engage in strategic bricolage, playing off differing definitions of legitimate citizenship in Malaysia and the second country, whose outcome is an example of what Ong (1993) calls "flexible citizenship."

Third, during and after the son's years of sojourning as a university student overseas, his status as an educated son provides elder males of the family—his father and frequently his eldest brother—with a legitimate pretext to visit the country in which he resides. In their visits these men assess the prospects for expansion in the line to which the family business belongs, explore other forms of investment, and discover new markets. They can accomplish these objectives while surveying the local and expatriate Chinese communities in and near where their sons and daughters study, and seeking out opportunities to build *guanxi* ties with expatriate and other Chinese businessmen.

Fourth, the several years required to receive a university degree overseas provides the male managers of the family business with the chance to assess comparatively the economic prospects for the family's children in both Malaysia and the country in which the son sojourns. Moreover, if the father seeks to retire from his profession or business, visits to sons overseas provide him and (usually) his wife with information about living conditions in one or more countries outside Malaysia to which they might wish to migrate.

In 1991 I visited Mr. Lim, in Seberang Perai. He is the owner of a small transport company whose trucks carry freight from northern and central urban areas to the east coast states of Pahang and Trengganu.

Lim looks much the same as he did six years ago, except for being a bit frail, though not much. He still is thin, wiry, and muscular. When I ask him today, he says his age is sixty-seven. Until he was sixty-five, he says, he would lift and carry freight to his trucks all day. Now, however, he says, he can lift only several pieces of freight before he is out of breath and then has to stop.

He says that he now has three sons who work in Australia. Two are medical doctors with their own clinics. The other, the youngest, is a computer specialist with an American company. His oldest son is the only one of his four sons here in Malaysia, and works with him in operating the trucking company. One of his sons (a doctor) has become an Australian citizen, while his youngest son has received permanent residence in Australia but—although he could do so—has not applied for citizenship because he is not sure whether he wishes to stay in Australia.

All three of his sons there are married, two to women who are Malaysian Chinese and have worked as accountants. The other wife is also Chinese. One of his sons, a doctor, has two children, and his youngest son has a child, so he is a grandfather. His wife went to visit his sons in Australia only last year, but he has not been to visit them since 1987. Next year, for Chinese New Year, all his three sons in Australia are going to come back to visit him and his wife.

It is crucial to observe that such strategic bricolage by elder men makes sense only within a familistic regime of power and discourse that allows them to authoritatively position the younger and female family members within spaces both in Malaysia (that is, "home") and beyond it, and to command family economic resources to do so. Yet among petty property owners this regime is poorly buttressed by their control of only modest economic capital, unlike the situation for elite Chinese transnational families. It is this weakness that allows the individual strategies of grown sons and daughters to operate within the penumbra, as it were, of this regime; a father can require them to accede to his sending them overseas, but once educated and employed, they cannot be made to return to Malaysia or to rejoin the family business.

When adult daughters are sent to universities overseas, their parents expect them to acquire not only degrees but often husbands as well, as part of a strategy of gaining citizenship through marriage—preferably to an ethnic Chinese man in Australia or wherever. Their presence overseas may then serve to provide the family with a social *pied-à-terre* there and, in a few instances, to recruit sons-in-law to the family business, though more often such men already have other work as affluent professionals or small businessmen. In any event, such men become family members familiar with the economic potential and political order of the other country. On the other hand, as with sons, the individual strategies of grown daughters once they are educated may lead them to act independently of their father's desires by cutting off ties, by moving back to Malaysia (but not to the parental residence there), and so on.

This pliable strategizing by Chinese transnationalists, focused on sending grown children for education and eventual employment overseas, provides an apt and timely response to the constantly shifting economic opportunities, largely independent of spatial constraints, that characterize flexible accumulation. It serves as a means to secure their adult children's entry into global and national professional elites and operates to gather information about emerging markets, market trends, new techniques in production, new technologies of advertising, communication and transport, and much more. Above all else, it expands the universe of potential *guanxi* relationships accessible to small-scale Chinese capitalists from/in/of Malaysia across national borders. This is the basis of what I call "middling" transnationalism.[6] Grounded in a familistic regime of truth and power, middling transnationalism also reflects the limits of this regime posed by petty property.

The narratives about Ang and Lim excerpted above illustrate particularly well two features of middling, as distinct from elite, transnationalism. One is that the determinate Malaysian space from which they come—an area near the border between the states of Penang and Kedah—is still for both men their "old native place" (*laoguxiang*): The space to which they affectively "belong" is not indeterminate and flexible but rather quite fixed in memory and association. On balance, it is affective "representational space" (Lefebvre 1975) in a way that New Zealand or Australia are not.[7] In the subjectivities of older men such as Ang and Lim, then, there is a painful tension between this affinity for specific Malaysian places and the space-independent sensibilities required for what could be called full-bore transnationalism, as observed, for example, among the wealthy male Hong Kong entrepreneurs discussed by Ong (1993) and Mitchell (in this volume).

The second point is that Mr. Lim's experience reinforces something repeatedly made clear to me: the *contingency* of transnational traversal—that among petty property owners such as Mr. Lim, not all resources held by Chinese capitalists are liquid economic assets shifted easily overseas, but are instead vested in persons working in specific Malaysian sites—in this case, in the goodwill of Lim's local customers, who require the services his trucking business provides, and in his relationships with foremen in truck repair shops and with the local police, among many others. On the one hand, the mobile business practices that Mr. Lim and those like him in other commercial businesses (wholesaling, distributing, etc.) engage in do "overcome space" and so predispose them to transnational moves.[8] On the other hand, profitable business requires they make time-consuming and vexatious visits to "provide service" to and "entertain" customers and suppliers dispersed regionally, and in this sense petty businessmen are confined by space in ways that wealthier entrepreneurs, employing deterritorialized investment strategies with greater liquid capital, are not.

The narratives of transnational traversals by Chinese petty business families discussed here point to the inextricably connected aspects of class and gender that are deeply implicated in diaspora life (Clifford 1994, 312–13), in its forms of symbolic violence and euphemizations, and in its unstated losses as well as its celebrated gains. Indeed, the narratives as such manifest a gendered imaginary of male mobility and achieved desire, an idealization of Chinese men who own and dispose of property, place family members where they wish, and move across national spaces and international boundaries as they are inclined.

"Airplane Jumping" and Gendered Imaginaries

In quite a different way, the interconnected aspects of class and gender are also evident in what I call transnational reversals—the movements associated with the sojourns of male Malaysian Chinese labor migrants in Japan and Taiwan.[9] If we view such movements as culturally creative strategic reversals—transnational endeavors achieved through return—rather than as passive or mechanical responses to the operation of international labor markets (Cohen 1987), we have much to gain theoretically, for it allows us to situate the practices of highly mobile working-class Chinese within the field of transnational practices.[10]

As part of the disaporic strategies by Malaysian Chinese, transnational reversals are gendered, for by and large they are undertaken by men.[11] Labor sojourning in Japan and Taiwan is almost exclusively the sphere of young working-class Chinese men, who thereby affirm the privileges of male mobility in contrast to the spatial constraints imposed on working-class women in general and on the women they know and have relationships with in particular. Among the working-class Chinese I knew in Penang, the familistic regime dictates that urban Chinese laboring women are to be confined to local spaces—to their natal residences while engaged in various forms of "homework" (such as sewing garments for piecework contractors) or to the nearby factories of local small-scale businesses or of the export-processing zones. Thus surveillance of them by older family members, if not continuous, takes place daily; this is true even when women move to other cities and towns for employment, for most live with older relatives already residing there (see Strauch 1984, 70). Younger working-class women not so confined because not under the control of families men or older women are "bad" women, and leave (or are ejected from) their families, typically moving to urban locales elsewhere. In contrast, some older women, no longer nubile and usually separated from husbands or widowed, have undertaken labor sojourns as domestics in Australia, but not in large numbers.

Those who organize international labor markets, such as employers overseas and labor recruiters, see certain kinds of labor as necessarily gendered—for example, construction work is male, while certain kinds of factory work are female and other kinds are male—and collude with state functionaries and with older male family members to reinforce the gender hierarchy associated with Chinese familistic regimes. It is within such a setting that male labor sojourning as a transnational practice takes place. As of 1992, Malaysians formed the largest contingent of estimated illegal workers in Japan—14,000, with the vast majority (79 percent) be-

Fig. 1: Chinese laboring men in urban Malaysia, at leisure. (Photo by D. Nonini)

ing male (Shimada 1994, 28, table 2.9); in Taiwan in 1992 there were about 4,000 Malaysians working illegally, although the figure had been as high as 16,000 in 1990 (Choi 1992, 9: see also Li and Wang 1992). The number of men engaged in such work has varied from year to year, depending on labor market conditions in Japan and Taiwan and the stringency of enforcement of immigration laws by Japanese and Taiwanese governments. I have been told by informants that they tend to concentrate in construction, certain factory jobs, and restaurant work; in the case of Japan, this is supported by official estimates provided of all illegal male laborers (irrespective of their nationality) in these categories of labor (Shimada 1994, 31, table 2.10). Large numbers of male Malaysian Chinese in Japan—along with other illegal labor migrants from the Philippines, South Korea, Thailand, China, Pakistan, and Bangladesh— have come to constitute the public "'problem' of foreign workers in contemporary Japan," in that they challenge Japan's hegemonic myth of racial homogeneity (Lie 1994).

Transnational reversals by Malaysian Chinese working-class men are called "airplane jumping" (*tiao feiji*). Recruited by Malaysian Chinese contractors working on behalf of Japanese and Taiwanese firms and flown to Japan and Taiwan, where they enter on tourist visas and then overstay, these men set out to spend from one to three years laboring as illegal workers to earn the relatively high wages, by Malaysian standards, paid by these firms. They live in dormitories or houses with the other men from Malaysia, at times cheek by jowl with Chinese and non-Chinese from other countries in Asia.

The experiences of "airplane jumping" form one substrate of the identity shared by Chinese working-class men who have returned from sojourning in Japan and Taiwan. My research from 1990 to 1992 focused on an informal peer group of more than fifteen working-class men, all but one married, who gathered in the afternoons and evenings in a roadside area they called "under the trees." More than one third of the group's "members"[12] either had sojourned as laborers in Japan or intended to do so. Other members of the group were off sojourning in Japan during my fieldwork. When members convened after working hours in their meeting place to talk, eat snacks, and drink tea, one of the most frequently discussed topics was their sojourning experiences in Japan, recalled vividly and often with nostalgia (see figure 1). These experiences were also narrated in the life histories of members I elicited.

In 1991 I interviewed Mr. Teoh, married and in his early thirties, then working as a stonemason near the town of Pekan Tebu.

Teoh: One of my younger brothers went to Japan to do physical labor.

DMN: Haven't you thought of going yourself?

Teoh: I went, but they would not allow me to enter [at Narita Airport]. I couldn't pass through.

DMN: If in the future you have an opportunity to go to Japan or Taiwan to earn money and return, what would you do with it?

Teoh: I haven't thought about what I would do with it. It's just that I'd heard that it was very well-paying there. We want to go look around. My younger brother went, and has just returned. He was there working for more than two years.

DMN: Was he able to save money?

Teoh: He was able to! He saved money, and he just returned.

DMN: What did he think of the life there?

Teoh: Life in Japan, you have to be frugal and thrifty [*shengchijianyong*]! You can still save money this way, but if you are going there to spend money, you don't have enough to spend. [Life working there is hard; one has to work long hours]. . . . My younger brother did two kinds of labor and worked until eleven o'clock before stopping.

DMN: Eleven at night?

Teoh: Yes! He began in the morning and went to a little after six P.M. He worked from eight in the morning until six P.M. From seven P.M. he worked

217

until eleven P.M. before stopping. By the next day at eight in the morning, he was out working again.

Several men I met have told me that in this way, if they labored continually, lived frugally, avoided the financial perils of excessive gambling, prostitutes, and sightseeing, and so saved their wages or remitted them back to their families in Malaysia, they could earn sufficient money for a down payment for a house or to start their own small businesses. This discourse of transnational reversal constructs a modal Chinese male imaginary—a fantasized life trajectory of upward mobility grounded in the privileges of male movement, a path marked also by formidable challenges to be heroically overcome by labor.

"Airplane jumping" doesn't pay off for everyone. In 1991 I spoke with Mr. Tan, at that time a truck driver living in Seberang Perai:

Tan: I sold my car and used the money to go to Japan to work. This was my capital [*benqian*]. I was in Japan for five months; at that time, my child had just been born.

DMN: Didn't you find this difficult, what with your child being born, to go overseas?

Tan: I didn't have any choice. For the sake of my future, for my life, I had to run off to Japan.

DMN: What kind of work did you do in Japan?

Tan: Refurbishing; I worked in construction. In a single day I could make 200 ringgit,[13] but the work was very filthy. . . . When I went to Japan, I expected that only after a year in Japan would I return. But I hadn't thought about the fact that in my dormitory there, everyone was gambling. So every day there I gambled. [He gambled all night long, and then was exhausted while he worked during the day. As a result one day he had an accident, falling down a story of the building. Fortunately he was not badly injured.] After that, I saw no meaning in the work, and came back.

DMN: At that time, were your family in Penang—your two small children, wife, parents, older brother, older sisters?

Tan: Yes.

DMN: Didn't you think of your family in Malaysia and feel lonely?

Tan: The first month I was in Japan, it was fairly difficult, but after that I became used to it. Still, I thought of them a lot and often called home on the telephone, and also sent them money.

DMN: So all this time, before your return, you were in Tokyo?

Tan: Yes. Especially, if I had time, I would go out and play, walk around.

DMN: So after five months you returned to Malaysia?

Tan: Yes. But I hadn't earned much money—it had been spent away. My capital in order to go there was about seven or eight thousand ringgit.

DMN: From selling your car?

Tan: Yes, I made eight thousand from the sale of my car. In going to Japan, I thought of changing my life, but I was not able to change.

In the narratives of Teoh and Tan, diasporic themes of male freedom and mobility, overseas economic opportunity, the temptations of single male company, waning and waxing attachments to family and Malaysian place, and the need for self-mastery all converge in the story of transnational reversal—this despite the fact that in Tan's case, sojourning is largely a failed strategy of mobility, of "changing my life." The modal male imaginary requires the possibility of failure to reinforce its hegemony.

The narratives of struggle, temptation, hard physical labor, triumph, or failure recounted by men "under the trees" who returned from Japan or Taiwan reflect a solidarity they share with other male groups to which they were connected by virtue of their transnational sojourns. In the illegal laborers' dormitory in Japan, Mr. Tan observed, "Everyone with me there were Malaysians. They were from Penang state, Kulim, Ipoh, Johore—many places. We rented a space together each of us paying five hundred ringgit per month. It was very convenient, with many facilities."

Although this gendered imaginary of self-uplift through labor sojourning takes a transnational form, it is but one of a class of such imaginaries narrated by Malaysian Chinese working-class men, a utopian fantasy that valorizes male mobility and labor power, cleverness and tricksterism, heterosexuality, male bodies, and bodiliness. At the same time, silently, it commits a kind of symbolic violence against working-class women, presuming while denying that its realization is dependent on their labor power and their confinement to domestic and adjacent spaces—in short, to their localization.

Men of "No Position": Fugitive Tactics, Fugitive Spaces

As was the situation for the transnational traversals discussed above, the transnational reversals of working-class Chinese men are grounded in the cultural politics of nationality, ethnicity, and race in Malaysia. However, they enter into these cultural politics in ways radically different from members of the urban Chinese middle classes who participate in the public sphere of antagonistic (if usually euphemized) polemics contesting the ethnic/racial and national identifications imposed by the Malaysian state.

Facing instead the harsh disciplinary and punitive apparatuses of the Malaysian state, working-class Chinese play little public role in the articulation of grievances about, for example, government universities admissions quotas or the use of English or Mandarin as languages of instruction in schools. Neither highly educated nor belonging to the preferred ethnic group, they are shut off from employment both in the government's bureaucracy and in the corporate sector, leaving them only poorly paid work for Chinese small-scale businesses or for the factories in nearby free-trade zones. Within a diasporic Chinese community that celebrates wealth above all other values, they have no "position" (*diwei*) that would allow their participation in the public sphere.[14] Moreover, their lack of *pangkat* (Malay for "status") in Malaysian society at large contributes to their identification by the Malaysian/Malay-nationalist state as a menace and danger to society—to state functionaries, offended by their lack of bodily deference and creolized Malay speech, they are even more "crude" (*kasar*), thus "more Chinese," and even more problematic as citizens than better-off, highly educated Chinese.

Working-class Chinese men compensate for their imperiled social and civil identities by resorting to two contrasting maneuvers. On the one hand, they explore the possibilities for transnational reversals that allow them bargaining power vis-à-vis domestic employers and labor markets and that free them from the daily regulation and surveillance by Malaysian state functionaries. Such strategems may not always succeed, as illustrated by Mr. Teoh's failure to slip by vigilant immigration officials at Narita, the point of entry into Japan, and by Mr. Tan's inability to save money once working in Japan. All the same, these strategems enact the imaginary that inspires the men. On the other hand, the men form defensive attachments to very specific Malaysian places and localizable persons—to their families and residences of birth and marriage, to their neighborhoods and to the "secret societies" (*sihuidang*) who dominate them, to the gods of neighborhood temples and shrines (especially sites for the place god Nadugong associated with the dangers of manual labor), and to fugitive spaces of occupation, such as the area "under the trees" they claimed for their leisure hours. Working-class Chinese men employ what de Certeau (1984, xix) refers to as fugitive tactics of opposition to state-determined identifications, as distinct from the overt strategies employed by affluent and educated Chinese. Even these informal and semi-covert engagements with the politics of national space are gendered and appear not to be available to working-class Chinese women.[15]

Networks of working-class Chinese men are, within the contrastive field of contested nationalities and "races" (*zhongzu*) in Malaysia, organized into transnational circuits consisting not only of male bodies rendering labor power to capitalists, but also of gendered cultural productions across vast spaces. They replicate, albeit at broader geographic scope, similar networks formed by working-class Chinese men who leave shared Malaysian native places to sojourn together in specific urban and rural sites within Malaysia—in timber camps, mines, factories, estates, truck transport depots, and other loci of male-centered economic production.

By insisting that the transnational sojourns of working-class Chinese be viewed as culturally informed transnational practices of reversal instead of as mere mechanical reflexes of international labor markets, I want to suggest the potential these experiences have for the formation of new cosmopolitan subjectivities and identities, many of which at present can only be imagined. In these experiences, these men acquire new patterns of commodity consumption and desire. They display new forms of habitus for coping with cultural and national differences encountered in their transnational travels. They have new perceptions of business opportunities (for example, smuggling, labor contracting, and petty trading). They form new self-definitions arising from exposure to the mediatized representations of Chinese in, for example, the kung fu films shown throughout the Asia Pacific. These and other aspects of transnational reversals represent forms of cultural production leading to new subjectivities and identities among working-class migrants.

I propose that the concept of a gendered imaginary can illuminate this process. Although both transnational reversals (and for that matter, traversals) have a rational-strategic dimension (and would make no sense if they did not), I also want to emphasize their symbolically mediated magical, projective, and imaginary aspects. These are deeply rooted in the identifications inscribed by familistic, workplace, and statist regimes of truth and power that, taken together, constitute gendered, race-identified and class-identified subjects. The effects of power acting through these regimes, however, are always incomplete and deferred; the impetus by subjects to agency and autonomy operates through psychic mechanisms of compensatory fantasy, the obverse side from the self-disciplining these regimes generate. Thus Chinese working-class male affect arises from a gendered imaginative construct of unbridled and unrestricted movement over spaces and through places within which others—women and children—are locatable and therefore serve as objects of the working of the men's powers, including sexual predation,[16] deployment of domestic labor, and so on. The fantastic dimensions of the male imaginary are firmly situated within a larger magic of desire for capital accumulation that is evident not only in gender relations, but also in religious worship, gambling practices, and other intimate dimensions of daily life (Nonini 1979).

In Inconclusion . . . A Cascade of Symbolic Violence

The triumphalist narratives of legendary Chinese tycoons and their family enterprises spanning the Asia Pacific nation-states should certainly continue to be grist for our theoretical mill as we seek to understand the transnationalization of overseas Chinese capitalism. Yet capitalism cannot be identified solely with a form of economic organization, nor Asian capitalism only with a family form of organization; rather, these must also be considered within the frame of associated modernities that encompass and position specific bodies, identities, and spaces within the Asia Pacific, particularly as these modernities are imposed by the interface between state powers and civil society (see the introduction to this volume and Ong's essay). Nor should diasporic Chinese throughout the Asia Pacific be reduced to being represented metonymically by a very few, spectacularly successful capitalist exemplars, however much rightful ethnic or racial pride might seem to call for it in the coming "Pacific Century."

These two related caveats suggest the virtue of investigating the full range of transnational practices available to diaspora Chinese throughout the Asia Pacific and beyond it. In this essay, I have merely begun to point to the extent of this range through the concepts of traversal and reversal. What this suggests, immediately, is the necessity for refiguring the tropes of Chinese subjectivities and identities inscribed *implicitly* in these narratives of triumph. Themes such as the incessant deterritorialized search for profits, the improvisational genius of founding fathers of business dynasties, the flexibilities in operation allowed family firms, the "bridgings" engaged in by Chinese capitalists acting as cultural brokers, and the instrumental deployments of *guanxi* and *ganqing* ("sentiment"), are standard features of the essentializing narratives of triumph. These themes need to be rethought, and they certainly require reframing in terms of broader considerations of the workings of fields of class, gender, ethnic/racial, and national relations and identities within the context of diaspora.

When examined within the field of transnational discourses and practices among diasporic Chinese, it is evident that the strategies of both elites and nonelites are grounded in imaginaries of desire in tension with cascades of symbolic violence. Symbolic domination works through the operation of nation-state, workplace, and familistic regimes of truth and power that constitute this person as a "citizen," "woman," "worker," or "Chinese," that person as "citizen," "male," official, and "*bumiputra*," and so on. The introduction to this book and Ong's essay on "flexible citizenship" (1993) point to the symbolic violence behind the elite discourse of *guanxi*—one euphemizing unequal interdependencies and interpersonal domination in terms of human "relationships." Similarly, as I suggested above, the elision of nonelites in the narratives of triumph centered on the wealthiest Chinese transnational capitalists represents the bracketing of shadowed, subordinate Others who are the audiences and objects of such narratives, never their subjects—a subtle intimidation and putting-into-their-place of those left out.

I propose that such narratives are merely the peak of a cascade of intimidation that "goes all the way down," distributing both agents and victims in its operation; moreover, with the exception only of those most dominant and those most dominated, this kind of intimidation makes certain persons perpetrators in some settings, acted-upon victims in others. Thus, for example, older Chinese male owners of petty property making transnational traversals to escape Malaysian state indigenist pressures aspire to position their grown children under their control, even if overseas; Chinese working-class men engage in transnational reversals to elude both capitalist and state disciplining in Malaysia while seeking to position their wives and daughters at home even as they themselves temporarily forgo their economic obligations to them. In connection to Chinese transnationalism, the cascade of symbolic violence operates most effectively through probabilities bearing on populations in which each person seeks the discursive and embodied localization of other subjects—putting people in their proper places within ordered national, workplace, and domestic spaces—while attempting to elude being so localized oneself. Mobility and modernity are thereby inextricably interlinked in forms of power.

Notes

[1] This is a revised version of a paper prepared for a conference entitled, The Transnationalisation of Overseas Chinese Capitalism: Networks, Nation-States, and Imagined Communities, held at the National University of Singapore, August 8–12, 1994. I am grateful to Judith Farquhar, Carla Freeman, Katharyne Mitchell, Sandy Smith-Nonini, Mayfair Yang, and above all to Aihwa Ong for comments and suggestions. I also gratefully acknowledge the support of the Social Science Research Council, whose Advanced Research Grant in Southeast Asian Studies made this ethnographic reseach possible.

[2] The term "symbolic violence," as used by Bourdieu (1977, 1991), refers to unconscious practices of intimidation euphemized both by those who dominate and by those who are dominated. It operates not so much by imperative language as by verbal insinuation, tone, tempo, and volume, and by gesture and other body language (see also Krais 1993). Symbolic violence "puts a person in his/her place."

[3] For example, widespread use of the language of "one big family" by factory managers to refer to their production workers in Chinese-owned enterprises.

[4] Here "Ali" is the fortunate Malay whose privileged access to government licenses and permits opens "the cave to riches," as in the fairytale, while "Baba" refers to the historic name given the Straits Chinese of Malacca and Penang. It is probably relevant that a related Malay word is *babi*, which means "pig"—an animal whose flesh Chinese are said to enjoy, while Malays, as Muslims, forswear it—and that *babi* is used by some Malays as a vulgar racial epithet for Chinese.

[5] I was asked frequently what I thought of "weighing males over females" (*zhong-nan qingnü*). Men who are family heads recognize a responsibility to pay for the education of daughters as well as sons. This may be the result of modernist discourses about gender acquired from the mass media. However, the degrees women earn tend to be in subjects with less commercial potential than those earned by men, such as business, accounting, and "helping" occupations such as nursing.

[6] I borrow this term from Rabinow's (1989) notion of "middling modernism" but give it a quite different inflection here.

[7] "Space as directly *lived* through its associated images and symbols [representation of space] . . . is alive: it speaks. It has an effective kernel or centre: Ego, bed, bedroom, dwelling, house; or: square, church, graveyard. It embraces the loci of passion, of action and of lived situations" (Lefebvre 1974, 38, 42).

[8] For instance, truck transporters and wholesalers have come to depend on the telephone and fax in their daily operations.

[9] Chinese labor migration out of south China to Southeast Asia is as long-standing as the history of European colonialism in the region (see Trocki's essay in this volume) and voluminously documented (see Pan 1994). Travel by Chinese laborers to work in Japan and Taiwan is but one of many migrations worldwide by working-class Chinese in recent years. Yet it is a qualitatively new process arising over the last two decades under the conditions of labor markets and labor control associated with flexible accumulation (Harvey 1989; see also the introduction to this volume).

[10] Cohen (1987, 109) writes that "the mass of illegal workers are usually neither romantic heroes of the wild frontier, nor amateur micro-econometricians. Rather they are sad, fearful, pathetic individuals desperate to escape intolerable conditions at the periphery of the regional political econmy, thrown about by forces they at first only dimly comprehend."

[11] This characterizes the larger pattern of Chinese laborers' migration worldwide. Kwong (1994, 2) describes Fuzhounese migration to the United States: "There are fewer jobs [in New York City] for women, because there are fewer undocumented women. Migration from China is a planned operation of extended families, who prefer to send young males first."

[12] They used this English word.

[13] The value of the ringgit, the unit of Malaysian currency, varied, but it was around 2.5 to the U.S. dollar during 1991–1992.

[14] Repressive labor laws, actively enforced, also mean that with few exceptions, working-class Chinese are allowed little collective expression through labor unions or occupational associations.

[15] All ethnography is partial and leads to limited insights. In a setting in which effective gender segregation is very strong, my closeness to male working-class informants "under the trees" precluded learning much about the strategies of the women related to them as wives and daughters. Evidence from elsewhere suggests that some Chinese women resist localization by men by seeking to opt out of familistic regimes (Stockard 1989).

[16] Resort to prostitutes, usually working-class Chinese and Thai women, works through displacement from the home setting. Certain places, such as border towns in Thailand, are "paradises" to be visited for male conquest marked by the presence and allure of purchasable female sexual services. This is not to imply that all working-class men engage in such practices; data on this topic is understandably anecdotal and uneven.

References

Basch, Linda, Nina Glick Schiller, and Cristina Szanton Blanc. 1994. *Nations Unbound: Transnational Projects, Postcolonial Predicaments, and Deterritorialized Nation-states*. Langhorne, PA: Gordon and Breach.

Bourdieu, Pierre. 1977. *Outline of a Theory of Practice*. Cambridge: Cambridge University Press.

———. 1984. *Distinction: A Social Critique of the Judgement of Taste*. Cambridge, MA: Harvard University Press.

———. 1986. "The Forms of Capital." In John G. Richardson, ed., *Handbook of Theory and Research for the Sociology of Education*, pp. 241–58. New York: Greenwood.

———. 1991. "The Production and Reproduction of Legitimate Language." In *Language and Social Power*, pp. 43–65. Edited by John B. Thompson. Cambridge, MA: Harvard University Press.

Certeau, Michel de. 1984. *The Practice of Everyday Life*. Berkeley: University of California Press.

Choi, Tuck Wo. 1992. "Rise in Illegal M'sian workers in Taiwan." *Star*, June 4. Penang.

Clifford, James. 1994. "Diasporas." *Cultural Anthropology* 9, no. 3: 302–38.

Cohen, Robin. 1987. "Policing the Frontiers: The State and the Migrant in the International Division of Labour." In Jeffrey Henderson and Manuel Castells, eds., *Global Restructuring and Territorial Development*, pp. 88–111. London: Sage.

Cumings, Bruce. 1993. "Rimspeak; or, the Discourse of the 'Pacific Rim.' " In Arif Dirlik, ed., *What Is in a Rim? Critical Perspectives on the Pacific Region Idea*, pp. 29–50. Boulder: Westview.

Deleuze, Gilles, and Felix Guattari. 1983. *Anti-Oedipus: Capitalism and Schizophrenia*. Minneapolis: University of Minnesota Press.

Foucault, Michel. 1978. *The History of Sexuality Volume I: An Introduction.* New York: Vintage.

————. 1979. *Discipline and Punish: The Birth of the Prison.* New York: Vintage.

————. 1980. *Power/Knowledge: Selected Interviews and Other Writings, 1972–1977.* Edited by Colin Gordon. New York: Pantheon.

————. 1991. "Governmentality." In Graham Burchell, Colin Gordon, and Peter Miller, eds., *The Foucault Effect: Studies in Governmentality*, pp. 87–104. Chicago: University of Chicago Press.

Gilroy, Paul. 1987. *"There Ain't No Black in the Union Jack": The Cultural Politics of Race and Nation.* London: Routledge.

————. 1994. *The Black Atlantic: Modernity and Double Consciousness.* Cambridge, MA: Harvard University Press.

Glick-Schiller, Nina, Linda Basch, and Cristina Szanton Blanc, eds. 1992. *Towards a Transnational Perspective on Migration: Race, Class, Ethnicity, and Nationalism Reconsidered.* New York: Transaction.

Hannerz, Ulf. 1990. "Cosmopolitans and Locals in World Culture." In Mike Featherstone, ed., *Global Culture: Nationalism, Globalization, and Modernity*, pp. 237–52. London: Sage.

Harvey, David. 1989. *The Condition of Postmodernity.* Oxford: Basil Blackwell.

Kao, John. 1993. "The Worldwide Web of Chinese Business." *Harvard Business Review* 71: 24–36.

Krais, Beate. 1993. "Gender and Symbolic Violence: Female Oppression in the Light of Pierre Bourdieu's Theory of Social Practice." In Craig Calhoun, Edward LiPuma, and Moishe Postone, eds., *Bourdieu: Critical Perspectives*, pp. 156–77. Chicago: University of Chicago Press.

Kwong, Peter. 1994. "The Wages of Fear: Undocumented and Unwanted, Fuzhounese Immigrants Are Changing the Face of Chinatown." *Village Voice*, April 26.

Lefebvre, Henri. 1974. *The Production of Space.* Oxford: Basil Blackwell.

Li, Qingyuan and Wang Xun. 1992. "Tong Shi Tianya Tiaofeijiren." ("All Are Faraway Airplane Jumpers.") *Xingzhou Ribao*, May 24, pp. 22–23. Kuala Lumpur.

Lie, John. "The 'Problem' of Foreign Workers in Contemporary Japan." *Bulletin of Concerned Asian Scholars* 26, no. 3: 3–12.

Nonini, Donald M. 1979. "The Mysteries of Capital Accumulation: Honoring the Gods and Gambling Among Chinese in a Malaysian Market Town." *Proceedings, First International Symposium on Asian Studies.* Volume 3: Southeast Asia, pp. 701–710. Hong Kong: Asian Research Service.

————. 1993. "On the Outs on the Rim: An Ethnographic Grounding of the 'Asia-Pacific' Imaginary." In Arif Dirlik, ed., *What Is in a Rim? Critical Perspectives on the Pacific Region Idea*, pp. 29–50. Boulder: Westview.

Ong, Aihwa. 1990. "State Versus Islam: Families, Women's Bodies, and the Body Politic in Malaysia." *American Ethnologist* 15: 28–42.

————. 1991. "The Gender and Labor Politics of Postmodernity." *Annual Review of Anthropology* 20: 279–309.

————. 1993. "On the Edge of Empires: Flexible Citizenship Among Chinese in Diaspora." *Positions* 1, no. 3: 745–78.

Pan, Lynn. 1994. *Sons of the Yellow Emperor: A History of the Chinese Diaspora*. New York: Kodansha International.

Rabinow, Paul. 1989. *French Modern: Norms and Forms of the Social Environment*. Cambridge, MA: MIT Press.

Shimada, Haruo. 1994. *Japan's Guest Workers: Issues and Public Policies*. New York: Columbia University Press.

Stockard, Janice E. 1989. *Daughters of the Canton Delta: Marriage Patterns and Economic Strategies in South China, 1860–1930*. Stanford: Stanford University Press.

Strauch, Judith V. 1984. "Women in Rural-Urban Circulation Networks: Implications for Social Structural Change." In J. T. Fawcett, S.-E. Khoo, et al., eds., *Women in the Cities of Asia: Migration and Urban Adaptation*, pp. 60–80. Boulder: Westview.

Chapter Eight

Transnational Subjects: Constituting the Cultural Citizen in the Era of Pacific Rim Capital

Katharyne Mitchell

How are subjects disciplined over a plurality of terrains? How is citizenship constructed within a context of transnational movement? What institutions of governmentality are brought to bear to "regulate the conduct of subjects as a population, and as individuals . . . in the interests of ensuring security and prosperity for the nation-state," yet at the same time are not bound by the territorially defined or rhetorically discursive spaces of the nation-state (Ong 1993, 748; see also Foucault 1991)?

The global restructuring of the past two decades has involved local transformations of both economy and culture, the interconnections of which are the subject of numerous theoretical inquiries (Appadurai 1990; Harvey 1989; King 1991, 1993; Featherstone 1990). As nations become increasingly interdependent and economies and cultures articulate across formerly regulated borders, the processes constituting "citizens as 'subjects' (in both of Foucault's sense of 'subjection'—subject of and subjected to the nation)" begin to assume a more global dynamic (Hall 1993, 355; see also Bhabha 1990 and Clifford 1992). Strong as they are, however, these forces of globalization are always tempered by local places and people; they "do not, contrary to popular opinion, lead to simple homogenization; globalization also initiates a myriad of local interpretations and transformations" (Olds 1995, 2; see also Pred and Watts 1992). At the same time, the interconnections of the global and the local perform in reverse fashion as well. Local constructions of citizenship, appropriate cultural taste, democracy, the public sphere, the environment, and many other arenas are active in the production of larger dynamic forces such as capitalism and modernity—so much so, in fact, that abstract theories of modernity, which are usually predicated on Western notions and assumptions, neglect the context-dependent nature of the beast and run the risk of reproducing the kinds of anemic geographies warned of by Sparke (1994) in his discussion of Robert Young's *White Mythologies*.

In terms of the global integration of people as well as places, "simple homogenization" is similarly inconceivable, despite the various state rhetorics of melting pots and cultural mosaics. Although immigrants may become legal citizens through a prescribed, state-regulated path, immigrants become *cultural* citizens only through a reflexive set of formative and locally constructed processes. This is not to suggest that the state-controlled or "regulated" path is not rife with the same kinds of racist, classist, and other roadblocks that beset the more informal channels. I am arguing, rather, that legal citizenship is not the end but the beginning of numerous, active local mediations over the "terms of the local-global integration"—in this case, the integration of people (Bright and Geyer 1987).

In the era of transnational flows of investment and investors, cultural citizenship involves acculturation to both global compacts *and* local traditions. In order to function effectively in an interconnected yet locally mediated global economy, the global subject must be attuned to the nuances of a particular locale as well as to the transnational flows characteristic of late capitalism. Concrete local details involving class lifestyle, state formations, neighborhood histories, and conceptions of race and ethnicity frequently undergird imagined communities of "nationness" and regional identity that impact transnational business and businesspeople in innumerable ways. Understanding these details aids the transnational in navigating complex local channels and avoiding blockages to the smooth flow of capital.

In addition to the conferral of legal citizenship, the state may aid transnationals and capital mobility in a number of ways. In Canada, for example, the liberal rhetoric of multiculturalism was appropriated and promoted by the state and by business elites in the 1980s in order to persuade the host society of the evils of racism and the benefits of cultural pluralism (Mitchell 1993). At a time of rapid immigration by Hong Kong Chinese businesspeople and their capital investment in Vancouver real estate, the message of what constituted "good" Canadian society and the "ideal" Canadian citizen—a message of tolerance toward racial and cultural difference—was heavily promulgated by officials at all levels of Canadian government. The particular timing of this state rhetoric of improved race relations indicated a desire to reduce the blockages of localism, patriotism, and racism that were affecting metropolitan land

and development policies and foreign direct investment in Vancouver real estate at that time.

Meanwhile, as the British-Canadian subject was being disciplined by a state rhetoric of multiculturalism in the 1980s, another discourse of cultural harmony involving Hong Kong immigrants was also under way. The desire by state leaders to reduce racial and cultural friction was clearly associated, at least in part, with efforts to further facilitate transnational capital flow and the integration of Vancouver into the global economy. But as greater and greater numbers of transnational businesspeople circulate among the new global cities of the Pacific Rim, the question of how these terrestrial astronauts themselves aid in the effort to reduce cultural antagonism becomes increasingly important.[1] How do transnationals become cultural citizens of particular national and metropolitan locales? How are citizens made and subjectivities produced in the interstices of national borders and cultural realms? In this chapter I examine the shaping of the Chinese investor-immigrant and address the issue of how stereotypes of the normative Chinese and the normative Canadian citizen are co-produced by both the Hong Kong and Canadian business elites and by the Canadian state. This production involves not just the workings of hegemony but also the refashioning of stereotypes by Chinese subjects themselves, who "selectively participate in Orientalist formations as they negotiate shifting discursive terrains in the world economy" (Ong 1993, 746).[2]

Class Distinctions and the Manipulation of Chineseness

The process of shaping cultural citizens is multilayered. It involves the self-fashioning of Chinese subjects and the efforts of the Canadian and Hong Kong business elites to shape prospective Hong Kong Chinese emigrants to Canada before their departure; it also involves the differentiation of emigrants by class fragments. Overtly, the education of future Hong Kong emigrants entails acculturation to a general British-Canadian subjectivity; more subtly, however, it can also be seen as an effort to indoctrinate the Hong Kong middle class into a kind of transnational cosmopolitanism.[3] The distinction between the extremely wealthy "superstratum" of Hong Kong transnationals and the *nouveau riche* or bourgeois middle class not only indicates the plurality of this immigrant group but also opens up some of the ways in which class and differences in taste may affect the constitution of cultural citizenship.[4]

Bourdieu, for example, has suggested that taste is one aspect of cultural capital that is intricately linked with economic capital. Taste, or the preference for one type of cultural consumption and lifestyle over another is a visible affirmation of economic as well as cultural difference. He writes, "Aversion to different life-styles is perhaps one of the strongest barriers between the classes. . . . At stake in every struggle over art there is also the imposition of an art of living, that is, the transmutation of an arbitrary way of living into the legitimate way of life" (Bourdieu 1984, 57). In Vancouver, the city that will be the focus of this chapter, cultural frictions involved in the shaping of a "legitimate way of life" for Hong Kong immigrants were bound up with the class dynamics of both Vancouver and Hong Kong societies. Some of the general differences in taste between the older, established, and wealthy residents of Vancouver's west side, most of whom considered themselves to be part of a British Anglo heritage, and the recent Chinese immigrants from Hong Kong were perceived and represented as racial or ethnic differences in the media; questions of class were rarely introduced. In the following section I examine a few of the distinctions that were made between the two groups and the frictions that these real and perceived differences in taste caused with respect to Vancouver's urban environment. I then investigate some of the urban transformations and social movements against change that resulted in efforts by the Canadian state and certain Chinese and Canadian business elites to shape the new Hong Kong middle-class emigrants to Vancouver.

Race and Class in the Formation of Taste

Hong Kong and Vancouver perceptions of house and home

Some of the general distinctions between Hong Kong Chinese and British Canadian tastes in the 1980s were described to me by informants in both societies.[5] Many people I spoke with in Hong Kong felt that overt manifestations of wealth—for example, in the choice of house or car or clothing—were fundamentally different between Anglo residents of Vancouver and recent Hong Kong immigrants. Several believed that this difference had led to jealousy and expressions of racism against Chinese people living in Vancouver.

The manifestation of prosperity, particularly the visible display of name-brand and high-status items, is generally considered appropriate in Hong Kong society, where differentiation between dominant class fractions is often predicated on an overt display of wealth. In middle-class and upper-middle-class circles in Hong Kong, visible displays of wealth are crucial for acceptance into the dominant group in society. And, as in most societies, acceptance into the dominant group is essential for continued access to the resources and networks of those holding the reins of economic power. According to Sally Liu, the daughter of a wealthy Shanghai businessman who emigrated to Hong Kong in the late 1940s, Hong Kong's culture of consumption was influenced by the lifestyles of early-twentieth-century Shanghai, where maintaining face was crucial for retaining one's place in a particular social circle. She described Hong Kong as a mix of Chinese regional cultures that had formed a distinct hybrid. She said in an interview:

> It's very different now because one becomes very half-merged, the Shang-hainese and the Cantonese—and we become very much a Hong Kongnese. We become very practical people. But because money in Hong Kong is so easy, has always been easy, so we have a wide section of *nouveau riche* people. And fiscal wealth is very important. We have, all of us, only been here forty, fifty years at the most. A few families will be over a hundred years. And basically, even though you might be very wealthy in China or you might be very poor, you all became quite poor to begin with because of the war, so you all have to start from scratch. So I think out of the necessity to survive and out of having no confidence, you have to be very physical, very physical with the car you drive, very physical with the jewelry you have, your address, your house, how to talk big, because this is the way you get into a particular type of circle.[6]

In Hong Kong, owing to the high cost of land, the automobile is a more ubiquitous symbol of wealth than the home. In the emigration to Vancouver, however, some attitudes about the importance of displaying wealth may have been transferred to the house. Bill and Jenny Leung, a middle-class Hong Kong couple who were emigrating to Vancouver and were familiar with Vancouver real estate, claimed that they could differentiate between the houses owned by long-time Vancouver residents and those owned by recent Hong Kong immigrants. Their criteria were the types of materials used and the amount of money apparently spent on the house by the occupants. Bill said in an interview:

> In Vancouver it's quite difficult for us to differentiate the rich class and the poor class since they all wear the same clothes. They are not showing off. In Hong Kong the behavior is different. When you're richer you use clothes, a precious watch to show off. The local people in Vancouver . . . they are so simple, not liv-ing a luxurious life. The one area that's most obvious is the house. When I look at houses, I can differentiate between whether they belong to the local people or the Hong Kong people. . . . For example, [in the houses of recent Hong Kong immigrants] the door is a golden color; sometimes the ground is all gravel. And all made with marble and glass. I can see they spend a lot of money.[7]

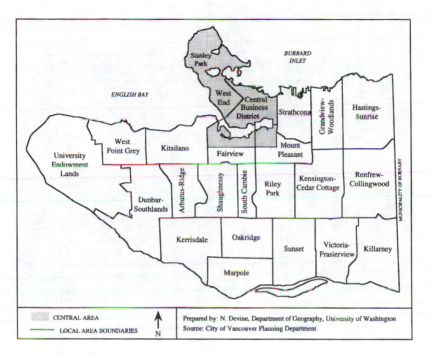

Fig. 1. City of Vancouver Local Areas

In Vancouver in the late 1980s these general differences in taste were quickly reflected in a new form of urban development, particularly in westside neighborhoods such as Kerrisdale and Shaughnessy Heights (see figure 1). Small houses were rapidly demolished, and numerous larger and glitzier homes were built in the hope of attracting the investment of recent Hong Kong immigrants. Although these new "monster" houses were the product of many forces, including the greater profit margins sought by developers, most older Vancouver residents blamed Hong Kong immigrants for the mammoth houses and perceived these immigrants as having a desire for more space, small yards, and expensive-looking house materials (see figure 2).

According to Holdsworth (1986, 28), early British Vancouverites saw themselves as part of a unique urban setting, one with a high standard of living predicated largely on open green spaces and detached single-family houses. Westside neighborhoods in Vancouver are characterized by open front yards with mature trees and wide, landscaped boulevards. The gently contoured lawns, scattered clumps of bushes

Fig. 2. A new "monster" house on Wiltshire and 54th Street in Oakridge. (Photo by K. Mitchell.)

and trees, irregular, curved shapes and natural-looking borders all draw from the landscape tradition of Capability Brown and Humphry Repton, British garden and park designers of the eighteenth century. The general ambience is unquestionably that of the English landscape tradition.

The use of British architectural and landscape symbols in Vancouver's westside neighborhoods was deliberate. Officials working for Vancouver's major landowner, the Canadian Pacific Railroad, intentionally modeled the elite subdivision of Shaughnessy Heights on the pastoral myths of the English countryside (Duncan and Duncan 1984, 270). By claiming this English tradition in the new spaces of Vancouver, an easy, unhurried grandeur and an idyllic, preindustrial way of life gradually became recognized and incorporated as part of the symbols and codes of the new suburban elite of "British" Columbia (see figure 3). The appropriation and reworking of these symbols over time operated on an aesthetic level that enabled residents of these neighborhoods to feel pride of place and to assume a universal notion of cultural propriety. Much of the anxiety of loss expressed in the late 1980s related not to the actual

Fig. 3. An English cottage-style house located on Wiltshire and 54th Street, opposite the house portrayed in figure 2. (Photo by K. Mitchell)

houses or trees that were demolished but to a more general fear of deprivation and dispossession of this way of life.

Reworking the art of living

The major cultural frictions in Vancouver in the 1980s thus centered on concerns about the changing urban landscape. Speculation in the housing market, the construction of extremely large houses, the removal of mature trees, and the open display of material wealth by a number of Hong Kong Chinese immigrants were among the many irritants that galvanized Vancouver homeowners into the formation of social groups opposed to urban change.[8] These urban social movements, which frequently introduced more protective neighborhood zoning laws, effectively blocked further redevelopment of a number of westside neighborhoods and slowed the free circulation of capital and commodities in the city (cf. Harvey 1985, 63–220).

Many of the worst conflicts over housing occurred in the westside, upper-middle-class areas of Kerrisdale, Oakridge, Dunbar, Granville-Woodlands, and Second and Third Shaughnessy. In these areas, hundreds of older houses were demolished and extremely large houses were constructed in their place. Based on interviews, surveys, observation, and archival evidence, it appears that many of the buyers of these homes in the late 1980s were middle-class Hong Kong Chinese immigrants.[9]

In an effort to counter the mobilization of British-Canadian homeowners of these neighborhoods, the wealthy transnationals of both Hong Kong and Vancouver attempted to lessen neighborhood friction by educating and disciplining (in the Foucauldian sense, see Foucault 1979) the future Hong Kong middle-class home-buyers about the cultural norms for the area. Meet with Success, a program hosted by the Canadian Club of Hong Kong, ran a series of twice-weekly seminars on Canadian society for Hong Kong citizens who had already received visas and were planning to emigrate to Canada. A substantial part of the video shown during the seminar focused on neighborhood and housing norms in Vancouver, as did the information packet distributed during the seminars. This program was funded by wealthy Hong Kong and Canadian patrons and backed by the Canadian Commission in Hong Kong.

In addition to the message of Canadian acculturation, Meet with Success introduced contemporary strategies of cosmopolitanism employed by the Hong Kong Chinese transnational elite. In this process, Orientalist stereotypes were aggressively refashioned. The self-representation of Asian Americans as model minorities and global economic subjects, for example, "is never simply complicit with hegemonic discourses, but seeks in this case to reposition Asian Americans as new authority figures" (Ong 1993, 769). In the context of increasing business opportunities across the Pacific, many Chinese transnational cosmopolitans represent themselves as Pacific Rim "bridge-builders," aiding and abetting in the production of what Donald Nonini (1993) terms the "Asia-Pacific imaginary."

Clearly the flexibility of this self-fashioning process can be useful in the contemporary global economy. As capitalist networks articulate, Chinese businessmen who speak the language of the global economic subject but are also imbricated in a Hong Kong Chinese discourse are able to operate as quintessential middlemen. With flexible citizenship and deterritoralized systems of credit, but with a durable and elastic business network established on the basis of the extended family (see Mitchell 1995), overseas Hong Kong capitalists can manipulate images of both the transnational cosmopolitan and the "ethnic Chinese," enabling them to position themselves at the lucrative center of Pacific Rim business. The strategic balancing that this requires, however, is threatened by the "inappropriate" cultural behavior of middle-class emigrants who exacerbate local friction through the overt display of material wealth or the expressed desire for "monster" houses and good *feng shui* in established Vancouver neighborhoods.

Middle-class or *nouveau riche* behavior, which was represented homogeneously as "Hong Kong Chinese" behavior by much of the Vancouver media in 1988, disrupts both capital circulation and the neutral, "transnational" image of Hong Kong investors. This disruption was particularly evident in the controversy surrounding residential housing in Vancouver's westside neighborhoods. As both commercial and residential real estate was a prime locus of investment by Hong Kong businesspeople in the late 1980s, efforts to reduce friction in this area were especially strong. Meet with Success and a number of other programs and media events in Hong Kong in the early 1990s were efforts to counter neighborhood frictions and to keep capital articulations and international business networking in the Asia Pacific fluid and faceless. In the following section I examine why Vancouver real estate was so attractive for international buyers during this period and how the state facilitated capitalist articulations between transnational players in Hong Kong and Vancouver.

Immigrant Investors and Transnational Capital Flow

In the late 1980s Vancouver was a primary focus of Hong Kong investment in real estate. Many factors were responsible for Vancouver's popularity, including the effort by the Canadian state and municipal politicians to attract Asian investors as well as the diversification of Hong Kong portfolios in advance of the colony's transfer to Chinese control in 1997. Government efforts to attract Hong Kong Chinese investors included the new business immigration program. Other draws included financial deregulation and the privatization of land initiated by British Columbia premier William Vander Zalm in the 1980s. Here I examine a few of these policy developments and their implications for land use and land contestation. Some of the friction over land that arose in the late 1980s was clearly exacerbated by the Anglo-Canadian perception of differing economic practices by Hong Kong Chinese investors in real estate—particularly the channeling of business opportunities along extended-family networks. Great friction was also caused by the construction of "monster" houses, speculation in housing, and the removal of trees in westside communities—actions that many residents felt were undertaken primarily by Hong Kong Chinese developers and buyers.

The immigrant investor program

The primary means of attracting Hong Kong investments to Canada was to attract the investors themselves via the lure of Canadian citizenship. Since many Hong Kong residents were hoping to establish citizenship in another country prior to the changeover to Chinese Communist control in 1997, the opportunity to qualify in the Canadian business immigration program and avoid lengthy delays in processing was highly desirable. The business immigration program was established in 1978 but was invigorated substantially in 1984, the year that the Basic Law treaty was signed in Hong Kong. The investor category, which was added in 1986, was the most important draw for Hong Kong immigrants to Canada in the late 1980s. The investor category required a significant investment in a Canadian enterprise and a personal net worth of at least $500,000 Canadian.[10]

Owing largely to the success of the business immigration program, emigration from Hong Kong to Canada jumped considerably in the late 1980s. From 1987 to 1989, the number of immigration applications from wealthy Hong Kong businesspeople leaped from 1,991, or 12 percent of all Hong Kong applicants, to 8,001, or 36 percent.[11] The total for all three years was nearly a quarter of all Hong Kong applicants. The number of business immigrants who chose British Columbia as their final destination in 1989 and the first six months of 1990 was significantly higher than for any other province in Canada. In 1989, out of a total of 1,121 "entrepreneurs" emigrating from Hong Kong to Canada, 384 (36 percent landed in British Columbia. In the same year, out of 406 "investors," 177 (44 percent) chose the province.[12] As with the general immigrant population from Hong Kong, the vast majority of business immigrants to British Columbia opted to settle and invest in the city of Vancouver.

Real estate and the immigrant investor

Despite government attempts to channel capital into productive sectors, the majority of business immigrant funds, particularly in the early years of the program, went into property investment. Rather than the creation of businesses and employment for Canadians, much of the capital invested early on actually served to subsidize developers in preplanned business ventures. The *Financial Post* estimated that in 1990, foreign investment in privately held real estate in Canada nearly tripled from the 1985 figure of $1.2 billion U.S. If the debt portion (bank financing) of the real-estate transactions was included, the total investments in 1990 would exceed $13 billion U.S.[13]

Vancouver was a particular favorite on the global shopping scene. A real-estate broker at Goddard and Smith Realty Ltd. said of the real-estate market in Vancouver in late 1989: "The saturation point for Hong Kong investment in Vancouver real estate hasn't been reached yet because people now look at this city in a global context, whereas ten years ago only western Canadians were considered potential purchasers."[14] Donald Gutstein, in his 1990 book on Asian investment in Vancouver real estate, chronicled numerous individual purchases of property and buildings in the city, demonstrating on a case-by-case basis the burgeoning investment in Vancouver property by Hong Kong buyers (Gutstein 1990, chapters 7–10).

Hong Kong immigrants in the "investor" category were responsible for a large portion of real-estate development in Vancouver despite the effort by the provincial government to channel the required $250,000 Canadian (later $350,000 Canadian) into manufacturing, trade, and research and development. Investment categories acceptable to the British Columbia government under the business immigration program included "developmental real estate," which was defined as real estate to which substantive improvements would be made in order to carry on a business of significant economic benefit. In practice, this meant investment in virtually all commercial buildings, including office buildings, hotels, tourist ventures, and shopping malls.

In addition to the commercial real-estate developments, speculative activity affected the residential housing market in Vancouver as well. The "flipping" of houses for profit became common in westside communities, where some houses prices tripled within the space of a single year.[15] In addition to the rapid rise of house prices (and taxes) in these neighborhoods, other changes included the demolition of hundreds of houses and three-story walk-up apartments and the construction of what became known as "monster" houses and luxury condominiums. In many cases, the large trees and natural-looking landscapes of the older homes were demolished along with the buildings, causing particular angst in a city that has long prided itself on its leafy suburban boulevards.

Selling the spectacle:
The privatization and sale of the Expo lands

Nine days after the closing of the World's Fair, Expo '86, a new Socred (Social Credit) government, under the premiership of William Vander Zalm, won the provincial election in British Columbia. Vander Zalm immediately initiated a sweeping land privatization campaign that necessitated the sale of vast quantities of undeveloped and enormously lucrative land in British Columbia—including the Expo site itself. This site comprised nearly one sixth of Vancouver's entire downtown land area. Under the new privatization strategy of the Vander Zalm government, these lands, which had been acquired at great cost under the previous govern-ment, were scheduled for sale back to the private sector.

In 1988 the Expo land was purchased by the Hong Kong property magnate Li Ka-shing. This sale, and the subsequent development of the land by Li's son, Victor, caused a heated controversy in Vancouver. Part of the local anger stimulated by this massive real-estate transaction was the belief that the provincial government had sold the land to Li at a frac-tion of its worth in order to attract even more investment to the city and the province from other Hong Kong buyers.[16] It was apparent to most Vancouverites that the effort to attract investment from Asia was linked to the desire to make Vancouver a "world-class" city, able to integrate and compete effectively with other global cities in the Pacific Rim mar-ketplace. The other source of local angst was the belief that both Li Ka-shing and his son, Victor Li, channeled real-estate opportunities and information primarily to other Chinese businessmen. This perception was fueled by the exclusive and rapid sale of 216 luxury Vancouver con-dominiums in a development called the Regatta to Hong Kong buyers in 1988 and by the sale of large chunks of the Expo land to Hong Kong and Singapore Chinese buyers in 1988 and 1989.

Urban megaprojects, flexible credit, and overseas Chinese capital networks

Urban megaprojects are "large-scale (re)development projects composed of a mix of commercial, residential, retail, industrial, leisure and infra-structure uses" (Olds 1995, 1). These urban projects are being developed around the globe in increasing numbers, and are responsible for the re-structuring of large chunks of the downtown cores of cities such as Sin-gapore, Shanghai, Yokohama, and Vancouver. In Vancouver, the largest and most highly publicized megaproject of the late 1980s and early 1990s has been the development of the former Expo lands by Concord Pacific, Inc., led by Li Ka-shing's son, Victor Li.

Urban megaprojects are usually financed through a consortium of in-ternational players. This global financing was greatly facilitated by the liberalization of finance systems worldwide in the late 1970s and 1980s, when liberalization and deregulation allowed finance and credit to become more available "on a global 'private' scale beyond the bounds of national control" (Olds 1995, 3; see also Leyshon and Thrift 1992). With credit operating globally through private and informal net-works, established Chinese business networks became increasingly im-portant systems for the circulation of credit during this time (see Mitchell 1995). In the expansion of urban megaprojects around the world, including the development of the Expo lands by the Li family in

Vancouver, these overseas Chinese business networks have been absolutely key.

One of the ramifications of the success of large-scale property developments by Chinese investors in the 1980s has been a cultural and racial backlash in many urban centers worldwide. In Vancouver, some of the friction over changes in the urban environment were related to a fear of the loss of local control as well as to a sense of exclusion from the business dealings of high-power, transnational Chinese players. These frictions culminated in a number of urban social movements with the express goal of impeding changes in Vancouver's urban environment. I will examine a few of these social movements in the next section and the analyze some of the strategies of Vancouver's foremost property developer, Victor Li, in combating these perceptions and political actions. I argue that in Li's efforts, as well as in the Meet with Success seminar, acculturation tactics and programs can be directly linked with the postcolonial strategies of transnational elites concerned with the development of urban megaprojects and the ongoing capitalist integration of the Pacific Rim.

Racism, urban social movements, and the promotion of cultural harmony

The friction caused by the massive changes in Vancouver's urban environment was expressed in a number of different ways. In 1989 a series of articles in the major local newspaper, the *Vancouver Sun*, focused on the connection between Hong Kong investments in real estate and the rapid rise of house prices. In an article entitled "The Hong Kong Connection: How Asian Money Fuels Housing Market," reporter Gillian Shaw discussed the large percentage (85 percent) of Asian buyers in offshore purchases, and noted that "the majority of those were from Hong Kong." She also stressed that many of the new buyers were paying for the houses *in cash* (Shaw 1989). Other article titles in the series included "Computer Shopping for B.C. Property"; "Investment Anger Confuses Hong Kong"; and "Money Is King in Hong Kong: Entrepreneurs Find Paradise in the Streets of Hong Kong." In many of these articles there was a strong emphasis on identifying "essential" Hong Kong Chinese characteristics; these were categorized as a tendency to speculate in the housing market for profit, an aggressive drive toward material wealth and its subsequent ostentatious display, and a general disregard for the natural environment.

These essentialized representations had an incendiary effect on Vancouver's residents, who were becoming increasingly anxious about housing affordability, neighborhood character and the loss of local control over urban development. Hong Kong Chinese investors and home buyers were increasingly targeted as the agents responsible for unwanted neighborhood change, and many urban social movements became imbricated in a racial discourse. Much of the growing antagonism against Chinese buyers was exacerbated by the wealth of many of the new immigrants and by some of these immigrants' purchases of "monster" houses.

Several of the social movements that were established during this period were expressly concerned with these kinds of neighborhood change. The Kerrisdale Concerned Citizens for Affordable Housing protested the demolition of walk-up apartments and houses, the Kerrisdale-Granville Homeowners Association battled the destruction of neighborhood trees, and the Shaughnessy Heights Property Owners Association attempted to amend zoning laws to limit the size of new houses that could be built in the neighborhood. Although these movements were publicly concerned with local control over the urban environment, the strong feelings against large-scale Hong Kong investment in commercial and residential real estate was made clear in association meetings and in a number of interviews with me.

In addition to state-sponsored efforts to redouble the emphasis on multiculturalism and cultural harmony in Canada in the 1980s, several private institutions were also quickly established to counter these growing urban frictions. The Laurier Institute, a non-profit agency concerned with "promot[ing] cultural harmony in Canada" and "encourag[ing] understanding among and between people of various cultures," began a well-publicized campaign to inform Vancouver residents that recent inflation in the housing market was *not* the result of speculation by nonlocal (that is, Hong Kong Chinese) buyers. The series of reports emphasizing this theme were picked up and reproduced with great fanfare by both a local newspaper, the *Vancouver Sun*, and a national paper, the *Globe and Mail*. By this point in time, the *Vancouver Sun* had been heavily criticized for its recent series of articles on Hong Kong and was eager to appear both objective and conciliatory concerning the issue (see Mitchell 1993). Vancouver's major newspapers, the Laurier Institute, and a number of other private organizations thus joined forces in the attempt to neutralize negative impressions of the impact of Hong Kong real-estate investments on Vancouver's rapid urban transformation.

The barrage of information that suddenly appeared from these sources and others in 1989 and the early 1990s represented efforts within the public sphere to discipline British-Canadians to the new global forces impacting their lives. Transnational flows and their local effects were both neutralized and normalized in a language of cultural harmony and general blamelessness. In one Laurier Institute report of 1989, the author wrote of rising house prices in westside neighborhoods: "If we seek someone to blame for this increase in demand, we will find only that the responsible group is everyone, not some unusual or exotic group of residents or migrants. In fact, there is no one to blame: the future growth in housing demand is a logical and normal extension of trends in the nation's population" (Baxter 1989).

With this kind of rhetoric, the construction of the "enlightened" Canadian urbanite of the Pacific Coast was advanced by both state leaders and private (business) concerns.[17] I will now turn to the mutual construction of the transnational Chinese subject by the Canadian state and by Canadian and Hong Kong elites. In both cases the connections between the shaping of a new kind of subjectivity and the movements of capital across the Pacific are my primary concern.

Fashioning the Transnational Cosmopolitan

In letters to the editor, to the city council, and to the Vancouver Planning Department, and in media articles in the late 1980s, it was evident that the two main sources of friction involving Hong Kong Chinese investors and older Vancouver residents were the fear of exclusion in business dealings and the anxiety surrounding the transformation of neighborhoods.[18] The barrage of articles in the media concerning both these topics and the linkage of Asian investment in the built environment with the profound changes that were occurring in the city spurred a strong local reaction against further investment and immigration from Hong Kong. In addition to the growth of social movements against urban change (some of which, such as RSVP and the Spokesman, were explicitly anti-Asian), racist incidents against Chinese Canadians increased during this time period.[19] Methods of combating the growing friction in the 1990s included appropriation of "positive" Orientalist representations of Chinese by wealthy Hong Kong-Canadian businessmen such as Victor Li, Stanley Kwok, and David Lam. At the same time, there was a strong effort to acculturate the middle classes to a new transnational cosmopolitanism through programs such as Meet with Success in Hong Kong.

Victor Li and David Lam: Good Canadian businessmen
When Li Ka-shing brought in three new Chinese partners into the Expo land deal in 1989, his son, Victor, reassured jittery Vancouver politicians that the Li family would maintain major control of the extensive downtown property. He emphasized that Concord Pacific, the company lead-

ing the development, was not a subsidiary of or related to the massive Hong Kong and Singapore conglomerates owned by the other partners, but a private company "financed mainly by family money."[20] Victor Li's remarks were intended to placate Vancouver citizens, politicians, and jounalists, who were becoming increasingly vocal against the perceived sellout of the Expo lands.

The strategy of winning acceptance on the local level was bolstered by the hiring of Stanley Kwok, a highly respected Chinese-Canadian architect in Vancouver, to become senior vice president of the company. At the time of his hiring, Kwok was a friend of the former Vancouver planning director Raymond Spaxman as well as an acquaintance of three of the major shareholders in Concord Pacific: Li Ka-shing, Cheng Yu-tung, and Lee Shaukee. Kwok was recruited by Li to "make Pacific Place happen and, not incidentally, to build bridges between Concord and Vancouver's business establishment." Grace McCarthy said of Kwok, "Stanley is a terrific bridge between the Chinese and Canadian business communities. He bridges it well and he brings them together, and that's very important."[21]

The necessity of a spokesperson to act as a bridge between the Chinese and Canadian communities was apparent as incidents of racism increased in Vancouver in the late 1980s. The perception of a difference in the economic practices of the Hong Kong Chinese capitalists and the fear of exclusion from family-oriented businesses was reflected in the vitriolic reaction against the 1988 sale in Hong Kong of luxury condominiums in Vancouver's Regatta complex. Following the uproar over Li's marketing of the condominiums, he again attempted to smooth local feathers in a press conference. He spoke of his commitment to Canada and of his Canadian citizenship, and he emphasized his intention for Concord Pacific to "be a good blue-chip Canadian company."[22]

Li's effort to appear as a "good Canadian businessman" was a position also advocated by British Columbia's lieutenant governor, David Lam. Lam, a Hong Kong Chinese immigrant who came to Canada in the late 1960s and who became a millionare from his investments in the Vancouver property market during that boom period, often spoke of the need to "keep what you have but be a Canadian."[23] When the Vancouver housing market heated up in 1988 and 1989, Lam worried that Hong Kong speculation in property would contribute to the growing racial discord in the city.[24] He spoke frequently of the need to assimilate to Canadian norms but at the same time to maintain traditional Chinese values. In his appearance in the Meet with Success video, Lam gave advice for new immigrants. He called on the immigrants to "adapt" and added, "Very quickly you'll join the mainstream. You can keep your culture, but be a member of your new community. It is possible to maintain your Chinese roots, but also develop the Canadian flower."

The connection between the particularist business practices employed by the Li family and the fear and antagonism expressed by Vancouver residents against the marketing of Vancouver condominiums in Hong Kong was apparent to many politicians and businessmen. David Lam's and Victor Li's awareness of the problem encouraged them to represent themselves as "good Canadian businessmen and bridge-builders" to the Vancouver public. Public attempts to herald their Canadian citizenship functioned also as a method of reducing friction and facilitating the articulation of international economic networks. These efforts were accompanied by a reminder of their superior economic power and the ultimate mobility of global capital. At the same time that Li made several moves to calm fears of marketing exclusion and of the future flipping of the Concord Pacific lands, for example, he also made it clear that he would not tolerate racial prejudice. He noted that the negative reactions to the Hong Kong investments in Vancouver were being perceived in Hong Kong (and elsewhere) as largely motivated by racism. He warned that racism was bad for the "business climate," that economic projects in the city were being adversely affected, and that Vancouver stood to lose millions of dollars in future capital investment. He said of the reaction of Hong Kong businessmen to the uneasy mood toward foreign property investment in Vancouver in 1989: "I think they're taking a cautious attitude. I don't think right now there's a mass pulling away of investments. . . . But I've seen and I've heard from close business associates that they are slowing down on activities and taking a wait-and-see attitude." To further his point, Li discussed the example of Australia, which had already lost foreign business because of its perceived racism: "Australia, we've absolutely pulled out. Most of the Australian investment is in small businesses, retail and those things. But I know a lot of friends, together with our group, that have absolutely pulled out, deliberately pulled out of that country because of the racist or the white policy there."[25]

As lieutenant governor of British Columbia, David Lam was in a good position to act as an advocate of cultural harmony. His primarily ceremonial position did not threaten the political interests of any particular group, and his personal background as a real-estate mogul and millionaire philanthropist indicated profound connections with both the business world and the art world in Vancouver. Buildings emblazoned with David Lam's name can be found in many areas of Vancouver, including the School of Commerce at the University of British Columbia. In light of this explicit and highly publicized generosity, Lam's self-appointed designation as a good Canadian *and* a good Chinese was thus difficult to contest and added a degree of legitimacy to his advocacy of self-fashioning and cosmopolitanism. Victor Li, in contrast, relied primarily on his Canadian citizenship and education to provide legitimacy for his claims to Canadianness. The implication, however, was that if these claims weren't considered adequate by Vancouver residents, his response would be summarily economic: He would pull out of his Canadian business ventures and lead the stampede of capital flight from the city.

These two fashioning strategies indicate some of the different ways in which economic capital may be converted to symbolic capital in a transnational setting. Lam's more conciliatory approach reflects an earlier reliance on cultural and political capital as a necessary accompaniment to the acceptance of cultural citizenship within the community. In Li's case, the rhetoric of Canadianness is similar, but the superior economic clout of the new immigrant investor group has allowed for a stronger insistence on the importance of legal citizenship and the protection of the liberal welfare state and its Canadian citizenry against racism or cultural antagonism. Thus Li's efforts at persuasion are Janusfaced: In addition to the rhetoric aimed at persuading immigrants to at least appear to assimilate and become good Canadians, Li also disciplines the British-Canadian residents to at least appear not to be racist and unwelcoming of the new immigrant investors. These ideological efforts were accompanied in the early 1990s by a program in Hong Kong called Meet with Success, to which I will now turn.

Meet with Success: Shaping the middle-class emigrant

> Cross-cultural training programmes have been developed to inculcate sensitivity, basic *savoir faire*, and perhaps an appreciation of those other cultures which are of special strategic importance to one's goals. (Hannerz 1990, 245)

Meet with Success was produced by the Canadian Club of Hong Kong in the spring of 1990. When a Hong Kong applicant to Canada was accepted as an immigrant, he or she was invited to attend a Meet with Success program. The invitation to the program was extended by the Commission for Canada in the same packet as the Canadian visa. Although attendance at Meet with Success was voluntary, there was a ninety percent turnout each week. One person involved in the program confided in an interview that "some think it is required because it comes from the commission."[26] The program was offered every week and consisted of a video, a slide show, and a question-and-answer session. An informational packet with a long survey entitled "Meet with

Success: Personal Inventory of Values" was handed to each person upon their arrival.

When I attended the program in Hong Kong, I realized that I had already seen the video, which is shown weekly at immigration and investment seminars in Vancouver as well.[27] The video, entitled "Being Canadian," depicts a young Hong Kong couple arriving in Vancouver. The film begins by describing Vancouver as a city "on the edge of the Pacific Rim." The narrator, who is a recent immigrant to Vancouver from Hong Kong, says in Cantonese, "Let me tell you about Vancouver." He is filmed in his home, an average-looking house on the eastside of the city. He says reflectively, "I love this city or else I would not have moved here . . . but lifestyles here are different.[28] The implication is that he chose to move to Vancouver for *love* rather than for the pursuit of profit. A Chinese woman then appears who reiterates the phrase, "Life here is so different." She adds, "The first thing to do was to learn English. Then the new culture and lifestyle."

At this point in the film there are a number of images of downtown Vancouver with a running narration that is consistently didactic. Some of the phrases are as follows: "People here are busy but orderly"; "They don't make unnecessary noise"; "In Canada most people are polite"; "People treat you nicely and politely." One scene involves shopping at the vegetable markets in Granville Island (Vancouver). The narrator says, "People don't bargain loudly. They are very polite to each other. I believe every immigrant will come to like this lifestyle." In another image, several cars are shown at an intersection. The narrator says, "They are patient. Each waits his turn so it doesn't become a traffic jam." There is a scene in a garden in which a Vancouver woman educates a Chinese man about gardening and Christmas. The Chinese man says thoughtfully, "You see, this is our neighbor. She not only helps her neighbors, she also makes her garden beautiful." Most interesting is that there are several images of flowers, large trees, and natural landscaping, which were obviously filmed in Vancouver's westside suburbs. While the camera pans over the gardens and homes, there appears an image of an extremely large, ostentatious house. The narrator says, "This is a Vancouver neighborhood. Residents are very proud of their gardens. Newer, bigger houses are a new trend. Sometimes the new houses look out of place."

According to two of my sources, who were involved with the planning of Meet with Success in 1989, the program was formulated as a direct result of the tremendous controversy and negative international publicity over the "monster" houses in Vancouver in 1988 and 1989.[29] One woman said that in addition to problems surrounding the "monster" house issue, there were other social conflicts, including "the ostentatious flaunting of wealth" and "double parking by Chinese students outside schools who just paid the fines and continued parking there." She noted that it was "not a smooth adaptation" when Hong Kong Chinese immigrants arrived in Vancouver and that in fact there was great resentment by many Canadians of the "yacht people." According to her, the Canadian Club organizers in Hong Kong were concerned about this friction, especially as they did not want Canada to be tarred with the same racist image that was being applied to Australia at that time.

Another organizer told me that the attempt to help Hong Kong immigrants learn about Canada was an attempt to avoid confrontation and "make life easier" for all involved. She noted that by showing various visual images of Canadian life it was possible to demonstrate cultural norms and unacceptable violations of those norms (such as removing trees and building large houses) without having to verbalize the problem, which might be interpreted as racist. The images of unacceptable violations were decided on by members of the board; according to a white Canadian member, the Chinese members of the board wanted to be tougher on cultural "problem areas" such as spitting. In the final decision, however, this was rejected as too patronizing.[30]

In addition to the video, a packet was given to each member of the Meet with Success audience. The packet contained a "Personal Inventory of Values" questionnaire, a series of fact sheets, and the list of contributors to the program. The questionniare, in both English and Chinese, addressed concerns about lifestyle and consumption. It began:

> The following questions represent a checklist for your reflection before and after you arrive in Canada. They introduce a wide range of issues and decisions that all Canadians face every day. These are personal values; the choices are yours but please make the commitment to understanding the economic, social and political environment within which you will be making them. Detailed information is contained in the accompanying "Fact Sheets" in this kit.[31]

The respondent is then asked to read several statements and circle *Important* or *Not So Important* in the margin to indicate his or her "personal values." Although it is stressed that these are individual, personal decisions, the didactic intent is clear. One of my informants involved with the program said, "It is their choice as to whether or not they want to modify their behavior. We are just alerting them as to possible conflict areas." The questions in the survey ranged from the work environment, housing, and family life to multiculturalism, social skills, and the assimilation process (see figure 4).

248

MULTICULTURALISM—FACT SHEET

The Canadian Mosaic All Canadians have a right to continue to enjoy the culture and language of their country of origin. Immigrants "integrate" rather than "assimilate" into Canadian society.

Multiculturalism: Multiculturalism has two official goals: the reduction of racism and the maintenance of minority languages. Unofficially, it is a way of thinking or an attitude. Canadians value diversity and tolerance protected by a democratic government with respect for human rights.

Too much concentration on their own separate identity can slow down or prevent cultural groups or new immigrants from entering the "mainstream" of Canadian society. "Hyphenated Canadians," such as Italian-Canadians, Chinese-Canadians, etc. maintain their own cultural values while participating in Canadian life.

Canada Needs Immigrants:
• to facilitate reunification of families
• to meet international commitments
• to increase the labour force
• to increase the population base
• to supply new capital
• to contribute to cultural diversity or the Canadian mosaic

Immigrants have both rights and responsibilities in their new homeland.

Immigrants Rights:

• Human Rights: Canada's Charter of Rights ensures that all Canadians (citizens with permanent residence) enjoy the benefits of a well established legal system regardless of race, religion, sex, or age. It reaffirms the basic human rights like freedom of expression and guarantees due process.

• Social Security: Education, universal medical insurance, and a variety of income supplements are provided for all qualifying Canadians.

• Preservation of Cultural Heritage: Minority languages are taught in the Heritage Language programs. Government services, educational programs and even street names appear in minority languages where numbers warrant. Multicultural festivals, cultural association, ethnic newspapers and minority language broadcasting on TV and radio are common.

Immigrant or Minority Group Responsibilities:
• to learn the language or languages of the host society: English and/or French.
• to tolerate cultural, racial and religious differences.
• to participate in the political process by voting.
• to contribute to social security through taxes and community involvement.
• to participate in and contribute to community life.
• to protect the natural environment and natural resources.
• to learn about the history of Canada.

Ways of Preserving Your Own Cultural Background:
• Join Chinese community groups.
• Teach your children the Chinese language.
• Participate in multicultural festivals such as Toronto's "Caravan".
• Listen to Chinese radio; watch Chinese TV; read Chinese newspapers.

Fig. 4: Sample "Fact Sheet" distributed to Hong Kong immigrants to Canada.

The "right" answers to the personal inventory of values were located in the "Fact Sheet" section of the packet. For example, in the category "Housing Options," statements such as the following educated the immigrant about the appropriate feelings to have concerning the home:

> Houses have historically been a good investment in Canada but the gains are not all financial. Communities of house owners tend to be stable and relatively friendly. Relationships with neighbours are important. Houses are a big commitment in time and lifestyle as well as money.

Here the warning against the disruptions caused by speculation are clear. As in the video, the correct purchase of a house was shown to be for the love of the neighborhood or the house itself, not for financial gain. In the section "Choosing a House and Neighborhood," the concern about frictions caused by the "monster" houses was broached in an even more warning tone. In this case, if the norms of the society were not willingly assumed, the legal system would be brought to bear on the most egregious offenders of good taste:

> The style of the houses and the amount of green space are serious considerations. Conformity to existing standards is a custom that in some cases is prescribed by municipal by-law. Plans to significantly enlarge houses, change the style of the exterior décor or cut down trees may be offensive if it is legal at all.

In the Multiculturalism Fact Sheet, the responsibility of the immigrants to become acculturated into Canadian society was underscored at the same time that the advantages of cosmopolitanism were upheld. Immigrant responsibilities included learning the language and history of the host society, participating in community and political life, and tolerating cultural, racial and religious differences. In a section called "Ways of Preserving Your Own Cultural Background," the manner in which both the responsibilities of acculturation and the rights of retaining some features of Chineseness could be accommodated was made clear. Possible ways of preserving Chinese identity were: "Join Chinese community groups. Teach your children the Chinese language. Participate in multicultural festivals such as Toronto's 'Caravan.' Listen to Chinese radio, watch Chinese TV, and read Chinese newspapers."[32]

As with the pragmatic advice from David Lam, the message of assimilating the cultural values from both the host society and Chinese society was fairly straitforward: It was possible, according to Meet with Success, to be both Canadian and Chinese through a strategic manipulation of cultural citizenship. Among the many silences in the video and packet, the question of the continuing transnational movements of both people and capital between Hong Kong and Vancouver was left undiscussed. Economic, class, and community frictions relating to this ongoing movement, which were among the most obvious sources of antagonism between British Canadian residents and the newer Chinese immigrants,[33] were elided as issues separate from the more fundamental cultural differences that were outlined in the seminar. This separation of cultural and economic concerns, which has a long history in Canadian multicultural policies as well, indicates the probable long-term inefficacy of the program's main agenda.[34]

This fashioning of the middle-class Hong Kong immigrant was promoted by the wealthy patrons and sponsors of both Canadian and Hong Kong society.[35] The video "Being Canadian" was filmed in Vancouver and funded by the Asia Pacific Foundation, a major organization involved with Canadian-Pacific Rim connections. Patrons of the Meet with Success program (contributing $25,000 Canadian or more) included David and Dorothy Lam and the government of British Columbia, in addition to many other individuals and organizations interested in improving Pacific Rim connections.

Conclusion

Hong Kong Chinese business information and networking involving overseas real estate was especially effective during a widespread period of deregulation and privatization in the 1980s. In Vancouver this networking translated into a number of successful real estate transactions involving the purchase and development of commercial and residential property. The remarkable scale of Hong Kong property investments in Vancouver during this time was made known through widespread media coverage of the sale and development of the urban megaproject planned on the former Expo site by Li Ka-shing, and by the public controversy over "monster" housing and tree removal in westside neighborhoods.

Owing to a strong public perception that Hong Kong Chinese immigrants were responsible for many of Vancouver's unwelcome urban changes, public disapproval of foreign investment and immigration policies grew considerably in the latter part of the decade. Anger toward the Hong Kong Chinese investors and immigrants focused on two areas: the exclusive marketing and sale of Vancouver property to other Chinese buyers, and the ostentatious display of wealth in a number of areas, most

notably in the purchase of "monster" houses. A number of social movements contesting urban change were initiated at this time, most with the
express purpose of halting demolitions and limiting house size and tree
removal, but some were also explicitly racist and xenophobic.

In reaction to burgeoning social and cultural antagonism, the Canadian and Hong Kong capitalist elites, backed by the Canadian state, established the acculturation program Meet with Success in Hong Kong.
This program was primarily targeted at middle-class emigrants to Vancouver, who were educated about Canada and about the necessity to
adopt a more flexible, cosmopolitan subjectivity. The manipulation of
Orientalist codings was employed at the same time by businessmen such
as Victor Li and David Lam, who represented themselves as good Canadians and also as key bridge-builders in the expanding Pacific Rim community.

In this setting, the ongoing framing of Chineseness and Canadianness
promoted by the Canadian state (Mitchell 1993; Anderson 1991), is simultaneously reframed by wealthy Hong Kong Chinese businesspeople
(Ong 1993). The ability to employ this kind of strategic repositioning,
however, is clearly predicated on the material wealth and cosmopolitan
savvy of this elite transnational group. Refashioning efforts by these
transnationals articulate with Canadian attempts to reduce cultural frictions caused by Chinese immigrants of other class fragments, who may
not share the same degree of cultural capital. In this manner, the positive
Chinese roles of bridge-builder and *homo economicus* (Ong 1993) can
be promulgated, while the negative, disruptive roles of profiteering spec-
ulator and *nouveau riche* are effectively elided. By reducing conflict
over the meaning of the urban environment and over differing economic
practices, foreign investment in real estate and the spatial integration of
the city can proceed more smoothly and efficiently.

In contrast with former state and civil representations of a dominant
British-Canadian cultural citizenship self-righteously resistant to Chinese immigrant outsiders, the contemporary promotion of the new cultural citizen in Vancouver is one that is multiply produced and
constituted. From coolie laborer to model minority, it is clear that the impact of cross-Pacific capital articulations in the last decade has profoundly influenced the promotion of new meanings of Chineseness and
Canadianness by both state and business leaders. In this extended effort,
Canadian multiculturalism and Hong Kong Chinese home ownership are
but two among many areas of increased intervention. Other efforts to
constitute cultural citizens abound, as the threads of ideological production are inexorably woven and resisted in concert with the ongoing economic and cultural transformations of the Asia Pacific.

Notes

[1] Because of the time spent flying back and forth, the term *astronaut* (*tai hong yan*) is a common label for Hong Kong businessmen who establish residency in Canada but continue to do business in Hong Kong. This oft-quoted pun has the additional meaning of "empty or absent wife," reflecting the considerable time that family members spend apart.

[2] My understanding of hegemony is as a highly contested process—one that is always a tendency rather than a realization (see Hall 1988). In this chapter my primary focus is on the process of hegemonic production rather than the experience and mediation of that process by Chinese or Canadian subjects.

[3] The cosmopolitan, in the sense employed here, belongs to a new international class of people able to manage meaning strategically in new environments (Hannerz 1990, 246).

[4] My focus in this paper is on wealthy immigrants and obviously does not address the constitution of cultural citizenship for the poor and the working class.

[5] Research in Vancouver and Hong Kong took place between 1990 and 1992. During that time I conducted sixty-five in-depth interviews in Vancouver and thirty in Hong Kong.

[6] Interview with Sally Liu, Hong Kong, September 26, 1991. The names of all informants have been changed to protect privacy.

[7] Interview with Bill and Jenny Leung, Hong Kong, September 3, 1991.

[8] Racism against the Chinese immigrants was also a factor in the formation of at least some of these social groups.

[9] My perception is based on a wide variety of sources, but exact figures on the original nationalities of buyers and their relative wealth are impossible to obtain and are widely contested. The term "middle class" as I employ it here, includes the middle strata of Hong Kong society, including the upper middle class and *nouveau riche*.

[10] It was also stipulated that the investor must have a proven track record in business. For acceptance into British Columbia before 1990, the investor had to commit $250,000 Canadian for a three-year period to a project approved by the Canadian government. After 1990 this figure increased to $350,000 Canadian.

[11] The total application numbers are calculated for an average of just under three people per applicant. (The applications include family members, not just individuals.)

[12] These statistics are from the Commission for Canada Immigration Section, Hong Kong.

[13] Victor Fung, "Hong Kong Investment Funds Pour into Canada," *Financial Post*, June 17, 1991, 18.

[14] Lawrence Lim, quoted in Moira Farrow, "Hong Kong Capital Flows Here Ever Faster," *Vancouver Sun*, March 21, 1989.

[15] See, for example, "Flippers Awash in Profits," *Vancouver Sun*, February 8, 1989; "City Housing Market Flipping Along," *Business*, September 9, 1989.

[16] Li's worldwide reputation for savvy real-estate deals was so strong that it was common knowledge that many buyers followed his global leads. Indeed, for two years following Li's purchase of the Expo lands, Vancouver became the hottest property market in the world.

[17] For an enumeration of the Laurier Institute's connections with Pacific Rim business leaders, see Mitchell 1993.

[18] As mentioned earlier, racism was also a factor, though rarely explicit.

[19] According to a coordinator at SUCCESS (United Chinese Community Enrichment Services Society), incidents of racism against Chinese Canadians rose markedly in the 1980s.

[20] *Globe and Mail*, June 21, 1989, A11. Li Ka-shing holds a 50 percent interest in Concord Pacific.

[21] Quoted in Robert Williamson, "Kwok's Connections Open Doors to Asia," *Globe and Mail*, April 6, 1992, B1.

[22] Quoted in Anne Fletcher, "Younger Li Tries Hard To Be a 'Good Canadian Businessman,' " *Financial Post*, January 9, 1989, 4.

[23] Quoted in *Seniors Advocate*, September/October 1989.

[24] See "Hong Kong-born Lieutenant-Governor Warns: Grabby Speculators Risk Creating Racial Discord," *Daily Commercial News*, February 23, 1989, 9, 11.

[25] See the interview in *Equity*, June 1989, 26.

[26] Interview with a Meet with Success volunteer, Hong Kong, July 1991.

[27] The immigration and investment seminars were given at the world trade center in Vancouver from January through June 1991. The seminar I attended was focused on the business immigration program. Although these programs were designed to facilitate business linkages, the "Being Canadian" acculturation video was shown at the beginning of every meeting.

[28] The narration is in Cantonese with English subtitles.

[29] There was a CBC Pacific Report on immigration to Canada, a TVB Hong Kong report, and a series of articles by the *Vancouver Sun* and the *Vancouver Province*.

[30] Interviews, Hong Kong, July 1991.

[31] From the "Personal Inventory of Values" section of the Meet with Success packet.

[32] From the "Multiculturalism—Fact Sheet" section of the Meet with Success packet.

[33] This friction was also felt between older Chinese residents a the new Hong Kong transnational immigrants.

[34] Many of the multicultural policies in Canadian history have been criticized as superficial efforts to promote cultural tolerance without any real advances in economic parity or reform (see, for example, Wardhaugh 1983, 201; Kallen 1982, 55). As noted earlier, I have not focused on how self-fashioning strategies and programs such as Meet with Success have been experienced by recent im-

migrants or by British-Canadian residents. I have chosen instead to investigate some of the shaping forces themselves rather than their relative success or failure.

[35] The Canadian Club program was ostensibly directed toward all Hong Kong emigrants to Canada. Most of the very wealthy, however, had already received Canadian citizenship or visas by the time the program was initiated in 1990. In my two visits to Meet with Success, it appeared to me from the questions asked and the apparel of the respondents that they were not of Hong Kong's superstratum. I was not allowed to interview members of the audience.

References

Anderson, Kay. 1991. *Vancouver's Chinatown: Racial Discourse in Canada, 1875–1980* Montreal: McGill-Queen's University Press.

Appadurai, Arjun. 1990. "Disjuncture and Difference in the Global Cultural Economy." *Theory, Culture, and Society* 7:295–310.

Baxter, David. 1989. "Population and Housing in Metropolitan Vancouver: Changing Patterns of Demographics and Demand." Laurier Institute Report.

Bhabha, Homi. 1990. "DissemiNation: Time, Narrative, and the Margins of the Modern Nation." In *Nation and Narration* pp. 291–322. London: Routledge.

Bourdieu, Pierre. 1984. *Distinction: A Social Critique of the Judgemen of Taste.* Cambridge: Harvard University Press.

Bright, Charles, and Michael Geyer. 1987. "For a Unified History of the World in the Twentieth Century." *Radical History Review* 39.

Clifford, James. 1992. "Traveling Cultures." In L. Grossberg, C. Nelson, and P. Treichler, eds., *Cultural Studies* pp.96–112. New York: Routledge.

Duncan, James, and Nancy Duncan. 1984. "A Cultural Analysis of Urban Residential Landscapes in North America: The Case of the Anglophile Elite." In J. Agnew, J. Mercer, and T. Sopher, eds., *The City in Cultural Context.* Boston: Allen and Unwin.

Featherstone, Michael. 1990. *Global Culture: Nationalism, Globalization, and Modernity*. London: Sage.

Foucault, Michel. 1979. *The History of Sexuality. Volume 1: An Introduction.* New York: Vintage.

———. 1991. "Governmentality." In G. Burchell C. Gordon, and P. Miller, eds., *The Foucault Effect: Studies in Govermentality*, pp. 87–104. Chicago: University of Chicago Press.

Gutstein, Donald. 1990. *The New Landlords: Asian Investment in Canadian Real Estate.* Victoria: Porcepic.

Hall, Stuart. 1988. "The Toad in the Garden: Thatcherism Among the Theorists." In C. Nelson and L. Grossberg, eds., *Marxism and the Interpretation of Culture.* pp. 35–73 Chicago: University of Illinois Press.

————. 1993. "Culture, Community, Nation." *Cultural Studies* 7, no. 3:349–63.

Hannerz, Ulf. 1990. "Cosmopolitans and Locals in World Culture." *Theory, Culture, and Society* 7, nos. 2–3: 237–51.

Harvey, David. 1985. *Consciousness and the Urban Experience*. Baltimore: Johns Hopkins University Press.

————. 1989. *The Condition of Postmodernity*. Oxford: Basil Blackwell.

Holdsworth, Deryck. 1986. "Cottages and Castles for Vancouver Home-seekers." *B.C. Studies* 69–70.

Kallen, Evelyn. 1982. "Multiculturalism: Ideology, Policy, and Reality." *Journal of Canadian Studies* 17, no. 1.

King, Anthony. 1991. *Culture, Globalization, and the World-System*. London: Macmillan.

————. 1993. "Identity and Difference: The International of Capital and the Globalization of Culture." In Paul Knox, ed., *The Restless Urban Landscape*, pp. 83–110. New York: Prentice-Hall.

Leyshon, A., and Nigel Thrift. 1992. "Liberalisation and Consolidation: The Single European Market and the Remaking of European Financial Capital." *Environment and Planning* A 24: 49–81.

Mitchell, Katharyne. 1993. "Multiculturalism, or the United Colors of Capitalism?" *Antipode* 25, no. 4: 263–94.

————. 1995. "Flexible Circulation in the Pacific Rim: Capitalisms in Cultural Context." *Economic Geography* 71, no. 4: 364–82.

Nonini, Donald. 1993. "On the Outs on the Rim: An Ethnographic Grounding of the Asia Pacific Imaginary.' In A. Dirlik, ed., *What Is in a Rim?* Boulder: Westview.

Olds, Kris. 1995. "Globalization and the Production of New Urban Spaces: Pacific Rim Mega-Projects in the Late 20th Century." *Environment and Planning A* 27, no. 11: 1713–1744.

Ong, Aihwa. 1993. "On the Edge of Empires: Flexible Citizenship Among Chinese in Diaspora." *Positions* 1, no. 3: 745–78.

Pred, Allan, and Michael Watts. 1992. *Reworking Modernity: Capitalisms and Symbolic Discontent*. New Brunswick: Rutgers University Press.

Shaw, Gillian. 1989. "The Hong Kong Connection: How Asian Money Fuels Housing Market." *Vancouver Sun*, February 18, A1.

Sparke, Matthew. 1994. "White Mythologies and Anemic Geographies: a Review." *Environment and Planning D: Society and Space* 12: 105–23.

Wardhaugh, Ronald. 1983. *Language and Nationhood: The Canadian Experience*. Vancouver: New Star.

Part 4

The Self-Making and Being-Made of Transnational Subjectivities

Preface

The working of postcolonial hegemonic discourses of statehood and citizenship in the Asia Pacific, the emergence of alternative imaginaries informing transnational publics that have been created by mass-media imagery, air travel, and global consumerism, and the pursuit of different kinds of capital are all processes making new Chinese identities and subjectivities, and are evident in the essays in part 4.

The *nouveau riche* Chinese families of Bangkok whom Blanc discusses adopt a conspicuous and self-consciously modern and up-to-date affect, style, and habitus focused on the syncretic consumption of both Western and Chinese cultural commodities, providing them with an explicitly new "Asian" identity that challenges older models derived from the Thai nobility; these trendsetters readily display their transnational connections and see themselves as associated with the new "Asian" affluence. In another setting, the Shanghai urban middle- and working-class audiences studied by Yang construct new subjectivities for themselves out of their fantasies of consumer desire and empowered mobility in adventures overseas, fed by the mass-media images of Hong Kong and Taiwanese stardom, which are promoted by the city's film and television industries. In so doing, these audiences elude the regime of governmentality and moral order set in place by the Chinese Communist state. The vicarious fantasies of consumption and travel on the part of Shanghai residents are embodied in a less utopian vein in the ventures of the overseas scholars in Great Britain studied by Liu (in part 1). At the same time, these Shanghai imaginaries of power and adventure represent the obverse of the subjectivities of the villagers of Zhaojiahe, Shaanxi, also reported by Liu, which are grounded in their perceptions of themselves as weak, powerless, and trapped by their lack of *guanxi* ties over space.

Chapter Nine

The Thoroughly Modern "Asian": Capital, Culture, and Nation in Thailand and the Philippines[1]

Cristina Szanton Blanc

The Intersection of National and Transnational Narratives

Driving on the new Bangkok highway just before reaching the town of Sri Racha (on Thailand's eastern seaboard), I remember that in the 1970s there were a few restaurants with gardens catering to highway traffic. Today it is dotted with colorful billboards advertising office constructions and residential compounds, some already built. Large cement buildings house businesses, restaurants, and even a formal clubhouse for evening entertainment that shows off the most up-to-date transvestite performers.

Just past the town, a peaceful Thai meditation temple faces a coastline now dominated by a huge white pipeline that channels tapioca straight onto international cargo ships far at sea. Japanese crew members in strange white uniforms—they look like Martians—wander the streets of the town. In the rural hinterland, scores of uniformed young Thai women stream out of the new Chinese-owned factories. A few miles down the road a large deep-water harbor is in process of construction.

In the center of Bangkok, where space is at a premium, imposing marble hotels, banks, and office buildings have replaced Thai-style wooden villas and peaceful canals. Multi-tiered shopping malls rise on both sides of busy main streets, bridged by brightly lit covered passageways.

Accompanying capitalist development in Thailand, Malaysia, Indonesia and now the Philippines, a new wind seems to be blowing. Changes in lifestyle, architecture, and behavior, their seeds sown in the 1970s, have become sharply visible in the early 1990s.

Fig. 1. Billboard advertising new construction projects by Sino-Thai companies on Thailand's eastern seaboard. (Photo by Cristina S. Blanc.)

These transformations are produced by a combination of state capitalism, Chinese-dominated businesses, and foreign investment. Increasingly complex alliances within and across countries connect these different sources of capital and the people administering them. Privatization, deregulated trade, and financial markets facilitate the movement of capital across nation-states. This capital is most often Western or Japanese, but it is also, increasingly, Southeast Asian. Each nation-state in the region has an important stake in these transformations. Also, populations variously involved in these sectors are on the move, thus developing new forms of interdependence across and between states (Basch, Glick Schiller, and Szanton Blanc 1994).

The novel ways in which the countries of Southeast Asia interact with this global restructuring are creating new geographies of power and new cultural constructions. People of Chinese background play an important role in these forms of capital accumulation, particularly in private business and banking (McVey 1992). From Singapore emerges a powerful discourse on Chinese capitalism as a new economic form that reinterprets the experience of overseas Chinese and forges new solidarities with mainland China (see Ong's essay in this volume). A closely related discourse on the advantages of Asian capitalism is emerging from Malaysia. Both narratives base parts of their appeal on reconstructions of what it means to be "Chinese" or "Asian." Inevitably they intersect with the shaping of ethnic identities that has taken place within nation-states, thus generating sharply different responses from Thailand and the Philippines.

During the twentieth century, as states marked their borders (Thongchai 1994), national communities were imagined by ruling elites, creating solidarities among sectors of the population that were, in fact, socioeconomically or ethnically different (Anderson 1991). These imaginings served to forcefully shape the populations of nation-states into appropriate subjects and control their desires. This essay examines how, given national ideologies and local circumstances in Thailand and the Philippines, the different class positionings and trajectories of local entrepreneurs of Chinese ancestry—core members of the new middle classes—affect the two countries' responses to these regional discourses. The essay also argues that taste and lifestyle, and the desires that they create, are an intricate part of emergent feelings of identity. New classes develop new preferred types of cultural consumption, tastes, and lifestyles, and most recently, new forms of symbolic capital, intricately linked with economic capital, are being deployed to affirm economic (as well as cultural) difference (Bourdieu 1987). This essay reflects on some of the "struggles that exist among the taste makers" (Harvey 1989, 77, 82) in the two countries, and it illustrates the local interpretations and transformations (Pred and Watts 1992) initiated by this global restructuring and the tensions they generate.

Recognizing that people operate with multifaceted identities that are both historically grounded and deeply affected by capitalist growth, this essay highlights how these identities are shaped and how they relate to power relations (Comaroff 1985; Basch, Glick Schiller, and Szanton Blanc 1994). They are dynamic, "complexly constructed through different categories, of different antagonisms . . . and locate [people] in multiple positions of marginality and subordination" (Hall 1991) as well as superiority. Individuals and groups constantly strategize within this constructed terrain of self-identifications and status markers.

While analyzing the responses of Chinese populations in Thailand and the Philippines to emerging narratives that reimagine Chineseness and Asianness, this essay tests the extent to which a new middle-class subjectivity has been emerging in these two countries, its degree of explicit Chineseness, and the ways in which it can bring together the descendants of "overseas Chinese and indigenous elites into a common, cosmopolitan *nouveau riche* consumer style which offers itself as the high culture model for modern capitalist Southeast Asia" (McVey 1992). It examines how populations of Chinese ancestry, born and raised in

Southeast Asia, and their indigenous counterparts are renegotiating notions of Chineseness and indigenousness which imply hierarchy.[2,3]

A Changing Context

The special role of Southeast Asian Chinese populations during the current transformations

Upwardly mobile people of Chinese ancestry have been key to the rise of powerful new industrialists, financiers, manufacturers, and businessmen (see McVey 1992; Hewison 1989; Blanc Szanton 1982; Mackie 1992; Suheiro 1985; Go 1994) as well as top-level bureaucrats and managers working in the enterprises generated by these transformations (Deyo 1987; Harrison 1994; Sassen 1997). Growing academic communities train professionals for businesses and state bureaucracies. Smaller companies and services are closely tied to but at times challenged by rapidly shifting capitalist growth.

As ongoing patterns of capital accumulation transform existing class relations and change the lives of most residents as well as the bases for their relationships to each other, new cultural modes of exclusion and inclusion are being developed. Consumption markets, tied to capital accumulation and to transnational consumerism, develop tastes and pin local identities to Asian (as opposed to Western) commodities. The extent to which these new forms of capital accumulation are still dependent on the older centers of capitalist growth such as the United States and Japan is the basis for extensive debate (Yoshihara 1988).

New imaginaries: From "Chinese" to "Asian" capitalism

Imaginaries producing new forms of difference are being proposed regionally and intersect national imaginaries (Redding 1990; Dirlik 1993; see also Ong's essay in this volume). The concept of a triumphalist Chinese capitalism represents an attempt by the modern, often transnational, capitalists of the rapidly industrializing Asia Pacific to position themselves and confront from a new standpoint, this time based on self-affirmed strength derived from the processes of rearticulation of capitalism that are occurring worldwide. First developed by Lee Kuan Yew for Singapore in the 1960s and 1970s, this model of a strong Confucian (read Chinese) capitalism, combined with an authoritarian state (in contrast to Western democratic models), is now supported by key Singaporeans.

In a similar mode, Malaysian government leaders, most recently Mahathir Mohamad, the current prime minister, have argued since the 1970s for a non-Western form of capitalism, initially focusing on the Japanese model. I encountered a modified version of this discourse in Penang when a Malaysian scholar contrasted an Asian version of development and industrialization to Western models and grounded the region's recent economic success in both Chinese and more generally Asian cultural and historical roots such as strong family values and communitarianism (Nagara 1993).

In 1993 Noordin Sopiee, the head of the Institute for Strategic and International Studies, an influential Malaysian think tank and Mahathir's close collaborator, was asked to set up the Commission for a New Asia to lay down a vision for the region in the year 2020. To Noordin, "the sense of 'West is best' has undergone a psychological transformation. . . . A great deal of Asia has started to rediscover Asia, to begin to have faith in Asia, to begin to be proud of being Asian."[4] The commission assembled eighteen leading Southeast Asian academics and politicians from Malaysia, Singapore, the Philippines, Thailand, Vietnam, and Indonesia, most trained at prestigeous Western academic institutions, and a few resource people from Japan, Russia, Hong Kong, and India. The commission's first report, issued in 1994, emphasized many of the elements of Confucian capitalism but transformed them into "Asian values and mores," such as an emphasis on consensus-building and communitarian values (rather than individualism), social responsibility (rather than welfarism), and pragmatism (rather than economic theology). "Doing what works" means selective government intervention, privatization of state enterprises, and full utilization of foreign investments. Singapore Foreign Affairs Ministry Secretary Kishore Mahbubani, a participant, boldly declared the dawning of a new era. Noordin recommended "above all, to harness everyone's energies. . . . and work like mad." The concept of Asian capitalism thus formally received an Asian rather than a purely Chinese stamp of approval. It articulated with the now core capitalist policies of economic liberalization, financial deregulation, and foreign investment.

These discourses, in both their Chinese and Asian versions, offer a new challenge for the Southeast Asian countries, where they do not yet represent official or even semiofficial government positions. The shift to a more generally defined Asian capitalism also facilitates the incorporation of less strictly Chinese state capitalists or of newly industralized countries (NICs) such as Japan, Korea, and potentially Vietnam. Southeast Asians are being reassured that through consensus building, strong family ties, and a different sense of community, industrialization in the region will lead to different social consequences than it has in the West. Ironically, these reassurances are coming at a time when the negative social consequences of industrialization are starting to be felt in countries of the region, and when governments, especially in Singapore and

Malaysia, are actively engaged in policies to offset these trends (Lai 1994; Soin 1994).

At an international regional conference in Singapore in 1994, the social consequences of industrialization and urbanization were hotly debated by Southeast Asian social scientists, officials, and nongovernment practitioners. Interestingly, two Japanese administrators joined their Singaporean and Malaysian colleagues in condemning American forms of development and their social consequences (Fukuda 1994; Ito 1994). They claimed that Japan too was on a somewhat different path than the West. Asian values, strong family ties, and a different sense of community were again invoked as major reasons for the difference.[5] An undifferentiated Asian claim of regional strength is particularly powerful symbolically because it builds on Chinese cultural elements but develops connections with what are perceived as the customary behaviors of indigenous populations (consensus building, maintaining a cool heart, a strong sense of community) and the orientalizing categorizations of past colonialists. In its specifically Chinese and generally Asian version, the argument obliterates local historical and cultural differences. It offers a new opportunity to culturally shape people's perceptions. Asian populations can now unify with their ruling elites in a common triumphalist anticolonial enterprise even though the position of many nonelite populations in this rapidly transforming social setting has in fact recently seriously deteriorated.

The new solidarities that these narratives are attempting to create specifically obfuscate, by evoking a single Asian category, existing class and speech-group differences among the Chinese.[6] These differences are often marked, and the networks and connections they fostered have been crucial to upward mobility. Now, with different class bases, the emphasis on Chinese particularities disappears. But these new solidarities mask the de facto exclusion of many sectors of their national populations from upward mobility and government services. As a result of structural adjustment, currency devaluations, and the need for cheap and docile labor forces, not everybody is profiting equally from the intensified capital growth of Southeast Asian countries.

One could argue that these new narratives are potentially liberating because they break away from Western hegemonic models. However, they may ultimately contribute to the creation of new forms of naturalized and essentialized difference that unite certain populations. In particular, the Chinese are being defined as Asians par excellence within those nation-states. These definitions potentially disenfranchise other groups that are often historically more ancient but now suddenly less clearly "Asian," such as the Malays (be they Malaysian, Indonesian or Filipinos). In other words, these constructions conceal the fact that the non-Chinese Asians have generally not been taking part quite as centrally in the region's rapid economic rise, even though Chinese Asians may be closely allied with non-Chinese Asian political leaders and work jointly toward the country's developmental goals.

How do Southeast Asian Chinese in each nation-state respond to these reformulations? What, given this fluid moment of transition, are the potentials for the selective adoption of such narratives across the region?

Thailand: Nation-ness, Transnational Processes, and New Narratives

In Thailand "nation-ness" is defined by practices. "Being Thai" after World War II meant acting as a Thai citizen (that is, going to Thai schools, doing military service, finding occasional refuge in Buddhist monkhood) and thus proving one's belief and loyalty in *chaat, satsana, mahakaset* ("the nation, the Buddhist religion, and the king") (Blanc 1982, 1985a and b).

This definition was consolidated during the transformations that occurred at the beginning of the century. The shift away from previously rigid, culturally defined categories of "Thai" and "Chinese" allowed the large number of Chinese who immigrated to Thailand between 1918 and 1931 to acquire a public veneer of Thai-ness, as Thai citizens, while retaining at the personal level some of their key advantages as Chinese. This has allowed people of Chinese background in Thailand relatively greater flexibility than that permitted to people of Chinese background in Malaysia or Indonesia, where ethnic boundaries were more firmly set by the state. Building on their support networks, Chinese in Thailand have been able to take excellent advantage of the economic opportunities of the twentieth century. This occurred despite government policies (often instigated by the more Thai-ified nineteenth-century Chinese migrants, now active in politics) that attempted to limit the newcomers' economic rise by reserving occupational niches for the Thais.

Sino-Thais, still identifiable through business practices and family strategies, predominate now among the top financial, industrial, manufacturing and agribusiness capitalists in the country (Suheiro 1985; Hewison 1989, McVey 1992). By the late 1980s, Sino-Thai family conglomerates such as Sophonphanich, Tejapaibul-U Chu Liang, Lamsam-Wang Lee, and Ratanarak owned 62 percent of all financial firms in Thailand and thirty-seven of the one hundred largest companies in the country. After the oil crisis of the 1970s, their alliances with industrial conglomerates such as Phornprapha (Siam Motors), Sethabutr (a brewery) and Chiaravanont (agrobusiness) provided the basis for a financial-industrial complex in which the Sino-Thais occupy a privileged position.[7] Sino-Thais represent about 40 percent of the population of Thailand's urban areas and a large proportion of the new middle classes.[8] As credentialism began to play an increased role in ensuring high income and prestigious employment, the children of upwardly mobile business-people became professionals during the 1960s and prepared for jobs as company managers and executives in the 1980s and 1990s. Many have started to penetrate the country's large government bureaucracy, while others remained in business. Only a small number are still struggling in more menial occupations. They creatively combine Chinese practices with the Thai behaviour expected from citizens.

During the immediate post-World War II period, the more successful Sino-Thai families continued to model themselves on upper-class Thais. As their representation in the urban middle class grew, these newly properous Sino-Thais were allowed to enter into politics. Often they walked a delicate tightrope between their business interests and popular consensus, especially after municipal politics started to be based on democratic elections. In the 1970s they were still struggling to conceal their Chineseness, which made them less acceptable to a mostly Thai electorate. National and local politicians wore dark glasses to conceal the shape of their eyes and were exposed to jokes about their relative lack of Thai education or their Chinese accents (always detectable during speeches, according to local commentators). Particularly successful local (and even national) businessmen would emphasize the importance of dedicating some of their profits for the good of the community, such as scholarships for the children of less well-off Thai bureaucrats or schoolteachers. Some preferred to support Thai candidates rather than run for office personally (Blanc 1982, 1985a and b).

At the same time there was a growing ambivalence among Sino-Thai parents in business about the relative importance of Chinese and English in education. Chinese-language schooling, available in Singapore or Hong Kong, reinforced the Chinese part of their children's identity and opened possibilities for expanding their national and regional networks by interacting with other Chinese. But English-language schooling offered an entry into new middle-class opportunities. This was the subject of much local debate in the 1970s, as parents increasingly tried to combine the two or opted for English alone.

Finally, while organizations of Chinese from the same regional native place, who spoke the same dialect, were still pitted against each other at the local level, there was the beginning of a joint Sino-Thai front. Organizations that prided themselves on being open to Chinese of all regions, speaking any dialect, were started. Again, this was the subject of much local debate and some resentment because of the relative local predominance of the Teochiu speech group, but this striving toward a united Sino-Thai front has continued, with mixed results, during the 1980s and into the 1990s.

There has been an increasing number of indications of the construction of a new Chinese modernity among these subgroups and classes. This modernity manifests itself through access to higher education (usually in English), a new and intense consumerism, shifts in food, fashion, and art styles, and a new interest in the most advanced technology. In the late 1970s and into the 1980s, one could see already a noticeable shift in the backgrounds of the students attending the major Bangkok and other Thai urban universities. Teachers and academics repeatedly commented to me during the 1980s that in high schools and universities, classes and student organizations now had a majority of students of clearly marked Chinese background, in contrast to earlier years, when they contained predominantly students of all-Thai background. This shift was facilitated by the lack of politicized categories of "Thai" and "Chinese," in contrast to Malaysia. The general opinion was that if people of Chinese background behaved like "appropriate citizens," they were welcome to attend any of the government-managed institutions of higher education.

At the same time, business schools such as NEDA and the popular Assumption Business College (ABAC) have been on the rise. English teachers in those schools were reporting in December 1993 that college students of both genders, when asked to describe a model hero or heroine, would almost inevitably describe their father—a reasonably predictable Confucian response, although the teachers had tried to encourage the students to select from multiple, less paternalistic models, usually to no avail. They were puzzled by this pervasive masculinist pattern among quite up-to-date young people who were to all effects considered Thai.

This modernity, with its Chinese features, connects with an advanced consumerism based on predominantly Asian modern goods from Hong Kong, China, Taiwan, and Singapore. Shopping in department stores, which are open late into the night and feature glaring lights as well as music and food from different countries, has become a main source of family entertainment since the mid-1980s. In the evenings the whole family goes to see what is new and browses for goods. Interest in advanced technology is clearly on the rise also, and now there are many more computer, video, and cassette stores.

A new class of *nouveaux riches* has become socially identifiable. In the prestigious and historic Polo Club in Bangkok, for example, where Thai families of royal blood regularly socialized with the business and government elite (including well-established Chinese immigrants now considered members of the Thai aristocracy), there is a new invasion.

Beginning in the 1990s, newcomers of more recent Chinese background have been filling the halls and grounds with their noisy parties and out-side barbecues. These newcomers are looked down on by the older Thai and Sino-Thai members of the club, who have for decades carefully pat-terned their behavior on the Thai aristocracy (Blanc 1982, 1985). "Mem-bership has changed," sighed former members in my presence. "We do not recognize it anymore!" And they would start talking nostalgically about the "old days," by which they mean less than a decade earlier. At the same time, a prominent Sino-Thai business family plans to open a new, expensive club for business executives in Bangkok in 1997 (*Bangkok Post*, August 1994).

Being modern (*than samay*) has acquired a character that is less Thai and more Chinese. While shopping for a reservation in a fashionable re-sort island on the southern coast of Thailand in December 1993, I was shown a whole array of possibilities at different prices. The brash young woman who was helping me insistently suggested three or four choices and showed me photographs of some of the rooms of these new beach resort houses. They represented a glorification of *nouveau riche*, Chi-nese-style wealth, with marble floors and large Chinese ceramic lamps, fancy paintings and golden decoration. When I asked her for tropical gardens and wooden Thai-style cottages—what I remembered as the fa-vorite resort style of the 1970s and early 1980s, evoking the lovely wooden palaces of the true Thai aristocracy—I was told that only old people still liked that "natural" (*thammachaat*) style. I was obviously quite out of date. Only grudgingly did she book an old-style spot for me—and it clearly commanded a lower price on the local resort market.

By the 1970s middle-class professionals and government officials—children of Chinese shopkeepers and traders—were proudly building stone, marble, and cement homes in the Bangkok suburbs rather than Thai-style wooden buildings along canals. They usually displayed in these "modern" homes a Buddhist altar, to show their allegiance to the re-ligion practiced by most Thais and their tacit acceptance of that religion as one symbol of their Thai-ness. Now their children, who are the young executives of transnational businesses, are being courted through news-paper advertisements to purchase or rent modern condo apartments rather than houses in order to prove their "modernity." This shift, which has al-ready occurred in the crowded Chinese city-states of Hong Kong and Sin-gapore, is a new and as yet only partially successful trend in Thailand, where apartment buildings have been for decades reserved for foreigners.

Home styles, clothing, food, and entertainment are progressively shift-ing from classical or folk Thai styles or clearly traditional Chinese styles to a "modern" corporate Chinese style. And it is these new professional

Sino-Thais and their children who are increasingly attracted to the new cosmopolitan offerings of Italian, French, and Japanese fashion designers (Armani, Benetton, Esprit, Noreko), as opposed to Thai-style silk and cotton prints. They eat in Japanese "suki" restaurants, play golf with their foreign counterparts, and practice baseball or tennis in their spare time.

Thus while upper-class Thai of earlier generations were often international, the new modernity is both distinctively Sino-Thai and generally more cosmopolitan than ever before. Being socially mobile means increasingly behaving like a successful Sino-Thai rather than like a Thai aristocrat. It is this cosmopolitan modernity that Thailand's film industry is presenting to its rural populations when it portrays the modern homes and lifestyles of urban professionals and that both the Thai and the lower-class or petty bourgeois Sino-Thai are now increasingly striving to imitate, even though not everybody partakes of it equally, and some may even resent it.

At the same time, the new narrative glorifies an Asian capitalism at the expense of American capitalism. If indeed Chinese business success and related upward mobility become thought of as "Asian," all Southeast Asian populations—including the non-Chinese Thai—can theoretically identify with it and feel proud of it. It becomes their success as well, at least in mythical terms. This defuses the danger that successful Sino-Thais, already quite involved in China's potential capitalist rise and thus more clearly identifiable with China, might run into problems. Categorizing the Sino-Thai capitalists as modern Asian businessmen rather than as explicitly Chinese facilitates the acceptance of their dominance within national politics, where "nationness" has been constructed on symbols that focus on non-overt Chineseness rather than thick Thainess. Thus if the regional narrative of Asian capitalism takes strong root in Thailand, and the new Sino-Thai middle classes and industrialists are increasingly perceived as embodying this thoroughly modern Asianness, in which being modern overrides being Chinese, the business involvement of overseas Chinese with China will be facilitated and become nationally more acceptable.

In characteristic Thai style, there is as yet little national debate about the new narratives. The issue was not discussed much in newspapers or at academic meetings. However one perceives that Sino-Thais are more at ease in manifesting their Chineseness as well as an active interest in internationalizing their businesses. For example, the next meeting of the Chinese Global Entrepreneurs sponsored by Chinese Chambers of Commerce across the region is scheduled to take place in Bangkok in 1996. As another example, in the mid-1980s Sino-Thai business managers and bankers entertained their mostly American counterparts at an international meeting of Young Managers Worldwide in Bangkok with Thai classical dance. Nowadays, by contrast, leading business figures meet to discuss whether the principles of Buddhism (a symbol of Thainess) and business success are mutually exclusive, in response to this new emphasis on the relationship between Confucianism and business success.[9]

Economically, Thailand's indicators look quite good, and the prognosis is for continued overall national growth. Given the strength of their capitalist enterprises and transnational networks, Sino-Thai businesspeople are likely to be very present on the China frontier. The narrative of Asian-capitalism-cum-modernity could then prove useful in sustaining this growth while contributing a hegemonic basis for political stability in Thailand itself.

The Philippines: Post-Colonial Dilemmas and the New Chinese Filipinos (*Tsinoys*)[10]

Several main characteristics distinguish the populations of Chinese ancestry residing in the Philippines from those of Thailand and are in part responsible for their different responses to the narratives. First, during the twentieth century the Philippine nation-state constructed "nationness" on different grounds than did Thailand. The descendants of Chinese immigrants, despite intermarriage, were repeatedly split into separate categories and had to adopt appropriate strategies. Second, the overall percentage of people of Chinese descent in the Philippines is much smaller than in Thailand.[11] Thus next to upwardly mobile Chinese, there is a substantial Filipino or Spanish-Filipino business elite and a well-educated Filipino middle class. Third, from the turn of the century to the present, the Philippine upper classes have been strongly connected to the United States. In Thailand these American connections, though powerful, have been balanced by continued relations with other European nations and with Japan (Yoshihara 1990). Moreover, in general, the immediate predictions about the future of the Philippine economy have been somewhat less optimistic than for Thailand. Serious damage was done by repeated structural adjustments and devaluations since the 1970s (Bello 1994), rising foreign debt, lack of productive investments, and the greed of elites. The regional narrative emerging from Singapore and Malaysia has thus been actively debated and vehemently opposed by Philippine spokepersons and by most Chinese-Filipinos.[12]

A less centralized and strong state than Thailand (Anderson 1991), the Philippines, after World War II, opted for a national narrative of pluralism and regionalism. National identity was created by a common colonial history as Indios, a strong nationalism, and a special attachment, inspired by the American colonial presence, to a democratic form of government. Citizenship acquired through blood (*jus sanguinis*) discriminated against non-Indio natives.

Successive waves of Chinese immigrants were split by the policies of the colonial and postcolonial Philippine state. A category of Chinese mestizos, distinct from Chinese and Indios, was established during the nineteenth century (Phelan 1959) but disappeared by 1900 as the Chinese mestizos moved up in society (Larkin 1975; Wickberg 1964) and the Philippines became a state under American rule. A new term was coined, *Filipino*, which included both local Indios and former Chinese mestizos, while the large waves of recent Chinese immigrants were considered distinctly "foreign." The disappearance of the mestizo category facilitated the absorption of long-established Chinese mestizos into the Philippine upper classes but now eliminated the possibility, despite continued intermarriage, of someone becoming a mestizo. This divided less-acculturated recent Chinese immigrants from the earlier mestizos.[13]

At independence, the Philippine nation state further consolidated the split. Citizenship was not automatically granted second-and third-generation Chinese born in the country because their parents were not citizens. Participation of Chinese in certain sectors of the economy was curtailed (Chinben See 1988). In the 1950s and 1960s the press and the public called the ethnic Chinese in the Philippines the "most legally undigested element" in all of Southeast Asia. While other countries had extended citizenship to their Chinese residents after World War II, this was not true in the Philippines until 1975, when President Ferdinand Marcos officially changed the country's policy toward the Chinese.

Despite these restrictions, many more Chinese residents requested naturalization into the new Philippine nation-state after World War II. However, they encountered legal blockages, long waiting periods, and requests for large payments of "grease" money to government officials in order even to be considered. Difficulties in processing citizenship applications have continued, and resident ethnic Chinese are still requesting that the Philippine government commit itself more decisively to the implementation of the new policy.

Thus despite policy changes, Chinese in the Philippines still face recurrent racial discrimination. They are singled out or used as scapegoats at times of economic hardship. The popular Filipino resentment against them was exemplified most recently by a number of abductions of Chinese businesspeople for ransom (Tulay 1994, 1995). Such abductions may have been politically motivated, but they fed upon a Filipino stereotype that views residents who are more culturally Chinese as usurpers of inalienable Filipino rights and as exploiters of the Filipino peasantry and small business.

The sharp line drawn by the Philippine nationalist state after World War II between the successful early Chinese mestizos, considered Filipino, and the more recent immigrants from China has contributed to hinder the continued incorporation of people of Chinese background into the Philippine upper classes in contrast to Thailand. Thus the upwardly mobile descendants of the twentieth-century immigrants, often quite filipinized and now members of the rising new middle classes, are still struggling to be accepted as full Filipinos.

Since 1987, a pan-Philippines organization Kaisa Para Sa Kaunlaran (Chinben See 1988; Wickberg 1992), is pushing for the adoption of a new term: *Tsinoy.* Their aim is to highlight the complex mixed identity of most people of Chinese background in the Philippines and their predominantly mestizo culture, a complexity denied by formal categorizations. Kaisa helps people overcome discrimination, freely express pride in their Chinese heritage, and deal with, even refurbish, their Chineseness. At the same time it expresses concern about the excessive consumerism and materialism of the new Chinese *nouveau riche* class and calls for renewed moral values and nationalistic concerns (Palanca 1995).

A few ethnic Chinese businessmen, often China-born, emerged in the 1980s as a gung-ho element on the big-business scene, allying themselves with Spanish mestizo families and starting a move from commodities into finance, media, and real estate (Tiglao 1990). They must, however, compete on that scene with Filipino big businesses owned by state capitalists who are either old-guard Chinese mestizo or full Filipino. In banking, for example, only four of the top ten banks in the country belong to ethnic Chinese families. The other six are Filipino-owned.[14] Thus, unlike in Thailand, a good number of successful indigenous Filipinos are also moving in to new business niches.[15] With respect to linkages to diasporic Chinese elsewhere in the Asia Pacific, ethnic Chinese billionaires in the Philippines have smaller businesses than their Sino-Thai counterparts and fewer (though growing) investments in China.

Furthermore, the wealthy and more filipinized former mestizo families, whose children, like those of the Filipino upper classes, have moved over the past few decades into top management, tend to still be very United States-oriented. The management specialists Sycip and Velayo, for example, opened branches in New York in the 1980s. Beniño Aquino and his Chinese mestizo wife, Corazon Cojuanco, the past president, studied in New York. Like other elite families of Chinese mestizo and Filipino background, they found refuge in the United States during martial law. (Cory's brother Pepeng and cousin Dading later became strong political rivals and important financial backers of Marcos and Aquino respectively.) In research towns in Iloilo province, wealthy middle-level

274

Chinese Filipino families were proud of having sent their children to study and work in the United States in the 1970s, and gloated over the consumer items they had received from them. Having been to the United States still commands considerable status in the Philippines.

Among Chinese-Filipino families involved in medium and small enterprises, which compose a significant portion of urban businesses throughout the country (Omohundro 1981; Mackie 1992), the younger generation—especially what Tan (1988) calls the third generation, 95% of whom are Philippine-born—has branched into education and the professions as well as into corporate and financial management (Chinben See 1988). They are thus now well represented in the new urban middle class, where they may carry recognizably Chinese names but often behave in quite filipinized ways.[16]

At the same time, the encouragement by President Aquino of Taiwanese investment in the Philippines fueled in the late 1980s recurrent feelings that transnationalized Chinese-Filipino big businesses are more interested in international deals than in protecting local businesspeople's interests, be they Chinese or Filipino. Newspapers in the Philippines frequently refer to the dissatisfaction of local businesspeople, who do not feel well represented, and there are calls for more protectionist measures. In other words, there is a recurrent split between the smaller, more nationally oriented business interests and the more global and internationally oriented capitalists. The government, on the other hand, is eager to obtain foreign investments and exchange, given the sizeable IMF repayment schedules of the Philippines (Broad 1988).

Finally, given their country's recently poor economic condition, a much larger proportion of Filipinos than Thais at all socioeconomic levels are migrating abroad in search of better opportunities. These migrations have been predominantly to the United States, other Western countries, or the Middle East (Basch, Glick Schiller, and Szanton Blanc 1993). Among them, the emigrating Chinese-Filipinos, well represented in business and the professions, are often more interested in accumulating legitimate political capital as Americanized patriots rather than as transnational Chinese. This is reflected in their consumption patterns, which do not show as strong a shift to the modern Asian *nouveau riche* lifestyles described for Thailand. While there are manifestations of this style, elite tastes and desires of former Chinese mestizos and Filipinos are still strongly patterned on European-American and modern Filipino styles.[17]

This is not surprising. Metropolitan Manila was proudly showcased during the late 1960s and early 1970s as the most Westernized city in Southeast Asia, with the exception of Hong Kong. Its modern sections had the tallest residential and office high-rises and the most up-to-date Western-style department stores (built by Filipino or Spanish Filipino families). Nowadays in Makati, where most Western, Philippine, and Chinese-Filipino-owned corporation have their offices, remodeled (Rostan) or new (Ayala) shopping compounds have a more subdued, Spanish-style appearance than the ostentatious East Asian-style multistory malls recently built in Kuala Lumpur, Bangkok, and Singapore.[18] New gentrified town centers (Magallanes, Alabang) are advertised for their relaxed old world charm and local neighborhood style as the 1990s alternative to the stress of "malling" (*New Chronicle* 1994).[19] These stores present the wares of top European and American fashion designers rather than Japanese or Chinese clothing. The remodeled hotels along fashionable Manila Bay are more Western cosmopolitan than they are East Asian, with extensive use of bamboo, wood and other natural products rather than cement or marble structures. Malls built by new Chinese tycoons, such as the Shoemart Megamall (developed by Henry Sy), Robinson (by John Gokongwei), and Uniwide (by Harry Gow) now have a more showy East Asian flavor, and do attract crowds.[20] But they have not displaced the elite malls described earlier.

The goods offered in the department stores catering to the local upper middle class are a mixture of Asian-made consumer items and U.S.-produced goods, the latter still having higher status. This is reinforced by the continued transference of U.S.-made high-technology items such as VCRs, TVs, and stereo equipment brought or sent home in "*balikbayan*" boxes by Filipinos resident abroad (Basch, Glick Schiller, and Szanton Blanc 1993). In the newspapers one finds prominent references to European and U.S. luxury goods. With the 1995 liberalization policies instituted by President Fidel Ramos, against which local businesses are strongly protesting, people are expecting a new influx of foreign investments, mostly American.

In the colonial Army-Navy Club along the bay or the elegant Polo Club in Makati, cosmopolitan industrialists and managers of Chinese background and their families, despite a greater social presence and acceptance, represent only a small number. Most educated professionals, both Filipino and Chinese, prefer professional clubs. Thus the elite upper-class style in the Philippines, although modernized, has not become quite as East Asian as in Thailand or Malaysia. At the same time, the Manila of the 1990s has started offering Chinese-style clubs in exclusive hotels catering to business executives, for businesspeople and managers often travel extensively with their wives to Hong Kong, Singapore, and Malaysia, where they are exposed to the Asian style.

The wind of a more Asian new consumerism is blowing, even though modernity is still primarily defined in Western ways. Most recently in the Manila metropolitan area, the sections of Makati, Fort Bonifacio (a military reservation near Makati), and Ortigas are experiencing a construction frenzy that is changing the area's skyline; funding for these projects involves joint ventures with both U.S. and Asian multinationals. Indeed, other Southeast Asian countries such as Malaysia and Singapore are starting to invest in the Philipines.[21] There are expectations that by the year 2000 half of all goods produced in the Asian region will be sold within it, even though the share of the Philippines as a producer or consumer of those goods is as yet unclear. At present the new Chinese and Asian narratives and the thoroughly modern Chinese-Asian consumer style are less clearly acceptable in the Philippines than elsewhere. A battle is obviously being waged between competing interests! This battle is in part ideological, attempting to shift symbols and trying to mark hegemonic terrains.

The Institute of Strategic and International Studies in Kuala Lumpur held a conference on Jose Rizal and the Asian Renaissance in October 1995 as the first step of its current project to highlight the achievements of Southeast Asian leaders. It was the first time that a conference focusing on the achievements of a foreign Asian leader was held in Malaysia. Both Philippine president Ramos and Malaysian prime minister Mahathir addressed the conference. It is significant that Rizal played a key role in Philippine history and imagination as the anticolonial hero par excellence and that the Chinese-Filipino organization Kaisa has made attemps to have him recognized as the offspring of a Chinese mestizo and a Spanish mestizo.[22] Taken in this light, the conference acquires new meanings in relationship to the forging of symbolic connections across the region.

The conference was heralded as a forum for the analysis of contemporary issues of democracy.[23] Concerns about democracy have indeed been one strong argument made by Filipinos against the Straits narrative, particularly the version promulgated by Singapore's Lee Kuan Yew. The reasons are important. During the American colonial period, the Filipino political system was patterned on the U.S. two-party system, and Filipinos were taught that democracy was the marker of political adulthood. Though martial law interrupted this narrative, the pride in the democratic outburst of "people's power" in 1986 brought it all back. Filipinos have thus found it difficult to accept those aspects of the new Asian narratives that emphasize an authorization form of government.[24]

How do the Chinese-Filipinos locate themselves in this conversation? I was fortunate to be the only Westerner to attend the First Tsinoy National Convention in Tagaytay, near Manila, in August 1994. The participants, Chinese-Filipino assembled from all over the Philippines, had come together under the sponsorship Kaisa with the specific aim of discussing their future.

In addressing questions of identity, community, discrimination, and change, the Tsinoys were asked to locate themselves with respect to the regional narratives emerging from Singapore and Malaysia. The participants—middle-aged and young businesspeople, professionals, and students—responded by highlighting the complexity of their position in the Philippines and their wish for increased participation in the country's political life. They emphasized how this represented a break from the strategies adopted by the previous generations of Chinese residing in the country. Many acknowledged that their wish was viewed with suspicion by their parents or grandparents, who still felt that the best strategy for people of Chinese background was to be neither seen nor heard, essentially to disappear into the woodwork, while continuing to carry out their business.

The response of these assembled Tsinoys to the Straits narratives was: How can we emphasize our Chineseness when we still need to make ourselves acceptable to a Filipino electorate? As the keynote speaker mentioned, access to government is key in a country such as the Philippines, where business depends more heavily on government concessions and export quotas than on control over productive labor.[25] But running for office was not always easy. The recent increase in the number of Chinese-Filipino candidates in Manila and in the provinces was creating a backlash that spurred a congressional controversy in 1994. Discrimination is to this date an active weapon against the Tsinoys.

By opposing the regional Asian narratives, the middle-class Tsinoys recognize that they are on a somewhat different trajectory than their Malaysian, Singaporean, or Sino-Thai counterparts. Young spokespersons stressed the importance of "building bridges" uniting them to Filipinos, of feeling enriched by their own biculturalism rather than identifying as either Chinese or Filipino, and of being modern without subscribing to the new materialism (Ong 1995). At the meeting, the Tsinoys reiterated how strongly committed they felt to the Philippines as a country while being proud of and wishing to connect with their Chinese heritage. At the same time, well-to-do Tsinoys, even those from the provinces, were privately intrigued by the possibility of investing in mainland China. In many cases they had visited sites in south China as tourists and as potential investors. Even though they felt quite apart culturally from the mainland Chinese, whom they described to me as arrogant and impolite, they were intrigued by the country of origin of their ancestors and recognized its business potential.

The politics of language during the meeting reflected Tsinoys' internal conflicts about their complex identities. Formal sessions were carried out in both Cantonese and English. Occasionally young Tsinoys from the provinces would slip into Pilipino. During the discussion groups it became evident that English (or Pilipino) was an easier means of communication than the many Chinese languages represented in the assembled convention, which were often poorly spoken by the younger generation of Tsinoys. But there was obvious distress at the loss of language ability. Many Tsinoys called for greater access to Chinese cultural performances and information and asked the organization sponsoring the conference, Kaisa, to help organize and distribute such programs.

A rallying call by a Chinese-Filipino Manila journalist to "become cosmopolitan, flaunt our wealth and use this cosmopolitan status and wealth to do good investments, wherever they may be" was answered by a renewed appeal for the need to become involved in Filipino politics and by a cautious regard for the constraints that such a need generated.

The cosmopolitan upper classes in the Philippines, which include Filipinos, very filipinized former Chinese mestizo families, and more-ethnic recent Chinese, have for a variety of reasons become "modern" without yet fully embracing the models of East Asian modernity that are coming to characterize some of their neighboring countries, even though these models are starting to affect them. They are, in effect, split between two forces. Those of Chinese background who are in the rising middle class, even though very upwardly mobile, model themselves accordingly: They do not feel they can easily embrace the new Straits narrative at this point, and although they are affected both personally and professionally by the economic attractions offered by mainland China and a broader Asia, they are still powerfully drawn to opportunities in the United States or Europe, where many of their relatives and friends have settled.

Cultural and economic variables are contributing just now to somewhat isolating the Filipinos from the rest of the region. There is a real danger, expressed at the Tagaytay meeting, that the country, which lost its position of advantage during the 1980s, may end up being rearticulated in a more dependent position as a labor-exporting and economically less successful ASEAN partner.

The Thoroughly Modern Asian or Asians?

New hegemonic narratives that originated in specific nation-states are being proposed to ruling elites and middle classes in other nation-states and finding multiple applications. Firmly anchored in the transnational linkages that helped generate them, they attempt to build on common elements across countries, encountering more or less favorable grounds depending on the national situations. The strength, current positioning, and trajectories of local class segments, however, affect the degree of commitment that the narratives can muster. The success or failure of these new politics of identity across the region cannot be fully understood unless they are connected to national circumstances and internal formulations.

The emergent new middle classes have not been equally shaped into ethnically marked subjects and are exposed to different modern lifestyles. A battle is obviously being waged between spheres of influence and hegemonic formulations that are more Southeast Asian or Asian and others that are more Western-based; yet another factor is the different formulations found within Southeast Asia itself. This battle, with all of its ideological components, primarily serves top capitalists' interests in the region. It offers, because of its lack of full closure, different possibilities on a country-by-country basis. Closure will occur when the narratives become fully naturalized and essentialized.

The narrative of "Chinese capitalism" is problematic because it clashes with competing national and local constructions of sameness and difference. It creates special problems for the Philippines, a country that culturally and structurally has been closely connected with the United States and in which populations of Chinese background, split by legal changes of categories, are on a trajectory of reunification with Filipinos, rather than wishing to differentiate themselves further.

In contrast, the category of undifferentiated Asian being constructed by journalists, academics, government spokespeople, and statesmen in Malaysia offers greater potential because of its more attenuated Chinese elements. This narrative's attempt to develop solidarity across the Asia Pacific, based on opposition to the United States, builds on a sense of regional pride that finds echoes among those who have received the least advantage from this new capitalism. By so doing it skillfully homogenizes diverging interests and minimizes class differences. Everybody is called upon to join forces and achieve success as Asians. The emerging new Asian narrative also connects to new forms of upper-middle-class modernity that are becoming powerful status symbols in many Southeast Asian countries. It may yet become one of the ideological linchpins of the current regional growth.

The Asian narrative powerfully reconstructs previous Chinese-indigenous binaries common across Southeast Asia. It inverts former hierarchical relations that gave precedence to the indigenous elites and replaces them with a new hierarchy giving precedence instead to the new self-orientalist construction of the Asian, still somewhat ethnically marked (read East Asian-Chinese). However, the thoroughly modern "Asian" that the narrative privileges is at this point still rather multiple and complex. As a member of different national ruling classes, this modern "Asian" remains primarily concerned with maintaining control over the large indigenous populations of his or her country. Thus McVey's

(1992) suggestion that a single modernized new Asian cultural model, based on a common cosmopolitan *nouveau riche* consumer style, will unify the Chinese and indigenous upper classes across the region has yet to be fully realized. The new consumer styles respond in part to national trajectories. What we see emerging are multiple Asians, unequally modernized, searching for new modes of hegemonic control that match their restructured social relations. The ethnic dimensions of the proposed new narratives are not equally acceptable to all of them.

Notes

[1] Many people contributed to this paper. I wish to also thank Don Nonini and Aihwa Ong for their constructive editorial comments.

[2] The paper is based on fieldwork in the Philippines and Thailand in the 1970s and early 1980s and subsequent revisits in the late 1980s and the 1990s to monitor changes. See Blanc 1982, 1985a, 1985b, 1990, 1991.

[3] Practically all descendants of Chinese immigrants currently living in Southeast Asia are of mixed descent with many cultural features from their Southeast Asian countries of birth. Their self-identifications vary according to the national constructions within which they operate. In this paper, *Chinese* refers to "all those residents . . . . of recent (i.e. the last few generations) Chinese inheritance . . . who consider themselves, or are considered by others, in some sense "Chinese" (Wickberg 1992, 44).

[4] *Asiaweek* 1994b.

[5] *Business Week* 1995.

[6] Southeast Asian Chinese generally came from Guangdong and Fujian and speak southern Chinese languages.

[7] The top industrialists families identified by Suheiro (1989) and Hewison (1989) are all Sino-Thai. See also *Asiaweek* 1994c.

[8] They were estimated at about 10 percent of a total population of 26,276,000 by the early 1960s (Ostaphan et al. 1978, 65, part I). These estimates do not include the more acculturated Sino-Thai.

[9] *The Nation* August 1994.

[10] *Tsinoy* combines *Tsino* (the Filipino term for "Chinese," as opposed to the pejorative *Intsik*) and *Pinoy* (colloquial word for "Filipino"). "Our blood may be Chinese but our roots grow deep in the Philippine soil and our hearts are with the Philippine people is the credo of Kaisa says Teresita Ang See (1990, see also 1994).

[11] The ethnic Chinese were estimated in 1970 at representing about 1.4 percent of a total Philippine population of 37,158,000. A somewhat larger number of Filipinos, however, have some "Chinese blood" (Somers Heidhues 1974).

[12] *Asiaweek* 1995a.

[13] "The Americans encouraged the Chinese to put up their own hospitals, their own schools, their own trade and social organizations" and to function as "self sufficient enclaves." "The long term effect of this policy was even more insidious than the legacies [of physical separation in parian] of the Spanish policies" (Ang See 1992).

[14] The ten top banks of the Philippines all ranked below the 230 mark among the top 500 banking institutions in the region. In contrast Thai banks ranked well above the 230 mark. Philippine banks owned by ethnic Chinese only represent 25.72 percent of the national commercial banking system in terms of total assets (Go 1994). Only Lucio Tan, born in China, was listed among the top twenty Chinese billionaires in Southeast Asia. In contrast, four Sino-Thai bankers appeared on that list (*Asiaweek* 1994c).

[15] *Asiaweek* 1995b.

[16] In contrast, Sino-Thais adopted very Sanskrit-sounding last names for general purposes while often using Chinese names in Chinese circles (Blanc Szanton 1982).

[17] Filipinos have created their own modern elite styles in architecture, painting, fashion, and the arts, inspired by the Westerners that colonized them but also uniquely Filipino.

[18] The Rostan Center was built by Imelda Marcos to offer highly prized Western imports to the elite.

[19] New shopping and housing projects are in part funded by Chinese-Filipino tycoons such as Gotianun (*Asiaweek* 1995d).

[20] The Fujian-born billionaire Henry Sy started in 1946 by selling imported shoes in Manila and later built Shoemart shopping malls across the country. In 1991 he invested in a five-story Manila Megamall with movie houses and ice-skating rinks, the world's third largest at the time, considered a kind of third-world Disneyland (*Tulay* 1994).

[21] *Asiaweek* 1995c.

[22] Since its beginnings in 1987, Kaisa organized exhibits and seminars on the contributions of Chinese-Filipinos to the Philippines. At a recent heritage ceremony, former President Corazon Aquino, after talking about her father and her China-born grandfather, concluded: "Just as I am proud to be of Chinese descent, the Chinese are also happy to have a daughter who became president" (*Tulay* 1995).

[23] *Philippine News* 1995.

[24] *Asiaweek* 1994a, 1994b.

[25] This became most evident during the martial law period, when a portion of the ruling elite (Filipino and Chinese mestizo) was cut off from government concessions by the Marcoses.

References

Anderson, Benedict. 1991. *Imagined Communities: Reflections on the Origins and Spread of Nationalism*. Rev. ed. London: Verso.

Ang See, Teresita. 1990. "Introduction." In *The Chinese in the Philippines: Problems and Perspectives*. Manila: Kaisa Para Sa Kaunlaran, Inc.

————. 1992. "Images of the Chinese in the Phillippines." In Aileen S.P. Baviera and Teresita Ang See, eds. *The Chinese Across the Seas: The Chinese as Filipinos*. Manila: Philippine Association for Chinese Studies.

————. 1994. "Tsinoys: Responding to Change and Challenge." *Tulay*, July 4: 12–13.

Asiaweek. 1994a. "Asia's Way." January 5: 17–18.

————. 1994b. "The Asian Way." March 2: 22–25.

————. 1994c. "Dragon Power: The Richest Chinese in Southeast Asia." August 24: 38–39, 40, 45.

————. 1995a. "Re-Inventing the Asian Miracle: Reform, Affluence, Intra-Asian Trade, and Huge Infrastrucure Projects Are Creating a New Regional Economy." January 13: 32–42.

————. 1995b. "Mr. Billion: How Cheap Homes Made a Filipino Rich." August 18: 46–48, 50.

————. 1995c. "The Sky's the Limit: Developers Rake It In as Manila Property Takes Off." August 18: 49.

————. 1995d. "The Asiaweek Financial 500: Gaining on the Giants." September 15: 90–107.

Bangkok Post. 1994. "A New Club Planned in Bangkok," August 12, 12.

Basch, Linda, Nina Glick Schiller, and Cristina Szanton Blanc. 1993. *Nations Unbound: Transnational Projects, Postcolonial Predicaments, and Deterritorialized Nation-States*. Langhorne, PA: Gordon and Breach.

Bello, Walden, with Shea Cunningham and Bill Rau. 1994. *Dark Victory: The United States, Structural Adjustment, and Global Poverty*. London: Pluto.

Blanc Szanton, Christina. 1982. "People in Movement: Mobility and Leadership in a Central Thai Town." Ph.D. dissertation, Department of Anthropology, Columbia University.

————. 1985a. "Thai and Sino-Thai in Small-Town Thailand: Changing Patterns of Inter-Ethnic Relations." In P. Gosling and Linda Lim, eds. *The Chinese in Southeast Asia*. Volume III: *Identity Culture, and Politics*, Singapore: Maruzen, pp. 99–125.

————. 1985b. "Ethnic Identities and Aspects of Class in Contemporary Central Thailand." Paper presented at the Symposium on Changing Identities of the Southeast Asian Chinese Since World War II, Australia National University, Canberra.

————. 1990. "The Construction of Gender in Lowland Philippines: Variation and Continuities." In Jane Atkinson and Shelley Errington, eds., *Power and Difference: Gender in Island Southeast Asia.* Stanford: Stanford University Press, pp. 345–383.

————. 1991. "Change and Politics in a Western Visayan Municipality." In Ben Kerkvliet and Resil Mojares, eds. *From Marcos to Aquino: Local Perspectives on Philippine Politics.* Manila: Ateneo de Manila University Press, pp. 82–104.

Bourdieu, Pierre. 1987. *Distinction: A Social Critique of the Judgement of Taste.* Cambridge MA: Harvard University Press.

Broad, Robin. 1988. *Unequal Alliance: The World Bank, the International Monetary Fund, and the Philippines.* Berkeley: University of California Press.

Business Week. 1995 "Japan's New Identity." April 10: 108–19.

Comaroff, Jean. 1985. *Body of Power, Spirit of Resistance: The Culture and History of a South African People.* Chicago: University of Chicago Press.

Chinben See. 1988. "Chinese Organizations and Ethnic Identity in the Philippines." In Jennifer Cushman and Wang Gangwu, eds., *Changing Identities of Southeast Asian Chinese Since World War II.* Hong Kong: University of Hong Kong Press.

Deyo, Frederic C. 1987. "Introduction," and "State and Labor: Modes of Political Exclusion in East Asian Development." In Frederic C. Deyo, ed. *The Political Economy of the New Asian Industrialism.* Ithaca NY: Cornell University Press; pp. 11–22 and 182–202.

Dirlik, Arif, ed. 1993. *What's in a Rim? Critical Perspective on the Pacific Rim Idea.* Boulder: Westview.

Fukuda, Tariho Ted. 1994. "For Children on Whom Our Future Depends." Paper presented at the International Conference on Children of Urban Families, Singapore, September 5–9.

Go Bon Juan. 1994. "Ethnic Chinese in Philippine Banking." *Tulay*, October 4, VI (5): 8–9.

Hall, Stuart. 1991. "The Local and the Global: Globalization and Ethnicity," and "Old and New Identities, Old and New Ethnicities". In Anthony D. King, ed., *Culture, Globalization, and the World-System: Contemporary Conditions for the Represenatation of Identity.* Binghamton: State University of New York Press.

Harrison, Bennett. 1994. *Lean and Mean: The Changing Landscape of Corporate Power in the Age of Flexibility.* New York: Basic Books.

Harvey, David. 1989. *The Condition of Postmodernity: An Enquiry into the Origins of Cultural Change* Cambridge, MA: Blackwell.

Hewison, Kevin. 1989. *Power and Politics in Thailand.* Manila: Journal of Contemporary Asia Publishers.

Ito, Yone. 1994. "Role and Responsability of the Family." Paper presented at the International Conference on Children of Urban Families, Regional Training and Research Center, Singapore, September 5–9.

Lai, Poh Guat. 1994. "Urban Families: Changing Trends and Challenges—The Malaysian Perspective." Paper presented at the International Conference on Children of Urban Families. Regional Training and Research Center, Singapore September 5–9.

Larkin, John. 1975. *The Pampangans: Colonial Society in a Philippine Province*. Berkeley: University of California Press.

Mackie, J.A.C. 1992. "Overseas Chinese Entrepreneurship." *Asian-Pacific Economic Literature* 6, no. 1, 41–64.

McVey, Ruth. 1992. "The Materialization of the Southeast Asian Entrepreneur." In Ruth McVey, ed., *Southeast Asian Capitalists*. Studies on Southeast Asia Series. Ithacany: Cornell University Press.

Nagara, Bunn. 1993. "A New Asian Model of Development." Paper presented at the International Conference on Communication and Development in a Postmodern Era: Re-evaluating the Freirian Legacy, University Sains Malaysia, Penang, December 6–9.

New Chronicle (Manila). 1994. "Future Shop." October 30: 22, 28.

Omohundro, John T. 1981. *Chinese Merchant Families in Iloilo: Commerce and Kin in a Central Philippine City*. Athens: Ohio University Press.

Ong, Lawrence. 1995. "Tsinoy: Identity, Integration, Involvement." *Tulay* VIII (5), August 21 pp. 10–11.

Ostaphan, Prasert and Nara Ratanaruth. 1978. "The Chinese in Thailand," In *Reader in Minorities in Thailand*. Ed. Likhit Dhiravegin. Bangkok: Praephittaya.

Palanca, Clinton. 1995. "Birth Pangs of Tsinoys." *Manila Times,* June 3.

Phelan, John Leddy. 1959. *The Hispanization of the Philippines: Spanish Aims and Filipino Responses 1565–1700*. Madison: University of Wisconsin Press.

Philippine News. 1995. "Malaysia to Hold Conference on Rizal." September 27–October 3: A7.

Pred, Allan and Michael Watts. 1992. *Reworking Modernity: Capitalisms and Symbolic Discontent*. New Brunswick: Rutgers University Press.

Redding, S. G. 1990. *The Spirit of Chinese Capitalism*. Berlin: Walter de Gruyter.

Sassen, Saskia. 1997. "States and New Geographies of Power." In C. Szanton Blanc, L. Basch, and N. Glick Schiller, eds., *Power and Territory: Transnational Processes, Identities, and the Repositioning of Nation-States* (forthcoming).

Somers Heidhues, Mary F. 1974. *Southeast Asian Chinese Minorities*. Studies in Contemporary Southeast Asia. Hawthorn Victoria, Australia: Longman.

Soin, Kanwaljit. 1994. "The Role of Government in Strengthening Families." Paper presented at the International Conference on Children of Urban Families, Regional Training and Research Center Singapore, September, 5–9.

Suheiro, Akira. 1985. *Capital Accumulation and Industrial Development in Thailand*. Bangkok: Social Research Institute, Chulalongkorn University.

Tan, Antonio S. 1988. "The Changing Identity of the Philippine Chinese, 1946–1984." In Jennifer Cushman and Wang Gangwu, eds., *Changing*

Identities of Southeast Asian Chinese Since World War II. Hong Kong: University of Hong Kong Press.

Thongchai Winichakul. 1994. *Siam Mapped: A History of the Geobody of a Nation*. Honolulu: University of Hawaii Press.

Tiglao, Rigoberto. 1990. "Gung-ho in Manila." *Far Eastern Economic Review*, February 15: 68–72.

Tulay. 1994. "Henry Sy: Migrant Shoe Merchant now a Shopping Mall King," VII/2, July 4. 7.

Tulay. 1995. "Breaking New Ground. Cory's Speech," VIII, 6, September 4. 15–16.

Wickberg, Edgar. 1964. "The Chinese Mestizo in the Philippine History." *Journal of Southeast Asian History* 5: 62–100.

———. 1992. "Notes on Some Contemporary Social Organizations in Manila Chinese Society." In Aileen S.-P. Baviera and Teresita Ang See, eds., *The Chinese Across the Seas: The Chinese as Filipinos*. Manila: Philippine Association for Chinese Studies, pp. 43–66.

Yoshihara, Kunio. 1988. *The Rise of Ersatz Capitalism in Southeast Asia*. Singapore: Oxford University Press.

Yoshihara, Kunio, ed. 1990. *Japan in Thailand*. Kyoto: Center for Southeast Asian Studies, Kyoto University.

Chapter Ten

Mass Media and Transnational Subjectivity in Shanghai: Notes on (Re)Cosmopolitanism in a Chinese Metropolis[1]

Mayfair Mei-hui Yang

In thinking about the history of the Roman Empire, Marshall McLuhan noted that writing and paved roads brought about "the alteration of so-cial groupings, and the formation of new communities" (McLuhan 1994, 90). They enabled the formation of an empire that broke down the old Greek city-states and feudal realms in favor of centralized control at a distance. A similar process can be seen in the history of the Chinese em-pire, where writing enabled the bureaucracy to hold together diverse eth-nic and linguistic groupings. However, it is with modernity and its new mass media that local and kinship identities come to be radically dis-solved by a more powerful national space of identity. Anthony Giddens has noted that an important feature of modernity is the "disembedding of social systems," or the "'lifting out' of social relations from local con-texts of interaction and their restructuring across infinite spans of time-space" (Giddens 1990, 21). In twentieth-century China, the mass media's disembedding operations have constituted first a new national commu-nity and then a powerful state subjectivity. This essay is an initial inquiry into a *third* disembedding process: the reemergence of a transnational Chinese global media public and its effects on the modernist project of the nation-state.

Benedict Anderson's (1991) thesis that a nation, a unit of identifica-tion larger than a village, local community, or region, could be concep-tualized only through the medium of mass print such as newspapers and novels is borne out by China's early-twentieth-century experience, in which print culture was intricately tied in with May fourth, republican, and Communist nationalism.[2] However, the point I would like to make is that the mass media are vehicles for imagining not only the nation but also the larger space beyond the national borders—that is, the wider world. This transnational aspect of media must not be neglected, because it harbors potentials for liberation from hegemonic nationalism and statism. Although both nationalism and internationalism composed the narratives of modernity, nationalism exerted a much more powerful influence, as it became implicated in nation-state territorial imperatives. However, with postmodernity, increasing transnational electronic linkages "all presage a delocalized, potentially nomadic future" (Friedland 1994, 15) which can offer post-modern challenges to state modernity. In post-Mao China, what can be discerned is a process in which the modern mass media, which had been (and continues to be) a central constitutive force for state projects of modernity and nation-state, has now also begun to construct a Chinese transnational imaginary world order.

Since media provide ways for audiences to traverse great distances without physically moving from local sites, they are crucial components of transnationalism. In China in the 1980s and 1990s, the media increasingly enable national subjects to inhabit trans-spatial and trans-temporal imaginaries that dissolve the fixity and boundedness of historical nationhood and state territorial imperatives. What is occuring via the mass media in China today is no longer the simple picture of a third-world culture "locked in a life-and-death struggle with first-world cultural imperialism" (Jameson 1987, 68) but a more complex variegated process of eager accommodation, appropriation, and resistance to foreign cultures. What can be detected is a culture now more confidently and creatively constructing a "third space" (Bhabha 1994) of transational Chinese identity through interaction with Hong Kong and Taiwanese mass culture. From a nationalist anticolonial culture, what is now starting to get created is a Chinese "traveling culture" (Clifford 1992) reaching out around the globe.

In recent scholarly literature, writings on diaspora comprise a body of work that deals with the traversing of vast distances of space (Clifford 1994; Chow 1993; Rouse 1991, 1995b). They chart an important phenomenon of modernity: the global movements of populations, especially from postcolonial places to the West. However, most of this writing is about how postcolonials become minorities in the West and the multicultural changes and challenges they introduce to Western hegemony, national identity, and academic curricula. While challenging the West, there is still a focus on the West as the central place of concern, the primary actor, and the key place of action. There is another important spatial transformation taking place among those who have stayed within their homelands, because a similar displacement is taking place there—

people in imaginary travel increasingly look outward and participate via mass media in what is going on with their fellow nationals in other parts of the world. This essay will document another reaction to colonialism besides nationalism: the increasing cosmopolitanism of the homeland.

The experiences of modernity and mass-media-induced consciousness in China challenge at least three common conflations dominant in Western critical theory. These conflations are those of *nation and state, state and capitalism, capitalism and the West.* In China we find that in each pair, the two processes have not always been the same, nor are they necessarily parallel; rather they have often been in conflict with each other. Understanding twentieth-century China requires the deconstruction of these ahistorical conflations, whose origins stem from the Western experience, for an approach emphasizing the historical fluidity of different forces that wax and wane, combine, diverge, counteract, and overpower each other (Deleuze 1980).

Shanghai's History as Media Capital[3]

As a treaty port opened up for trade and shipping with the West in 1842, Shanghai's history was inextricably tied up with the history of Western (and Japanese) colonialism as well as the development of native and Western capitalism in China.[4] Its Western influence meant that Shanghai always maintained a certain distance from the political centers of an agrarian bureaucratic state order, first the Qing imperial government and then the republican Kuomintang (Ding 1994). In the 1920s and 1930s, before the devasting dual processes of Japanese imperialist invasion in 1937 and the Chinese civil war, the city was the most urban, industrial, and cosmopolitan city in all of Asia.

In this bustling metropolis, there emerged what one historian has called "a new tradition, that of Chinese modernism" (Bergere 1981, 2). Shanghai saw the birth of a new modern, urban, commercial, and popular culture that, despite its foreign influences, was nevertheless Chinese. Shanghai was home to China's main publishing companies and printing presses, and to the greatest number of newspapers and magazines in the country. The city was also the cradle of a dynamic Chinese film industry in the 1920s and 1930s and had China's largest movie-going audiences (Leyda 1972).[5] Virtually all of the major film companies in the country were established in this city, and Shanghai films were distributed not only to all other regions of the country but also in Southeast Asia.

After the Communist victory, even an open port such as Shanghai became like the rest of China: closed to most foreign and overseas contact.

While Shanghai continued to be the major industrial center creating wealth for the whole nation, urban cosmopolitan cultural life saw a radical curtailment when, in the new ethos of revolutionary asceticism, it came to be labeled a decadent "bourgeois culture." With tight fiscal and political control by the center, the city focused on heavy industry rather than cultural production.

The Spatialization of National and State Subjects

Too often in Western academic discourse, *nation* and *state* are used interchangeably. Two exceptions are Arjun Appadurai (1990, 1993), who argues that diaspora populations around the world comprise emerging "post-nations" that deterritorialize states, and Katherine Verdery (1994), who has shown how, after the collapse of a super-state such as the Soviet Union, (re)emergent ethnic nationalist imaginaries (whose subjects are spread out across different East European states) seek to define and bolster themselves territorially with new and separate state apparatuses. My own concern to distinguish between nation and state stem's from a different historical situation as well as from as a different set of political and theoretical concerns. Rather than a nation in search of a state, I think that the Chinese situation in the 20th century requires that we examine how a powerful state apparatus came to overcode itself onto the nation, and how a reemergent nation or alternative community has now begun to decode or elude the state.

In China's transition from a traditional dynastic order to a modern nation-state, there was a "flattening" of a centripetal and hierarchical social realm, whose borders were hazy and indistinct, into a novel social space defined by horizontal linkages of comradeship inside and by distinct outer borders (Anderson 1991, 15; Foster 1991, 253; Chun 1994b). In the first three decades of the twentieth century, through the print medium, the urban reading public was exposed to the literature and culture of the West and Japan (Chow 1960) and came to share a growing alarm at the desperate poverty, "ignorance," and "backwardness" of China as compared to these foreign lands. At the same time, print also fanned the growing nationalist outrage at the imperialism of these same countries. The task of "saving the nation" (*jiuguo*) in the Darwinian struggle for existence between nations became a rallying cry that interpellated (Althusser 1971) patriotic subjects into the project of making the Chinese nation "prosperous and strong" (*fuqiang*).[6]

There is a historical significance to the fact that China's opening to the world was forced and its entrance into the world of nations was not on equal terms. China's encounter with global forces was disastrous for cultural self-esteem, and out of this was born nationalism. The violations of the empire's territorial space, first by Western powers in the Opium Wars and Treaty Port systems of the mid-nineteenth century, and then in the Japanese seizure of Shandong in 1914, annexation of Manchuria, and invasion of East China in 1937, propelled this traumatized new nation-state to close its doors for the first three decades after the Communist revolution of 1949. There followed the tight sealing of state borders. Outside contact was limited to government exchanges with the Soviet bloc and the nonaligned third world. Foreign visitors and returning overseas Chinese were relatively rare, as were emigrants leaving China. Few foreign films were shown; reading foreign literature was also frowned upon as submitting oneself to bourgeois culture; even letter-writing to people in foreign countries was severely curtailed. During the Cultural Revolution, it was politically dangerous to have "overseas connections" (*haiwai guanxi*) in one's family or personal past, and those who tried to flee across the borders in south China were often executed as "traitors" (*pantu*).

The first half of the twentieth century in China saw the emergence of nationalist consciouness and a concern for cultural survival in a colonial context. At the same time, the new nation sought to disengage itself from an older imperial state order and dynastic system. With the strengthening of the Kuomintang, a new state organization captured and harnessed nationalism to the project of the state. With the Communist revolution in the second half of the century, nation and state became fully coterminus, and the state took charge of all aspects of life. Beginning with Mao's historic talks at the Yan'an Forum on Literature and Art in 1942, all cultural and artistic production was harnessed to the task of state indoctrination and the upholding of party policies. Henceforth, nationalism as a critical discourse became a state discourse (A 1994). The Maoist period can be seen as the full appropriation of nationalism by the state, in which nation and state came to be fully integrated into a single entity.

By the mid-1950s, all private publishing firms, newspaper companies, radio stations, and film companies had come under centralized state administration, so that all the paths and networks of print and electronic media led to Beijing. The Central People's Broadcasting Station was established in Beijing in December 1949. All provincial, municipal, and local radio stations were required to transmit its news, commentary, and political programs (Chang 1989, 55) in Mandarin, the national language. Film in the Maoist era can be described in Walter Benjamin's (1969, 242) terms as both the politicization of art and the aestheticization of politics, but the former was more dominant than the latter, since aesthetic standards were often deemphasized (Clark 1984). The audience was constructed as an undifferentiated monolithic whole of "the masses" or "the people," so that gone were the variety and diversity of styles and tastes in the arts. During the Cultural Revolution, audiences across the country were restricted to a repertoire of nine "revolutionary model operas" (*yangbanxi*). In Maoist China, the mass media helped create a homogeneity of culture that played down regional identities, promoted the voice of the central government in Beijing in Mandarin, and reiterated the same state messages in all media, whether radio, newspapers, or film.

In almost all films of the Maoist era, family ties and personal sentiments were played down in favor of national and class commitments. The elevation of class also erased gender and gender discourse, as shown by Meng Yue's (1993) analysis of how *White Haired Woman* transformed the rape of a peasant woman Xi-er from a gender issue into a class issue. Film scholar Dai Jinhua (1995) has also noted the strange paradox whereby the Chinese film industry boasts many women film directors, but virtually none of their films have a female perspective. Although the state championed women's liberation, it did so by substituting for women's discourse a state discourse that was no longer as patriarchal but was part of a new masculinist national project (Yang 1995).

Running through many media messages was an "us vs. them" construction in which the sacred national space is constantly being threatened (as in the United States in the 1950s) and encroached upon by foreign interests and internal enemies who serve them. A binary classificatory system was set up of pure/impure and inside/outside forces of peasant and landlord, native and foreigner, in which the class opposition was made parallel with the native/foreign opposition as both struggle over the space of the state.[7] Thus, along with the centralization of all media in the Maoist era, the national identity that was first constructed by print capitalism in the early twentieth century came to coincide with the contours and logic of the state.

Mass Media Development in Post-Mao Shanghai

It can be said without exaggeration that in the post-Mao era there has been an explosion in the development of mass media. If the Maoist period can be described as a period in which the mass media sought to level, uniformitize, and homogenize the Chinese public, the post-Mao period can be said to have brought about the pluralization, differentiation, and stratification of media publics according to class, educational level, region, locality, gender, occupation, and leisure interests, fragmenting the state's mass public.

In Shanghai, radio culture was transformed with the establishment of the new Eastern Broadcast Station (*Dongfang Guangbotai* or DFBS) in January 1993, which quickly drew listeners away from the more "official" (*guanfang*) Shanghai Broadcast Station. When I first listened to this station in June 1993, I could not believe that I was in China. The Chinese media culture I was familiar with elsewhere in the country still featured broadcasters with solemn voices speaking in the standard Mandarin dialect about portentous affairs of the state. On DFBS, the serious voice and style had changed into a soft, fast-paced chatty style resembling that of Taiwan media culture. Programming content had switched to more market news, international news, and Shanghai local news (as opposed to Beijing news); there were interviews with Taiwanese, Hong Kong, and domestic stars of the film and popular music scene, and several times a day the stock market quotes would be read. What was different about DFBS was that all of its programming was live and it constantly solicited call-in comments and opinions from its listeners, so that all day long the voices of ordinary people talking about their everyday problems and dreams, in Shanghainese accents, filled the air (Bao 1993). I would walk into someone's home or get into a taxi, and eight times out of ten, this station would be playing in the background. A further novelty was that several late-night programs brought issues of the private sphere, such as marriage, romance, and the hitherto unmentionable topic of sexual life, to the public arena of radio.

At Shanghai Film Studio, the career of Xie Jin, its most well-known and successful director, spans the entire period from 1949 to the present. His films have always followed the changing Party policies and political vicissitudes of the country; however, in *The Last Aristocracy* (*Zuihou de guizu*), a 1987 film, Xie for the first time departs from politics and takes on the new theme of personal identity and cultural displacement in a foreign land. *The Last Aristocracy* embodies the very transformation of media addressed in this essay: a movement away from affairs of state toward personal issues and transnational wanderings of the imagination. The film expresses both the territorial restlessness and the longing for home experienced by a cosmopolitan Chinese woman whose identity is unmoored from her homeland. She flees war-torn Shanghai to study abroad. Prevented from returning home because of the Communist victory, she is cast adrift in a foreign land (the United States) to lead a lonely and alienated life. The nostalgia for old Shanghai is evident not only in the 1940s setting but also in the fact that the story is based on a novel of the same title by the Taiwanese ex-mainlander Kenneth Pai (Bai Xianyong), who now resides in Santa Barbara. The fact that the film was also shot on location in the United States and Venice, Italy, also exemplifies the growing transnational forays of Chinese media production. This combination of reconnecting with Old Shanghai, with Taiwan, and with the overseas world encapsulates the transformation of the imaginary taking place in Shanghai today.

New Technological Media and Publics

At least four important new media technologies have now become widely available: the cassette recorder, the telephone, the television, and the VCR. Two significant changes have accompanied the widespread adoption of these new media forms. First, in their contexts of use or reception, they have greatly expanded the private, personal and familial spheres. Take the telephone. In the Maoist era, telephones were very few and found mainly in work units, to be used in a public context for public business. Nowadays, of the 39 million telephones found in China in 1995 (up from 6.26 million in 1985), 70 percent are residential phones (*China News Daily*, May 17, 1995). For those who lived in China in the early 1980s, it is astounding to find that in some prosperous coastal cities today, 25 percent of the population now owns a phone. Urban neighborhood phone stands and booths have also multiplied, making it increasingly easy to transact personal business and weave countless *guanxi* or personal networks independent of state administrative organizations.

Whereas in the Maoist era information usually came from a centralized source, such as official newspapers and editorials, state documents (*wenjian*), or the radio, new media such as the telephone, cassette recorder, and VCR tend to decentralize information sources, making information flow more along the lines created by personal relationships (cassettes and videotapes are often circulated via personal and *guanxi* networks). In the Maoist era, state directives and didactic art were usually received in collective contexts: state directives were transmitted and newspaper editorials were often read in political study group sessions at the work unit; filmgoing was often organized as a work unit collective outing; revolutionary operas were viewed by the whole community in local theaters. Television viewing now, however, takes place in the private sphere among family, neighbors, and friends. Whereas in the public state-monitored context, one had to show one's acceptance of what was received from the state, in a private context of reception, one could also debate, mock, or reject the messages with one's family and friends, thus reducing the capacity for state media to sustain state subjects.

Another significance of these new media is that they have brought about increasing transnational connections for ordinary people. In the late 1970s and early 1980s, when cassette recorders and tapes first became widespread, they were primarily used to listen to music and to practice a foreign language such as English. Anyone wishing to listen to the sweet crooning voice and love songs of Taiwan's popular female singer Deng Lijun (Gold 1993, 909) had to have access to a cassette recorder because her songs were not played on the official radio stations. At that time most tapes were smuggled in from offshore, very similar to what is done today with videotapes. Now that telephone service has been established with Hong Kong, Taiwan, and virtually all countries of the world, those with relatives abroad can be constantly connected with life overseas. Via telephone, cassette, and videotape, they can be transported across the borders to be with their kin.

The television documentary *Their Home is Shanghai* (*Jia zai Shanghai*) illustrates well the role of the media in keeping people connected to their kin or fellow Chinese nationals in foreign lands. Its gripping portrayal of the lives and thoughts of Shanghainese studying and laboring in Tokyo emptied the streets in Shanghai as viewers crammed in front of televisions when it first aired in early 1994 (Guo 1994, 48). Shot on location in Tokyo by a Shanghai Television Station crew led by woman filmmaker Wang Xiaoping, with most of the interviews conducted in Shanghainese dialect, it made documentary more vivid and fascinating than fiction. In part 3 there is a poignant interview of a Shanghainese man who lives by himself in a cramped apartment and works three jobs a day to send money to his family back in Shanghai. He sits on the floor watching his daughter, whom he has not seen for four years, on a videotape the camera crew has brought from Shanghai, and tells the interviewer that he calls home once a week. Meanwhile, the Shanghai audience watching him being interviewed on their own screens collectively and vicariously experience not only his separation from and longing for home but also the foregrounding of his Shanghainese identity over his national identity in a foreign land, since he speaks in Shanghainese. Furthermore, in a more subtle way, they also experience his displacement from the confines and strictures of the Chinese state and the habitus of state subjects.

The Post-Mao Transnational Disembedding of Culture

The post-Mao era can be seen as a period in which a decoupling of nation from state takes place, so that Chinese identity becomes more culturally defined instead of defined only in terms of the state. While capitalism has brought back many disturbing tendencies to a state socialist society, such as increasing income disparities, the return of prostitution and child labor,

Fig. 1. The "Pearl of the Orient" television tower in Pu Dong New Area, across the Huang Pu River from downtown Shanghai. (Photo by Kathleen Erwin.)

and government corruption, it has also started the transnationalization of Chinese identity out of the confines of the state. What is developing in urban China, and especially in cities along the eastern seaboard such as Shanghai, is a fascination with and a hunger to learn about the world outside of the state borders. The new mass media both caters to and creates this interest and longing for the outside world, through linking up with the market economy and its global forays. The new Oriental Television Station (*Dongfang dianshitai*), which started broadcasting in Shanghai, is an example of this change in that its revenues come mainly from advertising, and its caters more to popular taste than the more official station. No longer relying on state subsidies, the media become increasingly independent of the state and dependent on the market.

Critiques of capitalism often assume that the logic and interests of *state* and *capital* are the same, or that they are coextensive. For advanced capitalist systems such as those in the United States and Japan, I would agree with Roger Rouse that "by and large, corporations and the state, as differently mediated forms of bourgeois practice, have worked together" (Rouse 1995a, 368) to serve as crucial media for a ruling bloc. The current situation in China of a transition from a state redistributive power to a new social form is different from this in that the moments of antagonism between state and capital are more evident and structurally deeper than they are in the United States and Japan. There is a major difference between theorizing a welfare state such as the United States and theorizing the state in state socialist systems. The Maoist state was not a welfare state in a capitalist mode of production, where the state regulates competition, assuages class tensions, and cleans up the environment. It was a system in which the state itself was the form that mode of production took, controlling not only production and distribution but also the determination of needs.[8] Therefore in the current period, when market forces are being introduced, the encounter between capital and state in state socialism will be marked by more conflict than that between capital and the welfare state.

What we find in post-Mao China is a new, complex political economy in which state and capital both converge and diverge at different moments. On the one hand, it is the state that initiates and sustains the new market-oriented policies and which eagerly lays out the welcome mat to overseas capital. On the other hand, the state also finds that the new forces it has unleashed often have a logic quite threatening to its own desire of fixing culture within territorial borders. The state redistributive economy of the Maoist period was a process whereby the state made the economy operate according to the logic of the state—just the reverse of what is going on in the United States on Capitol Hill, where the Republicans are engineering a deeper capitalist penetration of the state. It seems to me that since state logic classifies the population to enable it to measure, account for, and control it, therefore it would favor stability and a certain rigidity. This would be at odds with the nature of capitalism, which is restless and fluid in its class conflicts, constant overturning of productive forces, search for profit and new markets, and breaking up of established social relations. Marx himself pointed out the corrosive power of capitalism toward all traditional societies and values. What makes capitalism a deterritorializing culture is "the encounter between flows of convertible wealth owned by capitalists and a flow of workers possessing nothing more than their labor capacity" (Deleuze and Guattari 1983, 140) and the flows of desire which consumer capitalism unleashes. Just as "capitalism has haunted all forms of society [and] haunts them as their terrifying nightmare, [because of] the dread they feel of a flow that would elude their codes" (Deleuze and Guattari 1983, 140), so capitalism is often threatening to state-centered systems and the logic of state order and regulation over a delimited space.

There are countless examples of this tension between state and capital in the cultural realm (Yang 1993). Until 1995, the state limited the number of foreign (including Hong Kong and Taiwanese) films imported into the country to sixty films per year, chosen by the state film distribution bureaucracy. In the early 1990s there developed a widespread craving for American Oscar-winning films, which were seldom shown in Chinese theaters. Video technology solved the problem through the illegal private circulation of videotapes, most of which were smuggled in from Hong Kong or by Chinese returning from overseas. Although it was illegal to bring in videotaped programs from abroad, airport customs inspections were often lax. Often these videos were barely viewable, being second- and third-generation copies already viewed countless times before. College students were perhaps the biggest audience for such videos, and student entrepreneurs acquired videos and laser discs through various means and showed them in campus theaters on large video screens for four yuan a person. Sometimes there were no subtitles, but only a translator at the front of the cinema. At times it seemed that the films had been recorded on video directly in a Hong Kong cinema, because the sound quality was bad, and once in a while one could even see the heads of the Hong Kong audience on the screen or hear their laughter. *Lady Chatterley's Lover* was shown on one campus, but since it was considered a pornographic or "yellow film" (*huangse pian*), the police raided the crowded theater and stopped the showing halfway through the film. As a result of allowing Hollywood films to be shown in theaters, China's cinema attendance in 1995, especially in Shanghai, increased for the first time since its steady decline from the mid-1980s, almost doubling 1994 attendance (*China News Daily*, January 23, 1996).[9]

With television came the greatest exposure to the outside world and to the "culture industries" of Asia, the West, and other places. The Chinese urban television audience was only formed in the first half of the 1980s, and the rural audience in the second half (Zhang 1992). However, the growth of the television industry is quite astounding in this short period, contributing to the decline in the film audience. Already in 1986, 95 percent of all urban families owned at least one television set (Lull 1991, 23). Imported television programs from Taiwan, Hong Kong, the United States, and Japan (in that order), broadcasts of transnational sports and competitions, and TV guided tours of foreign cities all respond to a keen appetite on the part of the Chinese audience.[10] Many people have told me that when a domestically produced show (*guochan pian*) comes on screen, they or their children immediately change channels or turn off the television without bothering to check what it is about. Zhou Yigong, a division head at one of the two Shanghai TV stations, informed me that they often receive directives from the Municipal Party Propaganda Department to decrease their advertising for Hong Kong and Taiwan songs and TV shows, and to avoid showing them during prime time (*huangjin shijian*).

The Chinese audience's interest in the world outside China finds an economic expression and ally in the growing advertising industry and the business interests, both domestic and foreign, that it represents. Besides pressures from the government, Zhou's station must also respond to those who buy commercial time on their shows. Businesses refuse to buy ad time if there is a domestically produced show: "They don't even bother to check out the show to see if it's any good; they just don't want to have anything to with it," he said. The reason domestic films are not welcome by most viewers is perhaps because people no longer wish to plug themselves into the state imaginary; rather, they wish to cast their imagination outward.[11] Another reason is the poor quality of the technical production, the plot and narrative structure, and the stilted acting.

The pursuit of advertising patrons is why the station ignored a long-standing state regulation requiring stations to limit their imported TV series to two per year. Instead, they actually show about twenty per year, Zhou said. The authorities usually chose not to make an issue of this. Therefore, advertising has exerted a powerful influence on television programming, decreasing officially sanctioned, domestically produced didactic and political drama in favor of foreign and overseas Chinese products, as well as a new generation of innovative domestic dramas and soap operas.

Another point of contention between the public and the state is the issue of personal satellite television dishes, which receive programs from Hong Kong, Taiwan and Japan and (on more powerful receivers) from the United States, Russia, and Europe. In the early 1990s, many private Shanghai homes were equipped with satellite dishes, most of them made in China by rural factories hoping to profit from this highly valued product. State regulations forbid the setting up of personal satellite dishes, permitting only those work units dealing with international business to set up dishes (Anonymous 1993). The Public Security Bureau mounted periodic raids in Shanghai to confiscate private dishes, but the dishes always went back up after a while and the police chose to ignore it.

Thus the usual theory that conflates state and capital must be modified to one that can account for the changing moments or historical phases of convergence and divergence between state and capital and for the structural and discursive tensions that erupt in different situations. The case of China is especially illustrative of this tension, as it has experienced a shift from a state economy with territorially sealed activity and identity to a mobile capitalist transnational consumer economy without abandoning many features of state centralized control.

"The advent of modernity," writes Anthony Giddens, "increasingly tears space away from place by fostering relations between 'absent' others, locationally distant from any given situation of face-to-face interaction" (Giddens 1990, 18). Through the mass media of a growing consumer culture, the space of the state is becoming disembedded by transnational spaces of orientation. In the Maoist era, the "absent others" were the voice of the state and its symbolic leaders in Beijing. In the current commercialized period, Party leaders are being replaced in popular culture by new icons: pop singers and film stars located outside the national borders in Taiwan, Hong Kong, and beyond.

At least two mechanisms of spatial mobility of subjectivity can be discerned operating in the mass media and constructing a transnational Chinese imaginary. First, there is the mainland identification with roles played by Taiwanese and Hong Kong stars in films, TV shows, and popular songs. Second, there is the transnational Chinese imaginary at play, in the identification of the audience with a mainland character who goes to foreign lands.

Identifying with overseas Chinese others

Although American film and television have made some headway in China, they cannot compare with the influence of Hong Kong and Taiwan popular culture. One most vivid indication of this cultural invasion can be found in the pop songs that young people listen to and the popularity of karaoke singing. There is something mesmerizing about the repetition of endless stories of love and disappointment. Hong Kong and Taiwan popular culture has gained a firm foothold in the mainland (Zhen 1992; Gold 1993), with visiting singers giving concerts to packed halls filled with adoring fans paying high prices for tickets. Sixteen- and seventeen-year-old girls want to embrace and kneel in the footsteps of such male idols as Tong Ange and Tang Yongling. The longing to be a star oneself can be temporarily satisfied using the imported karaoke audiovisual systems now found in karaoke bars and in many work units, schools, and restaurants. Music stores have sprung up to sell this music on cassettes. Hong Kong songs are sung in Cantonese by young Shanghainese whose point of comparison these days is not Beijing but Hong Kong.[12]

A radio program host in his thirties who introduces Anglo-American rock music explained to me the appeal of Hong Kong and Taiwanese pop music in Shanghai: "It represents the modern for young people, and that is why it has replaced folk music [*minge*]," which used to dominate the airwaves during most of the 1980s. Chinese folk music is also about love between men and women, and the lyrics also depict scenes of nature, but "there is something old-fashioned about it; it's for middle-aged and old people, it feels rural and quaint now. In contrast, Hong Kong and Taiwanese pop feels new, advanced, and urban." It represents what young people aspire to, a faster-paced, prosperous life outside of the borders of the mainland. This life is thought to possess the cachet of sophistication.

In watching Hong Kong and Taiwanese shows, and in listening and singing its songs, the mainland mass media audience can be said to be undergoing four processes simultaneously: (1) identification with Hong Kong and Taiwanese people; (2) internalization of another kind of Chinese culture not so tied in with a statist imaginary; (3) differentiation of gender in identification and performance; and (4) insertion into a discourse of love and sexuality. In these four processes, karaoke singing has a deeper impact, because it involves the active performance and enactment of a different way to be Chinese, where state identity diminishes in importance and female and male genders become salient categories.[13]

Here A. L. Austin's speech act theory and Judith Butler's performance theory on the staging of gender and sexuality (Butler 1991) are relevant in thinking about the construction of the subject in karaoke.

> If the "I" is the effect of a certain repetition, one which produces the semblance of a continuity or coherence, then there is no "I" that precedes the gender [or national identity] that it is said to perform; the repetition, and the failure to repeat, produce a string of performances that constitute and contest the coherence of that "I." (Butler 1991, 18)

It is through repeated performances that gender and national identity are constructed and reconstructed and that subjects sometimes come to realize that no essence lies beneath or outside of performance. To be sure, karaoke singing in China is putting into place a new regime of normalized heterosexual male and female objects of imitation, but it is also instituting different ways of being Chinese. The subjectivities produced by karaoke singing and those produced by the Maoist loyalty dance are

301

vastly different. Whereas Maoist subjectivity sought to merge the self with the body of the state and its embodiment, Mao's body (Yang 1994c), karaoke places the subject in a narcissistic dynamic between self and the love object through which it learns to desire, and whose desire it needs, to fulfill and strengthen the fragile self. This Other through which the self yearns to be completed is no longer the larger and powerful collective "I" of the nation, but a Chinese cultural Other of Taiwan or Hong Kong who has a gender.

The longing to be reunited with or merged with the Chinese Other outside the borders of the Chinese state is given full expression in a popular song of the nineties, "My 1997 Hong Kong," written and sung by Ai Jing, a young mainland female singer who is also popular in Taiwan and Hong Kong. I translate some excerpts:

> The year I was seventeen, I left my hometown, Shenyang,
> Because I felt that the place didn't fulfill my dreams. . . .
> I sang from Beijing to Shanghai,
> And from Shanghai I sang to the South that I had dreamed of.
> My stay in Guangzhou was rather long,
> Because my Other, he is in Hong Kong.
> When will we have Hong Kong?
> When will we know what Hong Kong people are like?
> My boyfriend can come to visit Shenyang,
> But I can't go to Hong Kong.
> Hong Kong, oh, that Hong Kong!
> I should have gone out into the world to broaden myself when I was young. . . .
> Let me go to that dazzling world,
> Give me that big red official seal of approval to go abroad.
> 1997! May that year arrive quickly! . . .
> Then I can go with him to the night markets.
> 1997! May that year arrive quickly! . . .
> Then I can go to Hong Kong!
> (Ai 1993)

This song sends shivers of anxiety through the hearts of Hong Kong Chinese because it reminds them of 1997, when China will become Hong Kong's new master. However, mainland Chinese are impatient for the day when Hong Kong's dazzle, wealth, and cosmopolitanism will become accessible to them. In contrast to mainland official discourse about 1997, which stresses Hong Kong's "return to the embrace of the motherland" (*huidao zuguo de huaibao*), the song expresses a yearning to break out of the motherland and to cross the state borders that forbid another way of being Chinese, although this alternative involves becoming a consuming Chinese. Along with the strengthening of the desiring "I," what comes into being is not only a culture of individualism but also a culture of desiring, consuming individuals yearning to be fulfilled.

The incursions of Hong Kong and Taiwanese popular culture, called *gangtai wenhua* (Gold 1993), into mainland state culture also show that it is no longer adequate for critical theory to identify *capitalism* only as a *Western* force. What post-Mao China is encountering is the regional or transnational ethnic capitalism of overseas Chinese in Hong Kong, Taiwan, and Southeast Asia. In the past two decades, overseas Chinese economic investment has dramatically increased on the mainland (Harding 1993; Ong's essay in this volume; Ash and Kueh 1993). In 1990 Hong Kong surpassed Japan and the United States as the number-one investor in China, and Taiwan became the second-largest investor (Hsiao and So 1994, 2). As a Chinese scholar friend said to me, "For Chinese people today, cultural imperialism no longer means Western imperialism, because it's now also coming from Taiwan and Hong Kong."

Increasingly the West is no longer the only, or even the primary, outside influence in local cultures, as Leo Ching's (1994) work on the importance of Japanese mass culture in Taiwan shows. Rather than a center-periphery framework of the West versus the rest, or capitalism versus the third world, it now looks as if the West is just another node in a system of other nodes (Appadurai 1990). The outside capital moving in is not Western but of the same ethnicity as the labor force it is appropriating. Furthermore, while Hong Kong and Taiwan are the capitalists exploiting mainland labor, they must also answer to a powerful mainland state that has military superiority over them, as evidenced in the mainland's readiness for military action against Taiwan. Thus previous simple models of Western cultural imperialism overrunning the third world through capitalist expansion cannot capture the complex situation in China today, where critique must be directed at a Chinese state as well as Chinese capital.

Recent critiques of multinational capitalism (Wallerstein 1974, 1984; Jameson 1987; Miyoshi 1993) often suffer from the very same problem they are against. That is, in seeing the world engulfed by multinational capitalism, they do so from a very Western-centric perspective. They fail to take an on-the-ground perspective of the particular cultural formations that undergo this complex process. Their models fail to take into account how at the same time transnational capitalism introduces a new regime of power into China, it also serves to dislodge an entrenched and deeply rooted state power.[14] The binary constructions of center versus periphery and West versus the rest prove inadequate, as the outside "cen-

Fig. 2. A cosmetics display in one of Shanghai's leading department stores, for a company sponsoring the Fourth World Conference on Women in Beijing. (Photo by Kathleen Erwin)

ter" that is having the most impact on China today is not the West but the modernized and commercialized Chinese societies of Taiwan, Hong Kong, and overseas Chinese. In this second spurt of capitalist culture, China is not being ground underfoot by Western cultural or economic imperialism, but is being drawn into a regional or ethnic Chinese capitalist mode of power in which China is both the victim as well as a host that benefits, manipulates, and calls the shots.

Following mobile Chinese subjects in other lands
The second mechanism for constructing a new transnational identity is the imagining of a mobile Chinese identity moving through foreign lands. This is a process in which the media audience identify with main characters who are mainland Chinese experiencing life in an alien culture. In recent years bookstores in Chinese cities have been selling a new genre of semiautobiographical and semifictional writing: accounts or stories by people who have lived in the United States or Japan of their

experiences and fortunes. Theater, film, and television productions have also taken up these themes.[15]

The "leave-the-country fever" (*chuguore*) reached a peak after the Tiananmen tragedy of 1989. The phenomenon of urban Chinese going abroad to live, whether as students and scholars, émigrés, laborers, or entrepreneurs, has been satirically called "joining a brigade overseas" (*yang chadui*). This expression conjures up the image of city people in the Cultural Revolution going down to the harsh life of physical labor in the countryside. Like their predecessors in the Cultural Revolution, to-day's Chinese are going to alien lands where they must struggle to sur-vive through their own labor and wits.

The most famous book in this genre is *A Beijing Native in New York*, written by Cao Guilin, which was made into the first television drama series shot entirely on location in New York City.[16] This popular show aired in China in October 1993 and was made by Beijing Television Pro-duction Center. The story is about Wang Qiming, a cello player in the Beijing Symphony, who goes with his wife, Guo Yan, to New York City. There they do not receive the help of their relatives and have to start life at the bottom of American society, he as dishwasher in a Chinese restau-rant, she as a seamstress in a sweatshop owned by an ambitious Ameri-can named McCarthy. In his uphill climb to become a wealthy sweatshop owner himself, Wang Qiming employs some ruthless tactics, loses his wife to McCarthy, and joins up with his employer, A Chun, an astute, in-dependent single businesswoman from Taiwan.

By listening to the discussion of this series by twenty members of a workers' film criticism group in Shanghai, we can get an idea of how this show has engendered multiple effects, such as: transnationalizing the audience, tapping into feelings of unease and suspicion about capi-talism, giving vent to yearnings for a better life in the United States, dis-seminating a new model of independent womanhood that is sensual and hard-edged at the same time, and providing a forum in which to critique state policies.

Everyone agreed this was a popular series, and people were very in-terested in seeing what American streets and building interiors looked like. They were very curious about the life of Chinese abroad, especially since many of them had relatives or friends abroad. Five themes emerged in the discussion. First, a middle-aged man said that a feature of this film is international exchange. America is a place that is not xenophobic (*pai-wai*) and in which everyone is treated equally; different races and cul-tures in the United States are engaged in competition. The lives of Chinese in America are not ones of luxury, for they must work hard in order to get anywhere. Just as he was learning about America, he thought

Americans could also learn about life in China from watching a hypothetical show called *An American in Beijing* or *An American in Shanghai*. What can be detected in this statement is a subjectivity traversing great distances as well as a change of perspective that follows upon this. Through the medium of television, this man could imagine himself in another land, observing people there, and could even reverse the process and imagine himself as an American coming to China. The latter move of stepping out of his taken-for-granted subjectivity and assuming another would enable him to defamiliarize his native surroundings, to look at them with a fresh and different perspective. Indeed, in a popular-magazine discussion of the program, one reviewer quoted the old Chinese adage "Not knowing the real nature of Mt. Lushan is due to one's fate of living only in its midst (*bushi Lushan zheng mianmu, zhi yuan shen zai cishan zhong*) to say that the show enabled Chinese to metaphorically leave China to come to a new understanding of their own country from a new vantage point (Yang R. 1993, 12).

A second theme was that of losing one's status, privileges, and support network, things that give one an identity and social role at home, and being propelled into a different status in America, where everyone starts out equal and only some rise up to the top through their own efforts. Several people commented on how once Wang Qiming entered the United States he could no longer enjoy the "aristocratic" (*guizu*) status that being a musician brought him in China; instead he had to use those refined musician's hands to wash dishes, because in the United States one is judged not by one's status (*shenfen*) but by one's efforts and talents. One man said that it doesn't matter whether one is a professor or worker in China, for in the United States none of this is recognized. It was also an eye-opener for them to see how Wang's relatives treated the couple in such a distant impersonal fashion. In the show the relatives were late to pick up Wang and Guo Yan at the airport and did not take the new arrivals to their homes but unceremoniously dumped them in a wretched basement apartment for which they expected the rent to be repaid. One man said that the show not only smashed the Chinese fantasy that one could pick up gold on the streets in America but also the fantasy that one could rely on one's relatives abroad. What seems to be operating in this line of thinking is that viewers of the show see the stripping away of familiar ways of being Chinese, such as relying on prescribed social status and on relatives. Through imagining these different ways of being Chinese abroad, the possibility is opened up for a reconstructing of both subject and society at home. So, for example, one man said that Chinese should learn to be more self-sufficient, and he called for a different way to raise children so that they will not rely on their parents.

A third theme was the ferociousness of capitalism and its ruthless cut-throat competition of "big fish eat little fish." A middle-aged man repeated a refrain of the theme song: "America is neither heaven nor hell, it is a battleground." Several people commented on the intense competitiveness of American society. They said that a newspaper had started a lively discussion soliciting letters debating the question of whether Wang Qiming is a good or bad man and whether he deserves sympathy or not. Sun, a factory office worker in his thirties, identified two issues in the show: the conflict between a planned economy and a market economy, and the conflict between Chinese and Western culture. Sun thought that Wang Qiming had to compete in order to survive, and he resorted to some ruthless methods, such as using his wife to destroy a competitor. Sun could sympathize with Wang: Wang won the economic battle but lost his personal integrity. He became dehumanized in the struggle; his "human nature became twisted [*niuqu*]." This showed how deeply Western culture has penetrated Chinese culture, he thought. Why did Wang, a person from a culture over two thousand years old, lose himself to a culture only three hundred years old? Because he was shocked at finding out about the West's economic might. Sun consoled himself that the Chinese market economy will not be as twisted and dehumanizing as that in the United States.[17] What was perhaps being worked out through this show and through the discussions it generated was the anxiety and ambivalence of plunging into capitalism and into the global society it represents. There was the fear of being corrupted by alien outside forces, of losing one's self and identity. At the same time there was the feeling that this was the only way to go, that it was necessary to overcome one's scruples and hesitations and make the leap.

There was also a fourth discussion of the female characters in the show. A Chun, the Taiwanese lover, and Guo Yan, the mainland wife, were compared. A Chun won the admiration of both men and women for her economic astuteness and her knowledge of the market and Western culture. As a soft-spoken traditional woman who could endure hardships, Guo Yan won the approbation of the male film discussants, who thought she represented "Eastern beauty and virtue" (*dongfang meide*). A Chun was considered very Americanized, and there was the belief that she too had once been like Guo Yan when she first went to the United States. The men thought women like A Chun, who are astute businesswomen, are good to have in a market economy, but they would not like to have her for a wife. Sun said that in China it is not common to find a woman like A Chun, who is so successful in the market. He confessed that his "world view" had still not completely turned around to fully accept her, although he admired her. "It's as though we have to tear off a layer of skin before we can completely turn around," he said. It would seem that the disturbing thing about capitalism is not only the cutthroat competition but also the new kind of independent women, like A Chun.

In separate discussions with women, I found that women generally liked the A Chun character. They admired her independence, her no-non-sense toughness, and the way she managed to separate the economic re-lationship from her romantic relationship with Wang. However, one of the women said that she did not want to challenge the men openly about their preference for Guo Yan at a public forum, and that even though men and women are now equal, it was still not easy for women to speak out in public. Perhaps it was easier for Chinese audiences to accept A Chun's novel combination of toughness, feminine sexual allure, and caringness when it was presented in the character of a Taiwan Chinese.[18]

Finally, this television series also provided an opportunity for these film discussants to question the wisdom of past state policies, such as political campaigns, that have caused so many people to want so desper-ately to leave China in the hope of finding a better future. Referring to a well-known phenomenon, one man declared, "There is something deeply wrong when some Shanghai women want to flee abroad so much that they are even willing to become prostitutes in someone else's country in order to survive." Since this was a public discussion, criticizing the gov-ernment for past mistakes, which have made material and spiritual life so harsh in China, was a delicate and still potentially risky undertaking. This theme was expressed in so roundabout a fashion that I almost missed it until I sought clarification in separate private discussions.

This discussion of *A Beijing Native in New York* may seem to many in the West who have seen the show to be discrepant with the pervasive allegory of big-state rivalry and capitalist competition between China and the United States, personified by the characters Wang Qiming and David McCarthy. However, as Stuart Hall has shown, the process of au-dience *decoding* of media messages often "does not constitute an 'im-mediate identity'" with the process of authorial *encoding* of the messages, for there is a "relative autonomy" in decoding due to "the structural differences of relation and position between broadcasters and audiences" (Hall 1980, 131). As the recent flood of audience reception studies show (de Certeau 1984; Radway 1988; Ang 1990; Yang 1994a), a sole reliance on textual criticism by academics of media products can-not get at the full range of their social effects, because audiences selec-tively misread or read past the intentions of the producers. What I discerned in doing fieldwork on this film discussion group in 1993 was not a tendency to identify with the Chinese state against the United States, but rather an interest in exploring the possibilities of transnational mobility and displacement.

A deterritorialized Chinese subjectivity

In these two examples of a pop song and a television series can be detected a deterritorialized Chinese subjectivity that cannot be contained by the state apparatuses of either mainland China or Taiwan. What Homi Bhabha (1994) calls a "third space" of cultural hybridity has begun to spill out over the constrictive molds of a fixed, state-spatialized Chinese identity and homogeneous national culture. This "third space" is the "intervention of the 'beyond'. . . . [which] captures something of the estranging sense of the relocation of the home and the world—the unhomeliness—that is the condition of extra-territorial and cross-cultural initiations" (Bhabha 1994, 9). Whereas only a tiny proportion of people in Shanghai have been able to physically cross state boundaries and venture into the outside world, it is through the proliferating media that the mass of the people now also occupy a "third space" of transnational encounters.[19] In this space, the lines between home and world, one's own nation-state and another country, Chinese and foreign, socialism and capitalism get blurred through traveling identities.

The song "My 1997 Hong Kong" is heard on the airwaves of cities in mainland China, Taiwan, and Hong Kong, so that we may begin to speak of the emergence of a set of Chinese audiences who are viewing an increasingly common set of programs, although they are separated by state boundaries. This sharing of a common set of media products is developing across a broad space of the globe and creating a linked Chinese community of media audience stretching from China to overseas Chinese in Southeast Asia and the United States. So although it is still not fully or directly connected by satellite, transnational subjectivity in Shanghai has already entered into a shared space of a common nexus of Chinese popular culture programming around the globe. Don Nonini describes two new Chinese-Malaysian public spheres that look outward from Malaysia for news and entertainment: cosmopolitans who have traveled and worked abroad (including in China) and whose children attend universities in the West, and the Sino-internationalists who are involved in Chinese-language new media of videotapes, cassettes, films, and karaoke (Nonini 1995, 16). Here in the United States there are now three Chinese-language satellite television stations: North American TV, a station airing Taiwanese but also some mainland programs; Jade Channel/TVB, a Hong Kong channel; and the new Eastern Satellite TV, founded by mainland Chinese in Chicago and airing mainland shows (Qiu 1993; Sheng 1995; Hamilton 1995). Thus in Shanghai, Taiwan, Hong Kong, Malaysia, and the United States, there are increasing overlaps and commonalities in the programming that Chinese in these various places are viewing, making for the emergence of a transnational (read trans-state) Chinese-language imagined community in the next century (Lee 1993).

Since the media is caught up with the commercial promotion and celebration of material consumption, its detaching of subjects from the state is often at the price of what Benjamin (1969, 240) called the "distraction" of these liberated subjects from serious social reflection and critique. However, in the present historical moment, despite the commercialism, there is something implicitly oppositional about the new media. Most intellectuals I spoke with had a pained expression when asked about the influx of overseas popular culture. They were disturbed by this sudden shift to the vulgar, the shallow, and the commercial. Lan Tian, a college professor, had his own explanation: "Mainland Chinese are like children who have been shut up at home for years. When finally you let them out, everything outside is good in their eyes." However, he also saw the potential in this imported culture for a challenge to state culture. This wave of another type of Chinese culture is a relief from the "linguistic violence" or "rape" (*yuyan qiangbao*) that people were subjected to before, he thought. Popular culture threatens both "official discursive power" (*guanfang huayu quanli*) and "central core culture" (*zhongxin wenhua*). "Money knows no center," he said, with some sarcasm.

Zhang Daoming, a writer in his late thirties, was even more affirming of Hong Kong and Taiwanese popular culture. He wanted higher dosages of it: "Let's have more of this cultural garbage [*wenhua laji*], so that it becomes a flood and disaster, then people will get sick of it. It will make people feel isolated and displaced so that they can throw off this great monolithic unity [of the nation] (*da yi tong*)." Zhang is much more willing for people to be trodden down by economics rather than by politics. "At least in karaoke pop songs, people are singing their individual hearts, not that of the state."

Conclusion

The historical specificities of modern China have led me to challenge several assumptions in critical theory on the question of the spread of capitalism, modern mass media, and globalism. I have pointed out that three common conflations must be challenged when we look at the particular situation of China today. What I have outlined is a case of a newly created nation, or nationalist imaginary of print, first throwing off an old state (the imperial dynastic order), then adopting, or being adopted by, a new socialist state, which sealed the national borders and homogenized the interior with print, radio and film. More recently, new forms of mass media and popular culture have generated sentiments toward eluding and transcending this new state once again with the creation of a transnational cultural subjectivity in the exposure to an ethnic overseas Chinese capitalism. The recosmopolitanizing of Shanghai is part of this counter movement of a transnational Chinese cultural identity that shuts off state messages to wander imaginatively across the globe.

The focus here has been to show how transnational media have enabled the detaching of Chinese subjectivity from the state and its mobilization across imaginary space to link up with alternative Chinese subjectivities far away. Through the new mass media, those who have stayed in the country have started to undergo a change in subjectivity that is perhaps just as dramatic as that of those who have traveled abroad, so that returning Chinese often find themselves strangers upon their return. While the nation and state continue to be imagined, now they must contend with the splintering of subjectivities into pluralized media audiences of gender, class, and rural-urban differences, as well as the emergence of a regional overseas Chinese imaginary. However, even while liberated transnational Chinese subjects have begun to displace state subjects, they immediately face the danger of getting trapped in new and different tentacles of power.

It seems to me that today China is poised between two dangers, neither of which is Western, although both are shaped by forces of modernity that the West first launched. First, there is the state centralized power of the Maoist era, which was largely indifferent to the high toll in human lives and psychic misery produced by its various political campaigns to strengthen the state and ensure that state subjectivity was the only form of consciousness. This danger has not fully retreated, although there have been recent cultural departures from its grip. Second, the new danger is that this same state will adopt the model of Asian state capitalism in the rest of Asia, which Aihwa Ong has suggested is an emerging counter-West Asia-Pacific hegemony of the twenty-first century (see Ong's essay in this volume). In this second mode of power, there is a smoother alliance of state and capital, a novel appropriation of cultural tradition such as state Confucianism (Ong 1996; Chun 1994a; Heng and Devan 1992) as legitimizing device, a state management of labor through the deployment of consumerism, and the dominance of a male business culture that tolerates women as business partners but more often casts them in roles servicing men in a commercialized culture of male sexuality. In this period of transition, the second mode challenges and offers relief from the first; however, this should not prevent us from seeing what Foucault (1980) realized with the early-twentieth-century discourse of sexual liberation: that liberation is always a prelude to a new insertion into another mode of power.

Notes

[1] I wish to thank Aihwa Ong and Roger Rouse for providing me with insightful and helpful suggestions on my paper. Thanks also to Don Nonini for his incisive comments and for the idea of the title, and to Lydia Liui and Zhang Yuehong for their careful reading of the manuscript. This paper was also presented at the Chicago Humanities Institute, University of Chicago, in January 1996, and I would like to thank the many scholars there who provided stimulating comments.

[2] Anderson's work has also had an impact on studies of electronic media and national identity, such as recent works by feminist anthropologists who show how television is an important means of constituting national identity through gender, albeit through a contestatory process (Mankekar 1993; Rofel 1994; Abu-Lughod 1993; Brownell 1995). These works point to an important effect of print and television: the knitting together of a readership and audience scattered across vast regions into a national identity, sharing the same language, emotions, narrative structures, and political messages.

[3] Fieldwork and interviews on recent developments in mass media and media publics in the post-Mao market economy era were conducted over five months in the city of Shanghai between 1991 and 1993 among mass media professionals and intellectuals and among working-class film and television criticism groups (see Yang 1994a).

[4] In the 1920s, Shanghai's international settlement zones housed 23,307 foreign residents (out of a Chinese population of 2.5 million) (Bergere 1981, 6), the largest collection in any Chinese city. Shanghai was also the city with the largest Chinese migrant population from other parts of China (Ding 1994), and perhaps the city with the largest number of Chinese to go abroad and return from abroad. Shanghai factories in 1934 accounted for half of China's modern industrial production, and in 1935 the city received 46.4 percent of all foreign investments in China (Bergere 1981, 21–22).

[5] It was in the Shanghai film industry that the figure of the "modern woman" emerged as a new site of culture production. Zhang Yingjin has shown how it provided critiques of tradition and expressions of sexuality for male desire as well as new objects for modern male disciplinary knowledge (Zhang 1994:605). See also Pickowicz 1991 for a discussion of themes of urban and foreign decadence vs. native rural purity in 1930s Shanghai films.

[6] In its iconoclastic attacks against the traditional Chinese family, kinship, and religion and in its promotion of the individual and the nation, May fourth discourse laid the foundation for what later became "the masses," atomised individual state subjects (Wu 1992) who were more equal, and at the same distance from the political center (Yang 1994c; 1996).

[7] The category of "third world brothers" softens this dichotomy but retains the sense of state border separations.

312

[8] See Feher, Heller, and Markus 1983 for a Marxist critique of Soviet-type state-centralized economic systems.

[9] Shanghai film ticket sales in 1995 were 230 million yuan, up from 140 million in 1994 (*China News Daily*, January 23, 1996). One Chinese intellectual I spoke with said that many people are concerned about the damage done to the domestic film industry by foreign films, but others argue that what Hollywood films will do is to draw the Chinese audience back into the theaters, so that Chinese films will in the future find a more conducive climate among domestic, as opposed to foreign, financers for their films.

[10] Here is a sampling of some international programs on the four television channels in Shanghai in the week of November 1–7, 1993: World Heavyweight Boxing Championship live from Las Vegas; tours of Hong Kong, Japan, and Hollywood with various Shanghai TV hosts; a history of the world trade agreement; Japanese and English language classes; the American program *Matlock* (*Bianhu lushi*), dubbed into Mandarin; a Taiwan television serial *The Capital City and Four Youths* (*Jingchen sishao*); an American documentary about the KGB and CIA; a Japanese children's cartoon, *Hero of the Universe: Jack Automan,* dubbed into Mandarin; and *The News in English* every night at 1 A.M.

[11] One exception to advertisers' reluctance to buy commercial time on domestic programs are those shows made by Wang Shuo and crew at the Beijing Television Production Center, which produced the very popular *Yearning* (*Ke wang*, 1990) (Zha 1995; Rofel 1994), *Stories from the Editing Department* (*Bianjibu de gushi*, 1992), and *A Beijing Native in New York* (*Beijingren zai niuyue*, 1993).

[12] Of course, the cultural impact is not just one-way; Mainland media and popular culture have also influenced Taiwan and Hong Kong (see Shih 1995 on the impact of the Mainland on Taiwanese TV and popular music).

[13] See two other discussions of karaoke by Vincanne Adams (1994) Aihwa Ong (1996).

[14] The assumption that the center (which is always figured as the West) always dominates the periphery means that "we get the history of the impact of the center on the periphery, rather than the history of the periphery itself" (Hannerz 1989, 207). The actual interactive process of cross-cultural negotiation, interpretation, and specific strategies of appropriation are not examined at all.

[15] The books of this genre come with titles such as *Chinese Educated Youth Abroad*; *Manhattan's China Lady*; *The Moon Back Home is Brighter*; *A Beijing Woman in Tokyo*; *The Bright Moon of Another Land*; and *A Shanghainese in Tokyo*. There are also two successful plays, one called "The Wife Who Came Back from America" (*Meiguo lai de qizi*), by Zhang Xian, and "The Woman Left Behind" (*Liu shou nüshi*), by Yue Meiqin, both of which I saw in a small theater in Shanghai. The latter was made into a film of the same title by Shanghai Film Studio in 1992. Another play titled "Tokyo's Moon" (*Dongjing de yueliang*) was written by Sha Yexin, and a TV documentary shot by Wang Xi-

aoping on location in Tokyo called "Their Home is Shanghai" (*Jia zai shang-hai*), depicting the everyday life of Shanghainese working in Japan, was aired to great acclaim on STV

[16] For a critique of how this show promotes the consumerism of transnational corporate products and becomes implicated in the movements of transnational (Western) capital, see Liu 1995.

[17] In an analysis highly critical of the show and of his compatriots who accept it, a Chinese expatriate living in the United States wrote that the picture the show paints of an immoral dog-eat-dog society in America merely serves as an excuse for Chinese to practice a ruthless kind of capitalism, which they conveniently imagine exists in the United States (Ye 1994). I think the fact that Wang Qiming's moral character is the subject of debate shows that many people cannot accept him.

[18] In the imaginary of travel and transnational crossings taking hold in the coastal Chinese cities, there is a gender differential whereby women are imagined to be more mobile and successful in adapting to foreign cultures and places, whereas men are seen as more rooted to the culture and national space. Space limits require a separate treatment of this theme in another publication (Yang 1995).

[19] Mike Featherstone also has a similar notion of "third cultures," or transnational cultures that are oriented beyond national boundaries; however, his application of this concept is narrower than what I am trying to conceive. By "third culture" he means the world of transnational professionals in architecture, advertising, film, global financial markets, international law, and other international agencies (Featherstone 1990, 6–8; 1992, 146). I would like to include the transnational mass cultures created by mass media.

References

A Cheng. 1994. *Xianhua xianshuo: Zhongguo shisu yu Zhongguo xiaoshuo* (Leisurely Chats: Chinese Customs and the Chinese Novel). Taipei: Shibao wenhua chubanshe.

Abu-Lughod, Lila. 1993. "Finding a Place for Islam: Egyptian Television Serials and the National Interest." *Public Culture* 5, no. 3.

Adams, Vincanne. 1994. "Karaoke as Modern Lhasa, Tibet: A Western View." Paper presented at the American Anthropological Association meetings in Atlanta, Georgia.

Ai, Jing 1993. *Wode yijiujiuqi xianggang* (My 1997 Hong Kong). Cassette tape distributed by Beijing Film Academy Sound Production and Distribution.

Althusser, Louis. 1971. "Ideology and Ideological State Apparatuses." In *Lenin and Philosophy: Notes Towards an Investigation,* pp. 123–73. Translated by Ben Brewster. London: New Left Books.

Anderson, Benedict. 1991. *Imagined Communities: Reflections on the Origins and Spread of Nationalism.* New York: Verso, rev.ed.

Ang, Ien. 1990. "Culture and Communication: Towards an Ethnographic Critique of Media Consumption in the Transnational Media System." *European Journal of Communication* 5, nos. 2–3.

Anonymous. 1993. "Guanyu weixin dianshi dimian jieshou wenti" (On the question of on-the-ground satellite reception). *Mei zhou guangbo dianshi,* November 1–7.

Appadurai, Arjun. 1990. "Disjuncture and Difference in the Global Cultural Economy." *Public Culture* 2, no. 2: 1–24.

———. 1993 "Patriotism and Its Futures". *Public Culture* 5, no. 3.

Ash, Robert, and Y. Y. Kueh. 1993. "Economic Integration Within Greater China: Trade and Investment Flows Between China, Hong Kong and Taiwan." *China Quarterly* 136.

Bao, Ming. 1993. "Shanghai shiting dazhan" (The great wars of television and radio in Shanghai). *Zhongguo shibao* 66.

Benjamin, Walter. 1968. "The Work of Art in the Age of Mechanical Reproduction." In *Illuminations.* Edited by Hannah Arendt. New York: Schocken.

Berger, Marie-Claire. 1981. "The Other China': Shanghai from 1919 to 1949." In Christopher Howe, ed., *Shanghai: Revolution and Development in an Asian Metropolis.* Cambridge: Cambridge University Press.

Bhabha, Homi K. 1994. *The Location of Culture.* London: Routledge.

Brownell, Susan. 1995. "Women Who Represent the Nation: Sportswomen and Sports Media in Chinese Public Culture." Paper presented at the conference Mass Media, Gender, and a Chinese Public: Mainlan, Taiwan, and Hong Kong, University of California at Santa Barbara, April 1–3.

Butler, Judith. 1991. "Imitation and Gender Insubordination" In Diana Fuss, ed., *Inside/Out: Lesbian Theories, Gay Theories.* New York: Routledge.

Chang, Won Ho. 1989. *Mass Media in China: The History and the Future.* Ames: Iowa State University Press.

Ching, Leo. 1994. "Imaginings in the Empires of the Sun: Japanese Mass Culture in Asia." *Boundary 2* 21, no. 1.

Chow, Rey. 1993. *Writing Diaspora: Tactics of Intervention in Contemporary Cultural Studies.* Bloomington: Indiana University Press.

Chow, Tse-ts'ung. 1960. *The May Fourth Movement: Intellectual Revolution in Modern China.* Cambridge: Harvard University Press.

Chun, Allen. 1994a. "From Nationalism to Nationalizing: Cultural Imagination and State Formation in Postwar Taiwan." *Australian Journal of Chinese Affairs* 31.

———. 1994b. "Discourses of Identity in the Politics of the Modern Nation-State: Spaces of Public Culture in Taiwan, Hong Kong, and Singapore." *Culture and Policy* 5.

315

Clark, Paul. 1984. "The Film Industry in the 1970s." Bonnie McDougall, ed. *Popular Chinese Literature and Performing Arts in the People's Republic of China, 1949–79.* Berkeley: University of California Press.

Clifford, James. 1992. "Traveling Cultures." In Lawrence Grossberg et. al., eds., *Cultural Studies.* New York: Routledge.

———. 1994. "Diasporas." *Cultural Anthropology* 9, no. 3.

Dai, Jinhua. 1995. "Invisible Women: Women's Films in Contemporary Chinese Cinema." Translated by Mayfair Yang, *Positions* 3, no. 1.

de Certeau, Michel. 1984. *The Practice of Everyday Life.* Translated by Steven F. Rendall. Berkeley: University of California Press.

Deleuze, Gilles. 1980. *Nietszche and Philosophy.* New York: Columbia University Press.

Deleuze, Gilles, and Felix Guattari. 1983. *Anti-Oedipus: Capitalism and Schizophrenia.* Minneapolis: University of Minnesota Press.

Ding, Yi. 1994 "Shanghai shiluo 50 nian?" (Has Shanghai fallen behind by 50 years?) *Zhongshi zhoukan* November 13–19.

Featherstone, Mike. 1990. "Global Culture: An Introduction." In Mike Featherstone, ed., *Global Culture: Nationalism, Globalization, and Modernity.* London: Sage.

———.1992. Consumer Culture and Postmodernism. London: Sage.

Feher, Ferenc, Agnes Heller, and Gyorgy Markus. 1983. *Dictatorship over Needs: An Analysis of Soviet Societies.* Oxford: Basil Blackwell.

Foster, Robert J. 1991. "Making National Cultures in the Global Ecumene." *Annual Review of Anthropology* 20.

Foucault, Michel. 1980. *The History of Sexuality. Volume 1: An Introduction.* Translated by Robert Hurley. New York: Random House.

Friedland, Roger. 1994. "NowHere: An Introduction to Space, Time and Modernity." In Roger Friedland and Deirdre Boden, eds., *NowHere: Space, Time and Modernity.* Berkeley: University of California Press.

Giddens, Anthony. 1990. *The Consequences of Modernity.* Stanford: Stanford University Press.

Gold, Thomas. 1993. "Go with Your Feelings: Hong Kong and Taiwan Popular Culture in Greater China." *China Quarterly* 136: 907–25.

Guo, Ke. 1994. "'Jilupian bianjishi'zhendong Shanghaitan ([The show] 'Documentary Editing Room' shakes Shanghai). *Zhongshi zhoukan,* August 14–20: 48–49.

Hall, Stuart. 1980. "Encoding/Decoding." In Stuart Hall et al., eds., *Culture, Media, Language.* London: Hutchinson

Hamilton, Denise. 1995. "Providing a Space Link to Homeland: Chinese-Language Satellite TV Gets a Good Reception Among Immigrants in U.S." *Los Angeles Times,* August. 2.

Hannerz, Ulf. 1989. "Culture Between Center and Periphery: Toward a Macroanthropology." *Ethnos* 54: 200–16.

Harding, Harry. 1993. "The Concept of 'Greater China': Themes, Variations and Reservations." *China Quarterly* 136.

Heng, Geraldine, and Janadas Devan. 1992. "State Fatherhood: The Politics of Nationalism, Sexuality, and Race in Singapore." In Andrew Parker, Mary Russo, et al., eds., *Nationalisms and Sexualities.* New York: Routledge.

Hsiao, Hsin-Huang Michael, and Alvin Y. So. 1994. "Taiwan-Mainland Economic Nexus: Socio-Political Origins, State-Society Impacts, and Future Prospects." Hong Kong: Institute of Asia-Pacific Studies, Chinese University of Hong Kong.

Jameson, Fredric. 1987. "Third-World Literature in the Era of Multinational Capitalism." *Social Text* 15: 65–88.

Lee, Benjamin. 1993. "Going Public." *Public Culture* 5, no. 2.

Leyda, Jay. 1972. *Dianying: An Account of Films and the Film Audience in China.* Cambridge: MA MIT Press.

Liu, Lydia. 1995. "Disjuncture of Theory: Transnationals, (Im)migrants, and/or Diaspora?" Paper presented at the Conference on Mass Media, Gender, and a Chinese Public, University of California at Santa Barbara, April 1–3.

Lull, James. 1991. *China Turned On: Television, Reform, and Resistance.* New York: Routledge.

Mankekar, Purnima. 1993. "Television Tales and a Woman's Rage: A Nationalist Recasting of Draupadi's 'Disrobing.'" *Public Culture* 5, no. 3.

McLuhan, Marshall. 1994. *Understanding Media: The Extensions of Man.* Cambridge; MA: MIT. Press.

Meng, Yue. 1993. "Female Images and National Myth." In Tani E. Barlow, ed., *Gender Politics in Modern China: Writing and Feminism.* Durham: Duke University Press.

Miyoshi, Masao. 1993. "A Borderless World? From Colonialism to Transnationalism and the Decline of the Nation-State." *Critical Inquiry* 19.

Nonini, Donald. 1995. "The Chinese Public Sphere and the Cultural Boundaries of the Malaysian Nation-State," paper presented at the American Ethnological Society Meetings, Austin, Texas.

Ong, Aihwa. 1996. "Anthropology, China, and Modernities: The Geopolitics of Cultural Knowledge." In Henrietta Moore, ed., *The Future of Anthropological Knowledge.* London: Routledge.

Pickowicz, Paul. 1991. "The Theme of Spiritual Pollution in Chinese Films of the 1930s." *Modern China* 17, no. 1: 38–75.

Qiu, Xiuwen. 1993. "Heima chuangjing beimei huayu dianshi shichang (A black horse charges into the North American Chinese-language television market). *Zhongguo shibao,* September 12–18.

Radway, Janice. 1988. "Reception Study: Ethnography and the Problems of Dispersed Audiences and Nomadic Subjects." *Cultural Studies* 2, no. 3.

Rayns, Tony. 1991. "Breakthroughs and Setbacks: The Origins of the New Chinese Cinema." In Chris Berry, ed., *Perspectives on Chinese Cinema.* London: British Film Institute.

Rofel, Lisa. 1994. "Yearnings: Televisual Love and Melodramatic Politics in Contemporary China." *American Ethnologist* 21, no. 4.

Rouse, Roger. 1991. "Mexican Migration and the Social Space of Postmodernism." Diaspora 1, no. 1.
———. 1995a. "Thinking Through Transnationalism: Notes on the Cultural Politics of Class Relations in the Contemporary United States." *Public Culture* 7, no. 2.
———. 1995b. "Questions of Identity: Personhood and Collectivity in Transnational Migration to the United States." *Critique of Anthropology* 15, no. 4.
Sheng, Feng. 1995. "Beimei shangkong de Zhongwen dianshi dazhan" Chinese-language television wars in North American outer space). *Huaxia wenzhai* [Chinese electronic news service], April 15.
Shih, Shu-mei. 1995. "The Trope of 'Mainland China' in Taiwan's Media." *Positions* 3, no. 1.
Verdery, Katherine. 1994. "Beyond the Nation in Eastern Europe." *Social Text* 38.
Wallerstein, Immanuel. 1974. *The Modern World-System.* New York: Academic Press.
———. 1984 The Politics of the World Economy. Cambridge: Cambridge University Press.
Wu, Xiaoming. 1992. "Ershi shiji Zhongguo wenhua zai xifang mianqian de ziwo yishi" (Cultural self-identity in the face of the West in twentieth-century China). *Ershiyi shiji* 14: 102–12.
Yang, Mayfair Mei-hui. 1993. "Of Gender, State Censorship and Overseas Capital: An Interview with Chinese Director Zhang Yimou." *Public Culture* 5, no. 2: 1–17.
———. 1994. "State Discourse or a Plebeian Public Sphere? Film Discussion Groups in China." *Visual Anthropology* 10, no. 1.
———. 1994b. *Gifts, Favors, and Banquets: The Art of Social Relationships in China.* Ithaca, NY: Cornell University Press.
———. 1994c. "A Sweep of Red: State Subjects and the Cult of Mao." In *Gifts, Favors, and Banquets: The Art of Social Relationships in China.* Ithaca, NY: Cornell University Press.
———. 1995. "From Gender Erasure to Gender Difference: State Feminism, Mass Media, & Public Culture in China." Paper presented at the conference Mass Media, Gender, and a Chinese Public: Mainland, Taiwan, Hong Kong," University of Santa Barbara, April 1–3.
———. 1996. "Tradition, Traveling Anthropology, and the Discourse of Modernity in China." In Henrietta Moore, ed., *The Future of Anthropological Knowledge.* London: Routledge.
Yang, Rujie. 1993. "Jingcai yu wunai—cong 'Beijingren zai Neuyue' tan dongxifang wenhua chongji (Gripping and frustrating: on East-West collisions in 'A Beijing Native in New York.'" *Dianying wenxue* 12.
Ye Ren. 1994. "Xi 'Beijingren zai niuyue' de shehui xiaoguo" (An analysis of the social effects of 'A Beijing Native in New York') *Zhongguo zhi chun* 14.
Zha, Jianying. 1995. *China Pop: How Soap Operas, Tabloids, and Best-sellers Are Transforming a Culture.* New York: New Press.

Zhang, Hong. 1992. "TV, TV, fangcun shijie de jingcai yu wunai (TV, TV, the brilliance and frustration of that square world). *Shehui* 92.

Zhang, Yingjin. 1994. "Engendering Chinese Filmic Discourse of the 1930s: Configurations of Modern Women in Shanghai in Three Silent Films." *Positions* 2, no. 3: 603–28.

Zhen, Hanliang. 1992. "Wo liaojie sandi de Zhongguoren: zhuanfang Luo Dayou" (What I understand of the Chinese in the three Chinas: an interview with Luo Dayou). *Zhongguo shibao,* Aug. 23.

Afterword

Toward a Cultural Politics
of Diaspora and Transnationalism

Aihwa Ong and Donald M. Nonini

Modern Chinese transnationalism, arising in the context of European colonialism in coastal China, Southeast Asia, the Pacific islands, and the west coast of North America, is now inseparable from the networks, strategies, and cultural politics of global capitalism. As a distinctive postcolonial social formation, modern Chinese transnationalism is expanding ever more rapidly across the Asia Pacific and indeed launching the capitalist development of China itself. Taken collectively, the essays in this book challenge models of the world system, diaspora, transnationalism, and identity heretofore drawn almost exclusively from Western experiences. In this afterword, we mention briefly the implications of modern Chinese transnationalism for our thinking about the relations between capitalism and the nation-state, globalization and ethnicity, class and identity, and ethics and politics.

Transnational Capitalism

We have traced at least two major variants of capitalism associated with Chinese transnationalism. In one, Chinese transnational capitalists act out flexible strategies of accumulation in networks that cut across political borders and are linked through second-tier global cities (Sassen 1994) such as Shanghai, Guangzhou (Canton), Hong Kong, Taipei, Singapore, Bangkok, and Kuala Lumpur. These overlapping business, social, and kinship networks stitch together dynamic productive, financial, and marketing regions that are not contained by a single nation-state or subject to its influence.

In the other, Chinese transnational capitalists flourish not only outside "the striated space of the nation-state" (Kearney 1995, 558–59) but also within it, aligned closely to non-Chinese (and to a lesser extent, Chinese) state bureaucratic elites in joint ventures with state capital. Despite current conservative shibboleths in the West about the ways in which nation-states supposedly "fetter free markets," in fact much of the new capitalism of the Asia Pacific is state-driven and state-sponsored, and Chinese transnational capitalists, like those in other parts of the world, represent forces that nation-states can deploy and discipline to strengthen themselves. It is no accident that since the 1960s strong repressive-developmentalist state regimes (Feith 1981; Tanter 1981) have emerged in Asia in tandem with the economic dynamism of flexible capitalism: Many civil and political liberties have been curtailed in the name of furthering capitalist accumulation, whether we speak of Suharto's "New Order," the succession of juntas in Thailand, or the *chaebol*-dominated governments of South Korea. Transnational Chinese capitalists within the region have been the linchpin securing economic dynamism to authoritarian state systems. Ideologically, strong states in ASEAN countries and in China represent mobile capitalism as the means to nation-building and state-strengthening. While benefiting from the wealth and economic development that capitalism can bring, these states also seek to be strong by regulating the access of their citizens to culturally subversive ideas such as Western liberalism and democracy. The imbrication of the nation-state with capitalism challenges the popular view that transnational capitalism is eroding state power everywhere and in the same way.

Diasporas

In much recent writing, diasporic cultures are viewed as formations that resist the disciplinary state and capitalist exploitation (Gilroy 1991, 1993; Clifford 1995). The essays here in part support this claim. However, they also demonstrate that modern Chinese transnationalism reveals a whole range of cultural politics that can strengthen state discipline, on the one hand; on the other, they expand capitalist regimes of exploitation and regulation and are often intertwined with local modes of control.

Diasporas, like any cultural formations, are grounded in internal hegemonies and systems of inequalities. The powers associated with diasporic Chinese mobility can be coercive, subversive of existing structures, or both, depending on whether these powers promote capitalist and/or state interests. Wealthy Chinese capitalists such as Liem Sioe Liong have worked hand in hand with the Suharto regime to underwrite it financially and thereby helped solidify the repressive capacities of the Indonesian government. Malaysian Chinese investors help the Malaysian government invest in mainland China and thus simultaneously buttress two national systems of economic and social inequality that selectively exploit poor rural and urban women—who have become human fodder for the intensified productive arrangements (such as subcontracting) associated with flexibility—and set policies that disadvantage groups marked by specific civil identities, such as Chinese as a minority ethnic group in Malaysia. At the same time, diasporic capitalist interests can subvert state disciplining by transferring economic capital out of their host countries to overseas locations, and thus act to transform national economies under the rubric of "market forces." This transnationalization of family business interests over the interests of the nation-state has created tensions between ethnic Chinese and indigenous populations in Southeast Asia for generations. Here it is important to recall that not all Chinese engaged in transnational moves are capitalists. Some instead are among the "new helots" (Cohen 1987)—international labor migrants now engaged in mass migrations between their countries of birth and the emergent areas of high labor demand in this age of flexibility. Still other transnational Chinese are members of professional salariats and other groups and are not capitalists. Yet these other groups also suffer from the antagonism generated between Chinese and indigenous peoples when the cut-and-run business strategies of wealthy Chinese tycoons fuel hostile populist imaginaries about "disloyal" Chinese.

Thus there is nothing intrinsically liberating about diasporic cultures. Transnational Chinese capitalism has increased living standards throughout much of Southeast Asia and China and it is the engine driving the economic boom in the region. Of this Chinese are justifiably proud. Yet these economic gains have been underwritten by the emergence of gross disparities in economic, social, and spatial powers and by the revival of modes of gender exploitation that had previously been partially dismantled. Overseas Chinese investments have made Xiamen, just across the Straits from Taiwan, into a booming town of flashy bars and discos dubbed "Little Taipei." Capitalist development in coastal south China has brought on the exploitation of female sex workers and factory workers to a degree not seen since before the Communist victory in 1949 (Ong 1996). Some Taiwanese factories in Xiamen lock up their female workers and have not allowed even local authorities to visit their premises. Taiwan factory bosses may compel pretty "little younger sisters" to provide harem services in return for benefits such as better housing. Meanwhile, at the opposite edge of the Asia Pacific, professionals and family businesses from Taiwan and Hong Kong have settled in the community of Monterey Park near Los Angeles, California, transformed its commercial landscape, and challenged preexisting Anglo hegemony by winning control of its city council and imparting a salubrious air of multiculturalism and racial diversity to its civic life (Horton 1992); not far away, however, in nearby Alhambra and elsewhere in the Los Angeles area, Chinese entrepreneurs from Southeast Asia have established garment sweatshops that set new debased standards in low wages and coercive working conditions (see Davis 1990).

Thus diasporic populations can introduce new or revive older forms of oppression into a nation-state; overseas Chinese investors are able to escape punishment because of their extraterritorial status and investment clout. One should not assume that what is diasporic, fluid, border-crossing, or hybrid is intrinsically subversive of power structures. This reminder should not even be necessary: While "ethnic" diasporas such as those of Chinese or Jews have long been pointed to, the mainstream diaspora of peoples of European descent associated with two centuries of Western imperialism, settlement, and the erection of the racial color bar over two thirds of the surface area of the world's continents has gone unmarked and unnoted (Stavrianos 1991; Du Bois 1962).

Identities and Ethnicities

The essays in this book have discussed how the habitus, practices, and identities of overseas Chinese are constituted through transnational systems rather than in stable cultural entities (see Marcus 1995, 96). Differently situated subjects—merchants, revolutionaries, officials, bosses, laborers, professionals, housewives—are molded through links among sites of discipline, histories of elusion, and imaginaries of power. These subjects represent what James Clifford (1992, 99) has called "discrepant cosmopolitanisms"—the specific experiences of diverse groups at home, on the road, or in the air who participate unequally in the cultural production and time-space compression of late capitalism.

The chapters in our book thus deconstruct modern Chineseness. The mainstream tendency has been to ascribe contemporary Chinese identity to long-standing roots in China native places or to the heritage of China's civilization (see, for example, Tu 1991; Wang 1991). In contrast, Chinese transnationalists show that their identities are increasingly diaspora-based rather than land-based. Furthermore, the transformation of identities through capital's global mobility recasts class, gender, race, and nationality differences in new ways. In this book we have considered identity as formed out of the strategies for the accumulation of economic, social, cultural, and educational capital as diasporic Chinese travel, settle down, invest in local spaces, and evade state disciplining in multiple sites throughout the Asia Pacific. The obverse of such accumulation strategies, is of course, the cost or debits that have varied but clearly negative effects on migrant workers and on home-bound or displaced women and children.

Chinese transnationalists are thus prototypical people of modernity who, like diaspora Indians, emerged as modern trading subjects under European imperialism and are now extending their entrepreneurial and professional interests to former metropolitan countries. Those who were imperialized historically are now "striking back." Once derided in the West as imitative WOGs ("Westernized Oriental Gentlemen," existing "With Our Grace"), postcolonial Asian cosmopolitans, with their instrumentalist attitudes, accumulation strategies, and view of the world as their canvas, are the products of globalization. Our approach opens up the question of identity—racial, ethnic, cultural, spatial, gender, and personal—as a politics rather than as an inheritance (Clifford 1992, 116), as fluidity rather than fixity, as based on mobility rather than locality, and as the playing out of these oppositions across the world. Clearly the old East-West binary for understanding and crafting identity is obsolete. The varieties of Chinese identity thus emerge out of the continuous invention and reinvention of Chineseness as a product of the multiple and contradictory effects of ultramodernist attitudes, transnational subjectivities, and the nostalgic imaginaries marketed by late capitalism and its culture industries.

As we have shown, modern Chinese transnationalism not only is multicultural but also has produced transnational imaginaries of ethnic self-celebration. Scholars maintain that globalization engenders and profits from the "proliferation of difference" and multiculturalism (Hall 1991, 31). Masao Miyoshi (1993, 744) claims that with the onslaught of transnational corporations, nation-states in Eastern Europe "look more and more inoperable," and that as a result "neoethnicism" becomes "the refuge from the predicament of an integrated political and economic body." While racial and ethnic xenophobia among displaced ex-peasants and the unemployed laborers of "workers' states" is quickly publicized, there has been little scholarly attention paid to the ethnic chauvinism among the more privileged that is called into being by globalization.

Indeed, triumphalist discourses of Chinese exceptionalism are today rather commonplace in Asian elite circles and in sympathetic Western think-tanks. Discourses on cultural distinctiveness are also a way of avoiding or rationalizing the unpleasant realities of increasing class and gender exploitation across the region. The assumed cultural affinities between overseas and mainland Chinese seem to make such exploitation more tolerable to officials in south China, while the economic differences between, say, Singapore and the Philippines have been framed invidiously in terms of the possession or lack of certain "Confucian" attributes.

The essentialization of Chineseness as Confucian has become a convenient meta-inscription of, and prescription for, pan-Asianess among the elites of the so-called new dragon nation-states of the Asia Pacific. Asian politicians of many nationalities have come to find strategic resonance with the diasporic Chinese imageries of Asian modernity, especially in framing disputatious issues vis-à-vis the West, such as trade barriers and human rights. Such a new hegemonic concordance on the Asian difference challenges the preexisting American and Japanese leadership of the Asia Pacific associated with cold war politics (Dirlik 1993; see also Ong's essay in this volume).

David Harvey (1989) has observed that with increasing cultural integration and incorporation of the earth's peoples into the evanescent and constantly shifting processes of capitalist globalization, a dialectically opposed process has also set in—that of increasing attachment to specific places and locales combined with intensified allegiances to trancendental ideologies conferring stability on those most displaced by a changing world.

This observation has been confirmed not only in new forms of nativization on the Asian side of the Pacific (for example, the *dakwa* missionary movement and other forms of Islamic revivalism in Malaysia, see Ong 1995) but also—and more forebodingly—in the surge in reactionary movements in North America and Europe that make a strong, organic association among specific races, national spaces ("the land" of "the people"), and theological or political fundamentalisms. At its most extreme, this countertendency will lead to the formation of profoundly antimodernist, racist, sexist, and protofascist social movements against globalization and its cultural and political implications, that threaten the very fabric of civil society. These movements tend to gain purchase on populations during periods of protracted economic decline, one of which, we firmly believe, the core of the old world system—North America and Europe—has now entered. Thus while we appreciate the justifiable pride among Chinese transnationalists and others in Asia in throwing off imperialist domination, we fear that their ethnic chauvinism feeds larger global antagonisms expressed by reactionary attachments to locale in the West, racist absolutism, and religious fundamentalism—most recently the antiglobalist sentiments expressed by antigovernment militias in the United States and the bombing of the Federal Building in Oklahoma City, America's heartland.

For this reason alone we would do well to be apprehensive about the broader political implications of the new triumphalist narratives of Asian and Chinese "success." One of us (Nonini), while engaged in ethnographic research in Malaysia in the summer of 1992, had what can be regarded as a prototypical postmodern experience: sitting with middle-class Chinese Malaysians watching a CNN broadcast of the Los Angeles urban uprising and hearing their explanations for the chaos whose manifestations they saw in panoptic TV color—the "inferiority" of American blacks combined with the propensity in American society to "give too much freedom" to people. This leads us to infer that the new Chinese transnational triumphalism we have described here, with its elements of a reflex racism, has now percolated down to nonelite segments of Asian populations, with invidious and harmful effects on mutual understanding in a period of global integration.

We are also aware that one of the first targets of misplaced antagonisms toward the new Asia will be Asian Americans, whose civil liberties and rights to citizenship may, as in the past, be called into question by hostile non-Asian majorities. Katherine Newman, in her important recent study of downward mobility among the white middle classes of the United States, has called attention to the appearance of new racist discourses that declaim against illegitimate Asian elites taking advantage of "hardworking Americans who have forfeited the opportunity to live in their own communities to these interlopers" (Newman 1993, 150). The new ethnic exceptionalism promoted by Asian transnational elites as it is disseminated internationally will surely exacerbate such tendencies. On the eastern side of the Asia Pacific, the "flexible citizenship" exercised by Hong Kong and other Asian business elites relocated from Asia to the west coast of North America, grounded in an expanded sense of civic duties (Ong 1993), will provide little resistance to these developments. There is every reason for concern.

Transnational Publics and Ethics

The dynamic tension between the diversity of subjects, cultures, and identities, on the one hand, and the homogenizing ideologies of Chinese racial and cultural essences, on the other, holds the key to our understanding of identity-making in the new Asia. The synergy between flexible accumulation and mass markets has produced transnational publics in Asia in which essentializing symbols—of Chinese culture, capitalism, and other values—are absorbed, negotiated, deflected, mocked, or contested. Thus we must go beyond Habermas's notion of civil society as a realm of political freedom and free expression of ideas. Contemporary publics in Asia are not apolitical arenas but are thoroughly infused with the cultural politics of transnational capitalism. Identity formation is increasingly shaped by the struggles between dominant publics and counterpublics, heavily influenced by transnational markets, media, and capital.

What are the ethical implications of this intertwining of Chinese mobility strategies with the circuits of global capitalism? We need to counter capital's mobility by forming transnational linkages between persons and groups disempowered by globalization, whatever their ethnic or national affiliations. No formula for emancipation and no teleologies of liberation are sustainable in this postmodern, and perhaps post-Marxist, age. Nonetheless, we would argue for the need to develop a new utopian imaginary that combines the experiences of displacement, travel, and disorientation, which many Chinese transnationalists have successfully negotiated, with an emergent sense of social justice. The habitus, strategies, identifications, and subjectivities formed out of the matrix of Chinese transnational experience have generated and reinforced class, gender, and ethnic inequalities and violences, both symbolic and bodily. A self-critique is necessary for a cosmopolitan sense of social justice to be fully articulated within the diasporic transnational experience.

The new global cosmopolitanism of Chinese transnationalists needs not only a self-critique; it should also provide an occasion to reflect on the wastage and devastation caused by many peoples more "local" than diasporic Chinese. There is an imperative for all persons—whether transnational or not—to come to terms with the debris of contemporary history, caught so poetically in Walter Benjamin's image of "the angel of history": "His face is turned toward the past. Where we perceive a chain of events, he sees one single catastrophe which keeps piling wreckage upon wreckage and hurls it in front of his feet" (Benjamin 1968, 257).

Surely one of the promises of transnationalism is the new possibility of negotiating democracies that cut across gender, class, racial, ethnic, and national divisions. Modern Chinese transnationalism must grasp the opportunity to transform the old shibboleth of Chinese cosmopolitanism, "All persons are as older and younger brothers" (*jie ren xiongdi ye*), into the principle that all persons are equal the world over.

References

Benjamin, Walter. 1968. *Illuminations*. New York: Schocken.

Clifford, James. 1992. "Traveling Cultures." In L. Grossberg, C. Nelson, and P. Treichler, eds.; *Cultural Studies*, pp. 96–107. New York: Routledge.

Clifford, James. 1995. "Diasporas." *Cultural Anthropology* 9, no. 3: 302–38.

Cohen, Robin. 1987. *The New Helots: Migrants in the International Division of Labor*. Aldershot, UK: Avebury.

Davis, Mike. 1990, *City of Quartz: Excavating the Future in Los Angeles*. London: Verso.

Dirlik, Arif. 1993. *What's in a Rim? Critical Perspectives on the Pacific Rim Idea*. Boulder Westview.

Du Bois, W.E.B. 1962. *Black Reconstruction, 1860–1880*. New York: Harcourt Brace.

Feith, Herb. 1981. "Repressive-Developmentalist Regimes in Asia." *Alternatives* 7, no 4: 491–506.

Gilroy, Paul. 1991. *"There Ain't No Black in the Union Jack": The Cultural Politics of Race and Nation*. Chicago: University of Chicago Press.

———. 1993. *The Black Atlantic: Modernity and Double Consciousness*. Cambridge, MA: Harvard University Press.

Hall, Stuart. 1991. "The Local and the Global: Globalization and Ethnicity." In A. D. King, ed., *Culture, Globalization, and the World System: Contemporary Conditions for the Representation of Identity*, pp. 19–39. London: Macmillan.

Harvey, David. 1989. *The Condition of Postmodernity*. Oxford: Basil Blackwell.

Horton, John. 1992. "The Politics of Diversity in Monterey Park, California." In L. Lamphere, ed., *Structuring Diversity: Ethnographic Perspectives on the New Immigration*, pp. 215–46. Chicago: University of Chicago Press.

Kearney, Michael. 1995. "The Local and the Global: The Anthropology of Globalization and Transnationalism." *Annual Review of Anthropology* 24: 547–66.

Marcus, George E. 1995. "Ethnography in/of the World System: The Emergence of Multi-Sited Ethnography." *Annual Review of Anthropology* 24: 95–140.

Miyoshi, Masao. 1993. "A Borderless World? From Colonialism to Transnationalism and the Decline of the Nation-State." *Critical Inquiry* 19, no. 4: 217–51.

Newman, Katherine. 1993. *Declining Fortunes: The Withering of the American Dream*. New York: Basic Books.

Ong, Aihwa 1993. "On the Edge of Empires: Flexible Citizenship among Chinese in Diaspora." *Positions* 1, no. 3: 745–780.

———. 1995. "State Versus Islam: Malay Families, Women's Bodies, and the Body Politic in West Malaysia." In A. Ong and M. Peletz, eds., *Bewitching Women, Pious Men: Gender and Body Politics in Southeast Asia*, pp. 159–94. Berkeley: University of California Press.

————. 1996. "Anthropology, China, and Modernities: The Geopolitics of Cultural Knowledge." In Henrietta Moore, ed., The Future of Anthropological Knowledge, pp. 60–92. London: Routledge.

Sassen, Saskia. 1994. *Cities in a World Economy*. Thousand Oaks, CA: Sage

Stavrianos, L. S. 1991. *Global Rift: The Third World Comes of Age*. New York: Morrow.

Tanter, Richard. 1981. "The Militarization of ASEAN: Global Context and Local Dynamics." *Alternatives* 7, no. 4: 507–32.

Tu, Wei-ming. 1991. "Cultural China: The Periphery as the Center." *Daedalus* 120, no. 2: 1–32.

Wang, Ling-chi. 1991. "Roots and Changing Identity of the Chinese in the United States." *Daedalus* 120, no. 2: 181–206.

Notes on Contributors

CRISTINA SZANTON BLANC was born and raised in Rome. Currently senior associate at the Southern Asian Institute, Columbia University, her books include *A Right to Survive: Subsistence Marketing in a Lowland Philippine Town* (Pennsylvania State University Press, 1972); *Urban Children in Distress: Global Predicaments and Innovative Strategies* (Gordon and Breach, 1993); and *Nations Unbound: Transnational Projects, Postcolonial Predicaments, and Deterritorialized Nation-States,* with Linda Basch and Nina Glick Schiller (Gordon and Breach, 1993). Her currents projects focus on transnationalism, new social movements, and human rights.

PRASENJIT DUARA was born in Assam. He is professor of history at the University of Chicago. His publications include *Culture, Power, and the State: Rural North China, 1900–1942* (Stanford University Press, 1988) and *Rescuing History from the Nation: Questioning Narratives of Modern China* (University of Chicago Press, 1995). He is at present working on Japanese colonial discourses and East Asian identities with a special emphasis on the puppet state of Manchukuo.

YOU-TIEN HSING was born in Taipei. She is assistant professor at the School of Community and Regional Planning at the University of British Columbia. Her book *Making Capitalism in China: The Taiwan Connection* is forthcoming from Oxford University Press.

CHING KWAN LEE, a native of Hong Kong, is lecturer in sociology at the Chinese University of Hong Kong. Her research interests focus on gender, the sociology of work, and qualitative methodologies. She is writing a book called *Women Workers and the Manufacturing Miracle: Gender, Labor Markets, and Production Politics in South China.*

XIN LIU was born and raised in Beijing. He received his doctoral training at the School of Oriental and African Studies, University of London, and is now assistant professor of anthropology at the University of California at Berkeley. He is writing a book on the changing strategies of everyday practices in post reform rural Shaanxi.

KATHARYNE MITCHELL was born in Boston. She is assistant professor in the Department of Geography at the University of Washington and is the author of several articles focusing on questions of ideology, culture, and the built environment. She is currently working on a book entitled *Facing Capital: Ideology, Culture, and Politics in Vancouver's Urban Development.*

DONALD M. NONINI was born in San Francisco. He is associate professor of anthropology at the University of North Carolina at Chapel Hill. The author of *British Colonial Rule and the Resistance of the Malay Peasantry, 1900–1957* (Southeast Asian Monograph Series, Yale University, 1992), he was acting editor of the journal *Dialectical Anthropology* from 1991 to 1993. He is currently writing a book on working-class Chinese men and cultural politics in Malaysia.

AIHWA ONG was born into a Straits Chinese family in Penang, Malaysia. She is associate professor of anthropology at the University of California at Berkeley. Her publications include *Spirits of Resistance and Capitalist Discipline: Factory Women in Malaysia* (State University of New York Press, 1987) and *Bewitching Women, Pious Men: Gender and Labor Politics in Southeast Asia,* coedited with Michael Peletz (University of California Press, 1995). She is writing a book on new Asian immigrants and cultural citizenship in California.

CARL A. TROCKI is professor of Asian studies at Queensland University of Technology in Brisbane, Australia. He is the author of *Opium and Empire: Chinese Society in Colonial Singapore, 1800–1910* (Cornell University Press, 1990) and *Prince of Pirates: The Temenggongs and the Development of Johor and Singapore, 1784–1885* (Singapore University

Press, 1979). His current research interests include militarism and democracy in modern Southeast Asia.

MAYFAIR MEI-HUI YANG was born in Taiwan. She is associate professor of anthropology at the University of California at Santa Barbara. Her publications include *Gifts, Favors, and Banquets: The Art of Social Relationships in China* (Cornell University Press, 1994). She is currently working on Chinese mass media, urban women, and non-state organizations in rural Wenzhou.

Index